C000108944

Steve Cannane is an
Correspondent for th   :
                                                           ⅃.

FAIR GAME

STEVE CANNANE

SILVERTAIL BOOKS • *London*

First published in Sydney, Australia by HarperCollins Publishers Australia Pty
Limited in 2016. This edition is published by arrangement
with HarperCollins Publishers Australia Pty Limited.

This edition published in Great Britain and North America
by Silvertail Books in 2016

www.silvertailbooks.com

A catalogue record of this book is available from the British Library

ISBN 978-1-909269-46-0

CONTENTS

PREFACE

UNTIL 2010, I WAS ignorant of the activities of the Church of Scientology. I was 12 months into one of the best jobs in the Australian media, working as a reporter for ABC TV's *Lateline* program. I was looking around for a story to get my teeth into. I didn't have to wait too long. *Lateline*'s Executive Producer, John Bruce, called me into his office and in his formidable baritone said, 'I think I've got something for you …'

Quentin McDermott had just aired his *Four Corners* program 'The Ex-Files'. It contained a series of explosive allegations about forced abortions, punishment camps, abusive work practices and families being torn apart by Scientology. Quentin had two strong leads he had been unable to follow up on and had generously passed them on to *Lateline*.

The stories related to former Scientologists Scarlett Hanna and Carmen Rainer. Scarlett was the daughter of Vicki Dunstan, the head of the Church of Scientology in Australia. Scarlett wanted to blow the lid off one of Scientology's dark secrets – how children were treated inside the cult. She told me she had been separated from her parents and forced to live in a unit with 25 other children of Sea Org members. She said children were treated like cattle. Scarlett said she did not see her father, Mark Hanna, for several years after he was sent to the US as punishment for failing to prevent a critical story airing on Australian TV.

Carmen Rainer had been sexually abused between the ages of 8 and 11, by her Scientologist stepfather, Robert Kerr. She told me that a senior Scientologist, Jan Eastgate, had coached her to lie to police and community services about the sexual abuse she had suffered at the hands of her stepfather, an allegation that Eastgate denied. Carmen also said that Scientologists had told her the abuse was her fault because she had been bad in a previous life.

The Church of Scientology did all it could to prevent Scarlett and Carmen from telling their stories. *Lateline* was threatened with an injunction and defamation writs. Scarlett said her father had threatened to sue her if she went ahead and spoke to me. The night before the interview was due to be recorded, Vicki Dunstan spent the night at her daughter's unit pleading with her not to talk to me.

When it was clear the stories were going ahead, the Church of Scientology did all it could to make life hard for me. No-one at the centre of the allegations would speak to me. Negotiating an interview with their spokeswoman, Virginia Stewart, was a painstaking process. Finally, after much back and forth, she agreed to be interviewed. But when the cameras were due to roll, she simply failed to turn up. When we rescheduled for another day she brought along Sarah McClintock, a committed Scientologist, who disputed Scarlett's version of events.

The Church of Scientology wanted to film the interviews on a video camera, which was no problem to me. But when I started asking difficult questions of McClintock, Sei Broadhurst, the Scientology public affairs representative who was filming the interview, abruptly yelled out, 'I have to change my batteries!' It seemed like a preordained tactic to give Sarah thinking time once the questions got too tough.

When the stories aired, the blowback began. The ABC and *Lateline* were bombarded with complaints from Scientologists. I was accused of bias and interacting with members of a cyber terrorist group (by this they meant I spoke to members of Anonymous as a reporter might do while filming an anti-Scientology protest). They complained about my stories but never sued. They said the allegations were egregiously false but the organisation with a well-earned reputation for silencing journalists and publishers with aggressive litigation never took it to the courts.

Included in the correspondence I received following those stories was an email from Virginia Stewart's father, Allen Wright. In her on-camera interview Scientology's spokeswoman had denied that children and parents were routinely separated by the church. Her father, by now living in Switzerland, had seen the program and was disgusted by the comments. He wrote me the following note:

I am Virginia Stewart's father.
I was a Scientologist, doing up to OT 5 in the Church of Scientology and being on staff in Sydney, but I saw the whole place turn from something fantastic to a good approximation of a Nazi concentration camp after 1982, so I just left when my staff contract was up.
I still had great relationships with both of my daughters until 1988, when Virginia phoned me to say she was joining the Sea Org and could no longer have any communication or connection with me.
Since then she has kept that decision and never once originated a communication, or replied to any from me across the intervening 22 years.
I wished to grant her complete freedom of choice in her life, no matter how much I disagreed with her choice, and how much I missed her, but her directly lying publicly on your show has really pissed me off and I'm willing to make this story public, if you are interested.
Please feel free to email or phone me if it will help put some control in on this criminal organisation.
Regards,
Allen Wright

Virginia Stewart's father had made a similar post on an Internet forum known as the Ex-Scientologist's Message Board. He said, 'I even sent her a great gift for her 40th birthday, but not even a thank you card.' I quickly organised a camera crew to travel to Allen's home to do an interview, but he pulled out at the last moment. His daughter must have have seen the public relations disaster that was about to unfold. Allen wrote to me again.

Steve,
I have just had a long email from Virginia, the first communication in 22 years!

And I feel there is a chance of continued communication,
so I'd like to put a hold on the interview for now.
Sorry.
But this doesn't mean I don't applaud what you are doing.

The same organisation that could separate a loving father from his daughter for 22 years could suddenly allow them to communicate again if it meant that it helped close down the threat of negative publicity.

At every opportunity, before, during and after I covered the stories of Scarlett Hanna and Carmen Rainer, the Church of Scientology tried to make life difficult for me, my Executive Producer and the ABC. It was a common tactic designed to intimidate journalists, editors and publishers to the stage where they made a decision that these stories were simply too hard to cover. My instincts told me it was worth the trouble. I thought that if they were willing to carry on in this way to prevent two stories going to air, what else did they have to hide? To his credit, John Bruce agreed and backed me to keep going.

The more I looked, the more I found. I did further stories for *Lateline* and the reaction from the Church of Scientology was repeated. They threatened to sue me, sent complaints to the Managing Director of the ABC about me and sent me statements that at all times denied all allegations raised by former Scientologists. One thing, however, did change. They never again granted me an interview with Virginia Stewart or any other Scientologist.

As I researched the topic more I was struck by the extraordinary stories where Scientology and its founder, L. Ron Hubbard, were entwined with Australia. Hubbard had served in Brisbane in World War II and visited Melbourne in 1959, where he declared that Australia would be the world's first 'clear continent'.

Australia was the first country to have a public inquiry into Scientology and the first place in the world where it was banned. I discovered that many of Hubbard's harshest policies had evolved in response to that inquiry and the banning of Scientology in three states: Victoria, South Australia and Western Australia. Among these harsh policies was Fair Game, which (according to Hubbard) allowed critics to be 'deprived of property or injured by any means by any Scientologist without any discipline of the Scientologist. May be tricked, sued or lied to or destroyed.' Australia had changed Scientology forever and that story had never fully been told.

A number of Australians also had a major impact inside Scientology. Mike Rinder, who grew up in Adelaide in the 1960s, became its international spokesman and head of its feared Office of Special Affairs (OSA). He later became one of the cult's fiercest and most influential critics.

Former Brisbane kindergarten teacher Yvonne Gillham set up Scientology's Celebrity Centre in Los Angeles. Her daughters, Terri and Janis, were two of Hubbard's original messengers, responsible for everything from pulling his trousers on in the morning, to delivering abuse to subordinates. Both rose to be senior executives in Scientology and until now have never told their remarkable stories.

Then there are the big Australian personalities who collided with Scientology. James Packer was recruited into the organisation when he hit rock bottom after the One.Tel crash. Nicole Kidman had her marriage to Tom Cruise undermined by Scientology spies and wiretaps. Rupert Murdoch was spied on by the Scientologists after his newspapers took aim at them in Australia in the 1960s. Julian Assange was targeted when he helped publish one of the first anti-Scientology websites in the 1990s. Two Scientologists exposed one of the worst cases of medical malpractice in Australian history at Sydney's Chelmsford Hospital. The Church of Scientology even recruited elite rugby league players including State of Origin and Test prop Pat Jarvis. The more I looked the more extraordinary revelations I found.

Four years later, after conducting over 200 interviews, and spending countless days pouring over documents, files and transcripts, I finally managed to pull the story together.

In Scientology's foundation book, *Dianetics: The Modern Science of Mental Health*, Hubbard has an introductory chapter that includes a section titled 'How to Read this Book'. I feel like I need a similar section in my book because I think that as the reader there are a few things you need know about up front.

✻

The Church of Scientology would not put forward anyone to be interviewed for this book.
I tried to get interviews with church officials in Australia and the US, as well as practicing Scientologists at the centre of certain allegations – all requests were declined.

At times I had email exchanges with Vicki Dunstan, the head of the church in Australia, where she requested that I put all questions in writing before she would consider interview requests. I refused to comply with this. Former Scientologists I interviewed had not made the same request. I felt like it gave them an opportunity to rehearse their answers and would cut out the possibility of asking follow-up questions. I also believed they had no intention of giving me interviews anyway and this proved to be the case. I did manage to interview some current Scientologists but this was done without the church's knowledge.

After church representatives declined to do interviews, I laid out the key allegations in writing and requested written responses. Through their lawyer, Patrick George from Kennedys, the church accused me of being unreasonable and asked for further details including the names of sources. When I asked if I could publish online in full all correspondence between myself and the church so readers could make up their own minds about who was being unreasonable, I got another legal letter.

It said in part '… we expressly do not authorise, and indeed are instructed not to authorise, the publication or disclosure of our letters which were sent to you on a confidential basis. Further, publication of the allegations with knowledge of their falsity leaves you liable to substantial general and aggravated damages.'

Eventually I got written responses from Scientology's lawyers to the key allegations. This meant it was impossible to test their claims in an interview setting. The former Scientologists I spoke to were willing to have their claims tested and for me to follow up and further scrutinise their claims in subsequent interviews.

It is hard to know when the Church of Scientology is telling the truth.
I have come across evidence of Scientology officials being punished when critical stories have been published even when it's not been their fault. With that in mind a statement from a Scientology official has

all the credibility of a statement coming from the press office of the North Korean President Kim Jong-un. It might be true, but there are often good reasons why it might be a pack of lies. If the Church of Scientology is hiding something, why would an official tell the truth if it meant being sent off to a punishment camp?

Hubbard's internal justice system, known as 'ethics', punishes those who speak out against Scientology. In fact, inside Scientology's justice system, many High Crimes, the worst offences of all, relate to criticising or embarrassing Scientology in public. That means there is a powerful disincentive for any Scientologist to tell the truth if it will lead to bad public relations for Scientology. This makes it very difficult to ever trust any statement the church makes relating to serious allegations of abuse.

I have never seen a story about Scientology abuses where the church has admitted guilt or apologised. The closest I've seen them come to admitting a failure of some sort was in relation to the case of Paulette Cooper, the New York journalist who wrote about Scientology in the 1970s. Church operatives tried to get Cooper imprisoned by framing her for a bomb threat that she never made. She was facing 15 years in jail when the FBI raided the Church of Scientology over another matter and found documents that proved she was the victim of an elaborate conspiracy. The Church of Scientology has never apologised for this; instead it blamed the action on a 'rogue unit' that had been disbanded.

The Church of Scientology claims I am a bigot.

The Church of Scientology says I am a bigot and will inevitably make other false claims about me following the publication of this book. They have made similar claims of bigotry about other journalists and documentary makers who are determined to expose abuse inside Scientology. These include Pulitzer Prize-winning author Lawrence Wright; Academy Award-winning documentary maker Alex Gibney; Emmy Award-winning BBC journalist John Sweeney; and Tony Ortega, who blogs and breaks stories about Scientology on a daily basis out of New York. I consider all of these people to be fine journalists with a commitment to exposing the truth.

Similarly, former members who leave Scientology and become critics are labelled apostates, criminals, merchants of chaos, part of a posse of lunatics, liars, wife-beaters and egomaniacs. They are attacked in Scientology publications and dismissed invariably as either no-hopers or former executives who were removed from positions of power for incompetence or gross malfeasance. No ex-member who criticises Scientology is given any credibility at all. They are all slimed. Could it be true that not one of them has anything valid to say or any redeeming characteristic? I don't think so.

I'm not fussed about what Scientologists believe in. I am not interested in making fun of Xenu, volcanoes and thetans. If believing in Scientology helps its followers, I'm not going to judge them on it. As a journalist, what disturbs me about Scientology is the abuse of power that comes from the top: the forced abortions; the human trafficking; the underpaid and overworked staff; the families torn apart; the lies; the rips-offs; and the trauma experienced by its followers. It disturbs me too how the organisation has managed to avoid scrutiny through litigation and the intimidation of both its adherents and critics. I hope this book goes some way to exposing the truth of the abuses Scientology has managed to suppress inside its secretive organisation.

I also hope that by exposing the truth it helps in some way those who have suffered this abuse. The former members who spoke to me are extraordinarily brave. Many suffer from post-traumatic stress. All of them in their own way face repercussions for speaking out. It's been a privilege to meet these people and to be able to share their stories.

CHAPTER 1

THE ESCAPEE

JOSÉ NAVARRO WAS HOMELESS, hungry and hallucinating from sleep deprivation. He had one set of clothes, a quarter of a pouch of rolling tobacco and an empty wallet. Trapped in a foreign city, with no family or friends to fall back on, his passport held by the Church of Scientology, José had run out of options.[1]

The only people he knew in Sydney were trying to hunt him down and return him to Scientology's punitive re-education camp, the Rehabilitation Project Force (RPF). The RPF is reserved for members of Scientology's supposed elite unit, the Sea Organization, or Sea Org, who had fallen foul of the hierarchy. José had been a member of the Sea Org for 17 years. Now he was on the run, and consumed by the kind of fear only a wanted man knows. But the 37-year-old had one thing going for him. He was free from the soul-destroying enforced labour of the RPF.

José's fear of being recaptured was intense, but it was mixed with a sense of relief. A diary entry from 4 March 2010 read: 'Today was the day when I left, left, left.'[2] He'd repeated the words for emphasis to remind himself that he had somehow made it out. Above that sentence was a self-portrait sketched in blue pen. It depicts a free man, sitting barefoot in front of the Sydney Opera House. The sun was shining on José, bouncing off the sparkling waters of Sydney Harbour. But how long would his freedom last?

Freedom was one thing, but food was another. On his fourth day on the run he started eating the grass in Sydney's Botanic Gardens. He had learned how to get by on the primitive RPF diet of rice, beans and leftovers from the Flemington markets, but this was taking culinary deprivation to new levels. For a former head chef, trained in fine dining at international hotels, digesting a fist full of dry kikuyu lawn must have been a difficult prospect.

Most men sleeping rough in the Botanic Gardens raid the rubbish bins around Circular Quay, beg in the streets for money, or seek out a homeless shelter for a feed. But José was worried if the police discovered he was homeless they would send him back to the Church of Scientology, as his migration status in Australia was based on a religious worker visa granted through the church.

To avoid police scrutiny, José roamed the streets at night, and slept in the Botanic Gardens by day. He parked himself under a tree, a few metres from the footpath that hugs the shore of Sydney Harbour. He put his sunglasses on, placed a book beside himself and reclined. Passing joggers, if they noticed him, would never have guessed he was a Venezuelan fugitive on the run from a notorious American-born cult. In his blue shorts and blue work-shirt, he looked like a maintenance man on his lunch break, sent horizontal by a few sleep-inducing passages in his book.

Food and sleep were not the only things José was missing out on. Walking along the harbour foreshore at night, he watched enviously as young Sydneysiders laughed and drank and danced in the harbourside bars. On his fourth night of freedom, he gained the attention of a tall blue-eyed blonde in her late 20s drinking outside the Cruise Bar opposite the Opera House. She smiled at José; he smiled back. She asked him inside to dance. He could not believe his luck. The Sea Org, with its prohibitions on pre-marital sex, had already put him through an excruciating period of self-denial. His mind raced ahead with the possibilities on offer. A drink, a dance, a night alone with a beautiful woman, a bed, some breakfast, a hot shower, who knows, if things went really well, maybe even some long-term accommodation. Maybe his luck was about to change. But just as he was on the cusp of becoming the first homeless man to pick up at the Cruise Bar, the doorman spied his Sea Org issue work boots and shorts, and told him he did not meet the dress standards.

LESS THAN FOUR MONTHS before José escaped, Senator Nick Xenophon had stood up in the federal parliament and delivered a withering criticism of the Church of Scientology. He called it a 'criminal organisation', referring to allegations of 'false imprisonment, coerced abortions, embezzlement of church funds, physical violence, intimidation, blackmail'.[3]

Surprisingly, José had heard snippets of that speech. As a Sea Org member on the RPF, he was supposed to be denied access to all media. But while being ferried between Scientology work sites, he heard part of Xenophon's broadside on the car radio. The driver immediately lurched for the volume control and turned it down. 'That is the number one Suppressive Person in Australia right now!' he yelled at his downtrodden crew in the back of the van as they readied themselves for their next shift of hard labour.

At the time, Scientology spokeswoman Virginia Stewart dismissed Xenophon's accusations. 'I can tell you that allegations such as these do not happen in my church in Australia,' she said.[4] José knew these words were meaningless. Just months later, the Church of Scientology put men out into the streets of Sydney to round him up and take him back to their punishment camp.

The RPF is situated at Scientology's Australian and Asia-Pacific headquarters in Dundas, 22 km north-west of Sydney's CBD. The Continental Liaison Office, as it's known, is located in a suburban street, which backs onto St Pat's Oval, the home ground of the Shamrocks junior rugby league team. The sprawling brick building includes offices, kitchens and dormitories for the Sea Org members who live on site. The building was previously known as Champagnat College. Built in the 1950s by the Catholic Church, it functioned as a teachers' training college,[5] and operated as a home and a place of learning for over 500 Marist Brothers until 1984.[6]

The Church of Scientology says the RPF is a voluntary religious retreat. Religious scholar Professor Stephen Kent describes it as 'a program of hard physical labour, forced confessions, and intense ideological study within a prison-like environment'.[7] If members of the Sea Org breach Scientology policy or merely upset the wrong person they can be sent to the RPF.

At Dundas the RPF schedule was as follows: rise at 5.45 am for muster at 6 am. Breakfast for fifteen minutes, then physical labour from 6.15–10.45. A 15-minute meal break followed, before it was back to manual labour until around 3.30 pm. The work took on many forms, including sanding floors, cleaning bathrooms, painting, plastering, moving rocks, and cleaning out maggot-ridden dumpster bins. If targets were not met, RPF members had to do push-ups or run up and down stairs.[8] The RPF did not discriminate on the basis of sex or age. Some members struggling up and down the stairs were in their 60s.

After the hard labour was completed, the exhausted RPF members were given another 15-minute meal break. From 3.45–8.45 pm they had to study the works of L. Ron Hubbard, in what is known as Redemption Time. This was followed by another 15-minute meal break. At 9 pm they had to endure a half-hour meeting where they went over the day's statistics and whether they had met their goals or not. Next they were granted 15 minutes 'hygiene' time, before getting a quarter of an hour to themselves before the lights went out at 10 pm. This routine was repeated seven days a week, sometimes for years on end. One Sea Org member was on the RPF at Dundas for 12 years.[9]

The RPF at Dundas deprived Sea Org members of their liberties. They were not allowed to talk, unless someone from outside the RPF addressed them. They were denied access to newspapers, books, photographs and television. They were even denied toilet paper. They had no time off, not even on Christmas Day. When José Navarro was doing the RPF he was paid less than $20 a week for all that hard labour.

In the RPF, Sea Org members are paired up with a 'twin' who is meant to help them get through the program. If your twin does something wrong, you are punished as well. If you are assigned to the Sea Org's ultimate punishment, the RPF's RPF, your twin must go with you.[10]

José's twin was Darien Shea, an American Sea Org member who had been sent to the RPF in Australia for a bizarre indiscretion. He had been working in the roof of one of Scientology's buildings in the US when a thought crept into his mind. From this vantage point, someone could take a shot at Scientology's leader David Miscavige.

Shea was distressed by the idea. He was so committed to Scientology he would have taken a bullet for Miscavige.[11]

In a subsequent auditing session, he mentioned this innocent thought. It did not go down well. It was assumed Shea had 'evil intentions' against Scientology's leader and he was to be sent as far away as possible. Former Scientology executive Marty Rathbun remembers Miscavige making similar threats to others. 'I heard Miscavige refer to a couple of times in the early 2000s of threatening people: "I'm going to ship you off to Australia and nobody will ever hear from you again."'[12] Like Britain in the 18th and 19th centuries, Scientology had decided to use Australia as a far-flung penal colony. But their 21st-century version of transportation was done under the cover of religious worker visas.

In March 2010, José Navarro was sent to the RPF's RPF for flirting with a young Japanese woman who was on the RPF. It was the second time he'd been punished in this fashion for interacting with members of the opposite sex. The Sea Org's ultimate punishment meant less sleep, more work, even worse food. José's twin, Darien, had to share the burden.

On the first night of their second stint on the RPF's RPF, the pair were sent to Scientology's Advanced Organisation in Glebe, in inner-city Sydney, to clean the kitchen. AOSH ANZO, as it's known, is the place where Scientologists pay for services such as auditing. José was scrubbing pots and pans when an overwhelming feeling struck him. 'I started thinking I have to get out,' he recalls. But escape seemed impossible. The building at that time was full of loyal Scientologists, and he would somehow have to get past Darien, who would've taken a bullet for Scientology's leader.

Just after midnight, José decided to make his move. Most of the staff had left the building he just had to make it past his twin. 'I took a piece of cardboard to the rubbish bin,' says Navarro, 'Darien was going to follow me and I said "C'mon man, I'm just going to the bin!"'

For some reason, Darien cut his twin some slack. It gave José the opportunity he needed. 'I grabbed my backpack, opened the fire door and started running.' He turned left, and darted down Greek Street, a narrow lane that backs onto the car park of the busy Broadway Shopping Centre. He turned right down Bay Street before taking the first right into Francis Street and seeking refuge near a children's playground in Minogue Reserve just a few hundred metres from the Scientology building.

It was dark and silent and José kept still. He didn't move for another three hours. Heading straight into a park so close to Scientology's Advanced Organisation might seem counterintuitive, but he thought his pursuers would start looking further afield.

When the Venezuelan finally moved from the dark shadows of Minogue Reserve he headed towards the centre of Sydney's business district, just over a kilometre away. The streets were still awash with late-night drinkers, coming and going from the city's bars and clubs. He was seeing a part of Sydney he'd never seen before. Young men and women were out bar hopping. They were laughing, picking up, staying out late, all the things he'd been deprived of in his seventeen years inside Sea Org.

'Are you having a nice walk?' José was asked, as he was grabbed from behind. It was an official from Scientology's Advanced Org. There were two of them, the official and Darien, José's twin on the RPF. His escape had been thwarted, just hours after he'd pushed open the fire door and run for it. The Scientology official pulled out his mobile phone to call for reinforcements to haul in the escapee. But as he went to dial the number, the battery went flat. He would have to use a public phone.

José saw his chance. As the Scientologist wandered off to find a phone, the Venezuelan walked calmly in the opposite direction. Darien followed him. José looked for a dark street amid the bright lights of Sydney's business district. He walked down a lane; his twin followed. He pushed Darien over, shouting, 'Leave me alone. I'm not coming back'. The American got to his feet. 'If you don't leave me alone,' he yelled, 'I will put you on the floor.' Darien couldn't leave him alone. If he let him go, he would face further punishment back at the RPF.

Navarro punched Darien five times in the face and he fell to the ground. 'I was in a rage. I said if you keep following me, I will break your bones.' Darien was around ten years younger, but he couldn't defend himself from José's onslaught. The Venezuelan left him on the ground and ran for it. It was around 4 am. He decided to head for the Opera House. He is not sure why. 'I was just drawn to it,' he says. As the sun came up, he headed to the Botanic Gardens. It seemed like a safe place.

José had just $30 in his pocket. After buying some tobacco and cigarette papers, he worked out that he could afford one meal a day from McDonald's for the next three days. He got into his routine of catching the odd hour of sleep in the park by day, and walking the streets by night. By the end of his third day as a Scientology fugitive he didn't know what to do next. He was starving and skint, and roaming the streets in a desperate state. The grass he slept on doubled as his next meal. 'I was fucked,' he says. But no matter how bad things got, he could not go back. 'The RPF was like jail,' he says. 'I would rather eat grass for the rest of my life than go back to the RPF.'

By day six he was getting desperate and delirious. He started thinking dark thoughts. 'I was worried that if I didn't find anyone, I'd have to go back in and my life would be destroyed again.' José steeled his resolve to never return. 'I decided I would rather starve to death than go back in.' What he did next would change his life forever, much like the choice he made in Venezuela nearly 20 years earlier.

JOSÉ NAVARRO WAS BORN to a large family, in a small industrial town. He was the eighth of ten children, and, like many Venezuelans of his generation, dreamed of migrating to America. He left school at 17 and worked as a waiter in a local restaurant, before finding more permanent employment as a chef at a major international hotel. In his spare time, José studied English, French and Italian. His English teacher was a Scientologist. He was soon convinced that joining the Sea Org was his ticket to the United States. But it was a ticket that came with a massive down payment. Scientologists believe in past and future lives. When you join the Sea Org you sign a contract, promising to serve Scientology for one billion years – that is a thousand million years. He would only see his family once in the next 20 years.

Navarro started his training for the Sea Org in Mexico City, but had to move soon after. The local Scientology centre could not afford to pay the rent and they were kicked out of the building. José and his colleagues were relocated to a warehouse in the countryside until they were able re-establish an office in the city. After a few months of training, Navarro felt no closer to his dream of living in the US. But then he received an offer that made him the envy of all the other trainees. 'I got a call asking me to go to the *Freewinds*,' he says. 'They needed a chef. The others were very jealous.'

The *Freewinds* is Scientology's 440-foot luxury cruise ship, which sails the Caribbean. It acts as a floating study centre for wealthy Scientologists who can afford high-level courses such as Operating Thetan Level VIII (OT VIII). It's also the place where in July 2004, David Miscavige put on an extravagant birthday party for Tom Cruise that cost hundreds of thousands of dollars.

In the week leading up to Cruise's party, José and other kitchen staff were averaging two to three hours sleep a night. The chefs were under immense pressure to prepare a perfect banquet for the big night and meet the daily demands of David Miscavige's appetite for high-quality, low-calorie snacks and meals. 'We were warned,' Navarro says. 'Any mistakes and it would be straight to the engine room.'

The *Freewinds* was not only a place for celebration. While Cruise and his acolytes partied, there were others on board who were being held against their will.[13] The *Freewinds* is also part prison hulk – another place to punish and isolate Sea Org members who are deemed to have gone against Scientology policy or are considered a risk to the organisation's reputation.

In late 2006, Karleen Desimone, a young Scientology executive, was sent to the cruise ship. Her family was *Freewinds* royalty. Her father was a former Chief Officer, her mother had previously handled external relations for the vessel. Karleen had grown up on the *Freewinds*.[14] But her latest visit was no family reunion. She'd been sent to the *Freewinds* for punishment. While on board she and José fell in love.

Before she was banished to the *Freewinds,* Karleen Desimone was Deputy Executive Director of the International Association of Scientologists Administrations (IASA). The IASA solicits and banks donations for the International Association of Scientologists (IAS).[15] Desimone oversaw the fundraising for the IAS. In some weeks they pulled in US$5–10 million.[16]

The IAS was established in 1984 as a legal defence fund for the church. At the time the church was involved in dozens of multi-million-dollar lawsuits.[17] But the IAS grew into something bigger. Former Scientology executive Marty Rathbun says the IAS became a personal 'war chest' for its leader, David Miscavige, describing it as 'all offshore, out of the reach of tax authorities or civil lawsuits; all at his fingertips, to spend in whatever ways he sees fit'.[18] Former Scientology spokesman Mike Rinder estimated that by 2014 the IAS's cash reserves were probably in excess of US$2 billion.[19]

The IAS relentlessly solicits for donations. Nancy Cartwright, the voice of Bart Simpson in *The Simpsons*, was made a Patron Laureate of the IAS when she gifted US$10 million.[20] Scientologists will rack up huge debts to meet donation targets.[21] One Seattle couple that handed over US$160,000 were told their donation was not good enough and were reported to church officials for insufficient generosity.[22]

By 2006, questions started to be asked at the top of the IAS about the ethics of all this predatory fundraising and where the money was ending up. According to Mike Rinder:

Huge amounts of money were spent by the IAS to cater to POB [Pope on a Box – a disparaging nickname given to Scientology's leader, David Miscavige] and it was funded through a scheme whereby the staff of the IAS were paid 'bonuses' that they turned over to form a slush fund for POB/ Tom Cruise jaunts/parties/food/gifts.[23]

Janet McLaughlin was the President of the IASA, the organisation that managed the IAS and took care of its affairs. She was softly spoken, but hard headed, and Miscavige gave her power and status through the IASA, but after decades of playing the role of loyal subordinate she reached her breaking point. In late 2006, she made it known that she was not happy with the way IAS money was being spent and how her staff were being treated.[24] This did not go down well with Miscavige. McLaughlin's car was fitted with a tracking device, her calls were monitored, and she was tailed by private investigators.[25]

Janet McLaughlin and her husband, Colm, made plans to leave Sea Org. But before they could escape, Miscavige's agents swung into action. Around 15 Sea Org executives arrived at her LA office and separated her from her husband. Colm was dragged, kicking and screaming, into another room, where he was shoved into a closet.[26] Janet was sent to 'The Hole', Scientology's brutal punishment camp for executives, situated in a desert compound east of Los Angeles.[27]

It consisted of two trailers connected by a conference room. At times over a hundred Sea Org members were crammed into this building on the orders of David Miscavige.[28] Some stayed for months; others were trapped for years. There were bars on the windows and doors and a security guard stationed at the compound's only entrance.[29] Staff slept on the floors. Former Scientology Executive Debbie Cook testified that David Miscavige would have the electricity turned off for weeks at a time as desert temperatures nudged 40°C.[30] (The Church of Scientology denies the allegations concerning Janet McLaughlin.)

Janet McLaughlin paid a high price for standing up to Miscavige. Mike Rinder, who was in 'The Hole' on and off between 2004 and 2007, describes a *Lord of the Flies* style culture inside the compound where former executives were forced to confess to crimes against Scientology they had not committed, reminiscent of the outlandish confessions of those in Chinese thought control camps.[31]

While Janet McLaughlin was stuck in 'The Hole', her husband, Colm, and at least four other IASA executives were sent to the *Freewind*s as punishment. One of them was Karleen Desimone.

At first Karleen was sent to do hard labour in the engine room. 'It's hot, it's extremely loud, it's smelly, it's not nice,'[32] says Valeska Paris, a colleague of Desimone's on the *Freewinds*. Eventually Karleen graduated to the kitchen where she scrubbed pots and pans and peeled vegetables. It was here that she crossed paths with José Navarro.

José and Karleen already knew each other. When the Venezuelan had first arrived on the ship in 1993, Karleen was on board with her family. Already José sensed the chemistry between the two of them. He wanted to have a relationship with Karleen, but was overruled by senior Scientologists on board. 'They told me you can't have anything to do with her, because you're not a Scientologist yet.'[33]

The same excuse could not be used 13 years later when Karleen and José were reunited in the ship's kitchen. By this time José had more than paid his dues to the Sea Org. But the ship's hierarchy found new excuses to keep them apart. José was told he could not be friendly with Karleen. She was on the vessel to be punished and was to be treated as if she was on the Rehabilitation Project Force.

This was easier said than done. Karleen and José were working together in the confined spaces of the *Freewinds* kitchen. They would brush past each other, talk and flirt, and share cigarettes during meal breaks. After three weeks of simmering sexual tension they vowed to start a relationship once Karleen's punishment was over.

These plans were undermined when one of the kitchen staff told the ship's Master at Arms that something was going on between them. Security removed Karleen from the kitchen and the pair were given a one-month separation order. 'We were so angry,' says José. 'We hadn't even kissed yet!'[34] They became even more determined to be together and they wrote letters to each other in contravention of the separation order.

At 8 am, on the morning after the one-month separation order had expired, José woke and went to have a cigarette in the smoking area near the crew's dining room. Karleen was there. 'We started kissing,' he says. 'We couldn't stop. It was amazing.'

The couple made secret plans to get married. Karleen was still officially being punished, so they had to hide their feelings for each other. But rumours of their relationship filtered back to Scientology's security apparatus. They were hauled into an office where they were asked to explain themselves. They admitted to breaking Sea Org rules about pre-marital sex.

As punishment Karleen was sent back to the engine room, and José was forced to work on the decks. 'I tried to swap to make it easier for her,' he says, 'but they said no, she deserves heavy punishment.'[35] She sent a note to him telling him to meet her in the engine room at a designated time. Security found out. This time they would be separated permanently.

José was told he would be sent to the Rehabilitation Project Force, in Australia. 'They told me if you finish it, you can come back to the ship, and get married,' he says. He was sent to Australia, without even getting to say goodbye to the woman he wanted to spend the rest of his life with.

After his arrival in Australia he found out that Karleen had been pregnant with their child. Women in the Sea Org were banned from having children. According to Valeska Paris, who was on board at the time, Karleen was forced to have an abortion, carried out by a doctor on the *Freewinds*.[36] José wasn't even told. He had no say in the decision, and was unable to comfort Karleen through her grief. The

Church of Scientology would not directly respond to the allegation that she was forced to have an abortion, instead an email sent by Sydney lawyer Patrick George stated, 'The Church specifically denies that either Ms Desimone or Mr Navarro were ever forced to do anything in the Church.'[37]

José Navarro disembarked from the *Freewind*s in October 2007, on the island of Bonaire. He was escorted by a Sea Org legal officer, who made sure he did not escape. They flew to Amsterdam, then London, then Singapore, before arriving in Sydney. After a brief stop at Scientology's Advanced Organisation in Glebe, he was taken to the RPF's headquarters in Dundas.

On the RPF José was paid $17.50 a week. He worked 12–14-hour days, seven days a week. All Sea Org members assigned to the RPF wore dark work clothes to signify their status as 'degraded beings'. They were forced to run from job to job. The food was deliberately sub-standard and the sleeping quarters cramped. At Dundas, around 20 Sea Org members slept in a room that was around six by ten metres. Bunk beds were stacked up to the ceiling, four high.[38]

On the RPF in Sydney at the time was former St George rugby league player Chris Guider. After prematurely quitting his career as a professional footballer, Guider rose to be the Master at Arms at the Religious Technology Center in the US. He was the most senior ethics officer in the Church of Scientology, responsible for enforcing the will of the church's leader, David Miscavige. Guider says he was sent to the RPF in Australia, after he failed to comply with an order from Miscavige to hit an editor who was working on a Scientology promotional video.[39]

The RPF in Sydney was used as a dumping ground for troublesome people that David Miscavige wanted sent a long way away. 'The order came down from Miscavige that they were to be sent to the worst RPF on the planet,' says Guider. The worst RPF on the planet was in Sydney. The Church of Scientology, through its lawyer Patrick George, denied Australia was used as a dumping ground. 'On the contrary Australia is an important continental hub for the religion,' he said in a statement.[40]

Carol Miles, the public face of the *Freewinds,* was another difficult case banished to the RPF in Sydney. Valeska Paris, who'd also been sent there from the *Freewinds*, says Miles was held against her will. 'She told me she wanted to leave and have kids.'[41] The 'worst RPF on the planet' also detained local Scientologists. Mark Whitta, the former Captain of the Advanced Org in Sydney, was imprisoned there underneath a squash court. 'The poor guy was there for months, on a mud floor, under this building,' says Guider. 'Because he was high profile, they didn't want the public to see him, so he was put under the squash court all day long under guard.'[42] The deprivations of the RPF in Sydney were not restricted to adults. According to Valeska Paris, a 16-year-old boy was put on the RPF for four years after he stole from the canteen.

About a year and half into his punishment in Australia, José began to lose hope. 'I thought I was never going to see Karleen again,' he says. 'I tried to write to her, but they wouldn't let me.' The Church of Scientology had lied to him. Valeska Paris had heard Lurie Belotte, David Miscavige's representative on the *Freewinds*, say he would never be allowed to return to the ship.[43] He was now the responsibility of the Church of Scientology in Australia. He would languish in the RPF at Dundas for nearly two and half years before he found a way to escape.

ON HIS SEVENTH NIGHT on the run, José Navarro continued to roam the streets of Sydney. He was delirious with sleep deprivation and hunger as he walked past a group of carefree backpackers, towards the sandstone façade of Central Railway Station. Was it delirium? Or was the woman walking towards him really staring at him? As he got closer he recognised her. It was Ramana Dienes-Browning. When José last saw her, she was a senior executive on board the *Freewinds*. But now Ramana was living in the Blue Mountains and had travelled to Sydney for the day. She had just finished dinner with her mother, having told her for the first time about the physical and mental abuse she had suffered in Sea Org. Her mother had introduced Ramana to the *Freewinds*, and was still a practising Scientologist. The dinner was cathartic for Ramana, and traumatic for her mother. She had cried throughout the meal as Ramana told her of the ten long years she had spent in Sea Org.

Ramana had begun the day by meditating. 'I'd received a clear message to keep my eyes and ears open,' she says. With time to kill between dinner and the train home, she went for a walk. 'For some reason I decided to walk down to a part of the city which I never go to. As I walked down the street, I passed a man and we looked at each other and I couldn't place him. As I walked past him a few metres it suddenly hit me … I know him … I know him from the *Freewinds*! I hadn't seen him for over ten years!'[44]

Everything about their chance meeting was out of context. They were on land, not sea. They were in Australia, not the Caribbean. Neither was wearing their crisp white Sea Org uniform. In fact, both had escaped from Sea Org, but neither knew, in that instant, if the other was in or out. 'The last time I saw him [he] was in his cook's uniform in the crew galley on the *Freewinds*,' says Ramana. 'I immediately doubled back and walked up to him. Both of us couldn't believe our eyes. We hugged. He seemed relieved, almost tearful and couldn't stop saying, "I can't believe it's you."[45] I asked him what he was doing. I can't remember what he first explained, because it was tentative and wary … like he was trying to work out if I was there to catch him or whether it really was a chance meeting.'

'It was a long hug,' says José. 'Ramana asked, "What are you doing around here?" I lied and said, "I'm going to see a friend."' He wasn't sure if he could trust Ramana. What if she had been sent to track him down and lure him back to Sea Org? Conflicting thoughts competed inside his sleep-deprived brain. Was Ramana still in the Sea Org? Even if she wasn't, she might still be a Scientologist. Could he trust her? Informing on wrongdoers is a strong a part of the culture inside Scientology. He was overwhelmed to see Ramana. She had the potential to be his saviour, but he was paralysed by indecision.

They went to say goodbye to each other. 'As I went to leave, Ramana said, "Hold on, you look really bad. What's going on?" I told her I'd left Sea Org a week ago. She said, "Oh my God, you're coming with me!"'

The pair caught a train to the Blue Mountains. 'At this stage I didn't realise he was starving,' says Ramana. 'It took the whole trip back home to get the story out of him, he was so wary of which side I was on. As I told him bits of my story and reassured him I was totally out and he was safe, he filled in the blanks and gave me more information about his escape.' When they arrived home, José had a long hot shower and Ramana cooked him his first proper meal in four days. 'Oh, mate, it felt so good,' says José. 'I was very lucky.'

Scientologists are taught to fear the outside world. Hubbard referred to non-Scientologists as 'wogs' and the world they inhabited as the 'wog world', with its legal system of 'wog justice'. He picked up the racial slur while living in England, and fashioned it into his own disparaging term. Those inside are told the 'wog world' is a dangerous place, and that if they leave Scientology they will become failures. Former Scientologist Marc Headley says when he was in the Sea Org the general public were 'portrayed as drug addled criminals',[46] but after José Navarro escaped he came across a range of people from all walks of life who went out of their way to help him.

José stayed on Ramana's couch until she helped organise share accommodation with a close friend. They kept a close eye on him over that first six months. 'He had been one of the only people who was decent and kind to me when I was in serious trouble on the ship,' says Ramana. 'I'm so glad I had the chance to repay his kindness.' José was able to pay the rent at his share home because a local café owner took him on even though he was an illegal worker. The owner's son was studying psychology, and helped José out. 'I will never forget them,' he says of the family.[47]

Ramana's brother-in-law helped José get his passport and belongings from the Church of Scientology. When his visa was close to expiring, Gráinne O'Donovan, a lawyer with a deep knowledge of Scientology, came to the rescue, referring José to the Australian Federal Police's people-trafficking unit. 'Gráinne was my saviour,' says José. 'She was my mentor, she made me feel safe, she contacted the police, bought me food, told me that it was okay to be free, she organised everything. She saved my life.'[48]

Evelyn Eck, a senior adviser to Senator Nick Xenophon, accompanied José to see the Federal agents. He had heard Xenophon described inside the Sea Org as 'the number one Suppressive Person in Australia'. Now Xenophon was supporting his application for a protection visa.

José was terrified when he first met the Australian Federal Police. 'I was shitting my pants. I was really nervous. I thought I was going to be sent back to Venezuela.' He had no reason to worry. The police working in the Transnational Sexual Exploitation and Trafficking Team were experts in their field, and sensitive to the trauma he had been through.

José got further help from the Red Cross and Jennifer Burn, the Director of Anti-Slavery Australia. He qualified for assistance under the government's Support for Victims of People-Trafficking Program. Eventually they helped José get a protection visa and permanent residence in Australia on the grounds that he was a victim of human trafficking.

José found out that despite the propaganda fed him to him in the Sea Org, his life would not be an eternal misery once he left Scientology. He has made a new life for himself in Sydney and has never been happier. He works in a top restaurant, has a beautiful girlfriend and can speak his mind. He can watch TV when he feels like it, go to bed when he wants, and knock back a few cold beers after work. He is paid properly and has access to healthcare. He is a free man.

So how did it come to this? Why did the Australian government have to provide a protection visa for José on the grounds that a religious organisation it deems a tax-exempt charity had trafficked him? How could a church that claims to believe in freedom and human rights enslave and traffic its members? How could a church that in its own religious creed says 'that all men have inalienable rights to their own lives' separate a loving couple who wanted to get married and have a child, and force the woman to have an abortion?

How could a church use Australia as a penal colony in the 21st century?

To understand the madness of modern-day Scientology, you need to go back to the source, and the thinking that marked its very beginning.

CHAPTER 2

RON'S WAR

L. RON HUBBARD WAS not built to withstand the sweat and swelter of a Brisbane summer. His ruddy complexion was susceptible to sunburn; his eyes were sensitive to bright sunlight. Raised in the northern states of Montana and Washington he was not used to the heat and humidity that hit him when he arrived in Brisbane in January 1942.[1] It was a place, as the novelist David Malouf described it, where 'the pavements gave off a heat that rose right up through your shoes'.[2]

Hubbard wasn't meant to end up in Australia. A junior Lieutenant serving on the USS *President Polk*, his ship was diverted to Queensland after Japanese forces took Manila. Hubbard found himself in a subtropical town undergoing rapid change on the other side of the world. Brisbane at the beginning of 1942 felt more like a big country town than a city. Its shops and hotels were made of timber; its homes stretched high on stilts. The streets were lined with jacarandas and poinsettias. The backyards were fenced with corrugated iron. Its tallest building told the time. The clock tower above the Brisbane City Hall put surrounding structures in the shade.

The population of Brisbane, fewer than 350,000, was about to swell by a fifth, as Queensland's capital morphed into a garrison city and General Douglas MacArthur set up headquarters for the Allied Forces' South West Pacific campaign. US servicemen flooded the city, bringing jazz, the jitterbug, and nylon stockings. Local women flocked to the handsome GIs with their well-cut uniforms and healthy pay packets.

Tension between Australian and American soldiers spilled over into widespread street brawls in November that year. One Australian soldier was killed, and eight more received gunshot wounds when thousands of troops became involved in an infamous fracas that became known as the Battle of Brisbane.[3]

L. Ron Hubbard missed all of this, however. While the American servicemen based in Brisbane were commonly described as 'overpaid, over-sexed and over here', Hubbard's stint in Queensland is better characterised as overbearing, overzealous and over too soon. Hubbard would end up portraying himself as a war hero who helped save Australia from the Japanese. His arrival, his stay and his departure would all become subject of Scientology mythmaking. But the truth is that Hubbard was sent home from Brisbane in disgrace.

When L. Ron Hubbard enlisted in the Naval Reserve in 1941 he was already a widely published author, knocking out novels and short stories for a penny a word. The 30-year-old pumped out pulp fiction, science fiction and westerns as he struggled to support his first wife, Polly, and their two children, Nibs and Kay. Writing swashbuckling stories was obviously not enough for Hubbard. He wanted to live the adventurous life of his characters. He was desperate to join the military, and thought his country needed a man of his talents.

Hubbard soon found out the military could be just as brutal with rejection slips as the big publishing companies. In 1938, the Air Corps turned him down. In September 1939, he sent a letter to the Office of the Secretary of the War Department recommending himself. Once again he was rejected. By 1941, he had cultivated a broad range of references. The most colourful came from the desk of Robert M Ford, a politician from Washington State. The reference begins: 'This will introduce one of the most brilliant men I have ever known …'[4] Ford later admitted, 'I don't know why Ron wanted a letter. I just gave him a letter-head and said, "Hell, you're the writer, you write it!"'[5] But Hubbard's creative writing did not win over the military. In April that year he failed his Navy Reserve physical.

A month later, Hubbard was given a lifeline. In an address to the nation, President Roosevelt declared a state of emergency, warning Hitler that the US was prepared to go to war. For the US Navy, it became a case of all hands on deck. With recruitment standards lowered, Hubbard finally received his commission from the Naval Reserve in July 1941. After Pearl Harbor was bombed in December, Hubbard was meant to head to Manila. But the speed of the Japanese offensive in the Philippines took the military by surprise and the USS *President Polk* was diverted to Brisbane.

The official record of how Hubbard arrived in Australia doesn't quite match the story he would end up spinning to his military colleagues. Captain Thomas Moulton later testified in court that Hubbard claimed he made an epic journey from Java after disembarking from the US Destroyer the *Edsall*, 'He had been landed, so he told me, in Java ... and had made his way across the land to Soerabaja [Surabaya], and that is when the place was occupied. When the Japanese came in, he took off into the hills and lived up in the jungle for some time until he made an escape from there.'[6]

Hubbard, as Moulton told it, was machine-gunned while trying to out-fox the Japanese in the Javanese jungle. 'In the back, in the area of the kidneys, I believe on the right side,' the Captain recalled, 'I know that he told me he had made his escape eventually to Australia. I don't know just when it was. Apparently he and another chap sailed a life raft, I believe, to near Australia where they were picked up by a British or Australian destroyer.'[7]

Scientology's founder must have been superhuman with a paddle in his hands. According to Captain Moulton's testimony, Hubbard said he'd navigated his life raft to within 160 km (100 miles) of Australia. That is a trip of over 1600 km (1000 miles), in shark-infested waters, smack-bang in the middle of the monsoon season, the most dangerous period to attempt a sea crossing to northern Australia. Fishing boats carrying asylum seekers struggle to make it to Australia via this route, let alone men in rubber life rafts.

Hubbard's tall tale does not stack up with the official military record. Moulton said his navy buddy was in Java on 8 December. He didn't even leave the US till 17 December. There is no record of Hubbard ever being on the *Edsall*, which was sunk on 1 March. The Japanese invaded Java on 28 February; by this time Hubbard was already in the process of being sent back to the US for ill discipline. There is no evidence that Hubbard was wounded by machine-gun fire or by any other weapon. If he had been wounded in action he would have received a Purple Heart. Despite insistent claims from the Church of Scientology, military records show he received no such award. Hubbard's personal nurse from 1975 to 1980 testified that he had no scars from bullet wounds.[8]

In a 1956 lecture to Scientologists in London, Hubbard restated claims he was injured in the Pacific, further embellishing the tale by saying he was sent back to the US on the Secretary of the Navy's plane. 'I was flown in from the South Pacific as the first casualty to be shipped out of the South Pacific war back to the States,'[9] he told a captive audience. Perhaps the truth hurt Hubbard. The real reason he was sent back home had nothing to do with enemy fire.

Within weeks of landing in Brisbane, Hubbard took to writing. He would have been better off belting out one of his boy's own adventure stories than the five-page 'intelligence report' he eventually filed. The report dealt with a ship routing plan that had gone awry, and criticised his superiors including the Naval Attaché, Commander Lewis Causey.[10] Six days later, Hubbard was issued orders to return home.

Commander Causey accused Hubbard of acting above his rank. 'By assuming unauthorized authority and attempting to perform duties for which he has no qualifications he became the source of much trouble,' Causey wrote.[11] The Naval Attaché issued a blistering character assessment, as he punted the junior Lieutenant out of the country: 'This officer is not satisfactory for independent duty assignment. He is garrulous and tries to give impressions of his importance. He also seems to think that he has unusual ability in most lines. These characteristics indicate that he will require close supervision for satisfactory performance of any intelligence duty.'[12]

Hubbard was sent home in disgrace. Commander Causey cabled the Bureau of Naval Personnel, stating: 'He is unsatisfactory for any available assignment here.'[13] Hubbard was eventually sent packing to the Office of Cable Censorship where he could work on removing inappropriate sentences rather than writing them. At his new posting he would continue to be reminded of his embarrassing stay in Brisbane. He received ongoing correspondence about bad debts he left owing to Ryders menswear store in Adelaide Street and a missing Thompson machine gun he had borrowed from the Australian military.[14]

In less than two months in Australia Hubbard had racked up debts, lost a machine gun, upset the top brass and been sent home. Yet two decades later, Hubbard would portray his time in Brisbane as something Australians should be grateful for. In a statement to the press he said, 'In 1942, as the senior US naval officer in Northern Australia, by a fluke of fate, I helped save them from the Japanese.'[15]

The rest of Hubbard's war was equally inglorious. He was withdrawn from his only command after waging a 55-hour battle with what he claimed were two Japanese submarines but actually turned out to be a magnetic deposit off the Oregon coast, and for shelling a Mexican island for gunnery practice. In his report on these incidents, Rear Admiral Braisted, Commander of the Fleet Operational Trainer Command, Pacific, said: 'Consider this officer lacking in the essential qualities of judgement, leadership and cooperation. He acts without forethought as to probable results ... Not considered qualified for command or promotion at this time. Recommend duty on a large vessel where he can be properly supervised.'[16] Despite his claims, there is no record that Hubbard ever engaged in combat with the enemy.

The Church of Scientology argues there's a good reason for the discrepancy between Hubbard's tales of derring-do and the official military record. Colonel Leroy Fletcher Prouty was a chief of Special Operations for the Joint Chiefs of Staff under President Kennedy. In the Oliver Stone film *JFK*, Donald Sutherland plays an intelligence agent named X who believes the assassination of President Kennedy was part of a coup driven by the military industrial complex. The character X is based loosely on Fletcher Prouty, who worked as an adviser on the film, and as a consultant to the Church of Scientology in the 1980s.

Prouty was commissioned to write an authorised biography of Hubbard and contributed articles to Scientology's *Freedom* magazine. In 1985, he issued an affidavit defending Hubbard's war record claiming it had been 'sheep dipped' to hide Hubbard's role as an intelligence officer. He made similar claims in letters to CBS's *60 Minutes* and the publisher of Russell Miller's book *Bare-Faced Messiah*, arguing that Hubbard's military record 'is replete with markings that signify deep intelligence service at the highest levels'.[17]

Prouty wrote that 'nearly all official correspondence to and from Lt Hubbard bears the symbol "NAV-1651" (or other 1600 serial). This "1600" series identifies correspondence in the Intelligence series.' But Jon Atack, a former Scientologist who meticulously researched Hubbard's military record for his book *Let's Sell These People a Piece of Blue Sky*, says Prouty's claims do not stack up. 'His most significant evidence was the use of the code number "16" on Hubbard's orders,' he says. 'In fact, the code indicated that Hubbard was a member of the Naval Reserve, as documents within his Navy file, and comparison with other Navy Reserve officers' files, readily demonstrates.'[18]

Hubbard also claimed he was a widely decorated war hero who had received 27 medals including the Purple Heart.[19] The Church of Scientology at other times has argued the figure is 21 – taken from a copy of a US Navy notice of separation document they regularly distribute to journalists.

But this document has all the hallmarks of an amateur-hour forgery. It does not appear in Hubbard's naval records and is signed by Lieutenant Commander Howard Thompson, an officer who never existed according to naval records. Two of the 21 medals cited in this document were not commissioned until after Hubbard had completed active service; other medals such as the British Victory Medal simply didn't exist during World War II.

Hubbard's file shows he had been awarded just four standard issue decorations: the American Defense Service Medal; the Asiatic-Pacific Campaign Medal; the American Campaign Medal; and the World War II Victory Medal. None of these medals reward heroism or mark combat. They were awarded to everyone who served in these areas or, in the last case, served in the US military. There is no record of a Purple Heart, debunking Hubbard's claims he was wounded in action.

The missing Purple Heart undermines Scientology's key mythology that Hubbard's war ended in Oak Knoll Naval Hospital 'crippled and blinded'. As Hubbard wrote in *My Philosophy*, 'Blinded with injured optic nerves, and lame with physical injuries to hip and back, at the end of World War II, I faced an almost nonexistent future. My service record states: "This officer has no neurotic or psychotic tendencies of any kind whatsoever," but it also states "permanently disabled physically".'[20] Hubbard's military record states no such thing.

Hubbard did suffer from conjunctivitis, poor eyesight, a duodenal ulcer, arthritis and hemorrhoids. He also complained of urethral discharges, symptoms consistent with that common Naval affliction, venereal disease. When applying for a veteran's disability pension, Hubbard made no mention of war wounds or being blinded by the flash of a large calibre gun.[21]

If Hubbard was truly suffering from ill health following his war service, convalescing at home with his wife and family was not part of his recovery plan. Getting laid, and dabbling in the occult soon became part of his post-war rehabilitation program. On 5 December 1945, he was discharged from the Navy. The following day he applied for a military pension and headed straight to Pasadena and a share house with a reputation for debauchery.

Rocket scientist Jack Parsons owned a three-storey mansion at 1003 South Orange Grove Avenue, a street the *Los Angeles Times* once called 'the most beautiful residence street in the world'.[22] The 11-bedroom estate, once the home to the lumber millionaire and philanthropist Arthur Fleming, had been transformed into a bohemian flophouse following his death. Actors, writers, dancers and libertines moved in, much to the distaste of local residents. Pasadena police received official complaints about 'sex perversion'[23], while the local fire brigade were kept on their toes by Parsons' experiments with rockets and fireworks.

Jack Parsons was a true original. His work inventing a radical new form of rocket fuel paved the way for the moon landings and further space travel. He was a co-founder of the Jet Propulsion Laboratory, a research centre now run by NASA that oversees the Galileo mission to Jupiter and the Mars Rovers. As a child, Parsons experimented shooting off home-made rockets in his backyard. As an adult he began experimenting with black magic, becoming a disciple of the English occultist Aleister Crowley, and heading up the local Lodge of the *Ordo Templi Orientis*, a secret society that practised 'sex magic'.

L. Ron Hubbard didn't just move into 'The Parsonage' for the stimulating conversation. He was soon participating in occult rituals with Parsons including a bizarre attempt at creating a supernatural 'moonchild' during a 'sex magic' rite. Parsons detailed the ritual in *The Book of Babalon*. According to the diary, Hubbard wore white, carried a lamp and played the role of 'scribe', channelling the voice of the goddess Babalon who provided blow-by-blow instructions on how to impregnate Parsons' 'scarlet woman', the actress and artist Marjorie Cameron.[24]

Hubbard and Parsons performed the 8th ritual of Crowley's *Ordo Templi Orientalis* to incarnate the Anti-Christ. During the ceremony, Hubbard urged Parsons to 'Lay out a white sheet. Place upon it blood of birth. Envision her approaching thee. Think upon the lewd, lascivious things thou coulds't do. All is good to Babalon. All. Preserve the material basis. Thus lust is hers, the passion yours. Consider thou the Beast raping.'[25] The 'material basis' was Parsons' semen, ejaculated as Hubbard looked on.[26]

Hubbard's bizarre invocation did not work. No 'moonchild' eventuated. Aleister Crowley, a man not easily appalled, expressed his dismay in a letter to fellow occultist Karl Germer: 'Apparently Parsons or Hubbard or somebody is producing a Moonchild. I get fairly frantic when I contemplate the idiocy of these louts.'[27]

When *Sunday Times* reporter Alex Mitchell broke the story of Hubbard's participation in sex magic rituals, the Church of Scientology had an interesting take on why Hubbard had donned the white robes, and shouted incantations about menstrual blood and semen. Apparently he'd done it all for the good of his country.

In a statement provided to the *Sunday Times* in 1969 it was claimed, 'Hubbard broke up black magic in America ... He went to live at the house and investigated the black magic rites and the general situation and found them very bad. Hubbard's mission was successful far beyond anyone's expectations. The house was torn down. Hubbard rescued a girl they were using. The black magic group was dispersed and destroyed and has never recovered.'[28] No evidence was ever provided to back these claims up. The original copy of the statement was provided during a court case in 1984. It was in Hubbard's handwriting.[29]

When Hubbard mentions rescuing a girl from black magic, he is almost certainly referring to liberating Sara Northrup from her relationship with Jack Parsons. Sara, known as Betty by all those in The Parsonage, had first met Hubbard in August when he visited Pasadena at the invitation of science fiction fan Lou Goldstone.[30] Jack Parsons believed in open relationships, and Sara obliged, starting a sexual relationship with Hubbard. When Hubbard returned to Pasadena in December after driving straight from the Officer Separation Center in San Francisco, he and Sara resumed their affair.[31]

Sara was 21 when she met Hubbard. Just as she had taken on Parsons' appetite for 'sex magic', she soon adapted to the ways of her new beau. Hubbard was desperate for an income stream beyond his meagre military pension. He cooked up a plan that would see him take not only Parsons' girlfriend, but go after his life savings as well.

In January, Jack, Sara and Ron had formed a company called Allied Enterprises. Parsons kicked in over US$20,000, Hubbard around US$1200, Northrup not a dime.[32]

In late April, Northrup and Hubbard withdrew US$10,000 from the Allied Enterprises' bank account and headed for Florida. Parsons approved of the deal believing they would purchase a yacht and sell it for profit.[33] When Aleister Crowley heard of the plan he cabled Karl Germer with a warning: 'Suspect Ron playing confidence trick. Jack evidently weak fool. Obvious victim prowling swindlers.'[34]

Jack Parsons eventually came to the same conclusion. He headed to Miami to find that three boats had been bought including a schooner, *The Harpoon*, in which Ron and Sara had already set sail. Hubbard had written to the Chief of Naval Personnel seeking permission to visit South America and China.[35] After Parsons worked some black magic in his Miami hotel room, the weather remarkably changed. As he later wrote in a letter to Crowley, 'His ship was struck by a sudden squall off the coast, which ripped off his sails and forced him back to port, where I took the boat in custody.'[36]

Parsons kept two of the boats, retrieved most of his money, but never won back his girlfriend.[37] Hubbard's next act of deception would involve Sara, the woman he loved, and Polly, his wife and the mother of his children. On 10 August 1946, L. Ron Hubbard married his 21-year-old girlfriend. Hubbard now had two wives.[38] Sara found out her husband was already married when Polly filed for divorce in 1947 on the grounds of desertion and non-support.[39]

By this time, Hubbard had started beating Sara. In a testimony recorded in 1997 shortly before her death, she recalled a winter's night when Hubbard had pistol-whipped her after she had fallen asleep. 'I got up and left the house in the night and walked on the ice of the lake because I was terrified.'[40] Hubbard told her she was smiling in her sleep. He was worried she was dreaming about someone else.[41]

In October 1947, Hubbard asked for help. In a letter to the Veterans Administration, he wrote:

This is a request for treatment ... I was placed on certain medication back east and have continued it at my own expense. After trying and failing for two years to regain my equilibrium in civil life, I am utterly unable to approach anything like my own competence. My last physician informed me that it might be very helpful if I were to be examined and perhaps treated psychiatrically or even by a psycho-analyst. Toward the end of my service I avoided out of pride any mental examinations, hoping that time would balance a mind which I had every reason to suppose was seriously affected. I cannot account for nor rise above long periods of moroseness and suicidal inclinations ... I cannot, myself, afford such treatment. Would you please help me?[42]

Hubbard didn't get the help he was after. His pension was increased a few months later,[43] but the extra funds were not enough to stop him from taking desperate measures. In August 1948, Hubbard was arrested and fingerprinted by the San Luis Obispo County Sheriff, for cheque fraud. After initially pleading not guilty before the San Gabriel Township Justice Court, he changed his plea to guilty and was fined US$25.[44]

At the heart of Scientology's creation myth is the assertion that Hubbard cured himself from a state of permanent disability by using the power of his own mind. By 1947, he was said to be back to full health by using the same techniques that would form the basis for Dianetics and Scientology. As Hubbard's disciples wrote, in the 1992 edition of *What is Scientology?*, 'So complete was his recovery, that officers from the Naval Retiring Board reviewing Lt. Hubbard's case were actually upset. After all, they reasoned, how could a man physically shot to pieces at the end of the war pass his full physical examination?'[45]

But if Hubbard really did cure himself of his mythical injuries by 1947, why was he still claiming a part disability pension? Why did he write to Veterans Administration in October of the same year saying he'd been 'trying and failing for two years to regain my equilibrium in civil life' and asking for help paying for psychiatric treatment? Why did he continue to lobby for an increase to his pension over this period of time? And why was it the case that he claimed a disability pension for decades afterwards?[46]

Some of the answers can be found in excerpts from Hubbard's private journals, which came to light during the 1984 court case brought by the Church of Scientology of California against former Hubbard archivist Gerry Armstrong. The documents, commonly referred to as the 'Affirmations', were part of an archive compiled by Gerry Armstrong for a planned biography of Hubbard. Armstrong was a member of the Sea Org, but fell out of favour with Scientology's hierarchy when he wrote a report detailing the contradictions in Hubbard's personal history. Armstrong transferred a copy of the documents, including the 'Affirmations', to his lawyer and the Church of Scientology unsuccessfully sued for what they saw as the theft of private papers.

The 'Affirmations' are thought to have been written in 1946 or 1947.[47] They read like a detailed catalogue of self-hypnosis mantras designed by Hubbard to overcome his fears and troubles. A number of them refer to his naval record and his disability pension. Before listing the 'Affirmations', he writes, 'By hypnosis I must be convinced as follows: That I bear no physical aftermath of disease ... That I do not need to have ulcers any more ... That I am well and that there is no advantage in appearing ill.'[48]

The 'Affirmations' also read like admissions. Hubbard confesses to malingering, scamming and dodging military justice:

'Your eyes are getting progressively better. They became bad when you used them as an excuse to escape the naval academy.'

'Your stomach trouble you used as an excuse to keep the Navy from punishing you. You are free of the Navy. You have no further reason to have a weak stomach.'

'Your hip is a pose. You have a sound hip. It never hurts.
Your shoulder never hurts. Your foot was an alibi. The injury is
no longer needed. It is well. You have perfect and lovely feet.'

'In the Veterans' examination you will tell them how sick
you are. You will look sick when you take it. You will return
to health one hour after the examination and laugh at them.'

Hubbard also admits to feeling shame over the true nature of his military record, and tries to convince himself his time in the forces was not all bad.

'My service record was not too glorious. I must be convinced
that I suffer no reaction from any minor disciplinary action,
that all such were minor. My service was honorable, my
initiative and ability high.'[49]

After hearing extracts from the 'Affirmations' and other evidence while presiding over the Armstrong case, Judge Paul Breckenridge of the Los Angeles Superior Court wrote, 'The evidence portrays a man who has been virtually a pathological liar when it comes to his history, background and achievements.'[50]

Hubbard's lies and exaggerations went beyond his war record. He would later claim he was a nuclear physicist. He was not. He said he had many degrees. He had none. He called himself 'Doctor' for a while, claiming he had a PhD in Philosophy. The PhD came from Sequoia University, a shonky diploma mill that sold degrees to the unqualified. There are similar clouds over claims made about Hubbard's early years, his explorations and his relationships.

But it is the false claims about his war record that do the most to undermine both Hubbard's reputation, and the foundations of Scientology. Men of integrity do not lie about their war service. True war heroes are more likely to downplay their military service, not talk it up. Hubbard had been caught out lying about his rank, his war wounds, his war decorations, and where he served. In the United States it is referred to as 'stealing valor' and if Hubbard were alive today he could be subjected to laws that prevent fake war heroes from benefiting from false claims about their service records.

In 1948, as he planned his next move, hardly anyone would have expected that within two years he would become a wealthy man with a worldwide following. Following his visit to the San Gabriel Township Justice Court, Hubbard could have been classified as a petty thief, a con artist, a bigamist, a wife-beater, a dead-beat dad, a valor thief, a malingerer and a liar. Yet his next scheme was to convince others that he had found a way to solve any and all of their life problems. Hubbard was working on a book he would ultimately describe as a 'milestone for Man comparable to his discovery of fire and superior to his inventions of the wheel and arch'.[51]

CHAPTER 3

DIANETICS

BURIED DEEP IN A vault in the side of a mountain in the New Mexico desert lies a copy of *Dianetics: The Modern Science of Mental Health*. Etched onto stainless steel plates and secured in a titanium capsule, Scientology's most venerated text is barricaded against future destruction from nuclear war.

The vault's entrance is carved into the side of a rocky ledge in the desert near the ghost town of Trementina, and was covered by a three-storey house that was later removed in favour of a fake rock wall. Nearby, the logo for Scientology's Church of Spiritual Technology is tattooed into the landscape. The markings, which look like crop circles from the air, are designed to help survivors of a nuclear holocaust track down Hubbard's back catalogue so they can rebuild society based on his words of wisdom.[1]

Dianetics is Scientology's most sacred text. Scientologists refer to it simply as Book One. Hubbard even invented his own calendar off the back of its publication date. In his 1963 Christmas message to Melbourne Scientologists, Hubbard wished his 'cobbers down under' a Merry Christmas and a Clear New Year, dating it 13 AD (After Dianetics).[2] Hubbard claimed it took him only six weeks to write *Dianetics*,[3] but the truth is he had been working on and off for over a decade on what he privately referred to as his 'magnum opus'.[4]

In early 1949, Hubbard and his wife Sara moved to Savannah, Georgia, home then to the world's largest paper mill. The mill, known colloquially as 'The Bag', employed thousands of locals.[5] But the pulp fiction writer was no fan of the pulp mill. 'How it stinks,' he wrote to his friend the science fiction writer Robert Heinlein. 'Soon as I get myself in the chips I am going someplace where I can breathe!'[6]

To get himself 'in the chips' Hubbard had set out to revive *Excalibur*, an unpublished manuscript from 1938. In a letter he wrote to Heinlein in late 1948, he outlined his plans, 'I got a million dollar book ready to write ... I will soon, I hope, give you a book risen from the ashes of old *Excalibur* which details in full the mathematics of the human mind, solves all the problems of the ages and gives six recipes for aphrodisiacs and plays a mouth organ with the left foot.'[7]

The Church of Scientology regards *Excalibur* as Hubbard's 'first philosophic statement'.[8] It was in this manuscript, according to Scientology mythology, that Hubbard 'isolated the common denominator of existence: SURVIVE. That man was surviving was not a new idea. But that this was the single basic common denominator of existence was.'[9]

Hubbard claimed this 'breakthrough of magnitude',[10] as the Church of Scientology calls it, stemmed from an experience on the operating table. As his literary agent Forrest Ackerman described it, 'Basically what he told me was that after he died he rose in spirit form and looked back on the body he had formerly inhabited. Over yonder he saw a fantastic great gate, elaborately carved like something you'd see in Baghdad or ancient China. As he wafted towards it, the gate opened and just beyond he could see a kind of intellectual smorgasbord on which was outlined everything that had ever puzzled the mind of man.'[11]

Hubbard told his literary agent he absorbed all this information and re-entered his body. 'According to Ron,' said Ackerman, 'he jumped off the operating table, ran to his Quonset hut, got two reams of paper and a gallon of scalding black coffee and for the next 48 hours, at a blinding rate, he wrote a work called *Excalibur*, or *The Dark Sword*.'[12]

Gerry Armstrong is one of the few people to have read *Excalibur*. Before becoming one of Scientology's most trenchant critics, Armstrong worked as an archivist for the Church of Scientology. While researching an official biography of Hubbard in the 1980s, Armstrong came across the manuscript. He discovered it was happy gas, not a near-death experience, that inspired *Excalibur*. 'Hubbard had a couple of teeth extracted,' says Armstrong, 'and it was while under the effect of nitrous oxide that he came up with *Excalibur*.'[13]

There are conflicting claims about what happened to the original copies of *Excalibur*. The Church of Scientology says only small sections of the manuscript still exist because 'two copies were actually stolen by agents of foreign intelligence services who wished to appropriate those ideas for political ends'.[14] The Church of Scientology maintains Hubbard chose not to publish because 'it did not include an actual therapy for improvement'.[15]

However, Arthur J Burks, a friend and writer who claimed he was the first person to read the manuscript, says Hubbard was desperate to get it published. 'He was so sure he had something "away out and beyond" anything else that he had sent telegrams to several book publishers, telling them that he had written "THE book" and that they were to meet him at Penn Station, and he would discuss it with them and go with whomever gave him the best offer.'[16]

Hubbard would later tell his agent he withdrew *Excalibur* from publication because the first six people who read the manuscript went insane or committed suicide. But the reality is that Hubbard needed every cent he could get and was desperate to sell the manuscript. As he had written to his wife Polly in 1938: 'I'm still faced with the necessity of somehow getting lined up on steady money whether that be the sales of *Excalibur* or a movie job.'[17]

For Hubbard, the publication of *Excalibur* was not only about the money. He saw it as his way of making a name for himself. As Arthur J Burks wrote, 'He told me what he wanted to do with it – it was going to revolutionize everything: the world, people's attitudes toward one another. He thought it was somewhat more important, and would have a greater impact upon people, than the Bible.'[18] Hubbard's letter to Polly written a decade earlier laid out his vaulting ambition: 'I have high hopes of smashing my name into history so violently that it will take a legendary form, even if all the books are destroyed. That goal, is the real goal as far as I am concerned.'[19]

Hubbard's letter to his first wife, Polly, says much about his state of mind and his beliefs. The man who would later convince his followers that he held the secrets to eternal life shows no signs of believing in immortality himself. Hubbard bemoans that he will last only 'thirty-nine more years at the most' and sees his writing as his only hope for life beyond the grave. 'Personal immortality,' he wrote, 'is only to be gained through the printed word, barred note or painted canvas or hard granite.'[20]

Given his failure to have *Excalibur* published and recognised before the war, Hubbard must have placed himself under immense pressure to nail the expanded version of his ideas a decade later. Before he had completed it, he was already talking up the book's special powers in a bizarre letter to his agent Ackerman. 'I shall ship it along just as soon as decent,' he wrote in January 1949. 'Then you can rape women without their knowing it, communicate suicide messages to your enemies as they sleep, sell the Arroyo Seco parkway to the mayor for cash, evolve the best way of protecting or destroying communism, and other handy household hints.'[21]

As Hubbard battled away on the book that eventually became *Dianetics,* he updated his friends on its progress. He told Robert Heinlein his experiences in the Navy Reserve were having an influence on the re-write: 'When I re-read it, my war experiences pointed several necessary alterations and inclusions and I slave away.'[22] In the eyes of Hubbard, the book that would become the foundation stone of Scientology was not about religion. 'I fear the Catholic Church is going to take a look at that book and have a fit ... It aint agin religion. It just abolishes it.'[23]

In his letters to Heinlein, Hubbard says he has been experimenting on local children as well as Sara and himself. He claims he can double a person's IQ, and treat asthma, ulcers and arthritis. He boasts he can now sleep less and climax more. 'I am cruising on four hours sleep a night,' he wrote, 'but the most interesting thing is, I'm up to eight comes. In an evening, that is.'[24]

Just as Heinlein acted as a sounding board for Hubbard's ideas, another friend from the science fiction scene would prove critical in providing *Dianetics* with a launching pad. John W Campbell published much of Hubbard's and Heinlein's early work in his magazine *Astounding Science Fiction.* He was regarded as the most influential editor in what became known as the Golden Age of Science Fiction. After Hubbard moved to New Jersey in the spring of 1949, he started 'treating' Campbell, hypnotising him and retrieving real or perceived childhood memories. 'Ron's technique consists of bringing these old memories into view,' Campbell wrote, 'and then *erasing* the memory.'[25] The chain smoking, garrulous young editor was sold on *Dianetics* and he was about to help Hubbard sell it to the world.

Astounding Science Fiction had around 150,000 subscribers and in December 1949, before Hubbard had even completed his book, Campbell was already talking *Dianetics* up. 'The item that most interests me at the moment,' Campbell teased his readers, 'is an article on the most important subject conceivable. This is *not* a hoax article. It is an article on the *science* of the human mind, of human thought.'[26] Campbell promised a forthcoming article and in March once again pumped up Hubbard's new work in an editorial, writing: 'It is of more importance than you can readily realize.'[27]

In the May 1950 edition of *Astounding Science Fiction*, Campbell published a long essay by L. Ron Hubbard titled *Dianetics: The Evolution of a Science*. In an editorial, Campbell was again at pains to tell his readership Hubbard's work was not pseudoscience: 'I want to assure every reader, most positively and unequivocally, that this article is *not* a hoax, joke, or anything but a direct, clear statement of a totally new scientific thesis.'[28] On 9 May 1950, *Dianetics: The Modern Science of Mental Health* was released in book form. The publishers Hermitage House did not share John Campbell's faith; the initial print run was just 6000 copies.[29]

Dianetics was sold as a science, not a religion. Hubbard's 'science of the mind' carved the brain into two parts, the 'reactive mind' and the 'analytical mind'. Hubbard asserted the reactive mind was like a database, recording emotional trauma and physical pain. He called these recordings 'engrams'. Hubbard's theory was that engrams, unlike memories, could not be easily recalled. They could only be recovered through Dianetic counselling or auditing, a process that uses techniques from hypnosis to create a 'reverie' or light trance. According to Hubbard, once relived, these experiences are refiled into the analytical mind where they become part of the rational brain.

If the engrams are not sent to the analytical mind, so the theory goes, they can cause illness and anxiety. In *Dianetics*, Hubbard cites the story of a woman who has been knocked unconscious: 'She is kicked and told she is a faker, that she is no good, that she is always changing her mind,' he writes. 'A chair is overturned in the process. A faucet is running in the kitchen. A car is passing in the street outside. The engram contains a running record of all these perceptions.'[30]

According to Hubbard, these traumatic events can be easily 'restimulated' if the engrams are not processed. 'Running water from a faucet might not have affected her greatly,' he wrote, 'but water running from a faucet *plus* a passing car might have begun some slight reactivation of an engram, a vague discomfort in the areas where she was struck and kicked ... When the engram is restimulated in one of the great many ways possible, she has a "feeling" that she is no good, a faker and she *will* change her mind.'[31]

Like most forms of self-help, Dianetics provides individuals with a goal. That goal is to become 'clear', to refile all engrams from the reactive to the analytical mind. Hubbard argued that a 'clear' was free of 'any and all psychoses, neuroses, compulsions and repressions'.[32] He claimed that by removing engrams you could cure 'psychosomatic ills' including asthma, arthritis, sinusitis, ulcers, heart problems, tuberculosis, alcoholism, allergies and the common cold.[33] Once 'clear' an individual's IQ would skyrocket with the added bonus that 'the clear' would operate in a state in which 'full memory exists throughout the lifetime'.[34]

According to Dianetics, to get 'clear' you have to go and relive all the traumatic experiences filed in your reactive mind going back to conception. For Hubbard the womb was a world of pain. Engrams could be created *in utero* by a mother's farts, coughs, sneezes, bouts of constipation and sexual acts. Even dirty talk is off limits during sex with a pregnant woman. 'If the husband uses language during coitus,' wrote Hubbard, 'every word of it is going to be engramic.'[35]

But grunting and farting were not the greatest dangers when it came to generating prenatal engrams that could trigger psychoses and neuroses later in life. In Hubbard's view, that was reserved for failed abortion attempts. 'It is a scientific fact,' he wrote, 'that abortion attempts are the most important factor in aberration.'[36]

Hubbard's claims about the rate at which women attempt to terminate their pregnancies defy logic. 'Twenty or thirty abortion attempts are not uncommon in the aberee,' he wrote, 'and in every attempt the child could have been pierced through the body or brain.'[37] Hubbard argued that this epidemic of abortion attempts was responsible for filling the country's jails and asylums: 'However many billions America spends yearly on institutions for the insane and jails for the criminals are spent primarily because of attempted abortions done by some sex-blocked mother to whom children are a curse, not a blessing of God.'[38]

Perhaps Hubbard's distorted views on abortion attempts were coloured by his own experiences. In an interview over 30 years after *Dianetics* was published, L. Ron Hubbard Jnr said he'd walked in on his father conducting an abortion on his mother, Polly. 'He had a coat hanger in his hand. There was blood all over the place. I remember my father shouting at me, "Go back to bed!" A little while later a doctor came and took her off to the hospital.'[39] Hubbard's estranged son claimed he'd been born prematurely at six and a half months due to an attempted abortion. Hubbard himself had claimed his mother had tried to abort him as well.[40]

Hubbard wanted people to believe that all the 'breakthroughs' in *Dianetics* were original and based on his own scientific research. Yet he never provided a single case study on any of the 273 individuals he claimed to have worked on, nor did he offer his work up for peer review. Not one of these 273 'clears' has ever come forward.

Prominent scientists were scathing of *Dianetics*. Nobel Prize-winning physicist Issac Isidor Rabi began his review in *Scientific American* with a damning assessment: 'This volume probably contains more promises and less evidence per page than has any publication since the invention of printing.'[41] Professor Rabi accused Hubbard of quackery and deception: 'The system is presented without qualification and without evidence. It has borrowed from psychoanalysis, Pavlovian conditioning, hypnosis and folk beliefs, but, except for the last, these debts are fulsomely denied.'[42]

The American Psychological Association warned 'these claims are not supported by empirical evidence'.[43] A review in the *Journal of Clinical Medicine* described *Dianetics* as 'nothing but a rumination of old psychological concepts, popularized and oversimplified, therefore, misunderstood and misinterpreted'.[44] One doctor who did believe in Dianetics was Joseph Winter MD. The brother-in-law of John Campbell was an early convert to Dianetics, claiming it helped his six-year-old son conquer his fear of the dark.[45] Winter wrote the introduction to the first edition of *Dianetics* and became the medical director of the Hubbard Dianetic Research Foundation. But Winter's introduction no longer appears in *Dianetics*; he resigned from the board before the year was out, alarmed at Hubbard's attitude towards the medical profession, to scientific research and his developing belief in clearing engrams from past lives.[46] Later, publisher Art Ceppos withdrew *Dianetics* from sale, when he came to the conclusion it was a scam. He replaced it with Winter's critique *Dianetics: A Doctor's Report*.

Despite hostility from doctors, scientists, psychologists and psychiatrists, *Dianetics* took off. By June it was on the *New York Times* best-seller list, staying there until Christmas Eve. In some weeks, according to John Campbell, *Astounding Science Fiction* was getting over a thousand letters about *Dianetics*.[47] Enthusiasts embraced Dianetic counselling, known as auditing. As Hubbard's biographer Russell Miller put it, 'All over the country the same thing was happening: science-fiction fans were buying the book and auditing their friends, who then rushed out to buy the book so they could audit *their* friends.'[48]

Helen O'Brien, a pioneering executive in Hubbard's expanding movement, claimed thousands of Dianetics clubs were formed across the US. 'People everywhere embraced it as though they had found something which they had hungered for all their lives.'[49] Hubbard had tapped into a nation that was ripe for some therapy. Over 16 million Americans served in the armed forces during World War II and many returned from overseas deployments suffering from what we now call post-traumatic stress.

Hubbard was also able to feed into growing anxiety about the Cold War and the nuclear arms race with the Soviet Union. The year before *Dianetics* was published, the Soviets tested their first atomic bomb. In 1950, Harry S. Truman sent American troops to war in Korea. There was even paranoia about enemies from within, with Senator Joseph McCarthy rising to national prominence in February that year, with his Lincoln Day speech about communists working inside the State Department.

Hubbard's solution seemed so simple and cheap. For just US$4, you could buy a book that would unlock the secret to eradicating

all neuroses, psychoses and psychosomatic ills. All you needed
was a friend who had read *Dianetics* to audit you and you were
away. But this wasn't just self-help for the readers, it was helping
to line Hubbard's pockets in a way he could never have imagined.
By the end of 1950, there were six Hubbard Dianetic Research
Foundations across the country,[50] running one-month courses
that cost US$500 per student. One course in California had 300
participants.[51] Auditing cost US$25 an hour, far more than it cost to
see a psychotherapist.

The money was flooding in. As Hubbard's second wife, Sara,
recalled, 'He used to carry huge amounts of cash around in his pocket.
I remember going past a Lincoln dealer and admiring one of those big
Lincolns they had then. He walked right in there and bought it for me,
cash!'[52] Sara claimed the business turned over US$1 million in 1950,
and not all of it was accounted for. Helen O'Brien told the story in
Dianetics in Limbo of one member quitting Hubbard's first research
foundation in Elizabeth, New Jersey, over unscrupulous accounting
practices. 'He still retained copies of the bookkeeping records
that made him decide to disassociate himself from the Elizabeth
foundation, fast,' she said. 'A month's income of US$90,000 is listed,
with only US$20,000 accounted for.'[53]

While dodgy accounting practices were yet to catch up with
Hubbard, the lack of scientific evidence to back up his theories was
about to come under the spotlight. Given that the goal of Dianetics
was to eradicate engrams and produce individuals who were 'clear',
if there was no evidence of anyone reaching this state, Dianetics was
failing to deliver what it promised. Hubbard could vividly describe
the abilities of a 'clear'; for example, 'full memory exists throughout
the lifetime, with the additional bonus that he has photographic recall
in color'. But a key question remained unanswered. How could he be
so sure of the powers of a 'clear', if there was no evidence of anyone
attaining this status? The pressure was on Hubbard to publicly present
someone who had attained perfect recall through Dianetics.

In August 1950, Hubbard chose the Shrine Auditorium, a 6000-
seat theatre in Los Angeles, as the place he would present on stage
the 'World's First Clear'. The theatre was packed with a mixture of
Hubbard devotees, sceptics and reporters. Hubbard introduced to the

stage Sonia Bianca, a physics major from Boston who had 'full and perfect recall of every moment of her life'.[54]

The world's first 'clear' walked onto the stage to rapturous applause. A nervous Bianca explained to the audience that Dianetics had cleared her sinus problems and a painful itch she had in her eyebrows. Hubbard asked her a few questions before opening it up to the crowd. Not surprisingly, the audience questions were a little trickier than Hubbard's.

'What did you have for breakfast on 3 October 1942?' shouted one wag. 'What's on page 122 of *Dianetics: The Modern Science of Mental Health*?' asked another.[55] Sonia Bianca's purported perfect memory floundered. She couldn't even remember basic physics formulas she was studying at college. Audience members started to leave, many taking pity on the unfortunate Miss Bianca. Towards the end of the debacle one man noticed that Hubbard had his back to the student and yelled out, 'What colour necktie is Mr Hubbard wearing?'[56] Staring into the darkness of the crowd, Bianca racked her brain, desperate for some kind of cue. She could not remember the colour of her mentor's tie. Hubbard had humiliated both his first 'clear' and himself in front of 6000 people.

Most people would struggle to overcome such a public repudiation of their beliefs and reputation. Not Hubbard; he had an explanation for what went wrong. When he asked Sonia Bianca to step onto the stage 'now' he had given her a verbal command that froze her in present time, blocking her memory.[57] Hubbard would not make the same mistake again. Thousands more would be designated 'clear', but there would be no more public demonstrations of their special powers.

CHAPTER 4

DIANETICS GOES SOUTH

IT WAS IN AMONG Essendon's weatherboard homes, lock-up shops and manufacturing workshops, that Dianetics got its first, unlikely foothold in Australia. D'Arcy Hunt was Hubbard's pioneering messenger. The Californian had migrated to Melbourne's northern suburbs in 1951 to marry his sweetheart Dorrie. He would tell anyone who would listen about the marvels of the 'modern science of mental health'. Hunt's mission became his profession when he set up consulting rooms in Essendon, as Melbourne's first professional dianeticist.

While Essendon was one of the sprawling suburbs benefiting from post-war development, in many ways it was stuck in a bygone era. Lloyd's Ice Works still delivered large blocks of ice to homes that did not have refrigerators.[1] The local mayor's annual Egg Appeal collected tens of thousands of eggs to assist hospitals and charities.[2] The Essendon branch of the Housewives Association met regularly in nearby Moonee Ponds.

Still, Essendon in the 1950s was not completely immune from the shock of the new. In that decade, the local airport received its first international passenger flight,[3] entrepreneur Frank McEncroe opened up a factory to mass-produce his new takeaway snack sensation, the Chiko roll,[4] while 2 km down the road an unusual ambassador for Melbourne's northern suburbs emerged, in the form of Edna Everage, the housewife superstar of Moonee Ponds.

Into this environment rolled D'Arcy Hunt, pushing Hubbard's theories about engrams and reactive minds in a close-knit community more interested in going to the football, than going 'clear'. Fortunately, Hunt was familiar with lost causes. Like Hubbard, he had spent time in the Pacific during the war. But while Scientology's founder avoided action after his Navy ship was diverted away from the Philippines, Hunt found himself stuck in Manila as Japanese troops overwhelmed the capital.

The Stanford graduate had spent much of the 1930s and '40s working as a waiter on passenger ships that sailed between Manila, Honolulu and the US mainland.[5] In 1942, he found himself in the wrong port at the wrong time, becoming one of the over 5000 American civilians shunted into internment camps in the Philippines.[5] Hunt was to be a prisoner of the Japanese for the next three years, one month and 17 days.[7]

When the Philippines were liberated, Hunt returned home and set up a photographic studio in San Francisco. A friend in Pasadena alerted him to Hubbard's experiments with processing before *Dianetics* was even published.[8] After the book's release in 1950, D'Arcy Hunt rushed down to his local bookstore and ordered a copy.[9] He embraced *Dianetics* immediately, holding his first auditing session with a young engineering student. 'We flipped a coin to see who would lay down on the couch first,' recalled Hunt, 'and away we went.'[10]

Hunt and around 20 other Dianetics enthusiasts formed a group in San Francisco and co-audited each other.[11] When Hubbard lectured in Oakland in September 1950 over four consecutive nights, Hunt was among the crowd of devotees and curious onlookers.[12] Before long he was supplementing his photographic business with some after-hours auditing.

Almost a year to the day after Hubbard released *Dianetics*, D'Arcy Hunt flew to Melbourne to marry his fiancée Dorrie.[13] He set up a Dianetics group similar to the one he had been a part of in San Francisco. The group met informally in backyards on a Sunday afternoon.[14] As the informal sessions grew more popular, Hunt set up shop as a professional dianeticist.[15]

In November 1951, Don Greenlees, a reporter with *The Argus*, visited Hunt's rooms in Essendon, describing him as 'quiet-spoken, balding 30-odd,' with 'a reassuring manner'. D'Arcy Hunt explained that 'many members of Alcoholics Anonymous attributed their downfall to early compulsions over the milk bottle', and that 'phrases such as "drink up it's good for you" had set up a chain reaction which caused them to drink'.[16]

D'Arcy Hunt had a talent for recruiting. One Sunday evening he spied Treasure Southen lecturing at the Theosophical Hall in Collins Street. Afterwards, he approached her and asked, 'Have you read the latest American book on psychology?'[17] Grief-stricken after the death of her daughter, Southen had sought solace in theosophy. But Hunt quickly convinced her Dianetics would help her even more. He loaned her his copy and Southen read it three times. 'I felt this is what we needed,' she said. 'It had helped me so much that I felt I wanted it to help others.'[18]

Southen formed her own Dianetics group, advertising in the local press and holding group audits with around 20 people in her home at Balwyn in East Melbourne. Another group sprang out of her circle, meeting at Ascot Vale,[19] while a larger group evolved out of Hunt's backyard sessions, meeting in the city at the Victoria Railways Institute building in Flinders Street. A two-line advertisement was placed in *The Argus* spruiking for people interested in Dianetics.[20] Soon around 70 or 80 people were turning up to their Friday night meetings.[21]

The pioneering advocates of Dianetics were a colourful bunch. In Sydney, Edgar Oswald Haes held meetings at the Australian Psychology Centre in Pitt Street. The author of *The Release of Psychic Energy*, Haes was a man who was not afraid of unfashionable ideas. In the 1940s, he lectured about the harmlessness of masturbation and the importance of the female orgasm, while railing against corporal punishment in schools.[22] In 1951, he started advertising Dianetics literature.[23] The following year he started lecturing on the new 'science of the mind'.[24]

While interest was growing in Australia, things were not running smoothly in the birthplace of Dianetics. Hubbard was not behaving like a man who held the secrets to a happier, saner, more ethical life. His marriage to Sara was a trainwreck and his behaviour towards her was appalling. He beat her, strangled her, and at one stage ruptured the Eustachian tube in her left ear.[25] Sara wrote in an affidavit that strangulation was a 'frequent practice' of Hubbard's.[26]

Hubbard wanted Sara out of his life, telling her, 'I do not want to be an American husband for I can buy my friends whenever I want them.'[27] Divorce was not an option for Hubbard, he was concerned it would harm his reputation. He told Sara if she really loved him, she 'should kill herself'.[28]

Sara was not just Hubbard's wife, she was also the mother of his second daughter. Two months before *Dianetics* was published, Sara gave birth to a nine-pound redhead they named Alexis Valerie. Hubbard described her as the 'first dianetic gestation and delivery in history',[29] who was 'doing at three weeks what she should be doing at three months'.[30]

At 11 months of age, Alexis was exposed to the full force of her father's madness when Hubbard kidnapped his infant daughter and took her to Cuba. Concerned about the risks Hubbard's violent and irrational behaviour posed to her and Alexis, Sara had sought out a psychiatrist. After she documented the physical and emotional abuse she had been through, the psychiatrist advised that 'Hubbard be committed to a private sanitarium for psychiatric observation and treatment'.[31] When Sara confronted her husband with this assessment, Hubbard threatened to kill Alexis. 'He didn't want her to be brought up by me,' Sara said, 'because I was in league with the doctors.'[32]

On 24 February 1951, Sara went to the movies, leaving Alexis in the care of John Sanborn, a young staffer at the Los Angeles Dianetics foundation. At 11 pm, Hubbard and two colleagues abducted Alexis, then returned two hours later to kidnap Sara, threatening her that she would never see Alexis again unless she co-operated. Sara was then driven to San Bernardino where Hubbard tried to get her committed, but there were no doctors available at the county hospital in the early hours of the morning.[33]

Next, they drove to Yuma, Arizona, where a few hours later, a truce was negotiated. Hubbard would release his wife and tell her where Alexis was if she signed a statement saying she had travelled with Hubbard voluntarily. Sara agreed to the demands, and headed back to Los Angeles to be reunited with her daughter. Hubbard headed to the local airport, where he reneged on his deal, arranging for Alexis to be taken out of Los Angeles before Sara returned. A couple was then paid to drive Alexis across the country to New Jersey. Hubbard flew to the East Coast where he picked up Alexis then headed to Cuba.[34] Once there he placed her in a crib covered with wire while he binged on rum and rambled into a dictaphone. Richard de Mille, the adopted son of moviemaker Cecil B DeMille (the pair spelled their surnames differently), turned these ramblings into *Science of Survival*, the follow-up to *Dianetics*.[35]

Out of her mind with anxiety, Sara searched for Alexis throughout California for the next six weeks, before filing a writ of *habeas corpus*, accusing Frank Dessler from the Los Angeles Hubbard Dianetic Research Foundation of holding her child.[36] Sara's lawyers accused Hubbard, Dessler and Richard de Mille of conspiring to kidnap her daughter.[37]

On 23 April 1951, Hubbard received the divorce papers he was so keen to avoid. Sara filed a 13-page complaint in Los Angeles County that included allegations that Hubbard 'repeatedly subjected plaintiff to systematic torture, including loss of sleep, beatings, and strangulations and scientific torture experiments'.[38] Hubbard was accused of drugging his wife, kidnapping their child and forcing Sara to 'hourly fear of both the life of herself and of her infant daughter'.[39] The sensational allegations made news across the world. Brisbane's *Courier-Mail* led their coverage with the headline 'Sanity "Expert" Mad, Claims Wife'.[40]

At the time, Sara received support from the woman who understood most what she was going through. 'Ron is not normal,' wrote Hubbard's first wife, Polly, in an empathetic letter to Sara. 'Your charges probably sound fantastic to the average person – but I've been through it – the beatings, threats on my life, all the sadistic traits you charge – twelve years of it.'[41] Sara would eventually get her daughter back, but not before Hubbard wrote to the FBI accusing her of being a drug addict and a communist.[42] A follow-up letter to the Attorney-General two months later claimed Sara and 'members of the communist party' had destroyed his 'half a million dollar operation'.[43]

Hubbard was not only losing his wife, his child – and seemingly his mind – he had also lost his Dianetic research foundations. Original supporters like John Campbell and Dr Joseph Winter had given up on him. In April 1951, Hubbard resigned from the organisation that bore his name.[44] That same month he sent a telegram from Havana to Don

Purcell, a Dianetics enthusiast and the head of Omega Oil. In poor health and short of a buck, Hubbard asked for help.[45] After Richard de Mille called the Kansas-based millionaire to tell him Hubbard was dying, Purcell took action, chartering a flight that brought Hubbard back to the US.[46]

With Purcell's help, Hubbard set up Dianetics' new headquarters in Wichita, Kansas. The other foundations were closed and the debts from the New Jersey foundation became Purcell's responsibility.[47] Hubbard was in a bad way when he arrived in Kansas. When he summoned his young lover Barbara Klowden with a proposal of marriage, Hubbard did not present as Wichita's most eligible man. 'I went there and he was like Howard Hughes's last days, really in a bad depression,' Klowden told Hubbard's biographer Russell Miller. 'His fingernails were long and curved; his hair was stringy. He met [me] at the hotel and was in such bad shape, he was trembling, like someone who should be in a mental institution.'[48] Klowden, who also worked as Hubbard's PR assistant, left Kansas the day after.

The following month, Sara travelled to Kansas and agreed to drop her divorce action in California, and allow Hubbard a divorce on his own terms. This included having Sara sign a note that contained statements such as 'L. Ron Hubbard is a fine and brilliant man'.[49] The testimony carried the same level of authenticity as Hubbard's autobiographical references he had manufactured during World War II. Hubbard made out he was the victim, eventually being awarded a divorce on the grounds of Sara's 'gross neglect of duty and extreme cruelty'.[50] Sara later recanted her statement in an interview with Bent Corydon. 'I thought by doing so he would leave me and Alexis alone,' she said. 'It was horrible. I just wanted to be free of him!'[51]

Rejected by his lover, and divorced from his second wife, Hubbard was soon checking out the engrams on Mary Sue Whipp, a 19-year-old student from Houston, Texas. Mary Sue had travelled to Wichita with a friend who had read about Dianetics in *Astounding Science Fiction*.[52] The auburn-haired student moved in with Hubbard and was placed on the payroll as an auditor.[53] As Hubbard's relationship with Mary Sue flourished, his partnership with Purcell broke down. The foundation was bleeding money, and Purcell was uncomfortable with Hubbard's move into 'past life' recall.[54] At one Friday night lecture, Hubbard turned up with a limp, a result he said, of returning on his 'time track' to a Civil War battlefield.[55] When a court ruled that the Wichita Foundation was liable for the debts of the old New Jersey foundation, Purcell suggested the organisation be put into voluntary bankruptcy. Hubbard refused, but was outvoted at an emergency meeting.[56]

Don Purcell, the man who bailed the founder of Dianetics out of trouble when he was floundering in Havana, was about to get the full Hubbard breakup catastrophe – law suits, restraining orders, and accusations of criminal behaviour. Hubbard used the foundation's mailing list to accuse Purcell of accepting a US$500,000 bribe from the American Medical Association to destroy Dianetics.[57] When Purcell bought the Wichita foundation back in the bankruptcy court, Hubbard had to start afresh. In March 1952, he married Mary Sue and the following month the newlyweds moved to Phoenix, Arizona, where Hubbard reinvented himself once more by launching his latest discovery, a new 'science' and new belief system that built on the foundations of Dianetics and would change humanity forever. He called it Scientology.

Before they headed for the desert, the Hubbards introduced to their followers the E-Meter, a black metal box attached to two soup cans with a needle that swung back and forth. It was built and designed by chiropractor Volney Mathison in the 1940s. Like other lie detectors, the E-Meter measures the conductivity of skin and any activity in the sweat glands.[58] Simon Singh and Edzard Ernst, the authors of *Trick or Treatment*, describe it as 'nothing more than a piece of technical hocus-pocus'.[59] Hubbard argued it gave 'an auditor a deep and marvelous insight into the mind of his preclear'.[60] (A preclear is someone receiving auditing who has not yet achieved clear status.) It also gave Hubbard a revenue source, with his followers expected to buy the gadgets at inflated prices.[61]

The new headquarters in Arizona was called the Hubbard Association of Scientologists. Hubbard had not just come up with a new brand, he had also invented a new theory of the universe. Scientology's first text, *What to Audit*, later renamed *Scientology: A History of Man*, was released in July. Never one to undersell his work, Hubbard described it as 'a coldblooded and factual account of your last sixty trillion years'.[62]

Central to Hubbard's new cosmology was the theory that *thetans*, or *theta-beings* as he called them then, created the universe as their own playground. Thetans, according to Hubbard, are immortal spiritual beings. But having inhabited so many bodies over trillions of years, they have become so consumed by the universe they live in, that they have forgotten about their special powers and degenerated to the extent that they believed they were simply 'meat bodies'. Their super-powers could be restored through Scientology, the goal being to make an individual an Operating Thetan, or OT, who could 'operate' independently of the human body.

Hubbard's new belief system turned into a nice little earner. With Dianetics you only had one lifetime to audit. In Scientology, the 'thetans' running human bodies came burdened with engrams from past lives. That meant auditing past lives from this and even other universes. And it wasn't just the thetans that needed work, there were engrams lurking from the primordial swamp that needed clearing too. Hubbard told his followers their bodies were also occupied by another 'lower grade' soul called a 'genetic entity', or GE.[63] The GE, according to Hubbard, passed through an evolutionary line going back to molluscs, seaweed, right back to single atoms. Hubbard believed many engrams could be traced back to clams. He warned of the dangers of talking about 'clam incidents' with the uninitiated. 'Should you describe the "clam" to some one [sic], you may restimulate it in him to the extent of causing severe jaw pain. One such victim, after hearing about a clam death, could not use his jaws for three days.'[64]

In the lead-up to the publication of Hubbard's first book under the Scientology brand, he was reunited with his son from his first marriage, Nibs. Just a year younger than Mary Sue, Nibs moved into the newlyweds' rented home near Camel Back Mountain. If Hubbard's last book had been fuelled by Cuban rum, *A History of Man* seemed to have been inspired by more illicit substances. As Jon Atack wrote in *Let's Sell These People A Piece of Blue Sky*: 'The book leaves the strong suspicion that Hubbard had continued with his experiments into phenobarbital, and into more powerful 'mind-expanding' drugs as Nibs later asserted.'[65] Hubbard had frequently advocated amphetamines after the launch of *Dianetics*.[66] According to Hubbard's former medical officer Jim Dincalci, the clam story came from Nibs being pumped full of amphetamines: 'His dad kept giving him speed and all of a sudden he was talking about his history, when he was a clam and all these different situations in early Earth. And out of that came *A History of Man*.'[67]

BACK IN AUSTRALIA, TREASURE Southen was among the first to shift from Dianetics to Scientology. In her search for meaning as a former theosophist, she already believed in past lives. But D'Arcy Hunt was weirded out by Hubbard's latest book. He couldn't even finish it. 'I tried to read that,' he said. 'It was very disturbing to me. I did not like it.'[68] But Hunt stuck by Hubbard nonetheless, and played a critical role in establishing Scientology in Australia. 'We decided, all of us, by vote, that we would try to get somebody over here from America to train us under Hubbard's guidance,' Southen recalled.[69] The group raised the money to pay for the airfares to bring John Farrell and his wife Tucker to Melbourne.[70]

The Farrells had been running Scientology courses in Hubbard's old black magic beat of Pasadena[71] before they got married in Arizona in November 1954 in a service personally drafted by Hubbard.[72] Three months later, D'Arcy Hunt was one of the signatories on an application to the Department of Immigration to bring the Farrells out to Australia to give advice and assistance to their 'movement for spiritual and mental therapy' and to attend their Easter Congress.[73] The Commonwealth Migration Officer reported that the association was not financially sound and 'insofar as Australia is concerned, is a very minor and unimportant organisation'.[74] The Farrells were granted six-month visas and arrived in Melbourne in April 1955. The first Hubbard Professional Auditor course was run over eight weeks out of a rented home in Kew, attended by Treasure Southen, D'Arcy Hunt and around 20 others.[75]

Doug Moon, a local entertainer who was part of the early Dianetics groups in Melbourne, remembered John Farrell bringing a sense of structure to Scientology in Australia. 'Farrell would run professional courses, he would align our activities to the goals of Scientology, he would tell us what Hubbard wanted, and generally advise and monitor.'[76]

Scientology became formally recognised in Australia with the Hubbard Association of Scientologists International (HASI) registered in Victoria as a foreign company on 15 June 1955. The directors were all Americans – Hubbard, his wife Mary Sue, Burke Belknap, Robert Sutton and Ken Barrett. Their head office was based in Phoenix, Arizona.[77] The local agent was listed as Ron Chittock, an Electro-Medical Engineer from the General X-Ray Company in Fitzroy.[78]

Melbourne's Scientology headquarters was established at 157–159 Spring Street, almost directly opposite the Victorian parliament. 'It may be prime real estate now, but it certainly wasn't then,' says Roger Meadmore, who was involved in setting up the original association. 'Spring Street was an old building with lots of dirty rooms. The Farrells were living there with a small child. It was disorganised. Much of it was an empty building.'[79]

Australia's first Scientologists were an eclectic bunch. They included teachers, businessmen, accountants, housewives, musicians and public servants.

David Cooke, whose father, Alan, was involved in Scientology in Melbourne in the 1950s, remembers them fondly:

They were good people. These were among the bright young freethinkers of the post World War 2 generation, the 'angry young men' who prepared the ground for the counter-culture movements of the sixties. They could not accept the stupid, oppressive society of the day and wanted to try something – anything – that might be better. As a kid I met scientologists like Richard King, Ian Tampion, Les Verity, Roger Dunn, Jessie Gray, Doug Myers and loved their open discussions of past lives, lost civilizations, UFOs, alternative medicine, ESP and even political conspiracies.[80]

In April 1955, over four days, the first Australian Scientology Congress was held at Coppin Hall in Prahran. The Farrells, billed as Doctors of Scientology, were keynote speakers, along with Englishman Raymond Kemp, who had left the merchant navy to become a Doctor of Scientology. The advertisement, placed in a prominent spot on page five of *The Argus*, boasted that Scientology offered greater health, more energy, increased ability, broader knowledge, higher understanding.[81]

By the end of 1955, John Farrell was getting more entrepreneurial, advertising his services under the Personal Relations column in the classifieds: 'I will talk to anyone for you about anything. Phone FB3670. FB3396, between 12 and 1.30.' It was signed Rev. John R Farrell, Church of Scientology.[82] He was following a Hubbard directive.

Not only was he calling himself a Reverend, and Scientology a church, Farrell was getting around with a collar that made him look like a religious minister. 'Farrell used to tell us if we had a collar reversed we could walk into places where we may not otherwise be admitted,' recalled Doug Moon. 'If there were any questions asked about what we were doing we would raise a finger and say, "Would you interfere with the work of a man of God?"'[83] Again, Farrell took his lead from Hubbard, who gave this advice in a memo.[84]

George Maltby, a picture framer from Olinda and one of Melbourne's pioneering Scientologists, was not sure why Farrell was portraying himself as part of a religious movement. 'Farrell seemed to have got the idea firmly into his head,' said Maltby. 'I don't think anybody else was greatly impressed with it.'[85] But Farrell's dog collar was part of Hubbard's grand plan. He was determined to turn his re-branded form of Dianetics into something much bigger.

CHAPTER 5

OLD RON'S CON

DEATH AND TAXES, BENJAMIN Franklin's two great certainties of life, became two of the great motivating forces that helped transform Scientology into something beyond a self-help movement. By turning Scientology into a religion, Hubbard's new church would not have to pay tax, and his followers would not have to worry about the afterlife. He could provide Scientologists with the key to salvation and immortality while locking them into a lifetime of lucrative courses and auditing sessions. Religion at the price Hubbard would sell it, with no company tax obligations and lifelong proselytising customers, was a faultless business model.

Hubbard had been burned by the experience of losing both money and control of his failed Dianetics foundations. On 10 April 1953, he wrote to Scientology executive Helen O'Brien about his plan for a new type of franchise:

Perhaps we could call it a Spiritual Guidance Center. Think up its name, will you. And we could put in nice desks and our boys in neat blue with diplomas on the walls and 1. knock psychotherapy into history and 2. make enough money to shine up my operating scope and 3. keep the HAS (Hubbard Association of Scientologists) solvent. It is a problem of practical business.[1]

Revealingly, while outlining his plans of how to be 'swamped' with money, Hubbard wrote to O'Brien about the benefits of becoming a religion:

> *I await your reaction on the religion angle. In my opinion,*
> *we couldn't get worse public opinion than we have had*
> *or have less [sic] customers with what we've got to sell. A*
> *religious charter would be necessary in Pennsylvania or*
> *NJ (New Jersey) to make it stick. But I sure could make it*
> *stick. We're treating the present time beingness, psychotherapy*
> *treats the past and the brain. And brother, that's religion,*
> *not mental science.*[2]

Hubbard's religion angle became a reality by the end of the year when he incorporated three churches: the Church of Scientology, the Church of American Science and the Church of Spiritual Engineering.[3] In early 1954, the Church of Scientology of California was established, followed soon after by another church in Washington, DC. None of this would have surprised Nieson Himmel, the legendary newspaperman who covered the Los Angeles crime beat for over 50 years.

Himmel shared a room with Hubbard in Jack Parsons' Pasadena mansion in 1946. 'Whenever he was talking about being hard up,' Himmel recalled, 'he often used to say that he thought the easiest way to make money would be to start a religion.'[4] The Church of Scientology denies Hubbard said anything of the sort, attributing a similar quote to George Orwell. But Sam Moskowitz, Theodore Sturgeon and Lloyd Arthur Eshbach, three science fiction writers who were contemporaries of Hubbard's, back up Himmel's claims. All three say they heard Hubbard make comments about the money-making potential of starting your own religion.[5]

Money was not the only motivation, however. In a country where the right to freedom of religion is protected by the constitution, Hubbard could shield Scientology from attacks by doctors, scientists and psychotherapists by dressing his new franchises up as churches. In pursuing the religion angle, Hubbard's timing was immaculate. Belief was booming in the United States.[6] Church attendances were at record highs and fringe beliefs were starting to sprout. Historian

Robert Ellwood describes the US at that time as a supply-side 'spiritual marketplace'.[7] Even the state was in on the act. In 1956, President Eisenhower signed a law declaring 'In God We Trust' to be the official motto of the United States. Two years earlier, he signed the bill that saw 'One Nation Under God' added to the Pledge of Allegiance.

But in this growing spiritual marketplace was Hubbard buying what he was selling? Did he truly believe he had lived before and that he had the secret to eternal life? Back in 1938, he was certainly not an advocate of reincarnation. In a letter to his first wife, Polly, he wrote, 'Personal immortality is only to be gained through the printed word, barred note or painted canvas or hard granite.'[8]

Thirty years later, Hubbard was asked on Granada Television's *World in Action*, 'Do you believe that you have lived before? Hubbard paused nervously, before answering, "Now to answer that question would be very unfair."'[9] The interviewer Charlie Nairn followed up by pointing out that 'Scientologists believe they've lived before, though, don't they?' Hubbard, seemingly more comfortable answering questions about other people's belief systems replied, 'Oh yes, as a matter of fact it's quite interesting that exercises can be conducted which demonstrate conclusively that there are memories which exist prior to this life.'

It is rare to see the founder of a religion asked on television whether they believe in the fundamental tenets of the belief system they have created. Hubbard hardly passed the test with flying colours. He was nervous, evasive and unconvincing.

It's not surprising that Hubbard had difficulties answering the question. When the FBI raided the church in 1977, and top executives including his wife were indicted, Hubbard was trying to work out how they could increase their income to help bolster a legal defence. In a memo provided to me by former Scientology executive Nancy Many, Hubbard refers to one model for a non-profit fund that 'would fit better with the church mock-up'.[10] It was not the kind of language you would expect from a religious leader.

What went on in the hours before the Granada Television interview casts further doubt over the authenticity of Hubbard's claim that Scientology was a legitimate religion. For the first time, over 45 years after it was filmed, the documentary maker behind the Granada program *The Shrinking World of L. Ron Hubbard* has spoken out about the extraordinary story of what happened before the cameras started rolling. From the conversations he had beforehand, Charlie Nairn is convinced Hubbard did not believe in his own creation. 'He did not believe a single word of it, there's no doubt about it at all,' Nairn told me.[11]

The Scottish documentary maker had a deep fascination for people who invented religions. His mother, Lady Helen Nairn, the niece of Australia's eighth Prime Minister, Stanley Bruce, had developed something of an existential crisis when Charlie was a teenager, just after her beloved sister had committed suicide. 'I'd say she had or developed what has been called a God-shaped-hole inside of her,' says Nairn. His mother dabbled in a number of versions of Christianity and spiritualism before fashioning a personal faith that filled her 'God-shaped-hole'.

Charlie Nairn felt Scientology would provide the perfect vehicle to further explore this interest. His 1967 documentary *Scientology – A Faith for Sale* examined the Scientologists' need to believe in Hubbard. 'Having looked at the needy,' says Nairn, 'the next stage for me was to go off and talk to the inventor – the filler of their God-shaped-holes.'[12] Nairn got to work on his follow-up, *The Shrinking World of L. Ron Hubbard*.

At the time, Hubbard was bouncing between Mediterranean ports aboard his ship the *Royal Scotman*. Nairn worked out through marine radio channels that Hubbard had dropped anchor in the Tunisian city of Bizerte. The *World in Action* crew hotfooted it to North Africa. When they arrived, Nairn headed straight for the docks. It was after midnight, and the filmmaker was alone. He looked up at the Scientology ship and saw the outline of an older man in a Captain's hat smoking away. Nairn was sure it was Hubbard and decided to try his luck:

> *I went up the gang-plank, up to the bridge. He was alone.*
> *I said, 'Hello.' I made my excuses, told him that I wasn't a*
> *Scientologist like all those sleeping innocently below but that I*
> *was a young filmmaker fascinated by the process of inventing*
> *a religion. Immediately he seemed interested, intrigued – there*
> *was absolutely no whiff of a 'what are you doing on my ship?'*

response. I remember telling him about why I was interested in
this – about my mother.[13]

According to Nairn, Hubbard was undeterred by the provocative premise of his interest in him. He welcomed the conversation and the pair talked for over an hour. The filmmaker asked Hubbard why he invented Scientology. As around 200 Scientologists slept in their bunks on the *Royal Scotman*, he gave Nairn an answer he could never have uttered if his followers were awake: 'He said it started out purely as a way to make money,' says Nairn. 'This did seem to me the most extraordinary and fascinating opening. There he was saying this – that the whole thing was just a 'con' – very simply – with 200, or whatever it was, Scientologists innocently asleep just below us.'[14]

As the conversation developed, Hubbard told Nairn that making a buck was not the only motivating factor. 'He did say that although the initial thing was money, he had also become fascinated by "catching" people, especially clever people, at luring them in,' recalls Nairn. 'I remember him saying it reminded him of fishing with his father. You cast out your line to fool a beautiful silvery fish – that was the whole fun of it – of tricking it and luring it in, deceiving it.'[15]

Hubbard explained to Nairn that as a child, he and his father made fishing flies and lures together, experimenting with what would work, and what wouldn't. According to Nairn, Hubbard said, 'I never understood why a beautiful fish could be caught by a fake fly.' Hubbard was admitting his life's work was, like fly-fishing, all about camouflage and deception. Hubbard mused about how intelligent people got caught up in Scientology. 'I remember him specifically talking about two medical doctors (who got involved in Scientology) as if they should have known better,' says Nairn. 'I remember a sense of triumph from him over this idea – as if he felt some of his victims were maybe brighter than he was – but that they were needy, gullible – that he understood the human animal and its "needs" – exploitable needs – backwards.'[16]

But a sense of triumph was not all that Nairn got from Hubbard. 'I also got a feeling of someone who didn't actually seem to have much self-confidence, who was "boosted" by the respect and reverence that people he thought more intelligent than he was were prepared to pay him. And I'd say there was a funny mixture of triumph over his victims but then, once caught, a lack of respect for them – and now I wonder if that was what he ultimately couldn't stand – and so all those later stories of his towering rages ... Did he kind of "hate" his victims? I got that feeling pretty strongly.'[17]

As their late-night conversation continued on the bridge of the *Royal Scotman*, Nairn put forward his idea of why intelligent people were so easily conned. 'It's because you are filling up the God-shaped-hole,' Nairn told him. It must have been a confronting conversation for Hubbard. A young upstart filmmaker turns up unannounced and wants to ask provocative questions about how he invented a religion and how he was conning all those sleeping below the decks. Nairn says at no point did Hubbard argue with him, or shout at him, or ask him to leave. 'What he absolutely didn't say is, "No, that's not what I'm doing, you haven't understood."'[18]

Charlie Nairn felt Hubbard wanted to keep talking about the very topic you would least expect him to want to discuss with a documentary maker. 'He settled down, in relief I'd say, finally to be able to talk to someone about inventing a religion and conning people – and I'd now say the trap he found himself almost intolerably stuck in,' says Nairn.[19]

A thought nagged away at the young filmmaker as Hubbard expanded on the theme. 'I could well understand hopping into bed at night with one's wife, rubbing one's hands together and saying, "We made $10,000 today dear",' says Nairn, 'but I couldn't understand his own wife believing it all, believing in out-of-body experiences and previous lives. I couldn't imagine lying in bed with someone who "believed" my con. And being surrounded all the time only by believers – all those people sleeping peacefully below us, all believing in him.' Nairn asked Hubbard whether he felt trapped. Whether his situation made him feel utterly lonely? 'That's when he said – very, very slowly and with a smile that I can remember still – that was the first interesting question he had been asked in 20 years.'[20]

Nairn thought he had hit the jackpot. Not only had he tracked down the elusive Hubbard in a remote port, but he had got him to talk openly about the topic Nairn was so desperate to make a film about. He asked Hubbard if he would be interviewed on camera. Hubbard agreed. Nairn went away and woke up his film crew. By the time they had returned it was around 3 am. But the mood, the entire scenario had shifted significantly. There were now around 30 Scientologists surrounding Hubbard. He could not repeat the kinds of things he had been so happy to talk about just hours earlier. 'They were standing behind me, getting edgy if I pushed Hubbard,' says Nairn. 'I did try asking him "the first interesting question I've been asked in 20 years" again – but it didn't work. He was back in front of the conned – so therefore back in his trap.'[21]

Nairn could not replicate the frank and intimate conversation he had with Hubbard just hours earlier. The on-camera interview still provides extraordinary insights into the character of Hubbard. *The Shrinking World of L. Ron Hubbard* is still quoted and used by journalists and documentary makers across the world. But over 45 years later, Nairn sees what he missed, not what he captured. 'I've always hated the results because it was all a million miles from our conversation about dreaming up a religion and God-shaped-holes of an hour earlier,' says Nairn. 'Of course, thinking afterwards, he couldn't possibly have said any of this in front of his disciples, could he? Thinking about it now, how could Hubbard have ever got away from the monster he created? What would have been in it for him to stand up and say he didn't believe?'[22]

WHEN AUSTRALIA WAS FIRST sold Scientology in the 1950s, it wasn't quite the 'spiritual marketplace' of the United States, but it was a country in the process of opening up to the rest of the world. At the beginning of the decade, the population was just eight million – it would increase by another two million over the next ten years, due predominantly to immigration from war-torn Europe. In 1956, Australia held the Olympics for the first time, with Melbourne the host city. The same year saw the introduction of television, with American programs coming to dominate viewing habits. In August 1958, the ten most popular TV shows in Sydney included four sit-coms, five Westerns and *Disneyland* – all of them hailed from the US.[23]

But the American influence wasn't confined to Mickey Mouse and Lucille Ball. Music and movies from the US came to dominate popular culture. The American quest for perfection began to make headway into egalitarian Australia through the burgeoning self-help movement. Salesmen were sent off to Dale Carnegie courses. Norman Vincent Peale's *The Power of Positive Thinking* made its way onto many Australian bookshelves and Gayelord Hauser provided *Woman's Day* magazine with beauty tips from his bestseller *Look Younger, Live Longer.*

For those involved in the early days in Australia, Scientology was more about personal improvement, than salvation. Nightclub singer Doug Moon found it helped him with stage fright.[24] Businessman Phillip Wearne got involved to make more money.[25] Roger Boswarva wanted to become a better athlete.[26] Raised at Bronte Beach in Sydney's eastern suburbs, Boswarva was a champion swimmer and surf lifesaver. With its brutal rips, Bronte was the perfect training ground for an open water swimmer.[27] Boswarva beat all-comers from across Sydney at the New Year's Day surf carnival five years in a row. 'The joke among us,' Boswarva recalls, 'was that I was the only silly son-of-a-bitch who was sober or not hung over!'[28]

Boswarva was a sucker for punishment. Not only did he do constant battle with one of Australia's most treacherous rips, known as the 'Bronte Express', he put himself forward to be a human guinea pig for Forbes Carlile, a young Physiology lecturer at the University of Sydney. Carlile was a pioneer in applying sports science to swimming, experimenting with diet and hypnosis, and introducing training methods that would soon be mimicked across the world.

Carlile became Australia's swim coach in 1948 and produced a long line of Olympic gold medallists including Shane Gould, Gail Neall and Ian O'Brien. In the 1950s, he needed someone to experiment on. His Bronte neighbour Boswarva made the perfect lab rat. 'He was the most enthusiastic swimmer,' remembers Carlile, 'and he was always chasing new ideas.'[29] When an advertisement ran in a Sydney newspaper for a course in applied psychology, Boswarva couldn't contain his curiosity. He went into Marcus Tooley's Scientology Centre at Circular Quay and signed up for his first course. Boswarva soon found himself participating in Scientology's 'Confronting' drill:

> *The first night I did a straight hour of TR0 (Confronting). I did not notice much change in myself while doing the drill ... but*

once I got outside of the course room and drove home, I found myself 'feeling larger' and more aware as I would perceive in a 360-degree 'mental' manner about me … Also, events about me in the traffic appeared to be as though I was moving slower than usual. I recall having to check my speedometer to verify what the hell was going on. Next day, in my swim training session, I found my attention more directly under my control … and apparently less liable to physical fatigue.

On the second evening, we continued with more TR0 for an hour. On this occasion, I spooked out when the fellow in front turned into some sort of giant insect. At the time I had no idea what had happened or what the hell this was … but I knew there was something going on and that this stuff was producing change, which, if I could get control of it, might benefit me and my athletic performance.[30]

According to Steven Hassan, author of *Combatting Cult Mind Control*, the Scientology TR drills lead to an 'altered state of consciousness or trance induction, where all kinds of time distortions take place, things speed up, things slow down or people's faces turn into animals and insects … the brain is having a distortion effect – it's not functioning properly and our normal filtering mechanisms are being disoriented.'[31]

While Boswarva was seeing humans turn into insects, in Melbourne another young man with a thirst for new ideas and risk taking was experimenting with Scientology. Roger Meadmore lived to reach for the sky. After completing his six months national service in the air force, Meadmore flew Tiger Moths, Cessna Seaplanes and hot-air balloons, eventually winning the world ballooning championship in France. Scientology fit easily with his philosophy of life. 'When I went into it,' he said, 'it was more as an adventure.'[32] Meadmore embarked on that adventure with his brother Clem, who would later become a famous sculptor in New York. They started listening to tapes of Hubbard, and before long Roger was mixing with Dianetics groups and helping to set up Australia's first accredited Scientology franchise, the Hubbard Association of Scientologists International (HASI), opposite Parliament House in Melbourne.

Still in his early 20s, Meadmore had already run coffee lounges and a catering service. He would later establish the Pancakes chain of restaurants across Australia. Meadmore's entrepreneurial skills were needed at Melbourne's first Scientology office. They were short of money and needed recruits. 'I signed up 68 people to do the Hubbard Professional Auditor course,'[33] Meadmore recalls proudly. He was selling something he believed in. Meadmore says Scientology courses 'helped me enormously, raising my IQ from 115 to 156'.[34] His recruitment tactics were simple, entice them in with a free Personal Efficiency course and then sell them the whole box and dice.

Race Mathews was one of those who read Roger Meadmore's advertisement in the newspaper. Returning to Melbourne University to study speech pathology, he was drawn to the promise that the five-nights-a-week course would 'improve your study habits'. Mathews would later become the Principal Private Secretary to Gough Whitlam when he was leader of the federal Opposition. In the 1980s, he served as a Minister in the Cain Labor government in Victoria. Back in the late 1950s, he just wanted to get through university and signed up for Meadmore's classes. 'There was probably a dozen of us who did the course,' says Mathews. 'At the end of the course, everyone sat the Minnesota test. It was used to assess your need for processing.'[35]

According to Mathews, the idea of processing had been introduced to the students on the last night of the course and everyone was offered an estimate of how many hours they would need to become 'clear' or 'Operating Thetans'. 'The question I raised was wouldn't it be more credible if it was "cash for clarity" as the form of payment,' says Mathews. He felt he got nothing from the course, but remembers that 'one man expressed the intention of mortgaging his house to pay for more courses'.[36]

While not advertised as such, the 'Free Personal Efficiency Course' was in fact an introduction to Scientology course, and was described this way in internal Scientology documents.[37] Some students felt they were a 'bait and switch' scam and the courses even came under scrutiny from intelligence agents. In July 1958, Australia's domestic intelligence agency, ASIO, conducted an interview with an unnamed graduate of the course. According to one ASIO report, a student said he and other recruits were told, 'Scientology increased one's efficiency potential 100 per cent and built up a resistance that could even withstand the effects of atom bomb radiation.'[38]

The student told security agents he considered the Scientologists 'to be an organisation which extracts money from the naïve in an organised mass psychological appeal system'.[39] Even back in the early days of Scientology, courses were expensive. The Hubbard Professional Auditor course that Roger Meadmore was selling cost around eight weeks' worth of the average male wage.[40] Processing was sold in 25-hour bundles for £105,[41] which was over five weeks' worth of average earnings.

Scientology courses and auditing became a nice little earner for Hubbard. One recruit paid £3065 for Scientology services between 1957 and 1963,[42] or around three years' worth of average earnings. 10 per cent of the Melbourne Scientology office's corrected gross income was sent straight overseas into the bank account of Hubbard Communications Office (World Wide) Ltd.[43] Over five years, from 1 July 1958, over £25,000 was sent from Melbourne to Scientology's head office.[44]

By 1959, Hubbard was doing well enough out of Scientology to buy Saint Hill Manor, an expansive estate in the Sussex countryside. He soon moved his family and Scientology's headquarters to England. The Melbourne operation had little autonomy; it was under the control of a foreign company registered in Victoria under the Companies Act.[45] If Scientology was a religious movement, it certainly wasn't operating like one. On 30 June 1963, Saint Hill claimed the Melbourne headquarters owed them another £17,231 for management expenses, service charges and service expenses.[46] If that wasn't enough, both Hubbard and his wife Mary Sue had the right to draw cheques from any of the Melbourne accounts.[47]

The pressure to keep pumping money back to Saint Hill was felt keenly by new recruits. Max and Jenny Anderson received a letter from the Melbourne office's Director of Accounts asking that they help 'keep Scientology surviving' by paying their course fees sooner, 'because we have accumulated debts to the amount of £3000 to our own creditors in Melbourne'.[48] If the claims in the letter are true, the Melbourne headquarters was borrowing money so they could pay Saint Hill more training fees. While Hubbard was living the life of the landed gentry in his English manor, Australian Scientologists were struggling to get by on sub-standard wages. At times the highest paid person at the Melbourne office was the cleaner. One staff member received £4 8s for a 40-hour week – just a fifth of the average weekly male earnings at that time.[49]

The Melbourne Scientology centre was the focus of a number of allegations of rip-offs and rorts. Complaints came from both students and staff. Legal action was taken, and staff members were sacked or left in anger. Some of these disputes would have lasting consequences for the future of Scientology in Australia. Even John and Tucker Farrell, the founders of Scientology's first association in Australia, were at the centre of allegations involving stolen money, unpaid bills and visa rorts.

When the Farrells headed back to the US in 1957, they left a parting gift for their colleagues at the Melbourne office – an unpaid tax bill. Peter Crundall, one of the first staff members at Spring Street, was summoned by the tax department to deal with the money owed.[50] Crundall, a company director and father of four, was not impressed and wrote to Scientology's international headquarters asking that the debts be cleared.

After delays in getting the tax bill settled, Crundall fired off a heated letter to L. Ron Hubbard. 'I got quite upset, quite emotional,' Crundall later testified. 'Dr Hubbard said, "Well, now look, my fellow, you are temporarily suspended until you get yourself some retraining and some processing and let us see that you are handling things in a more rational manner."'[51] The retraining and processing costs would have been expensive for a father of four. Hubbard's punishments were akin to a judge finding an individual guilty, and issuing community service orders that came with a fee, with the money to be paid into a bank account in the judge's name.

The Farrells' visa for Australia was initially granted under guarantee that the local Scientologists would pay for their plane trip home.[52] Pat Krenik, a friend of the Farrells' who let them stay with her when they returned to the US, says the couple had to steal money from the Melbourne office to pay for their airfares home. 'They were good folks forced into an impossible position,' says Krenik. 'Their pay was so low they could never save up to get out of there. Finally, they stole the money out of the till and came here to Seattle.'[53]

The Farrells' status in Australia was the subject of much toing and froing behind the scenes. In February 1956, Immigration Minister and future Prime Minister Harold Holt wrote a letter to the Secretary of the Department of Immigration asking whether the Farrells could, 'remain in Australia indefinitely'.[54] Harold Holt followed up with a phone call to the department head and another letter in March asking for 'a speedy decision to be reached' as their visa was about to expire.[55]

But Harold Holt and the Farrells did not get their wish. The department refused permanent residency, instead extending their visa by just 12 months.[56] By the time it expired, it was decided their visas would not be renewed. A departmental file note says, 'these people are clearly charlatans … we may be criticised for having allowed them to stay.'[57]

The official explanation sent to the Australian embassy in Washington stated: 'In view of the dubious nature and activities of the organisation with which they were associated the application was not approved.'[58] The Department of Immigration was not impressed that the Farrells had entered Australia on a six-month visa and not declared the true reasons behind their visit: 'The original intention of the Farrells when they came to Australia was to remain here to expand the activities of the Association. They were therefore not bona fide visitors.'[59]

On 30 June 1957, John and Tucker Farrell and their two children left Australia aboard a Pan Am Boeing 377 Stratocruiser.[60] Hubbard's handpicked Scientology missionaries were being sent home in disgrace, owing money, labelled charlatans, accused of manipulating the conditions of their visa and rejected permanent residency at a time when Australia was undergoing a period of mass migration.

Scientology's early days in Sydney were not trouble-free either, with tales of stolen records, expulsions and a prominent tabloid exposé. In 1955, Marcus Tooley established a Scientology centre in the city's busy Martin Place. After a couple of months, the operation moved to 71 East Circular Quay where a sign outside the college described it as a Hubbard Association of Scientologists International (HASI) Scientology Centre.[61] Tooley later denied under oath he ran a HASI, even though he advertised it as such.[62] He was, however, accredited to train students who could then sit examinations through the Melbourne office in Spring Street.[63]

Marcus Tooley had completed a 'Doctorate' in divinity from the Church of American Science in Phoenix, Arizona, in 1954.[64] The course was only a few weeks long, rather than the three to five years required for a genuine university doctorate. Tooley's claims of being a doctor got the full tabloid treatment in Sydney's *Truth* in August 1955. 'He's the dux of the quacks,' screamed the headline on page three. Describing him as 'nothing but a phoney and a sham out for easy money', *Truth* mocked Tooley's qualifications, questioned the effectiveness of Scientology 'cures' and poured scorn on the price tag of £90 for an eight-week course.[65]

In the same month of the *Truth* exposé, Tooley was 'excommunicated' by Hubbard.[66] Apparently Scientology's founder was unhappy with some of his writings and sent John Farrell to see him. 'He came up to Sydney and sought to take over the Scientology centre and he (Farrell) was ordered off the premises,' Tooley recalled. 'That was my last contact with Scientology for quite some years.'[67] Tooley had already trained up a number of people who would play significant roles inside and outside Scientology. Peter and Yvonne Gillham did their first auditors' course under Tooley.[68] Roger Boswarva and Doug Moon also did courses through the Sydney centre, as did Ken Dyers, who would go on to found the notorious cult Kenja.[69]

After Tooley lost his Scientology training rights he renamed his practice 'The American College'.[70] The new business soon became a victim of corporate espionage. Moon, who was on staff with Tooley for around a week,[71] stole a copy of his register of students and sent it to the Melbourne Scientology headquarters.[72] The file was subsequently sent back to The American College, but not before Scientology executive Elizabeth Williams had written a letter to one of Hubbard's executives in England, saying, 'I am holding them [the files] until you or Ron tells me what to do with them.'[73]

Tooley called the police, and Moon was arrested. The Melbourne office pushed Tooley to drop any prosecution for fear of bad publicity.[74] Moon also leaked information to Scientology executives in Melbourne about the courses Tooley was teaching, the certificates he was giving out and how he went about his teachings.

In Victoria, private Scientology colleges sprang up in competition with the Melbourne centre in Spring Street, including one run by the

Gillhams in suburban Melbourne and another established by June and Eric Lake in Geelong. The Lakes ran a college of 'personnel efficiency', the Gillhams a college of 'personal efficiency'. Both were recognised by the Melbourne headquarters as independent franchises,[75] contributing money to Saint Hill.

Not everyone was happy with the way the Melbourne office was operating. Roger Meadmore set up his own college after he was sacked from the mission he helped found. 'I was really pissed off,' says Meadmore. 'I never got paid for the 68 people I signed up. I helped set the place up and Frank Turnbull came in and sacked me.'[76] While Meadmore was not impressed with the way Spring Street was run, nothing undermined his belief in Hubbard. 'He was fantastic,' declares Meadmore. 'One of the greatest human beings in the last five thousand years.'[77]

Putting behind his disappointments with the local Scientology operation, Meadmore visited Washington, DC to study under Hubbard before briefly moving to England. There he funded further Scientology training by selling fold-up ladders and advertising for estate agent maps. In late 1959, he returned home on the same plane as his hero. 'He was in first class, we were in economy,' Meadmore recalls.[78] Hubbard was returning to Australia in very different circumstances from his visit during World War II. This time he was in charge; he could be as garrulous as he liked, and no-one could send him home for insubordination.

There was no hero's welcome for Hubbard when his plane touched down at Melbourne's Essendon Airport on 5 November. 'He didn't get a big reception or anything,' says Meadmore. 'He was just regarded as a guy teaching us. No-one realised then how famous he should be.'[79]

Hubbard held his first lecture two days later in the Bamboo Room at Melbourne's Chevron Hotel.[80] Doug Moon, a man who appreciated good stagecraft, was impressed: 'He wore makeup, the lights were right, he was carrying a mike, it was professionally done, it was beautiful.'[81] Hubbard started with the obligatory 'down-under' joke, asking, 'How do they do their work standing on their heads?' before moving on to the importance of Scientology making money. 'Once in a while you think, well, Scientology is basically – must be very mercenary, very mercenary – thinks about money. You bet it thinks about money!'[82]

In his lecture, Hubbard criticised Russian communism and American capitalism, railed against the laziness of the British Labour Party, and took a swipe at the people who ran Melbourne's Scientology headquarters in its early days. 'It limped along and kept falling on its face,' he said dismissively.

But a large part of Hubbard's first lecture on Australian soil was dedicated to peddling more lies about his war service in Brisbane. 'Before the Yanks came,' Hubbard fantasised, 'I was Senior Officer Present of northern Australia, not because I had any rank, but because there wasn't anybody else there.' Hubbard claimed his service in Brisbane was the stuff of legend, and that after the war while 'kicking around an officers' club' he was recognised as the man who sent orders for a heavy cruiser to leave Australia. 'Good God, you're that fellow from down in Australia!' he said.[83]

Hubbard used this tall tale to ingratiate himself with his audience. 'So you see,' he said, 'I must be one of you.' He bounced between self-praise, and praise for the country he had returned to. He described Australia as, 'the country, perhaps, with the greatest and brightest future on the face of Earth today'.[84] He claimed Scientology could make Australia more economically productive and speculated that, due to atomic weapons, the Southern Hemisphere could be the 'only alive part of Earth within the next century'. Hubbard told local Scientologists that he believed Australia would be the world's first 'clear continent'.[85]

Hubbard delivered six lectures across two days to the Melbourne Congress. The Church of Scientology describes the weekend as a 'watershed in Scientology history'.[86] Scientology's current leader, David Miscavige, says the lectures 'marked a turn in the path and a rise in the road, from which the whole panorama of human potential came into focus.'[87] At the Melbourne Congress, Hubbard previewed his latest research that would allow 'clears' to become 'Operating Thetans'. The lectures would have Scientology public relations still gushing over 50 years later. 'He had now made the breakthrough to the accomplishment of an even higher state,' reads the promotional guff, 'a state long dreamed of in this universe but never, until now, able to be stably achieved – *Operating Thetan*.'[88]

While Doug Moon found Hubbard's Melbourne lectures too technical and difficult to understand,[89] local Scientologists lapped them up. 'Generally, they received him with hushed rapt attention,' Moon remembered. 'If he made a joke they would all laugh – almost obediently.'[90] But not all Scientologists who attended the Congress were in the thrall of Hubbard. Phillip Wearne, the businessman who was in Scientology to make more money, sent Hubbard a note requesting a meeting to discuss his processing goals.[91] When Hubbard couldn't make the suggested time, Wearne went apoplectic.

In a letter sent to Hubbard, Wearne fumed, 'I regard your request to "put it in writing" as most impertinent and offensive. I am not a subordinate on your staff, I am a client of your peculiar organisation who has spent nearly £2000 on auditing and I refuse categorically to make a submission in the manner of a mendicant.'[92]

Wearne called Hubbard 'insular' and 'supercilious' and threatened to stop paying for services until he received a 'satisfactory audience'. In response, Elizabeth Williams from the Melbourne Scientology office told Wearne, 'Ron will see you 3 pm Thursday – you will be sorry you came.' For reasons unknown, Hubbard never met with Wearne. Scientology's founder would soon be sorry he didn't take the opportunity to placate the disgruntled businessman. Wearne's anger at being ignored and ripped off would fester. His revenge was not swift, but it was brutal.

Wearne's payback eventually saw Scientology banned in three states in Australia and led to a chain of events that forced Hubbard to leave the UK and go into exile. Phillip Wearne was about to play a critical role in Scientology being discredited across the world; so too was another provocative Australian businessman.

CHAPTER 6

BUNKUMOLOGY

WHAT WAS RUPERT MURDOCH thinking? The veteran media mogul launched an extraordinary attack on Scientology in July 2012, following the marriage breakdown of Tom Cruise and Katie Holmes, 'Scientology back in news,'[1] Murdoch tweeted. 'Very weird cult, but big, big money involved with Tom Cruise either No. 2 or 3 in hierarchy.' In case anyone thought he didn't mean it, News Corp's CEO published a second edition a few hours later. 'Watch Katie Holmes and Scientology story develop,' he warned. 'Something creepy, maybe even evil, about these people.'[2]

Those two tweets became big news. Murdoch was calling the world's most litigious religion a weird, wealthy, creepy cult. In the US, Scientology had become a no-go zone for most media organisations. Murdoch's arch rivals at TimeWarner became bogged down in a costly decade-long legal battle after *TIME* published Richard Behar's searing exposé 'The Thriving Cult of Greed and Power' in 1991. Behar and TimeWarner were sued for libel for US$416 million.[3] The case was dismissed in 1996, but the Church of Scientology took it all the way to the Supreme Court. Ten years after Behar published his ground-breaking cover story, the highest court in the US refused to consider reinstating the libel case.[4]

So why would Rupert Murdoch tempt fate and brazenly bait Scientology and its golden boy Tom Cruise? Murdoch wasn't just a media proprietor; he also ran a movie studio, which could financially benefit from keeping one of Hollywood's most bankable stars onside.

What wasn't reported at the time was that Murdoch had a long history of going after Scientology. His views on what he called a 'very weird cult' were formed over 50 years previously, and can be found inside the fading pages of a muckraking Australian scandal sheet he published long before he became a global media player.

AT THE TAIL END of the 1950s, Sydney was blessed with a boisterous newspaper culture run by a trio of feuding autocrats. Warwick Fairfax published *The Sun*, the *Sydney Morning Herald* and the *Sun-Herald*. Frank Packer ran the *Daily Telegraph* and the *Sunday Telegraph*. Ezra Norton owned the *Daily Mirror* and the *Sunday Mirror*. All three proprietors used their papers to belittle each other. One disagreement between Norton and Packer was sorted out inside the members' enclosure at Randwick Racecourse. *Smith's Weekly* described Packer emerging from the punch-up as 'hatless, breathless and bleeding from a cut over one eye'.[5]

The ballet-loving Warwick Fairfax may have been more urbane, but he was no less competitive. In 1958, his deputy Rupert 'Rags' Henderson heard that Norton wanted to sell up. Determined to sideline Packer and any carpetbaggers from Melbourne, Henderson set up a shelf company financed by one of Fairfax's subsidiaries to purchase Truth and Sportsman Ltd. The deal was short lived. With Norton's old newspapers underperforming and Fairfax expanding into television, Henderson offloaded the renamed *Mirror* newspapers to a young Rupert Murdoch on 21 May 1960 for £2 million.[6]

Murdoch had finally cracked the Sydney market. Already he owned newspapers in Adelaide and Perth, now the *Daily Mirror* gave him a foothold in a big city for the first time. But as part of the deal he also acquired the *Mirror*'s wayward sibling. *Truth* was a newspaper shaped in the image of its most famous proprietor, John Norton. Like his son Ezra, John Norton was prone to acts of public drunkenness and violence. After *Truth* described local politician Richard Meagher as 'the premier perjurer of our public life',[7] Norton got his comeuppance at the busy intersection of Pitt and King streets. In front of a crowd of onlookers, the Honourable Member for Tweed flogged the startled newspaperman with a greenhide horse whip. In response, Norton drew his revolver and fired at the politician as he escaped in a cab.[8]

Sixty years later, *Truth* was still getting by on a staple of scandal, crime and racing form. But by the time Rupert Murdoch acquired it in 1960, it had also built a reputation for exposing scam artists and charlatans. As Mark Day, who worked on the Adelaide edition in the 1960s, recalls: 'It was an old-fashioned, muckraking, crusading paper. *Truth* had a long history of standing up for the battlers and it was forceful in its reporting of the underbelly of life.'[9] Rupert Murdoch would later reflect that '*Truth* deals with the seamier side of life.'[10] Describing it as a 'a knock-about newspaper', the proud newspaperman stated: 'Authority and Officialdom rest easy when it is NOT campaigning.'[11]

Owen McKenna was one of the journalists working on long form investigations for the Melbourne *Truth* in the 1960s. A relative latecomer to journalism, he was fortunate to gain a cadetship at the ripe old age of 27. McKenna was lucky to be alive. He'd spent five years in the Royal Australian Air Force, risking all as a dive bomber and fighter pilot. In 1943, McKenna survived a mid-air collision, bailing out of his stricken Wirraway. His wireless-airgunner Sergeant John Patrick was not so fortunate, perishing as he tried to parachute to safety.[12]

In *Truth*'s smoke-filled reporters' room on the first floor of 402 La Trobe Street, McKenna would take his turn at manning the phones. 'Before talkback radio, anyone who had a complaint would ring *Truth*,' McKenna remembers. 'It was like the people's ombudsman.'[13] While other reporters were out drinking with contacts, McKenna was happy to be taking calls. One small complaint could lead to a big scoop. Working the phones gave McKenna his first insight into the secretive world of Scientology. He received a series of calls from distressed family members complaining about the cult, and pitched a story to the Editorial Director, Lyle 'The Jockey' Cousland. McKenna was given the green light and got cracking. He was given two weeks to pull together his exposé.

On Saturday 2 December 1961, *Truth* published a 'special investigation' under the headline 'Bunkumology – cult of experts at smear tactics'. The former dive bomber didn't miss his target. 'They are operating one of the most dangerous but profitable schemes ever tried in Australia,' McKenna thundered. 'It is time they were put out of business.'[14]

Truth laid out a series of sensational allegations about the local Scientology operation. McKenna told the story of a 19-year-old chemistry student who had forgone asthma treatment because he was convinced his ailment was punishment for murdering his wife in a previous life. Another student who resisted signing up to Scientology was told 'he had homosexual tendencies which they could cure'. A young Polish migrant had gone into hiding because 'scientologists claimed to hold promissory notes he had signed for £600'.[15]

McKenna also exposed Scientology's bullying tactics when it came to silencing critics. *Truth* revealed that the Scientologists had threatened Catholic priest and broadcaster Dr Leslie Rumble and ABC TV journalist Gerald Lyons with security investigations.

Dr Rumble was not the wisest choice of targets. In 1928, five years after the first radio station was licensed in Australia, Dr Rumble was given his own Sunday night radio program *Question Box*. The program had a simple formula. A listener would write in with a question and Dr Rumble would respond with a mini-sermon. Expected to run for four weeks,[16] the show flourished for the next 40 years. Dr Rumble's answers were syndicated in Catholic newspapers across the country. His books sold over seven million copies worldwide.[17]

With a voice likened to worn sandpaper,[18] Dr Rumble was known for giving no-nonsense advice. When 'P O'N of Bexley' wrote in asking 'I would like your advice on the subject of Scientology,'[19] Hubbard's theology got the full sandblasting. 'Have nothing to do with it,' Rumble fulminated. 'Only credulous and gullible people will be impressed by the high-brow term, as a fruit-shop proprietor hopes simpletons will be by the description of himself as a Fruitologist. In case his listeners had any doubts where Dr Rumble stood he added, 'You flatter it by calling it a "science". *TIME* magazine recently described "scientology" as compounded of "equal parts of science-fiction, dianetics and jabberwocky"!'[20]

The year before Dr Rumble's tangle with Scientology, Hubbard urged vengeance upon his critics. 'People attack Scientology,' he told his followers. 'I never forget it, always even the score.'[21] In his *Manual of Justice*, Hubbard's form guide on how to deal with enemies, he encouraged the use of private investigators. 'Of twenty-one persons found attacking Dianetics and Scientology,' Hubbard wrote, 'eighteen of them under investigation were found to be members of the Communist Party or criminals, usually both. The smell of police or private detectives caused them to fly, to close down, to confess. Hire them and damn the cost when you need to.'[22]

Peter Williams, the head of Melbourne's Scientologists, took his cues straight from Hubbard's guidebook. He fired off a letter to Dr Rumble accusing the priest of allying himself with communists and threatened to investigate him. In part, it read:

> *You will no doubt find the attacked [sic] article of great interest, for apparently by your utterance you have not only divorced yourself from the main international body of Catholic attitude to Scientology but have allied yourself further with international subversive communism. By attacking Scientology you are attacking one of the most ardent and vigorous groups in the field of combatting communism and maintaining national security.*
>
> *It is our policy to investigate subversives through our own channels as well as to co-operate with national security organizations.*
>
> *Scientology has never been a threat to the honest and upright of any nationality or belief. Only those who tread dark paths or are on the payroll of a specialized interest seeking to profit by the sickness and troubles of man would fight a group of people trying to help man. May these sick and troubled offer their forgiveness.*[23]

Meanwhile, Denny Gogerly from the Hubbard Association of Scientologists sent a letter to the Catholic newspaper *Tribune*, warning that Dr Rumble was now being investigated and that from previous inquiries, 'facts uncovered in these investigations have generally been given to government security agencies, police etc'.[24]

The Australian public was getting an early insight into Hubbard's obsession with vengeance at any cost. McKenna's investigation in *Truth* had also revealed that Dr CH Dickson, the Victorian Secretary of the British Medical Association, was also subjected to intimidation tactics. After Dickson had asked the Victorian government to investigate Scientology, letters were sent to federal and state MPs alleging Dr Dickson was 'using smoke screen tactics to cover up his own irregularities'.[25]

Hubbard had already accused the Medical Association of collaborating with communists[26] and urged Scientologists to take on the doctors. 'We have the technology, they don't,' he wrote. 'We're the experts. They aren't.'[27] Hubbard thought Australia could not only be the first 'clear continent', but the first continent cleared of medical surgery. 'Let us pledge ourselves to work steadily and hard to make one nation on Earth free of knives, drugs and shocks used in the name of healing,' Hubbard wrote in his Special Project Australia HCO Bulletin. 'Let's declare war in our own way, in a Scientology way, upon the enemy.'[28]

Doctors soon found themselves being investigated for links to communism, with Hubbard boasting, 'We are having Dickson investigated for Anti-social background, and if it ever comes to a court case, we'll ruin him.'[29] But Dr Dickson was causing more harm to the Scientologists than they were to him. Dickson sent a report to the Deputy Premier Arthur Rylah that led to action by the police.[30] Under the headline 'CIB probes practice of Scientology',[31] the *Geelong Advertiser* on 7 June 1960 reported that Scientology was being investigated following orders from the Deputy Premier.

The wonderfully named Inspector Bent confirmed to the *Geelong Advertiser* that he had made inquiries into Scientology. Giving little away, Bent gave his local newspaper some cursory insights into his investigation.

Reporter: Is Scientology being practised in Geelong at present?
Inspector Bent: Yes.
Reporter: How many Scientologists do you know of?
Inspector Bent: One.[32]

A copy of the *Geelong Advertiser* must have somehow made it back to Hubbard's manor in the Sussex countryside. Three weeks after the article was published, he penned a bizarre letter to Inspector Bent.

The nature of letter, and the fact that Hubbard would be bothered writing to a Police Inspector who was investigating one Scientologist in a far-off regional city of less than 100,000 people,[33] gave some insight into the state of Hubbard's mind.

Hubbard told Inspector Bent that he had been given 'bad data' in relation to Scientology. He said Scientologists did not practice healing and mentioned that defamation action was already underway against media companies that had portrayed Scientology in a negative light. Hubbard warned Bent that, 'we are in communication with the government and will be conducting a broad investigation in your area.'[34]

Hubbard told Inspector Bent that he expected the police to be onside with Scientology, and raised a strange theory as to why the Geelong police were investigating his organisation:

> It is a serious thing when social organizations are attacked. Elsewhere in the world Scientology closely supports the police in their campaigns against subversion. Therefore it comes as a surprise to find an isolated case of attack by police. Scientologists are not doctors they are social workers.
>
> My personal feeling is that you have a subversive infiltration in your area. As one once trained as the Provost Marshal of Korea, I have a good grip on Asian subversion and do not intend it to ruin Scientology in any area.
>
> Just as we can undo brainwashing, so we can undo subversion as there are 12 Scientologists in Australia for every medical doctor. Please assist us to keep order in Australia.[35]

Hubbard's letter is notable for a number of reasons. He doesn't claim Scientology to be a religion, but a 'social organization'. He describes Scientologists as 'social workers', despite his internal demands for them to make more money. Once again he lies about his military record, stating he was Provost Marshal of Korea when his military files display no record of service in that country,[36] and for good measure he signs off his letter with a reference to the fraudulent PhD he sourced from a Californian diploma mill.

In case the Deputy Premier was interested in Hubbard's thoughts on 'Asian subversion', a copy of the letter was forwarded from

Inspector Bent to his office. A copy was also placed in the Department of Health's freshly minted file on Scientology. As government officials began to receive more complaints about the local Scientology operation, they could get a unique insight into its founder's mind by reading his bizarre letter.

For an organisation so obsessed about public relations, Scientology was doing a stellar job of alienating all the wrong people. It was picking fights with the medical establishment, the Catholic Church, the police and the expanding Murdoch media empire. *Truth* was eventually issued with a writ for defamation. But Murdoch's muckraking tabloid would not back down, launching a series of exposés over the next three years that would gleefully refer to Scientology, at all times, as 'Bunkumology'. Murdoch would later look back with pride at his paper's campaign against Scientology.[37] Paradoxically, it would be another victim of *Truth*'s robust reporting methods whose actions further exposed Scientology and led to the world's first state-sanctioned investigation into the cult.

CHAPTER 7

THE SCAMMER SCAMMED

EACH MORNING, PHILLIP WEARNE had to make a decision unfamiliar to most Labor men of his era. Did he drive the all-white sports MG to work or should he take the Jaguar?[1] Wearne's business, Australian Trade Union Press, had an office opposite Melbourne's Trades Hall, the world's oldest Trade Union building. Whichever car he drove, it always stood out in a sea of Holdens and Fords parked along Lygon and Victoria streets, near the eight-hour-day monument in inner-city Carlton.

Wearne's red and white Australian Labor Party (ALP) badge sat uncomfortably in the lapel of his expensive suit. Tall, dark-haired and well-fed, Wearne was a Toorak man making money out of Collingwood opinions. At the beginning of the 1960s, his business published over 50 trade union journals including *Transport Worker*, *The Tanner* and the gas workers' periodical *The Retort*. Wearne also published the official newspapers of three state ALP branches, *The New Age* (Qld), *The Western Sun* (WA) and the *Herald* (SA).

In the Melbourne telephone directory of 1961, Wearne listed himself as the ALP's Publicity Officer, even though no such position officially existed. This would not have troubled Wearne. At the age of 36, he already had a lifetime's worth of exaggeration and fabrication under his belt.

Sydney's version of *Truth* had exposed Wearne as a scam artist back in 1955. Under the headline 'Play safe, don't open your purse', the businessman was fingered as being part of 'a nest of Sydney's most prolific company promoters'.[2] Wearne had floated a company called Freehold and Brewery Properties Ltd, asking investors for £50,000. But the company had listed three companies, rather than individuals, as sole shareholders and directors, allowing Wearne and his colleagues to avoid liability if the money went missing.

In the same year, Wearne was exposed in parliament for making £1000 a week from a bogus organisation named the Citizen's Road Safety Council.[3] The group solicited donations from people who had mistaken them for the Road Safety Council. Another of Wearne's initiatives was to set up an Anti-TB Information Centre. The body had no concerns about public health. Wearne wanted to print pamphlets about tuberculosis so he could make money from selling advertising space.[4]

Even the spooks were onto Wearne. An ASIO report from 1962 said, 'There is little doubt that Wearne is certainly a go-getter, one might say con-man, who is prepared to approach anybody or anyone if he can see a chance of making a bit for himself.'[5]

When Wearne got involved in Scientology it was all about making a buck. In fact, the Toorak businessman and Hubbard had much in common. Their lives had been derailed by bankruptcy, mental breakdown and divorce and they both made money from elaborate scams. Even Wearne's war record read like Hubbard's. He had enlisted in the Royal Australian Air Force (RAAF) in 1944, but managed to avoid combat. He failed his pilot course at Elementary Flying Training School and never earned the respect of his commanding officers. His superiors considered him 'careless', too 'full of his self-importance' and not possessing the 'required aptitude'.[6] The similarities did not end there. Like Hubbard, Wearne had a love of science fiction. Before he started dabbling in the publishing business, he wrote and drew a comic strip called *The Legion of Space – An Inter-Planetary Adventure Strip*.

Yet even Wearne's brief comic strip career was based on a scam. He had ripped off the title and story, *The Legion of Space*, from American artist Jack Williamson, turning the concept into four books.[7] The original strip had appeared in *Astounding Stories* in 1934. After Williamson's version was published in paperback in 1947 and reprinted in magazine form in 1950, Wearne was exposed as a plagiarist and forced to find work in another industry.[8]

In many ways Wearne and Hubbard were similar characters. Yet Scientology's founder had a blind spot when it came to the Toorak businessman. When his publishing companies failed to profit from Hubbard's teachings, Wearne took action that would change Scientology forever. Hubbard would eventually find out the hard way about the perils of trying to shake down a fellow shakedown artist.

Phillip Wearne had first read *Dianetics* in the early 1950s[9]. A friend gave him an informal processing session, asking questions and giving instructions from Hubbard's book. But Wearne did not enjoy the experience. 'I found them quite upsetting,' he said. 'It made me feel somewhat ill and I abandoned it straight away.'[10]

Years later, when an entrepreneurial young Scientologist told Wearne he could help him increase his profits, Wearne had a change of heart. In January 1958, Roger Meadmore turned up unannounced at the businessman's home. A mutual friend had suggested he call by. Meadmore told Wearne that Hubbard had 'developed techniques of control and communication from his research in psychology, which showed tremendous advances, particularly in the field of selling and salesmanship'.[11]

Hearing Roger Meadmore describe Hubbard as a 'super salesman',[12] made all the difference. Wearne was always on the lookout for new ways to make money, and signed up for the Communication Course at Scientology's Melbourne headquarters in Spring Street. Wearne wrote down an ambitious list of goals, including slim the waistline, space travel, establish paper, control sex desires and making £50,000 a week.[13]

On his first night at Spring Street, Wearne listened to a brief lecture, before he and around 30 other new recruits were split off into pairs to do the first of their Training Routine Drills, or TRs as they are known in Scientology.

First, Wearne had to undergo the 'confronting' drills. He was asked to sit a metre apart from a colleague and stare at them for an hour without blinking, moving or laughing. The routine put Wearne in a hypnotic state. 'I was in a condition that I believed anything that was said to me and acted upon it,' he said.[14]

Next, he had to complete the 'bullbaiting' drill, once again staring at his opposite number, but this time with insults thrown in.

Paulette Cooper described the routine in *The Scandal of Scientology*: 'The other partner tries to make the immobile one "flinch" or react by insulting him, humoring him, taunting him, or leading him on – usually about his physical flaws or sexual problems.'[15]

The repetitive drills continued with Wearne and his new colleagues forced to undertake the infamous Scientology drill of shouting at an ashtray. 'They had everyone sitting down with an ashtray on a table,' Wearne recalled. 'One had to shout at this ashtray the same phrase over and over again until you became hoarse and exhausted.'[16] Among the phrases Wearne was forced to yell at ashtrays were, 'stand up', 'sit down on that chair' and 'thank you'.

Scientology historian Jon Atack says these drills can induce a state of uncritical euphoria: 'Repetition is another way of inducing an altered or trance state,' Atack says. 'Following these procedures definitely makes the individual more susceptible to direction from Scientology.'[17] Former Scientologist Margery Wakefield describes them as 'a sophisticated set of mind-control processes designed to convert a newcomer into a confirmed Scientologist'.[18] The drills certainly had that effect on Wearne. 'I had the delusion that if a person who had received training in Scientology gave me a command I would carry it out because it would carry with it this mystic power,' he said.[19]

Wearne claimed his publishing business suffered as a result of the hypnotic drills. 'I became confused,' he said. 'I could not make decisions. I could not handle the work.'[20] After confronting Meadmore about his problems, he was told, 'The only way out is through.'[21] Wearne was offered individual processing and 'intensives'. He was sold on the idea he could reach the exalted state of 'clear' or 'Operating Thetan' by signing up to another course.[22]

While Wearne had believed that Scientology would help him make money, the more auditing he sought, the less time he spent running his business. At the peak of his success, he had offices in Sydney, Melbourne and Adelaide, employed around a hundred staff[23] and was making profits in excess of £20,000 a year, or over $500,000 a year in 2016 terms.[24] He made enough to keep a home in Toorak, two houses in Sydney and two luxury cars parked in the garage.[25]

The business model that generated Wearne's wealth was simple. He published Labor Party newspapers and trade union journals at no cost to the labour movement, but made his profit by selling advertising space.[26] On the surface it seemed like a legitimate business. But Wearne never quite left behind the nefarious ways that led to his exposure as a scam artist by *Truth*.

In 1960, trade union membership was at record highs in Australia, with around 60 per cent of all employees unionised.[27] Wearne was able to leverage the threat of industrial action against businesses in return for guaranteed advertising space. Doug Moon described it as 'legal blackmail',[28] telling Hubbard, 'He would sell on an "or else" basis and he was doing quite well in his chosen rackets.'[29] Roger Meadmore described Wearne's operation as a form of psychological blackmail. 'Businesses felt if they didn't advertise they might be given a hard time.'[30]

In 1960, the year after he first visited Melbourne, Hubbard decided to expand his influence and launch a counteroffensive against his critics. In June, Scientology's Melbourne headquarters published Hubbard's latest bulletin, an ambitious call to arms titled, *The Special Zone Plan: The Scientologist's Role in Life*.[31] Hubbard urged Scientologists to infiltrate spheres of influence including governments. 'Get a job on the secretarial staff or the bodyguard,' he advised. 'Don't ask for permission. Just enter them and start functioning to make the group win through effectiveness and sanity.'[32]

Two months later, Hubbard announced he was setting up the Department of Government Affairs.[33] Australia came under its jurisdiction, with Denny Gogerly appointed as local Director. The goal of the new department was 'to bring the government and hostile philosophies or societies into a state of complete compliance with the goals of Scientology'. Hubbard's aims were clear. 'Introvert such agencies,' he demanded. 'Control such agencies. Scientology is the only game on Earth where everybody wins.'[34]

Hubbard advocated crushing Scientology's critics. 'Don't ever defend,' he wrote. 'Always attack. Don't ever do nothing. Unexpected attacks in the rear of the enemy's front ranks work best.'[35]

It seems Hubbard's decision to set up the Department of Government Affairs was influenced to a large degree by criticism he was receiving from medical authorities in Victoria. Hubbard's call to arms made a series of references to the peak doctors' group in Victoria at the time, the British Medical Association of Victoria:

'Example: BMA attacks Scientology in Australia via the government. Answer: throw heavy communication against the weakest point of the BMA – its individual doctors. Rock them with petitions to have medical laws modified which they are to sign. Couple the BMA attack with any group hated by the government. Attack personally by threats or suits any person signing anything for the BMA.'

Phillip Wearne took up Hubbard's rallying cry and designed his own zone plan. His goal was to take over the Australian Labor Party and run it along Scientology lines. In January 1961, Wearne wrote to Peter Williams, the head of Scientology's Melbourne headquarters, outlining his plans:

My goals for the Zone Plan are to make my organization a Scientology Organization with all executives HPA graduates, to use our publications to improve administration, management and communication in the Labor movement and interest the Australian Labor Party and Trade Union officials in taking scientology training.

The Australian Labor Party as an organization using scientology principles would soon win a [sic] Government as soon as the next Federal election.

With Australia led by a government employing scientology principles we should soon have a civilization which can extend influence overseas.[36]

Wearne's plan met with Hubbard's approval[37] and the publisher started placing Scientology propaganda in his journals. The April 1961 edition of his national publication *Reality* urged the trade union movement and the Labor Party to adopt personality testing and E-Meters.[38]

In the same year, Wearne published a journal called *Probe*[39] aimed at spreading Scientology techniques and principles into the federal public service. To help further his Zone Plan goals, Wearne sent his executives off to do the Hubbard Professional Auditor course and to have Scientology processing. Included was his Managing Editor, Harry Holgate, a future Labor Premier of Tasmania.[40]

Despite his intentions, Wearne was unable to follow through with his plan to infiltrate the Labor Party and the trade union movement. On 11 July 1961, he quit the ALP in dramatic circumstances, describing himself in a letter as having changed into a 'reactionary Tory Conservative' who had voted Liberal at the state election that month.[41] He would later blame Scientology auditing for changing his political beliefs.[42]

It wasn't just Wearne's political beliefs that were falling apart. His business soon went belly up as well.[43] Wearne claimed Scientology auditing had sent him mad and rendered him incapable of running his publishing business. Doug Moon felt auditing was to blame, but for different reasons. In a letter to Hubbard, Moon wrote, 'Soon after auditing he began to feel he should be more ethical, tried to be and went broke.'[44]

Despite Moon's assertion, the credit squeeze of 1961 and the chaos in Wearne's personal life seemed to have played a more critical role in his fall. Wearne had separated from his wife, who was the financial brains behind his business,[45] and by the time he resigned from the ALP, he'd stopped publishing trade union journals, the core part of his business. This was partly, he said, due to his new political beliefs, and partly because 'it became unimportant with the importance of Scientology'.[46] Wearne did the HPA course and became a professional auditor.[47] He claimed that after hundreds of hours of processing he was given 'clear' status.[48] He worked as an auditor at Scientology's Melbourne office for a fortnight in early 1963 before having a mental breakdown.[49]

AS WEARNE'S WORLD WAS falling apart, Hubbard was under siege from the US authorities. On 4 January 1963, the Food and Drug Administration raided the Church of Scientology in Washington, DC on the grounds that they were selling E-Meters which had false and misleading labels attached. This was no ordinary search and seize mission. Police blockaded both ends of 19th Street, while FDA agents and plain clothed US marshals jumped out of unmarked vans and stormed the building.[50] Employing tactics more commonly deployed on gunrunners, drug dealers or bomb makers, the FDA's actions only fuelled Hubbard's growing paranoia.

The FDA boasted it had seized more than three tons of literature and equipment.[51] In the end, the FDA won its case to have the E-Meter labelled as ineffective in the diagnosis or treatment of disease,[52] but the raid was a public relations disaster for the authorities. Hubbard was able to portray himself as a religious martyr, accusing the US government of burning books, attacking religion and ignoring the First Amendment.[53]

The Washington raid reinforced Hubbard's commitment to intensify the portrayal of Scientology as a religion. A week after the FDA's seizure of books and E-Meters, the Hubbard Communications Office in Melbourne issued a 'Stop Press' memo:

> *L. Ron Hubbard has cabled for us to sue the press, TV and radio.*
>
> *The FDA USA case is easily won and the meters and books will probably be returned in a few days.*
>
> *A MILLION DOLLAR DEFENSE FUND is already in view for defense.*
>
> *The Founding Church of Scientology of Washington, DC has just purchased all HASIs [Scientology Franchises]. We are to get its name on the door of every Australian office and issue Minster's certificates to all auditors.*[54]

Calling themselves a church, and ordaining ministers, would go against everything Australian Scientologists had been advocating. The Melbourne office described itself publicly as 'non-profit, non-religious and non-political'.[55] Elizabeth Williams, the Melbourne secretary, told the head of ASIO, Charles Spry, they were not a religious organisation.[56] In the short term at least, it seems like Hubbard's orders were ignored. The Melbourne organisation continued to call itself an Academy of Scientology, but not a church.[57] Six months after Hubbard made his declaration, *Communication*, the official journal of the Melbourne Scientology headquarters, published an article that described Scientology as being 'in a different realm from religion'.[58]

It was around this time, while working in the Melbourne office, that Phillip Wearne claimed he had an epiphany. He was auditing a young 'preclear' who was having financial problems and had made it his goal for that session to make more money. Wearne later said, 'I realised then how ridiculous it was that I had had this goal for hundreds of hours auditing and been reduced from a very wealthy person to making £4 a week working for Hubbard. So perhaps sanity started to shine through then.'[59]

The truth is that nearly a year earlier Wearne had started writing to the Melbourne office and to Hubbard asking for refunds.[60] He complained about threats of physical violence[61] and pointed out inconsistencies in Scientology texts.[62] Wearne claimed in a letter to Peter Williams, which he copied to Hubbard, that processing had led him to a 'complete mental breakdown' in February 1962 that had rendered him 'apathetic, sick at heart and completely incapable'.[63] Wearne was offered more processing and his thoughts about refunds dissipated. 'They processed me on that,' he later testified, 'and that went out of my mind.'[64]

But hostilities resumed in April 1963, when Wearne fired off a telegram to Hubbard threatening legal action:

> *HASI [The Melbourne office] postponed auditing before end of intensive and refuse repair work or refund. My communications ignored by Assoc Sec. Only your direct intervention before Tuesday will prevent litigation.*[65]

Hubbard was in no mood for conciliation responding:

> *Dear Phil,*
> *You be good, or we won't give you any more auditing ever.*
> *Sincerely,*
> *Ron*[66]

Like two hotheads on opposing football teams, Hubbard and Wearne were magnetically drawn to each other. Wearne was initially attracted to Hubbard's ideas simply because he thought they would make him more money. When the scam artist became the scammed, Wearne wanted a refund and revenge. Hubbard, by now used to subservience and sycophancy from his followers, could not abide Wearne's insolence. Instead of giving him a refund and shutting up a potentially dangerous critic, an arrogant Hubbard showed poor judgement, ignoring Doug Moon's advice that he pay Wearne off.[67] That decision would prove costly for Hubbard. The ensuing unnecessary dispute with Wearne kickstarted a chain of events that would lead to his own isolation and exile.

Wearne, furious with the dismissive tone of Hubbard's latest letter, fired back another missive to Saint Hill Manor. The businessman gave Hubbard both barrels, calling him on his authoritarianism, his deceits and his paranoia, and flagging the complaints that he would soon take to the authorities in Australia. Hubbard, who was used to being able to control his followers, could not control Wearne. He was the aggrieved customer from hell, and by letter he delivered Scientology's founder an epic smackdown, a taste of the grief that was coming Hubbard's way.

Dear Sir,[68]
In reply to your letter dated 26th April 1963, I agree that you won't give me any more auditing – ever.

Auditing is a covert form of brainwashing which uses repetitive commands to establish obedience, repetitive questions to elucidate confessions, and many forms of subtle suggestion and dogmatic assertion systemised into ceremonial rites, which implant a belief in the goodness, infallibility and desirability of scientology. There is no reasoning with this belief – after sufficient indoctrination adherents are deaf to argument and blind to refuting evidence.

The grandiose delusion that you are the focus of a concerted action to save the world from Communism and insanity and your organisation of deluded followers in terms of a paranoid pseudocommunity of 'mest clears' 'theta clears' and 'operating thetans' will soon be exposed as symptoms of a psychopathology cloaked to a disarming degree by an impressive façade of reasonableness, earnestness and normality.

Your suspiciousness of 'undercover' agents attempting to enter your organisation, persecution by governments, and your jealous protection of scientology dogma have developed over the past five years and gradually increased in number,

breadth, systemization and improbability. Your early feelings
of being slighted by the medical profession, unappreciated
by universities and disregarded by scientists have developed
into suspicions of being spied on by psychiatrists, slandered
by journalists, plotted against by communists and covertly
attacked by doctors. This requires 'explanation' which has
resulted in exalted ideas of great power, religious grandeur,
irresistible purpose, psychic ability, spiritual superiority etc.

It is interesting that you ascribe to others the deception,
irresponsibility and scathing criticism which you deny
in yourself by affirming the opposite. This mechanism of
'projection' is particularly evident in your use of 'security
checks' where questions of sex, sadism, guilt, betrayal etc.
are asked over and over.

You will regard any legal action as a natural outcome of
the great but unrecognised destiny of scientology and of the
envy and malice of an indifferent world.

But the result will be a breaking of the perpetual obsession
which binds your sycophantic followers and keeps them
hypnotized within a mystic circle of authoritarian doctrine
and ritual.

Yours faithfully,
PB Wearne

Within months, Wearne took the grievances aired in this letter to a range of authorities in Victoria. He sent what he called a 'detailed description of the hypnotic and brainwashing techniques of Scientology'[69] to the Attorney-General of Victoria, the Mental Health Authority, the Australian Medical Association, the College of Psychiatrists, the British Psychological Society, and the Psychology Department at the University of Melbourne.

Other authorities were already aware of the activities of the Scientologists and had noted their potential for mind control. An ASIO memorandum written in June 1962 stated, 'The Hubbard Association is not considered to be politically subversive but their activities are of marginal security interest because cranks are attracted and there is medical evidence that Scientology could establish control over the minds of some members of the public.'[70] Scientology first came on the security agency's radar in 1956 when John Farrell, the then head of the Melbourne office, asked the government for permission to publish the Scientology booklet *Brainwashing: A Synthesis of the Russian Textbook on Pyschopolitics*.[71] ASIO had kept a watching brief on them from that point on.[72]

In early 1962, the Department of Immigration had asked the Superintendent of Victorian Police for a confidential report on the activities of the Scientologists. The investigation found 'these people have a habit of trying to intimidate anyone who criticises them with threats that they will inform ASIO'. The report concluded that Hubbard 'considers himself a genius and regards anyone who is not a scientologist as an idiot'.[73]

In August 1963, Phillip Wearne took out a Supreme Court writ against the Melbourne office for the fees he felt he was rightfully owed.[74] On 11 October he settled for the sum of £1517 3s, agreeing to conditions that he not 'procure any adverse publicity' against Scientology and 'desist from soliciting any political, governmental or similar action' against Scientology and its Melbourne headquarters.[75]

But Wearne had no interest in fulfilling his promise of silence. Five days after the settlement, Labor MP John Walton rose to his feet in the Victorian parliament and called on the Liberal government to take action against Scientology. In a detailed speech, Walton questioned Hubbard's academic credentials, raised concerns about the use of E-Meters for security checks, warned of the potential for blackmail through intimate details given during processing and accused the Melbourne Scientology office of practising 'amateur psychology' without a licence. Walton also outlined the tactics Scientologists employed to attack critics. The information quoted by the Labor MP, though not attributed, came straight from Phillip Wearne.[76]

The tribal Labor connections Wearne had built up through his business were now being used for all they were worth. Next, he took his grievances to Jack Galbally, Labor leader of the Opposition in the Legislative Council. Galbally was a powerful advocate and a man not to be messed with. He had played football for the Collingwood Magpies during the Depression and set up a law firm soon after, where he developed a fearsome reputation for getting his clients acquitted. As a lawyer, he was best known for representing the Wren family in the criminal libel case against Frank Hardy over his book *Power Without Glory*. As a politician, he made a name for himself with his relentless campaign to end capital punishment, introducing 15 separate bills to abolish the death penalty in Victoria.[77]

Most of all, Galbally loved to antagonise Victoria's long-serving conservative Premier Henry Bolte. He introduced a private member's bill into parliament that led to the banning of live-trap bird shooting, a sport the Premier enjoyed in the open spaces of his rural electorate. When Wearne gave Galbally his brief on Scientology, the Labor MP took it on with relish, seeking to embarrass the Premier over his inaction on the cult's activities.

On 19 November 1963, Galbally got to his feet in the Legislative Council and moved an adjournment 'for the purpose of discussing the deliberate and obstinate failure of the Government to take appropriate action against a group of charlatans who for monetary gain are exposing children of a tender age, youths and adults to intimidation and blackmail, insanity and even suicide, family estrangement and bankruptcy'.[78] Galbally accused the government of ignoring warnings made by the influential head of the Mental Health Authority, Dr Eric Cunningham Dax, and the advice of its former health minister Sir Ewen Cameron, who wanted an inquiry into the cult.

Melbourne Scientology executives Peter Williams and Denny Gogerly hit back at Galbally and Walton, saying, 'The ridiculous and totally false allegations of these people would be a subject for a big laugh if it were not for the fact that people who do not know anything about Scientology might believe them.'[79] They described any prospect of a ban on Scientology as 'totally fascistic' and made the case that Walton's and Galbally's speeches were an unprecedented attack on Scientology. 'No other Parliament in the world,' they wrote, 'has done anything even remotely resembling this.'[80]

But Jack Galbally was not about to let up. A week later, he brought a private member's bill to the parliament to 'prohibit the teaching and practise of scientology for fee or reward and the use in relation to such teaching or practice of any apparatus or device for recording or measuring personal reactions, impulses or characteristics'. Before Galbally's Scientology Restriction Bill could be debated, Gilbert Chandler, the leader of the government in the Legislative Council announced that there would be an inquiry into Scientology. The following day, Kevin Anderson QC was appointed to run a one-man Board of Inquiry to 'inquire into, report upon, and make recommendations concerning Scientology as known, carried on, practised and applied in Victoria'.[81]

The response at the Melbourne Scientology headquarters was strangely euphoric. There was dancing in the halls of Spring Street with staff jumping up and down yelling, 'We've won! We've won!'[82] A banner was draped across the front of the Scientology building praising the parliamentarians across the road for the decision they'd just made: 'Scientologists thank parliament for the open inquiry,' it stated.[83]

Later, the Scientologists would claim that the descendants of convicts were incapable of holding a proper inquiry. An official release that had all the hallmarks of being written by Hubbard stated, 'The niceties of truth and fairness, of hearing witnesses and weighing evidence, are not for men whose ancestry is lost in the promiscuity of the prison ships of transportation.'[84] But at the time Victoria's most senior Scientologists had been actively lobbying for an inquiry. Four days before the inquiry was announced, Peter Williams and Denny Gogerly sent a telegram to government ministers Arthur Rylah and Rupert Hamer, stating:

Sir, Scientologists demand a full independent public enquiry to expose all the facts to public view. We will present all the material to prove our honest financial status. We will show many hundreds of documentary results. We will prove Scientology not harmful. We will give demonstrations of the practices of Scientology at work. We also demand a full public enquiry into those alleging blackmail and harm against us and their sources of information.[85]

Later on, when the true ramifications of the Inquiry were known to all, Hubbard distanced himself from the endorsement saying, 'I okayed only this: That we agree into an Enquiry into <u>all</u> mental health services and activities. This was the order.'[86] Hubbard blamed his former secretary Peter Hemery and Melbourne executive Peter Williams for the decision to narrow the Inquiry to just Scientology.

This seems like historical revisionism on Hubbard's part. There was no narrowing of the inquiry. It was never going to be about all mental health services, it was only ever going to be about Scientology. Furthermore, a letter whose contents have until now never been published, throws further doubt on Hubbard's take on events.

On 17 February 1964, Mary Sue Hubbard wrote a letter from Saint Hill Manor to Peter and Yvonne Gillham in Melbourne. After thanking the couple for a calendar they had sent, and passing on her best wishes to the children, Mary Sue asks the Gillhams, 'How goes the investigation of Scientology which we asked be made? Has the publicity increased or damaged your business?'[87] Mary Sue, in the middle of proceedings, is claiming they had asked for the Inquiry. There's no complaint that it's been narrowed, or that it's become a witch-hunt, Mary Sue simply asks whether the publicity has been good for the Gillhams' Scientology business.

Peter Gillham started making inquiries of his own. It didn't make sense to him that Hubbard would want anything to do with the Victorian inquiry. 'Well, one of his policies was we don't accept inquiries into Scientology,' Gillham asserts. 'We investigate other people or organisations.'[88] Gillham called Peter Williams to find out was going on. 'He said, "Well, Hubbard's authorised it."'[89]

If Hubbard did want an inquiry into Scientology, his judgement was way off beam. He certainly wasn't displaying the kind of supernatural powers that Operating Thetans were meant to have. The Inquiry would not be in the best interests of Hubbard or Scientology. It was to be long, bruising and humiliating for the organisation and its followers and it would have severe ramifications for its leader.

CHAPTER 8

THE ANDERSON INQUIRY

THE ANDERSON INQUIRY HAD a profound impact on the lives of Scientologists around the world. It led to other inquiries in Britain, South Africa and New Zealand, and formed the basis for many of the attacks in the parliament and the press in the UK, which ultimately forced Hubbard into exile. It changed Scientology policy too. Heavier 'ethics' policies led to a culture of punishment and abuse. In Victoria, Scientologists' lives changed almost as soon as the inquiry commenced. Some lost their jobs, others were humiliated in the media and children were bullied in school playgrounds.

Janis Gillham got a hint of what was coming when she lined up to run at her athletics carnival at Glenferrie Primary School. The youngest child of Peter and Yvonne Gillham loved to race. Normally before an event she milled around the marshalling area chatting with other girls her age. But this sports carnival was strangely different. Her usual pre-race nerves were instead overtaken by a form of anxiety that could not be alleviated by the starter's gun.

'Suddenly it was like people didn't want to talk to me anymore,' Janis recalls over 50 years later, 'I said to my friend Elizabeth. "No-one seems to like me." That's when I finally found out. She said she'd heard people say, "Don't talk to the Gillham children."'[1]

Janis Gillham's parents were two of the 151 witnesses[2] who gave evidence at the Anderson Inquiry. Their testimonies were quoted in the newspapers and their faces appeared on the TV news. The blowback wasn't confined to the playground at Glenferrie Primary School. Peter

Gillham Snr lost his job at an accounting firm after he testified before the Inquiry.[3]

Other witnesses were subjected to ridicule. Under the *Truth* headline 'Joined Sect; Stayed Bald' Lubomir Lutshetshko, an unemployed teacher who claimed he'd seen a fight between two robots in 9 BC, was described as a victim of a 'Scientology Flop' when he testified that Scientology had failed to cure him of his premature baldness.[4]

It was to be a long haul for Victoria's Scientologists and for Mr J May, the Chief Government Shorthand Writer. The Inquiry ran for nearly 18 months, with the evidence filling close to 9000 pages of transcripts that nudged four million words.[5] It was an inquiry worthy of Hubbard's own prolific word count.

The first formal sitting of Kevin Anderson QC's one-man Board of Inquiry took place on 6 December 1963 at the Flemington Court House. Later in the day, the hearing shifted to the Scientologists' headquarters in Spring Street where the contents of 35 filing cabinets and other records were tendered as evidence,[6] including the private auditing records of many of the Scientology witnesses.

In February, the Inquiry resumed in the rooms of the National Herbarium of Victoria, sharing a building with hundreds of thousands of dried plant, algae and fungi specimens from around the world. It was here that Scientology was put under the microscope in depth, in the world's first ever government-sanctioned inquiry into its practices.

Phillip Wearne's campaign against Hubbard was about to crank up a gear. He was granted special leave by Anderson to appear as a representative of the Committee for Mental Health and National Security.[7] This allowed him to give evidence and cross-examine witnesses. But the committee that gave him legitimacy had all the authority of Wearne's 'Citizen's Road Safety Council'. The group was formed just three days before the Inquiry first sat.[8] The meeting that nominated him to represent the committee at the Inquiry had only three members present – Wearne, his brother and his brother-in-law.[9] The only two other meetings held had attracted just two members.[10] An ASIO report from the time declared, 'It appears that this Committee exists in name only.'[11]

Wearne found a key ally to discredit Scientology at the Inquiry. Doug Moon was the former Melbourne Scientology staffer who had written to Hubbard in July 1963 warning him that he should refund Wearne.[12] In November, Moon reminded Hubbard, 'I advised you some months ago to give Wearne his money back ... had you listened to me in the first place instead of the idiot advisers you employ in this part of the world the parliamentary attack would probably not have occurred.'[13] When the Inquiry was announced, Moon offered Hubbard tactical help and warned that 'if it is allowed to run through the way it is planned the results will be disastrous'.[14]

Moon was a man who could not stand still. He worked as a nightclub singer in Sydney and Melbourne, had a bread delivery run in Perth, tried his luck with a vaudeville company in Mount Isa, and experimented in radio, TV and photography across three states.[15] His skittish employment record mirrored his relationship with Scientology. He was first excommunicated in 1959 after he criticised one of Hubbard's lectures for being too technical.[16] He was allowed back in briefly in 1962 before the E-Meter diagnosed him as having 'anti-scientology goals'.[17]

At various times, Scientology executives labelled him a communist, a spy, and a criminal.[18] The latter description bore some truth. Moon had some minor league form in obtaining money under false pretences, failing to pay a hotel bill and ripping off £30 from a department store.[19] But as long as Moon was paying for auditing, no matter where the money came from, the Melbourne Scientologists would eventually have him back.

In 1963, Moon joined Scientology's staff once more, only to leave again soon after. He moved back to Sydney where he found Wearne, in what he described as a 'dreadful state'.[20] As they helped rehabilitate each other, the nightclub singer couldn't make up his mind if he thought an inquiry was a good idea or not.[21] After returning to Melbourne, Moon offered his services to Scientology as a lobbyist and campaigner against Labor's attacks in parliament. But the Scientologists wanted him to do much more than that.

A message was delivered to Doug Moon, letting him know he could get back in good standing with Scientology if he signed a statement declaring that he, Wearne and another former Scientologist were 'practising homosexuals' who had 'signed a pact in 1959 to destroy Scientology and that all our activities since had been to that end'.[22] Moon seriously considered signing the statement.[23]

If Moon was to sign, he wanted to be compensated. As he told Hubbard, 'If my career was killed by the publicity and if this move was the only thing that would save Scientology then I would do it. £2000 would cover all my possible losses.'

Doug Moon laid out the conditions in a handwritten note given to Richard King, a Scientologist and bee removalist from Parkdale, who was a fan of Moon's nightclub act.[24] The note included the following criteria:

> *Not get booked on a homo charge.*
> *[Be paid] £2000*
> *That HCO (Hubbard Communications Office) Worldwide*
> *   has a record of this deal*
> *I shall give you no info that could conclusively prove a*
> *   homo charge*
> *Money to be paid when I show the Stat. Dec.*
> *All parties to realise that I did not come forward and offer*
> *   this deal. You came to me – these are my terms.*
> *My ex-wife and daughter not to be mentioned at any time*[25]

Peter Williams claimed Moon was trying to blackmail them and the deal never got off the ground.[26] According to Richard King, Williams was furious with Moon. 'He said that he had given Doug the chance to do the honest thing,' King said. 'And he was finished as far as he was concerned, he had better get out of the country or get a bullet-proof vest. He was really wild over this demand for money.'[27]

Within two months Moon was actively going after Scientology. He was adept, as he put it, at 'flipping in and out of the Scientology universe'.[28] One moment he was considering perjuring himself and outing Wearne as part of a fictitious homosexual love triangle, the next he was working with him to bring down Scientology. Moon joined the Committee for Mental Health and National Security[29] and got to work turning over another key Scientology witness.

Max Anderson worked as an industrial chemist at Shell Oil's Newport terminal in Victoria.[30] Within a week of the Inquiry being announced he had written a letter to the Board offering his services as a witness on behalf of Scientology. Anderson had worked at

Scientology's Melbourne headquarters in 1959 and was a friend of the former Bronte lifeguard Roger Boswarva. In his letter Max Anderson claimed Scientology had helped him get his Bachelor of Science and that he was concerned about 'the untruths and half truths which have been aired concerning this organisation which could prevent it being of use to this society'.[31]

But six weeks later, Max Anderson had changed his mind, withdrawing his offer to give evidence. In a letter to the Board he wrote, 'I believe that in the forthcoming mud-slinging match an amount of this mud will stick to me and adversely affect my future with the company for which I work. I am willing to clarify points in my earlier letter, in writing, but not by personal appearance.'[32]

Max Anderson had been got at by Doug Moon. In early 1964, Anderson was attending a 21st birthday party at Melbourne's Playboy Club when he bumped into Moon who worked at the club as a singer. When he told him he would be willing to testify at the Inquiry on behalf of Scientology, Moon replied, 'Oh God, we'll have to dig some dirt about you.'[33] A week later, Max Anderson wrote to the Inquiry to withdraw his previous offer.[34] He was frightened that Moon would blackmail him and ruin his career.[35] Five weeks after praising Scientology in a questionnaire that would be tendered to the Inquiry, he joined Wearne and Moon as a member of the Committee for Mental Health and National Security and began approaching key people to give evidence against Scientology.[36]

Max Anderson later testified that there was no pressure placed on him to change his position.[37] Instead he said Moon's threat, combined with his wife's disillusionment with Scientology and his own disgust at the 'phenomenally low salaries' at the Melbourne headquarters, had accelerated his change of view.[38] But Roger Boswarva, who was living with Anderson and his wife Jenny at the time, has a different opinion. 'He was blackmailed, Jenny confirmed it,' Boswarva told me.[39] He says Anderson was concerned that Moon, who'd had access to the auditor's records at Spring Street, would pass on confidential information to his employers and ruin any chance he had of a promotion.[40]

The champion swimmer was now feeling the pressure himself. According to Boswarva, Jenny Anderson urged him to side with Moon and Wearne and give evidence against Scientology.[41] Boswarva had previously been involved in a minor insurance scam and was warned it would be brought up at the Inquiry. Short of the money required to do a Scientology course, which he thought may help him treat his critically ill father, Boswarva had destroyed his prized violin so that he could make a fraudulent insurance claim which would then fund the course. Unbeknownst to Wearne and Moon, he paid the insurance company back of his own accord.[42]

When Wearne cross-examined Boswarva at the Inquiry he brought up the violin incident in an attempt to discredit him. It is likely Wearne had accessed the confession through the auditing records at Spring Street, possibly through Moon who had been on staff. But Boswarva had a surprise in return for Wearne. He told the Inquiry he made a decision to pay the insurer back after he'd had Scientology processing. As the former Bronte lifeguard put it, 'It is actually a *win* for Scientology, it helped me straighten out.'[43] Boswarva went on to tell the Inquiry that opponents of Scientology had tried to use the incident to blackmail him into not giving evidence at the Inquiry.[44]

'The truth is Scientology is a bad fraud,' reflects Boswarva 50 years on, 'but the truth also is Scientology got a raw deal. The Inquiry was not honest. It did not take honest evidence from both sides. It was designed to embarrass Scientology.' But Malcolm Macmillan, a psychologist who attended every day of the hearings, disagrees.[45] 'I certainly didn't think it was designed to embarrass,' he says. 'It was designed to explore the effects of Scientological practices. Everyone got a fair hearing. The Scientologists had the opportunity to defend themselves.'[46]

At the time, Malcolm Macmillan was working as a psychologist at Kew Cottages and was the Recorder (Secretary) of the Victorian Group of the Australian branch of the British Psychological Society. After the Inquiry was announced, the group decided to offer its services to the Board to give expert evidence on matters of psychological interest such as personality tests and E-Meters. It asked Macmillan to approach members to see if they would give expert evidence. Macmillan's boss, Dr Eric Cunningham Dax, who was opposed to Scientology and had met with Phillip Wearne before the Inquiry, also asked him to approach medical witnesses to appear. He gave Macmillan time off from Kew Cottages to co-ordinate witnesses for the Board.[47]

Gordon Just, the counsel assisting the Board, asked Macmillan to wade through the collected works of Hubbard to find any points of relevance to the Inquiry.[48] Macmillan provided the inquiry with 54 pages of quotes from Hubbard's writings on everything from the E-Meter, engrams and radiation sickness, to treatment claims about cancer, arthritis and poor eyesight.

Experts in the fields of physics, psychiatry, psychology, radiology, obstetrics, hypnosis and medicine were lined up by Macmillan to give evidence about Hubbard's claims. The Board's report later found, 'they were uniformly of the opinion that Hubbard's writings revealed him as ignorant and ill-informed in those sciences in which they were expert.'[49]

Dr Hendrik Van den Brenk, the doctor in charge of the Radio-Biological Research Laboratories at the Cancer Institute Board in Melbourne, testified that Hubbard's statements about cancer were 'quackery of the worst nature' and that in relation to his writings on radiation, 'basic and fundamental established truths of science are ignored and replaced by imaginative fiction, without a vestige of corroborative experiment designed to support such hypotheses'.[50]

The Board of Inquiry was wise to Hubbard's fraudulent claims about being a doctor, a nuclear physicist and a civil engineer. It asked Scientology executive Peter Williams to write to Hubbard and clarify his qualifications.[51] Hubbard was not impressed at being asked to justify his credentials. 'I keep forgetting Australia would not be conversant with standard biographical texts or reference works considered ordinary in civilised countries,' he huffed to Williams.[52] The Board received confirmation from George Washington University that Hubbard had not completed a degree there and had the Australian Consul-General in San Francisco check up on his diploma mill PhD.

Some claims made by Hubbard were so outrageous that they didn't need interrogation, just ventilation. The Inquiry heard he told his followers that he had visited the Van Allen Belt up in the earth's magnetosphere, had travelled to Venus and even been to heaven,[53] which according to Hubbard was 'complete with gates, angels and plaster saints – and electronic implantation equipment'.[54] Hubbard even had an arrival time for his first visit to the pearly gates: '43,891,832,611,177 years, 344 days, 10 hours, 20 minutes and 40 seconds from 10:02½ PM Daylight Greenwich Time, May 9, 1963'.[55]

Hubbard never appeared before the Inquiry to have his various claims tested. Scientology's defence was left mainly to Peter Williams from Scientology's Melbourne headquarters. The Scientologists claimed that Anderson made sure 'it was not possible for L. Ron Hubbard to testify in his own defence'.[56]

In September of 1964, Scientology's Melbourne lawyers wrote to Victoria's Attorney-General, offering Hubbard as a witness to the Inquiry. They were concerned that 'the pattern has emerged that Scientology may well be a great fraud and its founder, Mr Hubbard himself, may well emerge as a great fraud'.[57] Hubbard's lawyers said his appearance was conditional on his expenses being paid for by the government.

Victoria's Deputy Premier, AG Rylah, responded two weeks later:

> *I must inform you that it is not the policy of the Government to meet the costs of witnesses who wish to attend and give evidence on their own behalf before Royal Commissions or Boards of Inquiry, and consequently if Mr Hubbard decides to travel to Melbourne he must do so at his own expense.*[58]

The lawyers for Hubbard were outraged. They fired off another letter to the Deputy Premier claiming Hubbard could not afford to pay his own way and that 'the demands of natural justice require that he should not be – and that no person should be – put in a position of being bankrupted by this Inquiry'.[59] Kevin Anderson believed Hubbard had no intention of appearing. 'The applications for his expenses to be paid were made, knowing they would be rejected,' he wrote. 'They were made merely for the purpose of founding a criticism of the conduct of the Board and of this Report.'[60]

Kevin Anderson believed the bankruptcy excuse was a ruse. Through his own inquiry he had learned how much money Hubbard was making out of Australia. 'His financial resources and those of his organization were more than adequate to defray the expenses of his attendance at the Inquiry,' he wrote. 'It was his decision alone which resulted in his non-attendance.'[61] Just three months before his lawyers raised fears of bankruptcy, Hubbard had told the *Saturday Evening*

Post he was independently wealthy. The *Post*'s descriptions of the Georgian mansion, the butler serving Coca-Cola on a silver tray, and the chauffeur polishing the new Pontiac and Jaguar seemed to confirm that Hubbard could afford to travel to Melbourne.[62]

Besides, why would Hubbard leave such luxuries to face what he now saw as the barbarity of Australia? In *Kangaroo Court,* Scientology's official response to the Inquiry, fears were raised that Hubbard could have been imprisoned and lobotomised if he had gone to Melbourne to give evidence. 'What better way of ruining Scientology than by getting hold of the Founder, jailing him for purposes of his "own protection" and then quietly taking the opportunity to have Dr Dax perform one of his special, guaranteed to depersonalize, dehumanize, to idiotize and zombiize, operations.'[63]

Hubbard's contempt for Anderson and his investigation came to a head on 30 November 1964 when Ian Abraham, counsel for Scientology, announced that following instructions from his clients he would be withdrawing from any further participation in the Inquiry.[64]

Abraham told the Board: 'When the Inquiry was first proposed, my clients welcomed it in the hope and expectation that their ideas and practices would be examined in an atmosphere free from bias, prejudice and bigotry. The Board, however ... has allowed it to degenerate into a witch hunt.'[65]

At the point at which Scientology's counsel withdrew, 56 out of the 93 witnesses called had been pro-Scientology.[66] The Board heard further evidence in the New Year before wrapping up hearings on 21 April 1965.

On 28 September 1965, Kevin Anderson handed down his much-anticipated 173-page report.[67] The first paragraph set the tone for what was to follow:

> *There are some features of Scientology which are so ludicrous that there may be a tendency to regard Scientology as silly and its practitioners as harmless cranks. To do so would be gravely to misunderstand the tenor of the Board's conclusions. This Report should be read, it is submitted, with these prefatory observations constantly in mind. Scientology is evil; its techniques evil; its practice a serious threat to the*

community, medically, morally and socially; and its adherents
sadly deluded and often mentally ill.[68]

Hubbard himself was described as having a 'morbid preoccupation
with perversion' in relations to 'sex, rape, and similar topics'.[69] He
was deemed 'intolerant of opposition' and 'autocratic and harsh in
his treatment of the dissident'.[70] The Board concluded: 'Hubbard is a
fraud and Scientology fraudulent'[71] and asserted that his 'sanity is to
be gravely doubted'.[72]

Scientology's theories were found to be 'fantastic and impossible,
its principles perverted and ill-founded, and its techniques debased
and harmful'.[73] Anderson concluded that 'Scientology is a delusional
belief system, based on fiction and fallacies and propagated by
falsehood and deception. While making an appeal to the public as
a worthy system whereby ability, intelligence and personality may
be improved, it employs techniques which further its real purpose of
securing domination over and mental enslavement of its adherents.'[74]

Anderson considered Scientology to be a massive rort. He
documented justifiable concerns that Hubbard was profiting from
ripping off vulnerable people. But there was also a moral dimension to
Anderson's criticism of Hubbard and Scientology that was harder to
justify. Anderson was a devout Catholic. When he became a Supreme
Court judge, he prayed every morning before court. 'Each time I
mounted the Bench,' he wrote in his autobiography, 'I fortified myself,
almost instinctively, with a mental petition to God for guidance.'[75]

As a Catholic whose beliefs were formed before the second Vatican
Council modernised the doctrine of his own faith, Anderson seemed
to be repulsed by certain aspects of Scientology. One of his chapters is
titled 'Moral Laxity'.[76] He used terms like 'revolting', 'disgusting' and
'perverted'[77] and wrote that 'the filth and depravity recorded in the
HASI files as being discussed between preclears and auditors almost
defies description'.[78]

Russell Miller, the author of a highly critical biography of
Hubbard, thought some of the language used by Anderson was over
the top: 'In its intemperate tone, its use of emotive rhetoric and its
tendency to exaggerate and distort, it bore a marked similarity to the
writings of L. Ron Hubbard,' he wrote.[79] As a counter to this, however,

Scientology historian Jon Atack says the report 'contains much sound, factual information and many perceptive remarks'.[80] Atack disagreed with the subsequent ban on Scientology, however, believing it achieved little except helping to promote the cult internationally.[81]

Miller makes the point that 'in his determination to undermine Scientology, Anderson completely ignored the fact that thousands of decent, honest, well-meaning people around the world believed themselves to be benefiting from the movement'.[82] *The Anderson Report* had concluded the Board 'has been unable to find any worthwhile redeeming feature in Scientology'.[83]

Peter Gillham believes the Board didn't find any redeeming features because it wasn't looking for any. 'During my time as a witness they never asked me anything about what has Scientology done for you? How has it helped others? None of that. The questions for me were hostile, and rigged in such ways so they didn't get anything out of what Scientology did, or the benefits it gave.'[84]

The Anderson Report recommended that the Victorian government kill off the business of Scientology through regulation, by setting up a board that registered all psychological practices and restricted the practice to those who met minimum standards for registration.[85] But the Victorian government would take it a step further, becoming the first place in the world to ban Scientology. Peter Gillham would be at the forefront of the fight to undermine that ban.

CHAPTER 9

THE RIFF-RAFF OF AUSTRALIA

HUBBARD HAD SPOKEN OF Australia as if it were a promised land for Scientology. In 1959, he boasted that Australia would be the world's first 'clear continent'.[1] He described it as 'the country, perhaps, with the greatest and brightest future on the face of Earth today'.[2] But Hubbard's views changed markedly following his rejection and humiliation in Victoria. Now, in the eyes of Scientology's founder, Australia was a brutal, backward, unjust society incapable of escaping its criminal past.[3]

Kangaroo Court was Scientology's official response to *The Anderson Report*. It is unclear who wrote it, but it bears all the hallmarks of Hubbard's colourful turns of phrase and his lust for revenge. If Hubbard was not the author, it certainly met with his approval. Published by the Hubbard College of Scientology, bound in black and gold and featuring a kangaroo resplendent in a judge's wig on the cover, *Kangaroo Court* was scathing in its judgement of *The Anderson Report*:

> *Only a society founded by criminals, organized by criminals and devoted to making people criminals, could come to such a conclusion. A criminal society would applaud brutality, would regard leucotomy, lobotomy, and other major operations depriving a being of the use of his brain, as necessary to relieve a desperate situation.*[4]

Kangaroo Court gave an abridged history of transportation to Australia and pointed out that Samuel Speed, one of the last of the transported convicts, died in Perth less than 30 years before the Inquiry.[5] Australia, so the logic followed, was incapable of removing the convict stain from its people and its institutions:

Though memories are dim, patterns remain to determine action. Patterns of behaviour laid down in the days of imprisonment without trial, arrest without warrant, when justice was the tool of a few families, when politicians could demand a result and get it, persist.[6]

The state of Victoria, until recently home to one of the largest and most vibrant Scientology operations in the world, was not spared the vitriol in *Kangaroo Court*. 'The foundation of Victoria consists of the riff-raff of London's slums – robbers, murderers, prostitutes, fences, thieves – the scourings of Newgate and Bedlam.'[7]

Though the reaction was churlish, the Scientologists did have a right to be upset. Five weeks after *The Anderson Report* was published, the Psychological Practices Bill was presented to parliament.[8] Victoria became the first place in the world to ban Scientology. The act banned the teaching, practice, advertising or application of Scientology for fee or reward, prohibited use of the E-Meter, except by a registered psychologist, and demanded that any person in possession of Scientology files or records hand them over to the Attorney-General, who had been given expansive powers to issue search warrants on anyone suspected of keeping such records.[9]

Jack Galbally, who considered Scientology to be a racket, and whose speeches in parliament led to the Anderson Inquiry, refused to vote for the bill. 'It is a direct assault on freedom of speech, thought and ideas,' he thundered, 'and it puts practically the whole adult population under the thumb of the Executive. The Government has adopted a tactic familiar to Goebbels and the infamous leaders of the Nazi world. This measure, if enacted, will prevent parents from telling the little ones at home to abide by the Ten Commandments.'[10] Galbally didn't want Scientology outlawed; he wanted restrictions placed on its ability to rip off unsuspecting customers.

The psychologists weren't happy either. The Victorian Group of the Australian Branch of the British Psychological Society actively lobbied against the legislation.[11] The Act set up a council to oversee psychological practices, but only 50 per cent of the Board's members would be psychologists. This would make them the only regulated profession that did not have a majority on its own council. The Society was also uncomfortable that the bill that registered its practitioners was so closely aligned with Scientology.[12]

The Group's Recorder, Malcolm Macmillan, was annoyed that the legislation banned hypnosis, an area of research he had been exploring.[13] But he was also critical of the legislation from a civil liberties perspective. 'Most of us concerned about fringe practices were also concerned about infringement on the right to free speech and the right to believe in nonsense,' he said.[14] The Society tried to have the legislation amended, but to no avail. Macmillan watched on from the gallery in despair as the bill passed along party lines.[15]

When Macmillan testified before the Inquiry, he proposed the idea of an ombudsman who oversaw 'fringe practices'. If a customer paid money for a service and thought it had harmed them, they could then appeal to a tribunal for repayment of that money.[16] Anderson ignored Macmillan's advice, instead making recommendations that led to legislation that upset both the psychologists and the Scientologists.

On 21 December 1965 the ban on Scientology came into force. Law enforcement officials did not muck around. At 4.55 pm, three policemen and two officers of the Attorney-General's office raided Scientology's headquarters in Spring Street, seizing thousands of files.[17] The Scientologists had already got to work destroying documents. Police discovered papers being burned in two bins at the back of Scientology's headquarters. Another file was passed through a window into a getaway car.[18]

Scientologists who broke the new laws faced fines of up to £250 and two years in prison.[19] Peter Gillham took the law into his own hands when he smuggled E-Meters over the border into South Australia. He rented a station wagon, built a false bottom in it, and stacked it full of E-meters. The wagon was then filled with camping equipment for extra cover, before making the 1500 km round trip to Adelaide.[20]

Most Scientologists decided to get out of Victoria – either moving interstate or overseas. Annie Tampion wrote to Premier Henry Bolte expressing her disgust at being forced into exile in England. 'I wish to formally inform you that I have ceased to be a Victorian citizen,' she wrote, 'and no longer live in Victoria due to the suppression of Scientology by your Government. I will also do all I can to dissuade others to live there too.'[21]

According to Janis Gillham, around a hundred Australian Scientology families moved to England, where they could do courses with Hubbard at Saint Hill and practise their belief without state sanction.[22] Hubbard may have thought Victorians were descended from 'the riff-raff of London's slums'[23] but he was more than happy to take their money.

Yvonne Gillham was one of the first to lead the Australian pilgrimage to Saint Hill. But she left under duress, a victim of Hubbard's new policies. In 1965, Hubbard had introduced an 'ethics' system, which included the ability to declare someone a 'Suppressive Person'.[24] According to Hubbard 2.5 per cent of the population are suppressive or 'anti-social'. These people are considered enemies of Scientology. According to her daughters, Yvonne Gillham had been declared suppressive because her College of Personal Efficiency was taking customers from Scientology's headquarters in Spring Street. To get back in good standing she had to travel to Saint Hill and get her 'Suppressive Person declare' status dealt with.

The move devastated the Gillham family. Before she left for England, Yvonne had to separate from her husband and could no longer run the family's college. Hubbard had introduced a series of policies that year that forced Scientologists to 'disconnect' from a 'Suppressive Person' until that person was back in good standing.[25] She could not even attend her daughter Terri's 11th birthday party because her old Scientology friends would be there. In December 1965, Yvonne departed Australia, leaving behind her husband and three children. She never returned to her country of birth.

Six months later, the Gillham children, Peter Jnr, Terri and Janis, were sent by boat to England to be reunited with their mother. Later that year, Peter Snr sold the family home and his accounting practice so he too could head to Saint Hill.[26] The separation and dislocation put immense strain on the family. This was of no concern to Hubbard. 'He knew we were all slaves to him,' says Terri Gillham. 'He manipulated and controlled us into being that way.'[27]

Around this time Treasure Southen, one of Scientology's founding figures in Australia, and a witness supportive of Hubbard at the Inquiry, wrote to the government requesting a secret meeting.[28] In 1963, Southen had written to Premier Bolte praising Scientology. 'Any money I paid to these fabulous people,' she wrote, 'could <u>never</u> pay for the joy of living I found with their help.'[29] Three years later she wanted to dump on them.

The Police Commissioner dispatched a senior detective to Southen's home in North Balwyn on 22 July 1966. She asked that the meeting be treated as confidential because she feared that 'her life would be in danger'.[30] Southen provided details of where and when undercover Scientology meetings were being held, claimed Scientologists were being urged 'not to pay taxes or obey laws' and were being pressured into leaving Victoria.[31]

According to the report filed by Senior Detective SJ Houghton, Ms Southen said:

> *Literally hundreds of couples with children had been*
> *pressurized into selling their homes in Victoria and*
> *going to HUBBARD'S Headquarters at Saint Hill,*
> *Sussex, England, where they hand the money over to*
> *the Organization and are given a job for £8 a week.*[32]

Peter Gillham Snr says he never heard of anyone being pressured into selling their homes. 'No, definitely not,' he told me. 'I think it was more that they desired to sell their homes. They wanted to go to England.'[33] But an Ethics Order published in May 1966 made it clear Scientologists could no longer live in Victoria and must 'refuse to pay it taxes, refuse to vote for its so-called government, refuse to obey its laws, and refuse to reside within its State.'[34]

Hubbard had a strong financial incentive to get all Scientologists to move out of Victoria. When the Melbourne office was operating in Spring Street, 10 per cent of all fees were making their way back to Hubbard in England. If Scientologists were operating underground in

Victoria he got no financial benefit from it. If he could get them over to England he would probably do even better than before.

The Gillhams were a driving force behind the scores of Australian Scientologists who flocked to Saint Hill. Terri Gillham wonders whether Hubbard had conspired to have Yvonne declared 'suppressive', so he could get her and her clients over to England:

> *Hubbard had visited them in Melbourne. My mum and dad were very popular. There was no yelling and screaming at their college, there was no nasty conditions and evil stuff going on, it was all really good happy fun stuff, and I think that he saw that it was something that he should control. My guess is that he somehow manipulated the Suppressive Person declare and made certain it could only be handled at Saint Hill. Then she has to go, then Dad has to follow and then he's trying to get all these Scientologists sent over too and it ends up making Saint Hill look like a very vibrant wonderful place. Scientology was suddenly booming at Saint Hill and then everybody thought, well this has got to be the real deal.*[35]

Hubbard may have financially benefited from suddenly having around 100 Australians on course at Saint Hill, but he could not avoid the fallout from the Australian inquiry. As Roy Wallis points out in his sociological history of Scientology, *The Road to Total Freedom*, 'It was not until 1965 that mention of Scientology began to appear systematically in the British Press.'[36] The reports invariably referred at length to the inquiry in Melbourne.[37]

The increased scrutiny in England was dangerous for Hubbard. Saint Hill was where he lived, had based his Scientology headquarters and made much of his money from trainees. He could not afford to upset authorities in the UK. How Hubbard handled this threat would change Scientology forever.

In February 1966, the pressure on Hubbard began to build. Lord Balniel, Conservative MP for Hertford, and the chairman of the National Association for Mental Health, asked the Health Minister in the House of Commons whether he would initiate an inquiry into Scientology, stating, 'In view of the scathing criticism by an official

Board of Inquiry in Australia into the so-called practice of scientology, surely the right Hon. Gentleman considers that it is in the public interest to hold a similar type of inquiry in this country?'[38]

The Health Minister Kenneth Robinson told the parliament he had no plans for any form of inquiry. But the Scientologists were planning some investigations of their own. Within two days of Lord Balniel asking questions in parliament, Hubbard had published a memo laying out a plan to 'get a detective on that Lord's past to unearth the tid-bits. They're there.'[39] In the same document Hubbard wrote, 'England's Parliament is not about to pass or even introduce law barring religion or philosophy. After all these aren't ex-convicts.'[40]

In reality, Hubbard was concerned about developments in the UK parliament. Ten days after Lord Balniel's intervention, Hubbard set up a 'Public Investigation Section', which would employ private detectives from outside Scientology ranks.[41] In a memo titled 'Project Psychiatry', Hubbard laid out his plan to dig up dirt on psychiatrists and eventually eliminate them from the UK. 'We want at least one bad mark on every psychiatrist in England, a murder, an assault, or a rape or more than one,' he wrote.[42]

Vic Filson answered an advertisement in the *Daily Telegraph* and was the first to be hired. 'I was told that the first victim who was to be investigated was to be Lord Balniel,' Filson said.[43] The detective eventually resigned from the job in disgust and took his story to the press.

Burned by his experience with the Anderson Inquiry and fearful he may now face similar scrutiny in the UK, Hubbard formulated an official policy on how to deal with investigations. 'NEVER agree to an investigation of Scientology,' he wrote. 'ONLY agree to an investigation of the attackers. This was the BIG error made in Victoria.'[44] The correct procedure was laid out in the same policy letter.

Spot who is attacking us.
Start investigating them promptly for FELONIES or worse
using our own professionals.
Double curve our reply by saying we welcome an investigation
of them.

Start feeding lurid, blood, sex, crime actual evidence on
the attackers to the press. Don't ever tamely submit to an
investigation of us. Make it rough, rough on attackers all
the way.[45]

Hubbard's mission to protect Scientology's reputation didn't just rely on Black Ops. Desperate for some positive publicity, he announced his world's first real 'clear'. John McMaster was an articulate and charismatic former medical student from Durban. McMaster swore that Scientology helped him deal with the intolerable pain he suffered after having had part of his stomach removed due to cancer. He joined Hubbard's staff at Saint Hill in 1963 and was pronounced 'clear' three years later.[46]

McMaster couldn't really be categorised as Hubbard's first 'clear'. He had made the same claim about Sonia Bianca, the physics major from Boston 16 years earlier at the Shrine Auditorium in Los Angeles.[47] But Hubbard was a master of reinvention, and this time round he made sure he didn't put his first 'clear' on stage to perform unachievable memory tricks in front of 6000 people.

McMaster would, in the short-term, become an asset for Scientology. Hubbard, at one point, referred to him as Scientology's 'first Pope'.[48] He toured the world evangelising, delivering a message that was caring and non-threatening, devoid of all the aggression and exaggeration that so often filtered through Scientology's public pronouncements. But McMaster's gentle proselytising could not mask the fact that Hubbard's moods and his policies were getting darker, and that many of the changes he was making to Scientology doctrine reflected a deepening paranoia that followed on from the Anderson Inquiry and the increased scrutiny that flowed from it.

On 1 March, the Public Investigations Section, which bungled the Lord Balniel muckraking exercise, was ditched and replaced by the Guardian's Office.

As Jon Atack wrote: 'After the false starts of the Department of Official Affairs and the Department of Government Affairs, Hubbard at last had his own private Intelligence Agency.'[49] Hubbard's wife Mary Sue was to run the organisation, which would soon gain worldwide notoriety. Ted Gunderson, a former head of the FBI's Los

Angeles office, would later claim that Scientology 'has one of the most effective intelligence operations in the US, rivalling even that of the FBI'.[50]

The Guardian's Office would not only gather intelligence covertly, it would also conduct 'noisy investigations' designed to intimidate its critics and destroy their reputations. Family members, friends and work colleagues would be called or paid a visit and told the relevant person was being investigated for criminal activities. Cathy Gogerly, who moved to Adelaide following the ban in Victoria, gave some helpful hints on noisy investigations that Hubbard then forwarded on to Scientologists across the world:

> *Find out where he or she works or worked, doctor, dentist, friends, neighbours, anyone, and 'phone 'em up and say, "I am investigating Mr/Mrs _____ for criminal activities as he/she has been trying to prevent Man's freedom and is restricting my religious freedom and that of my friends and children, etc."*[51]

An 800-page training manual was developed for all Guardian's Office members – known as the 'B-1 Hat'. Jon Atack describes it as 'a scandalous compilation of harassment techniques, many derived from the confessions of former military intelligence agents and constructed around Hubbard's interpretation of Sun Tzu's *Art of War*. Staff were taught how to lie and how to break and enter, among other scriptural requirements.'[52]

Armed with Hubbard's brutal Fair Game policy, the Guardian's Office and other Scientologists could attack their critics with impunity. The Anderson Inquiry had scarred Hubbard and he wanted revenge. Two days after Scientology was banned in Victoria, Hubbard released a policy letter that stated, 'A truly Suppressive Person or Group has no rights of any kind and actions taken against them are not punishable under Scientology Ethics Codes.'[53]

Hubbard wanted his new Guardian's Office to go after judges and politicians in Australia. He wrote that 'Principals of the Victorian government such as the "Prime Minister" [sic], Anderson the "QC" and hostile members of the "Victorian Parliament" are continued as Suppressive Persons and they and their families and connections may not be processed or trained and are fair game.'[54] According to Hubbard, under the policy of Fair Game a Suppressive Person could be 'deprived of property or injured by any means by any Scientologist without any discipline of the Scientologist. May be tricked, sued or lied to or destroyed.'[55]

Scientologists claim that Hubbard later cancelled Fair Game. However, what he said in a revised policy letter was, 'The practice of declaring people Fair Game will cease. Fair Game may not appear on any Ethics Order. It causes bad public relations.'[56] In other words, the policy was never cancelled, but the term was not to be used any more because it had damaged Scientology's reputation. Scientology continues to attack critics to this day. As Heber Jentzsch, the President of the Church of Scientology once boasted, 'We're not a lie-down-and take it type of church. We're not going to turn the other cheek. If they slap us on one cheek, we'll slap them right back on both cheeks.'[57]

As Hubbard ramped up his policies for shutting down critics, he also began to look for a safe haven for Scientology. In 1966, he headed off to Rhodesia, which just months before had unilaterally declared independence from the UK, and was under the white minority rule of Ian Smith's Rhodesian Front.

Rhodesia at the time was subject to trade sanctions after UN officials described it as an 'illegal racist minority regime'.[58] This did not deter Hubbard. He believed he had been the country's founder, Cecil Rhodes, in a previous life and saw his trip as a homecoming.[59] According to his biographer Russell Miller, Hubbard thought he could solve the political crisis in the capital, find a safe environment for Scientology and recover gold and diamonds he believed that Rhodes had buried there.[60]

Hubbard was unable to achieve any of these outlandish goals. He did manage to buy a four-bedroom house in one of Salisbury's exclusive suburbs,[61] draft an unsolicited constitution for the government and put a down payment on the Bumi Hills resort hotel on Lake Kariba,[62] which he hoped to turn into a luxury learning resort for high-level Scientologists. But none of this impressed the government. After a stay of around three months, the Rhodesian Department of Immigration refused to renew Hubbard's visa and he had to return to England. Scientologist Morley Glasier told Jon Atack that Hubbard was actually refused a visa after Glasier – Hubbard's assistant – was caught trying to take government documents. Glasier served a prison term rather than implicate his boss. Hubbard was simply deported.[63]

Hubbard may not have deserved a hero's welcome at Heathrow, but he got one anyway. On the morning of 16 July, a fleet of buses had been hired to transport around 600 Scientologists to London's main airport.[64] Janis Gillham was one of those who celebrated Hubbard's arrival at the terminal. 'No-one knew he had been kicked out of the country in disgrace,' she says. 'It was a typical Scientology thing to cover that up by having hundreds of Scientologists there to cheer him.'[65] Gillham and the other members of Scientology's reception committee returned to East Grinstead by bus. Hubbard was driven back in his sumptuous yellow Pontiac convertible.[66]

The situation did not improve for Hubbard on his return to Saint Hill. By the end of the month the Church of Scientology in the US had lost its tax-exempt status after the Internal Revenue Service found that it was a commercial enterprise serving the private interests of Hubbard.[67] In August, there were further calls for an inquiry into Scientology in the UK, after revelations that a 30-year-old Sussex woman had ended up in psychiatric care following Scientology processing.

Karen Henslow, who had a history of mental illness, had written to her mother two weeks after joining the staff at Saint Hill, to tell her she was a 'Suppressive Person' and that she would be disconnecting from her immediately. Her mother, Hilary Henslow, and the psychiatrist looking after her, demanded the Health Minister set up an inquiry into Scientology.[68] Initially the Minister resisted, but the case of Karen Henslow gained national media attention and led to a debate on Scientology in the House of Commons.[69]

Hubbard was feeling the pressure and looking for an escape route. The master of reinvention was about to blindside even his closest followers. His 'Pope of Scientology', John McMaster, got a hint of what was coming. 'You know, John,' Hubbard told McMaster, 'we have got to do something about all this trouble we are having with governments. There's a lot of high-level research still to be done and I want to be able to get on with it without constant interference. Do you realize that 75 per cent of the Earth's surface is completely free from the control of any government? That's where we could be free – on the high seas.'[70]

Hubbard's most dedicated followers were about to get a crash course in paint scraping, bilge cleaning and the art of triple expansion steam engine maintenance. A committed band of Scientologists would leave their homes, hit the high seas and sign their lives away to Hubbard. But first their man had some business to do in North Africa with the head of the Galactic Confederation.

CHAPTER 10

ALL ABOARD

L. RON HUBBARD'S NEXT move was more typical of a rock star than a religious leader. He hung out in Spain and Morocco, took a lot of drugs, drank a load of rum, did some writing and had a breakdown.[1]

First stop was Tangier, a city that attracted writers, artists, swindlers, dope fiends and rent boys. It was the place the Rolling Stones escaped to following their infamous drug bust at Keith Richards' Sussex manor, where William S. Burroughs wrote his acclaimed novel *Naked Lunch*, and Hubbard started his work on Operating Thetan Level III (OT III).

While Burroughs' work was fuelled primarily by opiates, Hubbard had a history of using amphetamines, barbiturates, opiates and booze.[2] In a letter to Mary Sue at the time, he admitted to 'drinking lots of rum and popping pinks and greys'.[3] Pinks and greys are a street name for Darvon or propoxyphene,[4] a narcotic prescribed for pain relief. Whatever Hubbard was taking, it wasn't working.

After a month in Tangier,[5] Hubbard headed to Las Palmas in the Canary Islands. Virginia Downsborough, a staff member at Saint Hill, had been summoned to the Spanish city where she found Scientology's founder in a bad way:

> When I went in to his room there were drugs of all kinds everywhere. He seemed to be taking about sixty thousand different pills. I was appalled, particularly after listening to all his tirades against drugs and the medical profession.

There was something very wrong with him, but I didn't know
what it was except that he was in a state of deep depression;
he told me he didn't have any more gains and he wanted to die.
That's what he said: 'I want to die.'[6]

Out of Hubbard's North African drug binge came Operating
Thetan Level III (OT III). According to Scientologists, an Operating
Thetan is 'one who can handle things without having to use a body
of physical means'.[7] Scientologists believe Operating Thetans have
superhuman abilities including telepathy, recalling past lives and
the power to cause physical events through willpower.[8] Once a
Scientologist becomes 'clear' they can make progress up 'the Bridge to
total freedom' right up to Operating Thetan Level VIII (OT VIII). To
get to the higher OT levels, a Scientologist needs to commit to a period
of intense study and hand over hundreds of thousands of dollars.

In what the Church of Scientology describes as 'a research
accomplishment of immense magnitude',[9] while popping pills and
slugging rum, Hubbard discovered the myth central to OT III.
According to Hubbard, 75 million years ago, Xenu, the head of a
76-planet Galactic Confederation, solved an overpopulation problem
by sending billions of excess aliens to Teegeeack (Earth) in DC-8 style
spacecraft, placing them at the base of volcanoes and wiping them out
with hydrogen bombs.

The disembodied souls or 'thetans' were then forced to watch a 3D
film for 36 days, which indoctrinated them with false information about
the world's religions. According to Hubbard, these corrupted 'thetans'
then latched onto the bodies of humans. As a result, individuals began
carrying hundreds or thousands of invisible 'body thetans', that can
only be removed by an expensive form of Scientology auditing.[10]

Hubbard claimed obtaining this information nearly cost him
his life. 'In January and February of this year,' he told his followers
in a lecture recorded at Las Palmas, 'I became very ill, almost lost
this body, and somehow or another brought it off and obtained the
material, and was able to live through it.'[11] Hubbard said he broke his
back, his knee and his arm in the course of gathering his research, but
refused to give in. 'I am very sure that I was the first one that ever did
live through any attempt to attain that material.'[12]

In the same lecture, Hubbard revealed that the Guardian's Office, functioning under the leadership of his wife Mary Sue, had been able to isolate the source of all attacks against Scientology. 'Our enemies on this planet are less than twelve men,' Hubbard proposed, 'They are members of the Bank of England and other higher financial circles. They own and control newspaper chains, and they are, oddly enough, directors in all the mental health groups in the world which have sprung up.'[13]

The speech is significant in that Hubbard talks about the Sea Organization, or Sea Org, for the first time to a broader audience of Scientologists.[14] In November of 1966, a mysterious note appeared on the bulletin board at Saint Hill, calling for volunteers with naval or seagoing experience.[15] The note was taken down within an hour and those who had seen it were sworn to secrecy.[16] Yvonne Gillham was part of the elite group who answered the call, joining the secretive Sea Project (later to be renamed the Sea Organization) without even telling her family.[17] In the same month, the Hubbard Explorational Company Ltd was incorporated in London.[18]

Hubbard got busy accumulating a flotilla for his new exclusive sea-born unit. He bought an old North Sea fishing trawler, the *Avon River*, a former channel ferry, the *Royal Scotsman*, and a 60-foot ketch, the *Enchanter*, which Virginia Downsborough helped sail to Las Palmas. In March 1967, Yvonne Gillham and 18 other Scientologists were sent to the docks at Hull where the *Avon River* was moored. They worked long hours getting the vessel ship-shape for their trip to Las Palmas.

Just eight months after she had been reunited with her children, Yvonne Gillham was about to leave them again. At the time, Peter Jnr was 13, Terri 12, Janis 10. The former Brisbane kindergarten teacher told her children she was responding to a special invitation from Hubbard to join the Sea Project and that she would send for them soon.[19]

After a difficult journey made in rough weather with an inexperienced crew, the *Avon River* finally made it to Las Palmas in late May. Captain John Jones, one of only two professional seamen on board, described it as the strangest trip of his life:

My crew were sixteen men and four women Scientologists,
who wouldn't know a trawler from a tramcar. But they
intended to sail this tub 4,000 miles in accordance with
the Org Book. I was instructed not to use any electrical
equipment apart from the lights, radio and direction finder.
We had radar and other advanced equipment which I was not
allowed to use. I was told it was all in the Org Book, which
was to be obeyed without question.[20]

After the *Avon River* arrived in Las Palmas, Hubbard ordered a refit and his new elite unit got to work sanding, painting and building new bunks.[21] At the time, Gillham was acting as Chief Steward of the vessel and personal steward to Hubbard. Gillham was a beautiful woman, with a personality to match. She was full of energy, enthusiasm and empathy and Hubbard found her irresistible.

On 12 August 1967, Hubbard issued Flag Order #1, officially establishing the Sea Organization, appointing himself the Commodore and making Yvonne Gillham the Commodore's steward.[22] Her duties included looking after Hubbard's meals, clothes and quarters on the *Avon River* and reporting to Villa Estrella where Hubbard was based at Las Palmas.

Each day, Hana Eltringham would drive from the *Avon River* to Villa Estrella to deliver Hubbard's mail and make any deliveries back to the ship. The South African was the officer on board responsible for the crew's ethics and morals. On one trip to the villa she noticed Yvonne looked unhappy. 'I took her aside and said what's going on?' says Eltringham. 'And she burst into tears and said, "He's trying to hit on me. I'm so scared I don't know what to do."'[23]

Hubbard told Gillham she was a loyal officer of Scientology, and the key person who prevented Xenu from turning everyone on Earth into a complete slave.[24] As Hubbard made a move on his steward, he told her special people like them had to stick to together. Gillham tried to keep her distance from Hubbard and maintain her composure. When she rejected his advances, she was demoted.[25]

Yvonne Gillham was in an awkward situation. She desperately needed Hubbard onside if she was to be reunited with her family. 'LRH (Hubbard) kept promising that us kids would be sent,' says

Janis Gillham, 'because she did not agree to join the Sea Project unless she knew we'd be sent over.'[26] Rejecting Hubbard's advances did not help. It was nine months after Yvonne had left Saint Hill that arrangements were finally made to reunite the family. It was to be a false dawn. 'We flew into Valencia where the ship was,' recalls Peter Gillham Jnr. 'We were told that my mother wasn't there. She had sailed on the *Avon River* the day before. I realised then I'd just been shanghaied.'[27]

Peter Gillham Jnr is sure that Hubbard was behind the move that devastated the whole family. 'He was like a puppet-master and he liked to play people and I got to see more and more of that later, but at that point what the heck do I know? I'm barely 15, I'm going to see my mother, families are meant to stay together, even Hubbard says that, he doesn't practise that, but that's what he says.'[28]

Around a month later, Peter Gillham Jnr was able to transfer to the *Avon River* and see more of his mother, but it was different for his sisters. They were stuck on the *Royal Scotman*, as it became known after a spelling mistake was made while registering it in Sierra Leone,[29] 'We didn't see her but once in maybe three to four years after that – he made sure of it,' says Terri Gillham. 'It was like he was punishing her and making sure he could have us as his slaves with no control from parents.'[30]

The Gillham children joined the Sea Org, signing the standard one-billion-year contract. Janis was just 11 at the time. 'I had no choice,' she says. 'I'm on a ship. I had no parents there and I'm told if I want to stay on the ship I had to sign. Where do I go if I say no?'[31] Even though they were of school age the Gillham children were put to work full-time. If they were lucky they would get three hours a day of reading, writing and arithmetic to supplement their work schedule.[32]

Peter Gillham Jnr went to work in the engine room on the *Avon River*. Within six months he had been promoted to Chief Engineer at the age of just 15. His younger sisters were considered too young to be on the *Avon River* but not too young to be given senior positions on the *Royal Scotman*. When Hubbard issued orders, he wanted to know for sure that they were carried out. He set up the Commodore's Messengers Organization (CMO) for this purpose. The first two messengers were his son Quentin and Janis Gillham.[33] Soon after,

Terri joined the CMO. Aged just 11 and 13, Janis and Terri would soon become two of the most powerful people in the Sea Org.

The messengers were the eyes, ears and mouthpieces of Hubbard. They were expected to deliver a message with the same words, the same emphasis and the same tone that Hubbard had relayed it to them. If this included abuse and strong language, so be it. Hubbard frequently blew his stack and the messengers had to channel this anger. Even though they were 11 and 13, Janis and Terri, like the other messengers, were to be called 'Sir' at all times, and treated with the utmost of respect by all members of the Sea Org. The messengers were placed on six-hour shifts, seven days a week.

Delivering messages was just one part of the job. They also had to light Hubbard's cigarettes, carry an ashtray beside him, run his bath, swat flies, tell the captain which way to steer the ship, and even pull the Commodore's trousers on. 'He always wore these boxer shorts,' recalls Terri Gillham in disgust. 'Young girls should not be around that. He could have pulled his own trousers on. It's just ridiculous.'[34]

As a Commodore's Messenger, Terri Gillham was exposed to Hubbard's sleazy side. 'He tried to kiss me one time,' she told me. 'It was disgusting. I was 16 years old and up on the sun deck with him, Doreen was on watch with me and he had sent her off on a message; it was evening and getting dark. He had rotting teeth and such bad breath. Oh, God, he was disgusting. He was disgusting to look at and to touch and he thought he was God's gift.'[35]

As they became more experienced, the messengers assumed more responsibility, eventually handling the management team, enforcing orders and making sure Hubbard's programs were properly implemented.

Because they worked so closely with Hubbard, and were passing on his messages to various other Sea Org members, the messengers got a unique insight into Hubbard's character and how he treated his followers. 'He was bipolar!' says Janis Gillham. 'He could be so sweet and nice and friendly and very personable and sometimes he would just go into these tantrums and you'd just have to calm him down.'[36]

Terri Gillham concurs. 'He was always angry, always yelling and screaming at people. It was always in the back of my mind – why is he so angry?'[37] It's a question Terri has pondered for most of her life. She feels part of his anger was driven by self-loathing and guilt from not being the man he claimed he was. 'He knew he didn't have the good intentions that he claimed he had. He knew we were all slaves to him, he knew he manipulated and controlled us.'[38]

These were not just random acts of anger. Hubbard had institutionalised a culture of control and punishment through what he ironically titled 'ethics'. By the time the Sea Org was functioning, Hubbard was already using Scientology policy to control his followers. He had the power to declare someone a 'Suppressive Person' and force them to disconnect from a friend, colleague or family member.

Hubbard had pulled together a battalion of 'Ethics Officers' to report on and monitor the behaviour of his followers. If someone saw another person doing the wrong thing by Scientology they could write a report and send it to the Ethics Officer. Hubbard was building a system of spying and informing of which the East German Stasi would be proud.

Next he introduced 'Ethics Conditions', laying out formulas to measure the ethics of an individual or a group. He called these the 'Conditions of Existence' that included the states of 'power', and 'affluence' at the top and 'liability', 'enemy' and 'treason' towards the bottom. On 18 October 1967 Hubbard issued a list of penalties for those on 'lower conditions'. Someone assigned the condition of 'liability' would have their pay suspended and have a dirty grey rag tied to their left arm. Anyone given the condition of 'treason' would have their pay halted and a black mark placed on their left cheek.[39]

Hubbard defined his 'Conditions of Existence' in terms of degrees of success or survival.[40] 'Ethics' were the key to an individual's ability to improve and for an organisation's ability to survive and flourish. Hubbard's concept of ethics did not match up with the traditional meaning of the word. 'We are not in the business of being good boys and girls,' he wrote in *Introduction to Scientology Ethics*. 'We're in the business of going free and getting organization products roaring.'[41]

Through his 'Ethics' policies Hubbard introduced an authoritarian regime of measuring and monitoring statistics. Each Thursday at 2 pm, Scientology staff had to turn in the weeks' sales figures and achievements. Hubbard demanded that these statistics improve every week; otherwise lower ethics conditions were imposed. He had created an impossible regime of accelerating achievements where staff and Sea Org members had to work harder and harder each week or face punishment.

Terri Gillham, who saw the policies developed up close, says Hubbard constructed them to enslave his followers. 'I think it's all designed to teach you how to submit and give in and be monitored and be controlled. It's all about controlling the person and getting them under submission and control.'[42]

According to Terri, Hubbard was smart enough to know how to control his followers, and smart enough to know better. 'He was intelligent, he could read something and then duplicate it and understand it and take it and rewrite it in his own way. He was very clever as a writer – incredible at marketing, that's how he boomed Scientology, he was a marketing genius.'[43]

In the early days of implementing his new policy, Hubbard decided a whole vessel was under the condition of 'liability'. After an incident where the *Royal Scotman* had crashed into a dock, all the crew was forced to wear dirty rags. Even the ship's funnel had a grey tarpaulin wrapped around it.[44] While dirty rags and hard labour were humiliating, Hubbard was only just getting started.

At the front of a ship like the *Avon River* or the *Royal Scotman* is a narrow compartment called the chain locker. When the anchor is not in use, its chain is coiled up and stored there within the bow. In Hubbard's mind, it was not just a place to store the anchor chain, but Sea Org members he considered to have low 'ethics conditions'.

Hana Eltringham, a former captain of the *Avon River*, knew the chain locker well, describing it as 'a closed metal container, it's wet, it's full of water and seaweed, it smells bad'.[45] Terri Gillham cannot believe Hubbard used it to punish his followers. 'That chain locker was evil,' she says. 'It was a hellhole. It was worse than prison. The chain locker was stinking, disgusting and dangerous. If the chain had been let out while someone was in there, they would've died.'[46]

Peter Gillham Jnr was given the condition of 'enemy' and sent to the chain locker for making a wisecrack about oil on the floor of the engine room on the *Avon River*.[47] His father, who joined the Sea Org briefly in March 1968, and was in charge of the finances on the *Royal*

Scotman, ended up in the chain locker after he was falsely accused of trying to steal money.[48]

Even small children were sent to the chain locker. Because Scientology treats children as if they are small adults, minors were not protected from the growing culture of punishment and abuse aboard the *Apollo*. As Hubbard wrote in *Scientology and Your Children*, 'They are (and let's not overlook the point) men and women. A child is not a special species of animal distinct from Man. A child is a man or a woman who has not attained full growth. Any law which applies to the behaviour of men and women applies to children.'[49]

Derek Greene, a four-year-old boy who had dropped a Sea Org member's Rolex watch overboard, was sent to the chain locker for two days and two nights.[50] The boy's mother pleaded with Hubbard to let him out, but Scientology's founder would not relent.[51] Alone in the dark, with no blankets or potty, the four-year-old sobbed until his punishment was up.[52]

Tonja Burden, a former Sea Org member, swore in an affidavit she'd seen a boy held in the chain locker for 30 nights. 'He was only allowed out to clean the bilges where the sewer and refuse of the ship collected,' she said.[53] Scientology's 'Pope' John McMaster claimed Hubbard sent a deaf mute girl of around five years of age to the chain locker for ten days, assigning her an 'ethics condition' where she was meant to 'find out who you really are'.[54]

When Terri Gillham had difficulties dealing with a naughty child on board the *Apollo*, Hubbard dreamed up a form of punishment you wouldn't even inflict on an adult. 'He said lock him in the cupboard overnight,' she says. 'I was 13 or 14 years old but I knew that's not what you do. I knew I would never tell him that I wasn't going to do it – I just didn't do it. Because if I told him I'm not going to do it I'd be busted and he'd have somebody else do it so I figured the best thing to do was pretend I did it and not say anything further about it. I always looked back at this and thought there was something wrong with a man that would consider locking people up like this.'[55]

Even Hubbard's special messengers were subjected to cruel punishments. When Janis Gillham finished last in the messengers' Scientology dictionary exam, she had to spend 24 hours up the crow's nest on the top of the ship's mast. 'I was 12,' says Gillham. 'It was a big metal mast. You climb up the ladder, which was pretty high, and then you climb into it and you can't lay down, you're sitting up there with your knees pulled to your chin for 24 hours.' As the youngest messenger it was almost inevitable that Janis would finish last in the exam. Hubbard was punishing a small girl for not keeping up with older children.[56]

John McMaster was to experience first-hand the expanding punishment culture within Scientology's elite unit. In May 1968, Hubbard started giving orders that Sea Org members be thrown overboard from the ship from a height of around six to seven metres.[57] Hubbard did not consider his 'Pope' of Scientology to be infallible. McMaster was overboarded on six separate occasions, the last time breaking his shoulder as he hit the water. He left Scientology soon after and had lost all respect for Hubbard, referring to him in published interviews as 'Fatty'.[58]

Victims of overboardings were fully clothed when thrown into the sea. Some had their hands and feet tied together, others were blindfolded.[59] For those who couldn't swim it was a terrifying experience. There was no mercy shown for older Sea Org members either. Julia Lewis Salmen was pushing 60 when Hubbard issued the order that she be tossed overboard. 'She screamed all the way down,' says Hana Eltringham.[60] 'Once she hit the water the screaming stopped. Nobody did anything. Finally Hubbard shouted down, "For God's sake, what is she doing in the water?" He then told someone to jump in and save her.'[61] One Sea Org member suffered the indignity of losing his toupee after he was thrown off the deck.[62]

Sea Org members could be overboarded for the most minor indiscretions. Peter Gillham Jnr was thrown overboard for turning up 15 minutes late to a shift in the engine room.[63] He was just 15 at the time, but being a strong swimmer, was not traumatised by the experience like some of the American and English Sea Org members. The British *Sunday Times* reported that children as young as eight or nine were being thrown overboard.[64]

It was the *Sunday Times* journalist Alex Mitchell who first broke the story of Scientology's brutal overboarding rituals, and his exposé could be traced back to Australia and *The Anderson Report*. The

Townsville-born journalist had already antagonised the Scientologists while writing about them for Sydney's *Daily Mirror*. When Mitchell moved to London in 1967, he brought with him copies of *The Anderson Report*, and was happy to share them with other journalists.

Mitchell's copies of this sought-after document soon made their way around the bars and newsrooms of Fleet Street. The report helped many British journalists write about Scientology. 'Because the report had been tabled in parliament,' says Mitchell, 'its contents were "privileged" and could be used without fear of legal action by the vexatious litigants of Scientology. The report was widely used by UK newspapers during that time and provided a platform for most of the exposés.'[65]

After arriving in London, the Australian reporter decided to go undercover and sign up to the Church of Scientology in Tottenham Court Road. Mitchell must have been good at hoodwinking the E-Meter. Despite believing in none of Hubbard's doctrine, he reached Operating Thetan Level I (OT I) before he put his newfound knowledge to work.[66]

The Sea Org dropped anchor on the Greek Island of Corfu in August of 1968.[67] Hubbard was so enthused by the hospitality he'd received from the Greek military junta, he renamed the *Royal Scotman* the *Apollo*, and rechristened the *Avon River* the *Athena*. The British Home Office had asked its Vice-Counsel on Corfu, the formidable Major John Forte, to tell Hubbard he was no longer welcome in the UK.[68] Alex Mitchell was sent to Corfu to investigate Hubbard's plans on the island, which were said to include a proposal for a University of Scientology.[69]

Mitchell was able to document Hubbard's bizarre punishment rituals and uncover the story of a woman with two children who had tried to escape one of the ships. She had apparently run screaming down the gangway before she was restrained and returned.[70] The reporter was unable to put any of the allegations to Hubbard, who had instructed the local police to keep the media away.

But the *Sunday Times* journalist was a graduate of Sydney's then boisterous tabloid newspaper culture and was not easily deterred. Staking out the dock one night, he saw what he described as 'a rotund figure dressed in the preposterous white uniform of an admiral'[71] climbing into a limousine. He followed the car to the local casino. Mitchell tried to get into the roulette room, but the doorman told him he did not meet the dress regulations. The journalist picked a spot at a bar with a view of the high rollers and waited. Two hours later Hubbard went to the men's room and the intrepid Mitchell followed him in.

As Hubbard stood at the urinal, Mitchell sidled up alongside him. As both men took a leak, the journalist turned to Scientology's founder and asked for an interview. 'Alex, you're wasting your time,' Hubbard responded. 'I know where you're coming from and it's been very nice meeting you. Goodbye.' Hubbard zipped up his fly and was on his way. Mitchell filed his Sea Org exposé from Corfu and would later break the story of Hubbard's links to Aleister Crowley and occultism.[72] His name was eventually placed on Scientology's enemies list and he came under surveillance.[73] 'When I saw the list with my name on it,' Mitchell says, 'I was immensely proud. A Badge of Honour, I thought.'[74]

By now the culture of abuse inside the Sea Org had further torn apart the Gillham family. After Peter Gillham Snr had reported excessive spending by Scientology executives, he was accused of planning to take money from the ship. As the banking officer on board, he was meant to carry around money in a briefcase. When he was asked to go and manually flush out toilets as punishment for a crime he did not commit, Gillham refused. As a result he was sent to the chain locker and declared a Suppressive Person. His daughters, Janis and Terri, were called in and told to write letters of disconnection to him. Just 11 and 13 years old, the two girls were crying their eyes out as they were forced to write the letters.[75]

After Gillham had finished his punishment in the chain locker, he wrote to Hubbard to tell him that the Sea Org was not the right place for him. 'He had been so knocked down,' says Janis Gillham. 'He came and saw Terri and me and told us he was leaving and he'd be in touch. He had thought it was just him that was in trouble.'[76]

Peter Gillham Snr flew to Valencia where his son was in port. 'I saw my dad getting out of a taxi and I went down the gangway to talk to him,' recalls Peter Gillham Jnr. 'He said he was leaving and going back to England because he had some stuff to take care of. He didn't tell me what had happened. I said, "Well if you're going back to England, how come we can't too?"'[77]

The 15-year-old boy just wanted his family to be together. But he didn't get the answer he wanted. 'Not at this time,' his father said.[78] Hubbard and Scientology's intelligence division had other plans for Peter Gillham Snr.

CHAPTER 11

THE CHURCH OF SPYENTOLOGY

AS A PRIVATE INVESTIGATOR, Rex Beaver was used to asking people uncomfortable questions. Now he was on the receiving end of an interrogation. 'Are you a pervert?' he was asked. 'Are you or have you ever been a communist?'[1] Beaver gripped his hands on a pair of tin cans attached to an E-Meter as the questions kept coming: 'Are you a homosexual? Have you ever had unkind thoughts about L. Ron Hubbard?'

It was the morning of 10 September 1968 and Beaver was being given one of Scientology's notorious security checks at the organisation's Sydney headquarters at 340 Pitt Street. Beaver was not a Scientologist. He had merely answered an advertisement in the previous day's *Daily Mirror* that said, 'Investigator – Services of Trained Personnel Required for Interesting Work'.[2] Already things were getting interesting, and the work had not even started yet.

After the security check was finished, and Beaver had let go of the cans on the E-Meter, he was asked another question by a member of Scientology's feared Guardian's Office. 'Would you be worried if you had to get tough? Because you would have to get tough in the course of any employment with the Hubbard Association of Scientologists.'[3] Beaver could get tough all right. He was awarded the Queen's Commendation for bravery after he tackled a man armed with a shotgun who had been aiming it at police.[4] The Scientologists would soon find out just how tough Rex Beaver could play it.

After Beaver passed the security check, the Scientologists hired him to spy on a number of prominent Sydney figures including newspaper publisher Rupert Murdoch, journalist Anne Deveson, five psychiatrists, one clergyman and fourteen parliamentarians.[5] The politicians targeted included: future Deputy Prime Minister Lionel Bowen; the next Premier of NSW, Tom Lewis; future Liberal leaders Peter Coleman and John Mason; and a Deputy Premier in the making, Jack Ferguson.[6] It is unclear why these parliamentarians were targeted; only one on the hit list had been publicly critical of Scientology.

Martin Bentley from the Guardian's Office made it clear to Beaver what the first priority was: 'Your assignment is RO Healey, Liberal member for Wakehurst. I want everything from his birth certificate to what he's doing today.'[7] Dick Healey had been asking questions about the Scientologists in parliament and Beaver was told they wanted him to dig up dirt on the MP. 'Bentley said that any detrimental information I gathered about Mr Healey would be used to bring pressure to bear on him to stop him attacking Scientology in Parliament,' Beaver said.[8]

Rex Beaver didn't think much of the Scientologists. 'I thought they were a bunch of ratbags,' he says. 'I didn't want to waste my time working for them.'[9] The private investigator came up with a better idea. What if he played double agent? What if he took the job, pocketed the pay and fed information back to the politicians the Scientologists wanted him to spy on? Three days after the Scientologists had interrogated him, Beaver rang Dick Healey at his Forestville home. The Liberal MP and former ABC sports broadcaster was happy to work with the private investigator. He provided Beaver with personal details and access to his newspaper files to make it look like he was gathering information on him, in exchange for information about the inner workings of Scientology and the organisation's use of private investigators on critics.

Beaver was to be paid $60 a week plus expenses, and bonuses if he uncovered any dirt on his suspects.[10] He reported back mundane personal details to Martin Bentley, but also fed him a fictional story that the Liberal MP was having an affair. 'I asked Bentley if I could catch Dick Healey committing adultery just what would he want,' Beaver wrote in a statutory declaration. 'Bentley said just the photographs would do.'[11] There's little doubt what Bentley was planning to do with any photos that might come his way. As Hubbard wrote in his policy on how to deal with critics, 'Start feeding lurid, blood, sex, crime, actual evidence on the attackers to the press.'[12]

If the Scientologists wanted to get the tabloid press on side to run their lurid, blood, sex, crime stories, they weren't exactly going the right way about it. When Beaver returned to Scientology's head office he was shown a longer list of surveillance targets. He was asked to investigate Rupert Murdoch, the ambitious young publisher of Sydney's most popular evening tabloid the *Daily Mirror*. Around this time, Murdoch was getting his first foothold into the lucrative English newspaper market as he began buying up shares in *News of the World*.[13]

Rex Beaver took on the assignment and headed straight to the office of Brian Hogben, the editor of the *Daily Mirror*. The private investigator again offered to act as a double agent, spying on Murdoch for the Scientologists, while feeding information back to the newspaper for a future tabloid exposé. Hogben arranged for a meeting between Rex and Rupert Murdoch.

'Rupert was rapt,' says Beaver. 'He even volunteered to have a photograph taken of himself emerging from a motel with his secretary!'[14] Beaver told Murdoch there was no need for mocked-up photos. All that was required was some personal details. Murdoch obliged, telling the investigator his home address, where his yacht was moored and giving him free access to the newspaper's clippings library. Hogben loaned Beaver a special spy camera so he could take a photo of Scientology's surveillance hit list, but the investigator could not get a clean shot of it, with so many Scientologists hustling their way through the office.[15]

The surveillance operation expanded. Anne Deveson, who had produced a radio documentary on Scientology, was also investigated. 'I got a call out of the blue from someone who said he was a police detective,' recalls Deveson. 'He said he'd heard the Scientologists were watching me and that I should be careful.'[16] At the time, Deveson lived at Clareville on Sydney's northern beaches, and was concerned someone could try and run her off the road at the Bilgola Bends, the winding and dangerous stretch of Barrenjoey Road that runs between the southern and northern headland of Bilgola beach.

Martin Bentley continued to provide more names to Rex Beaver. 'He instructed me to check on Doctors William Barclay, AG Bennetts, Reverend Coughlin, Dr E Fischer, Dr Carl Radeski and Dr Scott Orr, also the Minister for Health Mr Jago,' Beaver said.[17] Harry Jago was hardly a crusader against Scientology. When asked in parliament by Dick Healey if there were any plans to ban Scientology in New South Wales, the Minister for Health responded that in that state there was 'little incidence of the more unfavourable features of scientology'.[18] That response did not make Jago immune from investigation. Bentley wanted Beaver to find out if the Minister for Health had ever visited a psychiatrist.[19]

Harry Jago was one of 14 NSW parliamentarians placed on the list. Besides Dick Healey, none of them seemed to be speaking out against Scientology. Some had the same surnames as members of the NSW Association of Mental Health, which Bentley wanted investigated.[20] Perhaps the Guardian's Office considered the others to be influential politicians or future leaders who they should start building files on.

With bonuses included, Rex Beaver was now pulling in over $100 a week to spy on critics or suspected critics of Scientology. But after a month of operating as a double agent, he pulled the pin. Rupert Murdoch was ready to run with the story. On 20 October 1968, the *Sunday Mirror* splashed its exposé on the front page with the headline: 'Blackmail! Detective says cult hired him to spy on city MP – sensation expected'.[21]

The *Sunday Mirror* reported that 'A private detective revealed yesterday that he had been hired to get blackmail evidence to silence a member of state parliament.' The story also mentioned the surveillance of Rupert Murdoch: 'The scientologists have declared Mr Murdoch an official "enemy" since the *Sunday Mirror* challenged the cult: sue and be damned!'[22]

Two days later, Dick Healey stood up in parliament and accused the Scientologists of 'a wicked, deliberate plot to inhibit and intimidate members of Parliament'.[23] Healey argued the Scientologists had breached parliamentary privilege. 'This is a diabolical threat from an outside group who seek to prevent members in the free execution of their duties. Here is an organization, which now poses as a church and indulges in a kind of pernicious practice which is bordering on criminal.'[24]

In ruling on the matter of privilege, the Speaker, Kevin Ellis, described the actions of the Scientologists as 'repugnant' and 'abhorrent' but said he could find no evidence that Martin Bentley had followed through with his plans to intimidate Dick Healey or any other members of parliament.[25]

While Scientology's Guardian's Office had asked Rex Beaver to find out if Harry Jago had ever visited a psychiatrist, the Minister for Health stuck to his principles. He would not be motivated by anger, and had no plans to follow the Victorian example and outlaw the organisation. 'I do not believe it is a function of parliament to exorcise false ideas and crazy beliefs,' Jago stated.[26]

The *Sunday Mirror* was not so forgiving. With the help of Rex Beaver they had secured a photo of Martin Bentley. The following Sunday, they ran the picture accompanied by the headline 'This is the face of Scientology'.[27] An accompanying editorial described Scientology as a 'money-making racket which encourages fanatics and charges high fees for using harmful psychological practices on the sort of people most likely to be harmed by them'.[28]

In attacking Scientology, the *Sunday Mirror* had also identified the organisation's plans for a counter-attack: 'Scientology's latest ruse to beat any restrictive legislation is to declare itself a "church" and claim freedom of worship. As a "church" scientology hopes to stage a legal comeback in Victoria where it has been banned for several years.'[29] The *Mirror* anticipated the tactics Peter Gillham was about to employ when he returned to Victoria the following month.

After Peter Gillham had said goodbye to his son in Valencia he returned to the UK. He found a country that was becoming increasingly hostile to Scientology. As had happened in Australia, critical reports in the media led to calls for action in parliament. Harold Wilson's government was under increasing pressure to act. In July 1968, the Health Minister Kenneth Robinson made a special announcement to parliament:

> *The Government are satisfied, having reviewed all the available evidence, that scientology is socially harmful. It alienates members of families from each other and attributes squalid and disgraceful motives to all who oppose it; its*

*authoritarian principles and practice are a potential menace
to the personality and well-being of those so deluded as to
become its followers, above all, its methods can be a serious
danger to the health of those who submit to them. There is
evidence that children are now being indoctrinated.*[30]

The Minister admitted there was no existing law he could use to
'prohibit the practice of scientology',[31] so instead he would set about
taking action to curb its growth. The Aliens Act would be used to ban
foreign nationals from coming to the UK to study or work at Saint
Hill, and those already doing so would not have their visas renewed.
Hubbard was being driven out of Britain. No longer could he enjoy
the simple pleasure of having his butler serve up his afternoon Coke
on a silver tray at his English manor.

Hubbard telexed Saint Hill to protest that 'England, once the light
and hope of the world, has become a police state and can no longer be
trusted'.[32] The UK government announced it would be commissioning
an inquiry into Scientology to be conducted by Sir John Foster. The
Scientologists would call on Peter Gillham to do some investigations
of his own. Jane Kember from the Guardian's Office ordered him to
return to Australia to lead the fight against the ban in Victoria.

Peter Gillham arrived home in November 1968. 'I am here to
establish the organisation again in Victoria,' he told Melbourne's
Sun newspaper, 'and I defy the Government to stop me.'[33] Premier
Henry Bolte, outraged by Gillham's impertinence, warned, 'People
who flouted the law would get their just desserts.'[34] But Gillham was
not intimidated by Victoria's long-serving Premier, accusing Bolte of
being 'too frightened to order his police force to prosecute practising
scientologists'.[35]

His brief was not just about reviving Scientology in Victoria.
Like Martin Bentley in NSW, Gillham was ordered to dig some dirt
on high-profile critics: including the Victorian Minister for Health,
Vance Dickie; the Opposition Leader in the Legislative Council,
Jack Galbally; and the former head of the Scientology inquiry, Kevin
Anderson QC.[36] But a week after Gillham arrived home, Scientology
suffered a further blow. The Liberal government in Western Australia
became the second state in Australia to ban Scientology. The Health

Minister Graham MacKinnon had described it as 'an insidious cult' and had urged a nationwide ban at a conference of health ministers in Darwin.[37] When other states refused to act, he moved to have Scientology banned in WA. The legislation passed despite opposition from the Labor Party.[38]

In the same week Scientology was banned in Western Australia, a parliamentary inquiry into its prohibition in South Australia was already underway. Premier Steele Hall had told parliament he considered the organisation to be a threat to mental health. 'It is my opinion that the possible indoctrination of children with its pernicious theories and illusory goals is a definite threat to the future mental health and emotional stability of these young people,' he said.[39] Soon after the inquiry was completed, South Australia became the third state in Australia to ban Scientology.

In Victoria, the authorities were coming to grips with the difficulties of implementing a ban on a belief system. The Scientologists were becoming increasingly defiant, holding open meetings and daring the police to arrest them. In October, a group of Scientologists invited the Minister for Health, police and members of the public to attend a 'church service' at the Noble Park home of Harry Baess.[40] Four Russell Street detectives promptly raided Baess's home, seizing a number of books, pamphlets and teaching manuals.[41]

The raid underlined the problems facing the police. One Scientologist left the home with a suspicious bulge beneath his shirt. While the police suspected he was concealing an E-Meter, they did not have the power to apprehend or search him.[42] There was also a broader problem with the law. The police found a large number of manuals and books on the premises, but how did they prove that the teaching of Scientology was actually taking place? As the Secretary of the Department of Health put it to the Minister: 'This will probably always be the case when the police raid premises.'[43]

The Scientologists were declaring publicly they would break the law, but the police could not find the evidence with which to charge them. It was like raiding an illegal casino and finding the roulette tables but no gambling taking place. Flaws in the Act meant the police struggled to get search warrants. The Attorney-General had to be satisfied that the premises contained 'scientological records' before he signed a warrant. When Ian Tampion advertised a Scientology meeting at his home in Hawthorn, Senior Detective Henderson, who was in charge of all Scientology investigations, was unable to enter the premises to gain evidence.[44]

As part of their campaign, the Scientologists went hard on what Hubbard referred to back in 1953 as 'the religion angle'. Ian Tampion and Peter Gillham started referring to themselves as 'ordained ministers' and 'Reverend' in their correspondence with government officials.[45] The pair described themselves as representatives of the Church of Scientology California in Victoria, which had registered itself at 'the Titles Office under section 33 of the Religious Successory and Charitable Trust Act'.[46] Ian Tampion even sought recognition of the 'Church of Scientology of California' with the trustees of the Necropolis at Springvale so that he could perform burial rights.[47]

As the Health Minister Vance Dickie described it, the Scientologists 'were becoming vocal again under the veil of religion'.[48] Was it just a campaign strategy, or did they truly believe it was a religion? 'I never considered it to be a religion while I was running the Melbourne College of Efficiency,' says Peter Gillham. 'Later on I went to Saint Hill, which is the Centre of the Scientology religion, so you gradually get into the idea of okay, it's a religion, because there are a number of things in it that coincide with religion.'[49] Australia's domestic security agency wasn't buying it; an internal ASIO report from the time said they had adopted a religious profile, 'to impress authorities and gain respectability, but these postures have not been taken seriously'.[50]

How seriously Scientologists took this religious posturing is perhaps best measured by what they were saying in their own publications at the time. Issue XVI of *The Bridge: The Official Publication of Scientology in Sydney* makes no references to the Church of Scientology, instead calling itself the Hubbard Scientology Organization. It refers to Scientology not as a religion, but as the 'fastest-growing self-improvement and philosophic movement in the world'.[51]

The publication reads nothing like a journal of religion, instead resembling a retail catalogue. Eighty-five per cent of this 1968 issue of *The Bridge* is dedicated to advertising, including selling memberships, books, E-meters, auditing courses, Scientology processing, tickets to a congress, and long-play records of L. Ron Hubbard's lectures. The publication carries an explainer written by Hubbard titled 'What Is Scientology?' At no time in the article does he describe it as a religion or a church. He draws a parallel with Buddhism, but only in the sense that they were both interested in 'the goal of Freedom'.[52]

At the beginning of 1969, L. Ron Hubbard released a message from the Greek isle of Corfu designed specifically for his followers in Australia and New Zealand: get things right down there or get ready to be taken over taken by 'Asiatic hordes'.[53]

Hubbard issued a special memo for Australian and New Zealand Scientologists, which stated that the intensity of the attack against Scientology was at its greatest in the antipodes. He claimed that Australian governments were taking orders from communists and what he called the 'International psychiatric front organization' and that this would have catastrophic consequences. 'If the US pulls out of Vietnam, that's it for Australia and New Zealand,' Hubbard warned.[54]

Four years after *The Anderson Report* had been handed down, Hubbard still felt aggrieved, and blamed a communist conspiracy for the ban in Victoria: 'We are gradually turning up more and more red cards connected to this Melbourne mess,' he said.[55]

Scientology's founder had a three-point plan for salvation that he laid out for his followers:

1. *Revitalize ANZO [Australia/New Zealand/Oceania] society with Gung Ho groups.*
2. *Solidly oppose the election of psychiatric political stooges and*
3. *Set up agitation and committees to achieve US statehood quickly.*

This is the only way I know of to keep ANZO from being deluged with Asiatic hordes.[56]

Meanwhile, in Corfu, the Greeks were at risk from being deluged by Scientology's hordes. Hubbard was planning to open an 'Advanced Org' in some disused local government offices.[57] Little did Hubbard realise, but at the same time he was railing about the communist infiltration of Australian governments, the anti-communist military junta he'd been cosying up to in Greece was seeking information and advice from Australian authorities about Scientology.[58]

For six months Hubbard's vessel the *Apollo* had been moored in Greek waters. The foreign ministry was considering a request from Hubbard to open an office in Corfu.[59] Australia's ambassador Hugh Gilchrist gave one Greek official some stern advice. A cablegram from the embassy in Athens stated, 'I suggested to him that Greek authorities would be well advised not to allow its practitioners a foothold here.'[60]

The Greeks were also seeking advice from British and American diplomats. Both embassies urged the foreign ministry to keep the Scientologists off Greek soil, but they had little documentation to back up their views.[61] The Australian embassy asked for relevant parts of 'judicial reports or state parliamentary debates' to be cabled through to 'help us and colleagues stiffen ministry's case'.[62] *The Anderson Report* continued to haunt Hubbard even on the isle of Corfu.

On 18 March, the Nomarch of Corfu, acting on instructions from the Deputy Prime Minister, Brigadier Stylianos Pattakos, ordered the Scientology vessels be removed from Greek waters within 24 hours.[63] The Scientologists complained the *Apollo* was not fit to sail, but a group of Greek officials headed by the local Harbourmaster pronounced the *Apollo* seaworthy.[64]

Hubbard had already advertised that he would be opening his school of Scientology on Corfu, in Dallietos House near the Phoenix Cinema,[65] urging Scientologists from around the world to come to Greece and study. He then had to hastily put out a note explaining why they were no longer there. He did it in classic Hubbard style: 'Due to unforeseen foreign exchange trouble and the unstable Middle Eastern situation we are not opening the new AOSH in Greece but in Denmark … Go now direct to Scientology Organization Denmark Hovedvagtsgade 6 1103 Copenhagen.'[66]

The following month, the Guardian's Office kickstarted a series of protests against the Scientology bans in Australia. On 27 April, four coach loads of Scientologists arrived at Australia House in London carrying placards with slogans such as 'Australia – A Police State', 'Thought Police Ride Again' and 'Emigrating? Go to New Zealand'.[67] Wayne Gibney, a representative from a group calling itself the Committee of Australian Refugees from Religious Persecution in London, delivered a letter to the High Commissioner in which he complained of being 'driven out from the country of my birth' and 'subject to persecution of religious belief that is equalled only by Adolf Hitler's vitriolic campaign against the Jews'.[68]

There were follow-up protests in May to coincide with Sir Henry Bolte's visit to London[69] and in October when Australia House had an open day to encourage migration.[70] At the latter protest the Scientologists handed out pamphlets trying to discourage emigration. Included in the list of 'ten reasons not to move to Australia' was the claim that *Jack and the Beanstalk* and other fairy stories were banned in state schools, and that Australia was responsible for myxomatosis that caused the 'lingering DEATH of millions of rabbits from the SUPPURATING eyes and SWELLING HEADS'.[71]

The head of the Guardian's Office, Jane Kember, led a delegation to Australia House to complain about what they saw as religious persecution. The delegation told a representative of the High Commissioner they were not satisfied with the results of the Anderson Inquiry and wanted the case reopened. If it wasn't, they would continue their protests, consider legal action, and employ any means possible to embarrass Australia, in any country, especially in the US.[72] Soon after the protests expanded to Los Angeles, with around 500 Scientologists gathering outside the Australian Trade Commission on Wilshire Boulevard. Many of the placards drew on Nazi analogies, with one banner reading, 'Australia – The Fourth Reich – Is Hitler Alive and Well in Melbourne?'[73]

But there was one Australian in Los Angeles the Scientologists were happy to call their own. After the UK government had cut off Saint Hill as a training ground for foreign Scientologists, Hubbard moved to established new training centres around the world, with one of the critical offices set up in Los Angeles.[74] After doing her Class VIII Auditing course with Hubbard in Corfu, Yvonne Gillham had been sent to the new Advanced Org in LA. She was about to get to work on developing the first ever Celebrity Centre, a move that would play a critical role in the marketing of Scientology in the years ahead.

CHAPTER 12

CELEBRITY AND NEW FAITH

L. RON HUBBARD HAD long seen the potential benefits of recruiting celebrities to Scientology. In 1955, he announced 'Project Celebrity', a plan to recruit big names to boost numbers. 'It is obvious what would happen to Scientology,' he wrote, 'if prime communicators benefiting from it would mention it now and then.'[1]

Hubbard drew up a hit list, including Greta Garbo, Walt Disney, Liberace, Bob Hope, Billy Graham, Groucho Marx and Edward R Murrow. The idea went nowhere. Not one of the celebrities targeted in 'Project Celebrity' became a Scientologist. But at that time, Hubbard did not have someone of Yvonne Gillham's charm and persuasion at his disposal.

In October 1968, Gillham was the most qualified auditor on deck in Los Angeles. Being close to Hollywood, she was auditing young people who were involved in the movie business. The former Brisbane kindergarten director started keeping separate files on celebrities and dreamed of setting up an exclusive facility where they could get together and access Scientology services.[2]

Yvonne Gillham wrote to Hubbard aboard the *Apollo* outlining her concept for a Celebrity Centre. Hubbard embraced it immediately. Gillham's concept worked on a number of levels. Hollywood was full of young people trying to make it; a battalion of potential new recruits for Scientology, creative and open-minded, emotionally vulnerable and economically insecure, all willing to try anything that would give them an edge in the pursuit of their dreams. Once recruited, these artists could then help create a vibe around Scientology. If they became famous, they could be used for recruitment purposes.

However, Yvonne Gillham did not set up the Celebrity Centre as a marketing strategy. She enjoyed being surrounded by creative people and loved to see them succeed as artists. 'The whole idea was to get celebrities into Scientology to help them become a success, not to benefit Scientology,' says Peter Gillham Snr. 'It was about what we could do for them, not what they could do for us.'[3] Yet despite her motives, Yvonne was laying the groundwork for what was to be Scientology's greatest marketing tool, the use of celebrities like Tom Cruise and John Travolta to help sell their services.

After much planning, Yvonne found a suitable building for Scientology's first Celebrity Centre in July 1969. It was an old supermarket at 1809 West 8th Street[4] in a rough part of Los Angeles. The feel was bohemian, with no uniforms, no overboarding, no militaristic air. 'It had that hippie vibe that people responded to at the time,' said Chris Many, a musician who worked at the Celebrity Centre in the early days.[5]

Yvonne Gillham ran the Celebrity Centre like she ran the Melbourne College of Personal Efficiency in Hawthorn. She created an environment that was warm, friendly and fun. She enticed people in with her personal charm and kept them there with her enthusiasm. She flattered the artists and performers, appealing to their neediness with what she called 'admiration bombing'.[6] Even the landlord was not immune to Yvonne's dazzling personality. Theodore Freistadt had planned to charge the centre $1200 a month rent, but Gillham bargained him down to $800. When asked why he acquiesced, Freistadt responded, 'You know Yvonne don't you? Well, then you know the way she is, nobody can say no to Yvonne!'[7]

The Celebrity Centre attracted artists, musicians and actors. Among the attendees at the packed opening night were the actress and star of *Easy Rider*, Karen Black, jazz fusion pioneer Chick Corea and the musician Stanley Clarke.[8] The centre was an instant success. 'She held socials, parties, dances, workshops, meetings, Sunday services and was constantly brainstorming with everyone for ideas on how to draw more people into her doors,' wrote her biographer Howard Dickman, 'at first the building was mostly a big open space.

Then, booths were set up. They were varied; for example, there was a calligraphy booth, a candle-making booth, tie-die and many others.'[9]

The Celebrity Centre's most successful recruit during Yvonne's time at the helm was John Travolta. The young actor had battled depression and insomnia as his career struggled to take off. 'She just loved Johnny,' recalls Spanky Taylor, who worked with Yvonne. 'She believed in John, when John didn't believe in John.'[10] Travolta took the Hubbard Qualified Scientologist Course at the Celebrity Centre just before he auditioned for a part in the television show *Welcome Back Kotter.*[11] After he landed the role of Vinne Barbarino, he gave credit to what he'd learned at Celebrity Centre. 'I would say Scientology put me in the big time,' he said.[12]

While the Church of Scientology was courting celebrities in the US, in Australia it was busy lobbying politicians. At the beginning of 1969, Scientology was under immense pressure in Australia. It was banned in Victoria, South Australia and Western Australia, and under further parliamentary and media scrutiny in New South Wales following the Rex Beaver spying scandal. The main game was convincing elected representatives to change the legislation. The focus of much of that lobbying was Lionel Murphy, a left-wing labour lawyer and atheist with a love of science rather than Scientology.

Senator Murphy was an advocate for human rights and social justice. He campaigned against the death penalty, and fought for the introduction of no-fault divorce, racial discrimination legislation and legal aid for the underprivileged. He was exactly the kind of man that L. Ron Hubbard would have labelled a communist. But the Shadow Attorney-General was about to become Scientology's unlikely saviour in Australia.

On 28 January, six detectives raided Perth's Scientology headquarters in Hay Street seizing stationery, records and electrical equipment.[13] Included in the haul were 4000 stamped, addressed envelopes. The Hubbard Association of Scientologists (HASI) and 15 individuals were charged with practising Scientology.[14] The Perth HASI was eventually found guilty and fined $200,[15] but the Supreme Court quashed the conviction later that year.[16]

South Australian Scientologists dealt with the ban in their state by pursuing Hubbard's 'religion angle'. Three days after the Perth raid, they changed their name, incorporating the Church of the New Faith under the Associations Incorporation Act. Branches in Sydney and Perth were formed later that year.[17] When the new church registered in Victoria under the Companies Act, the authorities were not too concerned. George Rogan, the Secretary of the Victorian Department of Health, wrote in a memo to his Minister that the move would 'not in any way legally improve the position of the scientologists'.[18] Rogan did not see what was coming.

Tom Minchin was an energetic 24-year-old Arts graduate with libertarian instincts. The younger brother of an Anglican priest, he was ordained as a Scientology Reverend on 3 March 1969, in a chapel in Peel Street, Adelaide, less than five weeks after the new church was incorporated.[19] Minchin took on the critical role of chief lobbyist for the Church of the New Faith. Scientology's future in Australia depended on him. Minchin took on the new role with vigour, bombarding the offices of politicians with letters and phone calls, making the case for recognising the religious status of Scientology.

It helped that Tom Minchin was also a member of the Australian Labor Party (ALP) and was able to gain access to the South Australian Premier Don Dunstan. Minchin was a member of the St Peters branch of the ALP. Dunstan and Minchin would have known each other from branch meetings. St Peters was part of Dunstan's electorate.[20] At one point the Premier was forced to distance himself from the cult, denying that the Scientologists were raising campaign funds for Labor. Minchin had promoted a party fundraiser that Dunstan was a guest speaker at in a Church of the New Faith newsletter. 'They may have told some of their members it was on,' Dunstan told the local media, as he tried to hose down any connection between his party and the banned organisation.[21]

An interesting link between Scientology and that fundraiser went unnoticed at the time. The event had been held at the home of Brian and Marjorie Fitzgerald, a prominent Labor couple who had previously dabbled in Scientology. 'Doug Joyce was a lecturer in management and my husband Brian did his course,' Marjorie told me. 'Doug came back from England where he had learned from Hubbard. Doug talked about self-improvement, which interested me. Later it became all about money and power and they starting talking about it being a religion and I dropped it like a hot scone.'[22] Marjorie was also friends with Ian and Barbara Rinder, the parents of Mike Rinder who later became Scientology's international spokesman. She also babysat Cherie Joyce, the daughter of Doug, and the mother of future Freedom Medal winner Kate Ceberano.

On the surface it might seem like an obvious plot on behalf of the Guardian's Office to have Tom Minchin infiltrate the ALP and help overturn the ban. But his brother, the Anglican priest James Minchin, suspects Tom had joined the Labor Party before he moved to Adelaide.[23] [Tom Minchin would not talk to me for this book. When I knocked on his door and asked to speak to him, he would not even come to the door. His wife asked me to leave from behind the locked door.]

However, there is evidence that at least one other Scientologist was acting covertly inside the Labor Party at the time. With his platform boots, green bell-bottom flares and strong commitment to the Labor cause, Eric Kleitsch did not seem like an undercover operative. Tom Minchin had introduced him to Scientology when both were members of Young Labor. Soon after, Kleitsch joined the Sea Org, and studied at Saint Hill. When he returned to Adelaide, the Guardian's Office had a job for him. While Minchin lobbied the politicians, Kleitsch was meant to find out what was going on inside the South Australian government.

Ron Payne was the Labor member for Mitchell and a friend of Kleitsch's father. Kleitsch began meeting with Payne once a week. 'I told Ron Payne my shore story (story designed to cover real story) was that I was a disaffected Scientologist who had been declared suppressive and that I was investigating Scientology,' says Kleitsch. 'I told him I needed information from him so I could help destroy the cult and he bought it lock, stock and barrel.'[24]

Kleitsch's weekly meetings with Payne continued for close on a year. 'Ron told me everything the Labor Party and the government were planning on doing about Scientology,' says Kleitsch. After each conversation, the young Scientologist would return to the Guardian's Office around midnight for a debrief with Scientology's intelligence operatives. While feeding internal Labor Party secrets to the Guardian's Office, Kleitsch was also sitting on the Young Labor executive as a Senior Vice-President.

Andrew Mack, who was in Young Labor at the time, remembers both Minchin and Kleitsch. 'Eric did a fine job of hiding his job as a Scientology agent,' says Mack. 'A decent enough character, he seemed very keen to get Labor up in the state and federally. Tom, to the contrary, was a single-minded protagonist for Scientology, specifically aiming to ditch the ban in South Australia and coming up with pamphlets for Young Labor people on the evils of psychiatry.'[25]

While his Young Labor colleagues spent most of their time campaigning against conscription to the Vietnam War, Minchin somehow managed to turn that issue into a Scientology crusade. He had been a key witness in a landmark court case in Western Australia in 1970 when Jonathan Gellie successfully claimed he was a minister of the Church of the New Faith and therefore exempt from national service. Dressed in a suit with a clerical collar, Minchin helped convince magistrate Con Zempilas that the church was a religion within the context of the National Service Act.[26]

Earlier that year, Scientology's great nemesis in Australia passed away. On Friday, 7 March 1970, Phillip Wearne died aged, 44. Scientologists spread false rumours that he had been assaulted outside a nightclub,[27] but Wearne's death certificate states he died from an overdose of the sedative Methaqualone, otherwise known as Mandrax or Quaaludes. Wearne had been admitted to Sydney's Prince of Wales Hospital four days earlier, but never recovered.[28]

The life of luxury that Wearne enjoyed in Melbourne in the early 1960s had evaporated in his final years. After his house was sold and his debts were paid, his estate left just over $12,000 to his wife, Jillaine, and a $30 oil painting to his friend John Willis. Phillip Wearne was living on the pension at the time of his death. His relative poverty might help explain why he signed a bizarre statement a year earlier that helped the Scientologists argue they had been victims of a conspiracy involving two intelligence agencies.

On 6 January 1969, Wearne signed an affidavit, witnessed by Scientologist Ron Segal, that stated throughout the Anderson Inquiry he kept in close contact with Earl Wilkinson, a man he believed to be a CIA agent.[29] Wearne said Wilkinson 'wined and dined' him, helped him with 'certain financial problems' and would turn up at his flat regularly with a bottle of Scotch.

The affidavit was used by the Scientologists to try and prove there was a conspiracy between ASIO and the CIA to target them, leading to the banning of Scientology in three states.[30] The Scientologist who organised the meeting with Wearne was Martin Bentley, the same operative from the Guardian's Office who had recruited Rex Beaver to spy on Rupert Murdoch and 14 parliamentarians. With both Wearne and Bentley now dead, it's unlikely we will ever know who organised that meeting and whether money changed hands to secure the statement.

As Tom Minchin continued to lobby South Australian politicians to repeal the local Act that prohibited Scientology, he also wrote letters to federal politicians asking that they recognise the Church of the New Faith as a religion under the Marriage Act and to allow him to personally conduct weddings. Recognition under the federal law was critical. In Victoria, Scientology was banned by the registration of all forms of psychological practice. An exemption was given to any religious minister recognised by the federal Marriage Act. If the Church of the New Faith could get recognition under the Act they could override the ban in Victoria.

Two successive Liberal Attorneys-General, Tom Hughes and Ivor Greenwood, rejected Minchin's arguments.[31] Senator Greenwood stated: 'If the practice of Scientology is unlawful in Victoria, South Australia and Western Australia, I don't believe that I should go around authorising members of that church to celebrate marriages.'[32] But over 20 years of Liberal government was coming to an end and Minchin set his sights on Lionel Murphy, Labor's Shadow Attorney-General, and leader of the Opposition in the Senate.

On 11 April 1972, Tom Minchin wrote to Senator Murphy, asking that 'in the event of a Labor Government coming to power in Canberra, you would recommend a proclamation for our Church under the Marriage Act.'[33] Four months later, Minchin got the answer he was looking for. Lionel Murphy announced that if Labor won government they would recognise the Church of the New Faith.[34]

For Murphy, the lawyer and human rights activist, the decision was about equal rights. 'Under the constitution, all religions are entitled to equal treatment,' he said. 'Whether churches are big or small, orthodox or unorthodox, they are entitled to equal treatment.'[35]

But not all of his Labor colleagues agreed. Gil Duthie, Labor's Whip in the House of Representatives and a former Methodist Minister, could not understand the decision. 'A lot of my colleagues would also oppose it,' he said. 'I agree that all churches are entitled to equal treatment, but scientology is not a religion.'[36]

Three days after the announcement, Murphy sought to clarify his position on Scientology. In a press release he stated:

> *I wish to make it quite clear that I have expressed no approval of or endorsement of the beliefs of the Church of the New Faith, founded by people who call themselves scientologists.*
>
> *In fact, I do not agree with their beliefs.*
>
> *However, I am concerned that principles of freedom of religion be upheld.*

In his press release, Murphy mentioned the incorporation of the church in 1969 and the 1970 decision in regard to the National Service Act, before launching into an impassioned defence of an individual's right to start their own religion, even if as an atheist he considered this a form of irrational behaviour:

> *If certain citizens choose to found their own church, then provided they observe the law, they are entitled to equal treatment with other churches, whether their beliefs are generally approved or not, be they big or small, old or new, orthodox or unorthodox.*
>
> *It is an important aspect of freedom of religion that except where there are breaches of the law, governments should not interfere in religious matters and especially not examine the validity of religious beliefs.*
>
> *This must be accepted or there would be no religious freedom. If governments assume the function of deciding which are true religions and which are false religions, none will be safe. History has demonstrated this.*

Murphy stressed that there were safeguards within the Marriage Act to deal with any abuses, and ended his statement by saying:

Some people are concerned that adherents of the Church of the
New Faith may break the law. If they do, there are civil and
criminal remedies which may be invoked to enforce the law.[37]

In December 1972, Labor was swept to power under the
reformist leader Gough Whitlam. Lionel Murphy became Attorney-
General. Two months later, it was announced that the Church of the
New Faith had been proclaimed a recognised denomination under the
Commonwealth Marriages Act.[38]

The following Sunday, Melbourne Scientologists held a special
'Service of Thanks' in honour of Lionel Murphy. The Church of
Scientology of California in Victoria presented the Attorney-General
with a blue leather-bound folder embossed in gold writing featuring his
name, title and the Scientology symbol on the front cover. Inside were
the signatures of 67 Scientologists who had attended the ceremony in
Melbourne.[39]

Jane Kember, the Guardian Worldwide, Scientology's most senior
executive, visited the office of the Australian High Commission
in London to present a scroll of thanks.[40] The nation, which
Scientology headquarters had previously dismissed as 'founded by
criminals, organized by criminals and devoted to making people
criminals',[41] was suddenly worthy of appreciation. Michael Graham,
the Australian President for the Church of the New Faith, lauded
the new Attorney-General. 'All praise should go to the Senator for
the bold and enlightened decision he has taken,' he said.[42] Mary Sue
Hubbard was happy to report that 'honest politicians do exist and
Australia can look forward to an exciting future under the Labor
government'.[43]

But not everyone was celebrating. TM Jensen of Essendon
wrote to the Victorian Minister for Health, saying, 'The Scientology
organization is apparently wasting no time in preparing to exploit
the loophole in the Psychological Practices Act brought about by the
recent action of the federal Attorney-General. A member of my family
who underwent a very severe and unhappy personality change at the
hands of this organization some years ago has made it clear to me
that she has now been induced to embark on further treatment at
Scientology courses.'[44]

Jensen was worried his relative would hand over most of their inheritance to the local Scientologists. 'It is difficult to understand,' he wrote, 'the readiness of present Labor Governments to recognize as a Church what is patently one of the most wicked financial rackets ever conceived.'[45]

TM Jensen of Essendon may have been onto something. A year before, Hubbard had issued a 12-point policy governing Scientology Finances. Points A and J were both 'MAKE MONEY', point K was 'MAKE MORE MONEY', the final point was 'MAKE OTHER PEOPLE PRODUCE SO AS TO MAKE MONEY'.[46]

The ban on Scientology in Victoria was effectively over. As Robin Youngman, a Scientology official, said, 'The Victorian ban against Scientology is now null and void as it specifically exempts organisations so acknowledged under the Marriages Act.'[47] Malcolm McMillan, from the Australian Psychological Society, who had initially proposed the definition of 'recognised religion' for the Victorian bill as all those listed under the Marriage Act, says that definition 'became the Achilles heel of the bill. It made the whole thing inoperable.'[48]

In the eight years after the Victorian legislation was introduced, there was not one successful prosecution against a Scientologist or a Scientology organisation.[49] Two stage hypnotists were prosecuted; there were four charges of practice of hypnotism without consent (three sustained, one dismissed); and two successful prosecutions for the unregistered practice of psychology.

In May 1973, the Labor government in Western Australia lifted the ban on Scientology, despite opposition from Liberal MPs.[50] In South Australia, Labor Premier Don Dunstan repealed the Scientology (Prohibition) Act the following year. Dunstan had spoken out against the legislation while in Opposition. When Labor announced its plans to overturn the legislation, L. Ron Hubbard gave all the credit to Tom Minchin. Under the Heading 'Big Win', Hubbard wrote:

The Adelaide Ban is to be repealed according to the Attorney General at the Adelaide Labour Convention.

This is a GO victory. The A/G there Tom Minchin did it. He is being made a Kha Khan.

So the tide rolls back the way it came.

A lovely birthday present for Mary Sue. The Telex arrived
in the first few minutes of her birthday today.
LRH, COMMODORE[51]

The newspapers reported the first official Scientology wedding
on 13 January 1974 when Reverend Michael Graham married Gary
Clark and Ruth Roots in Perth.[52] The following month, Hubbard
released a triumphant directive titled GO-ANZO-GO:[53]

ANZO (Australia/New Zealand/Oceania) is free to GO-GO-
GO,' wrote Hubbard. 'Psychiatry lost. Scientology won. When
you have won you take advantage of your victories. Psychiatry
wanted joyless, apathetic people totally controlled and
suppressed. Scientology wanted friendliness and freedom for
ANZO's people. Scientology won ... Scientology has a mission
to rescue all of ANZO from the darkness that was spread by
the Nazi philosophies of psychiatry and psychology.

Scientology had 'won' because they had convinced local politicians
that either they were a religion, or that it wasn't a government's role
to decide. Two of the key politicians they targeted, Don Dunstan and
Lionel Murphy, were both social libertarians opposed to discrimination
against minority groups. Sir John Foster, who had conducted an
inquiry into Scientology in the UK in 1971, was opposed to the kind
of prohibition that had been temporarily pursued in parts of Australia.
'Such legislation appears to me to be discriminatory,' he wrote, 'and
contrary to all the best traditions of the Anglo-Saxon legal system.'[54]

But in pursuing Hubbard's religion angle so publicly, Scientology
had caused itself a problem. Some potential young recruits who had
rejected organised religion found it a turnoff. As Peggy Daroesman,
a young musician who embraced Scientology in Sydney in the 1970s,
recalled: 'We were somewhat put off that it called itself the Church of
the New Faith.'[55]

However, Scientology was expert at manipulating its image to
accommodate just about anyone. 'We were assured by almost everyone
we met,' Daroesman says, 'including ministers of the church such as
Peter Sparshott, Martin Bentley and David Graham – that it wasn't

really a religion but that it had to adopt the practices and appearance of a religion so that the government would not harass it.'[56]

Lionel Murphy was right to argue that if Scientologists broke the law, there were 'civil and criminal remedies which may be invoked'. This is exactly what was happening to Hubbard elsewhere. In the same month Murphy became the Attorney-General, Hubbard was expelled from Morocco and had the French authorities pursuing him for fraud.[57] He flew to New York with a briefcase full of banknotes and went into hiding in Queens for nine months with two Sea Org members.[58] It was here he began planning what became popularly known as Operation Snow White, a covert mission that saw his wife Mary Sue end up in jail for her role in a massive criminal conspiracy.[59]

Also in that month Lionel Murphy recognised the Church of the New Faith and Scientology as a religion under the Marriage Act, a grand jury investigation in the United States showed the outrageous lengths the Church of Scientology was prepared to go to silence its critics. If Murphy the human rights activist had been aware of what was going on inside the American judicial system, he would have been appalled.

Operation Dynamite and Operation Freakout were covert missions designed to destroy Paulette Cooper, a New York journalist who had written *The Scandal of Scientology*. For daring to expose the inner workings of Scientology, Cooper faced 19 separate lawsuits and untold harassment.[60] Her phone was tapped, a spy moved into her apartment and her psychiatrists' files were stolen. When she moved apartment buildings, 300 of her new neighbours were sent letters that claimed she was a child molester and a prostitute who carried venereal disease.[61]

In February of 1973, the New York journalist was called to testify to a grand jury.[62] Cooper thought she was being summoned as an expert witness on Scientology and was looking forward to it. When she arrived, she found out she was under investigation. The Church of Scientology in New York had been mailed two bomb threats; one of them had Paulette Cooper's fingerprints on them. Cooper denied the allegations but was indicted for the bomb threats and for perjury.

The trial was delayed. Evidence eventually emerged that the Church of Scientology had attempted to frame her. Cooper believes her fingerprints were accessed as she signed a petition. 'A mysterious girl named Margie Shepherd came by with a petition for me to sign supporting the United Farm Workers,' she later told journalist Tony Ortega.

Margie Shepherd was wearing gloves. Cooper believes she placed a piece of stationery under the clipboard, which would have picked up her fingerprints.

That piece of stationery, the theory goes, was then used to write a bomb threat against the Church of Scientology. It was five torturous years before Cooper was exonerated. The lawsuits with Scientology continued until a financial settlement was reached in 1985.[63] They were still spying on her up until at least 2010.[64]

It wasn't only Scientology's critics who were becoming victims of L. Ron Hubbard's paranoia. Those close to him in the Sea Org would soon face a new regime of punishment. As Hubbard found it harder to find countries that would accept him, it would be those on his ship who found themselves in the firing line.

CHAPTER 13

THE ROCK CONCERT

MIKE RINDER WAS IN deep shit. Outside his apartment on the remote Portuguese island of Madeira was a baying mob full of beer and bravado. Portugal had just undergone a coup, the locals believed Rinder was an American spook and the locals were letting him know about it.

'Apollo is CIA! You're CIA!' the crowd chanted from the square below. This was no peaceful protest. The locals were armed with rocks and Rinder's neighbour, a captain in the Portuguese army, offered some ominous advice: 'Don't leave the apartment,' he told the young Australian. 'Turn out all the lights and stay on the floor.'[1] Rinder expected adventure when he signed up to the Sea Org, but not this. The captain left in haste with a comment that did little to ease Rinder's growing anxiety: 'Stay here,' he said. 'I'm going to get a helicopter and pick you off the roof of the apartment.'

The 19-year-old South Australian had become the focal point of an unruly protest. As three truckloads of soldiers surrounded his apartment building with machine guns pointing outwards, Rinder decided to take a look through the peephole in his front door. The scene did not fill him with optimism. 'I saw the ship sail past and I'm thinking, what? They left me?'[2] The *Apollo* had set sail for safer waters after Hubbard and his crew had been bombarded with stones thrown from the docks. Rinder was now the only Scientologist left in the port of Funchal. 'I felt very alone and quite scared. I didn't know if the *Apollo* was leaving for another country or if anyone even knew I was there.'[3]

The young Scientologist grew up in an Adelaide suburb where young boys routinely dodged projectiles aimed at the head. Down the road from the Rinders', the Chappell brothers turned backyard cricket into a form of suburban warfare, with their cut-throat games providing a foundation for their future success as Test cricketers.

The eldest of three children, Mike Rinder had his own youthful trials. His parents became Scientologists a few years after he was born. After Scientology was banned in South Australia, auditing became an undercover operation. Family legend has it that their collection of Hubbard's books was hidden under the floorboards of the family home.

Educated at the elite private school Kings College, Rinder sung hymns in the chapel each morning and recited the Lord's Prayer. He kept his own beliefs to himself: 'I gotta tell you when I was growing up it wasn't something that was talked about. You didn't publicly announce yourself as a Scientologist because it was like oh my God! You don't wanna to say that.'[4]

Rinder cruised through school, getting good grades without having to put too much work in. When he graduated from school in 1972, he turned down a full scholarship at Adelaide University. The 18-year-old had other goals. 'From the time I was 10 or 12 years old I wanted to join the Sea Org and I wanted to work with Ron Hubbard,' he says.[5] He moved to Sydney and signed the billion-year Sea Org contract.

After a few months working in the 'Tours Org', driving a Torana GTR between Melbourne, Sydney, Adelaide and Perth, and selling Scientology services, he headed to Saint Hill in the UK to do his formal Sea Org training. Once qualified, he set off for Lisbon, where he boarded the *Apollo*. They were the first steps in a journey that would see Mike Rinder rise to the top of the Church of Scientology, becoming its international spokesman and the head of the feared Office of Special Affairs.

In September 1973, Rinder was put to work doing menial tasks on the *Apollo*. He started off as a deckhand and a pinholer before becoming a messenger. Rinder had dreamed of meeting Hubbard as a child; now he was living and working with him on the same ship. One of their first interactions was physical. 'I ran up the stairs and sort of ran into him and he started laughing and said never stop a busy man.'[6] Rinder got to know Hubbard a lot better in the coming years as the Australian made his way up Scientology's hierarchy:

> *I don't think there is anyone who has met the guy who doesn't say that he was larger than life. He was a presence. He was someone that walked into the room and you knew he walked into the room. He was highly intelligent, astonishingly well read and claimed knowledge about so many things. He had a great sense of humour and he was very polite and concerned about the wellbeing of people around him. You hear some people tell stories about how he was like a madman, and I've seen him get upset with people and lose his temper. But that is not what defined him in my experience. In hindsight, and knowing what I now know, I saw what I wanted to see in him – but still, there is no doubt he was larger than life.*[7]

Mike Rinder didn't know at the time, but Hubbard's time on the high seas was drawing to a close. By 1974, Portugal was one of the few countries in the Mediterranean where the *Apollo* was still welcome, but that was about to change. On 25 April, members of the Portuguese military pulled off a coup, restoring democracy, ending conscription and halting the colonial wars being fought in Angola, Mozambique and Portuguese Guinea.

The coup was organised by the Movimento das Forcas Armadas, or MFA, a group of left-wing military officers. The MFA were worried that the CIA was trying to undermine them.[8] The rumours of CIA subversion reached as far as the remote port of Funchal, 1000 km from Lisbon. Graffiti appeared on the walls near the docks stating: 'Apollo = CIA'.

It didn't help the Scientologists that they had told Portuguese port authorities that the *Apollo* was owned by a successful business consultancy.[9] That little piece of deception was an attempt to shield Hubbard from the kind of scrutiny that lead to Hubbard's ill-fated TV interview in Bizerte with Charlie Nairn.[10] Hubbard's medical adviser Jim Dincalci had made contacts among the locals in Funchal and was disturbed by what he found out. 'It seemed to be common knowledge in Madeira that the ship was not what it was supposed to be and most people seemed to think it was a CIA spy ship.'[11]

Dincalci had telexed Hubbard warning him not to dock anywhere in Madeira, but the Commodore had other plans. In early October, Hubbard brought the *Apollo* into Funchal Harbour. He wanted to stage free concerts promoting the ship's band, the Apollo Stars.[12] Hubbard got his rock concert, but not the type he was hoping for.

As Mike Rinder says:

Funchal is a funny place because Madeira is a tiny island and it's in the middle of the Atlantic, there's nothing, and the people there go kinda stir crazy. There is this little section beside the port where there is a row of six cafes where everyone sits around and drinks beer, drinks coffee and talks endlessly. There was an infamous incident where a Dutch naval ship had been in port and some Dutch sailors came in and had been insulting some Portuguese woman so it ended up with a running battle through the streets of Funchal and this became the stuff of legend. So the 'Apollo is CIA' thing started when a bunch of these guys in the cafes stirred themselves up and said let's go get rid of them. So they took a bunch of taxis and they filled the trunks up with stones and they drove the cabs to the docks where there's 500 or 1000 people there who then started chanting 'Apollo is CIA!' and throwing stones.[13]

The protestors meant business. The red Mini Clubman station wagon that Rinder had driven around the island was thrown off the wharf and into the harbour. The ropes that moored the *Apollo* to the docks had been cast off and the ship was now drifting. The crew was being bombarded with rocks. Peter Gillham Jnr witnessed the battle from the sun deck: 'They started pelting us with river stones and then a bunch of the guys on deck got fire hoses out and started hosing them down and it became a bit of a free for all. A few people tried to board but not many. Most of them were content to stay on the dock and throw rocks. They also threw crew members' motorcycles in the drink. I'm standing up there watching this all, going this is really crazy!'[14]

Hubbard stormed onto the deck armed with a bullhorn, and began yelling at the mob, calling them communists and criminals.[15] The locals returned fire. Kima Douglas, standing just a metre away from the Commodore, had her jaw broken by a rock. The *Apollo* pulled up anchor and headed to safer waters. The protestors' attentions now shifted to Mike Rinder who was anchored in his apartment.

The chants of 'Apollo is CIA! You're CIA!' continued outside his apartment from late in the evening till early the following morning. Rinder endured an agonising night. Alone and lying on the floor in the dark he wondered who would come for him first? The protestors? Or the helicopter? By the time the army captain returned it was 5 am. There would be no dramatic rescue from the rooftop. The captain had not been able to secure a chopper, but he did have another plan. If Rinder let a delegation of the protestors into his office, which was connected to his living quarters, they could look through their files and find out for themselves whether they were CIA or not.

The protestors eventually overtook the Scientology apartment. It was bedlam. 'These people came in and start ripping the office apart,' recalls Rinder, 'turning the tables upside down and emptying everything.'[16] They did not find the evidence of CIA infiltration they had been hoping for and the mob soon dissipated. After drawn-out negotiations with customs police, Rinder was eventually allowed to leave at about 9 am.

A lifeboat from the *Apollo* was sent out to pick up the 19-year-old. 'I was greatly relieved,' says Rinder. 'I had a lot of friends in Funchal and I had enjoyed living there, but by this time I knew it would never be the same and I could not stay.' Rinder had survived the first of many dangerous missions on behalf of Scientology. He was happy to be reunited with the crew of the *Apollo*.

With the latest crisis averted, Hubbard realised he had a much broader problem to tackle. The *Apollo* had been kicked out of ports in Greece, Spain, Morocco and Portugal, while the French were investigating him for fraud. Hubbard decided it was time to take a new course. Much to the delight of all the Americans on board, the *Apollo* headed due west, bound for Charleston, South Carolina.

As the *Apollo* cruised towards Charleston, a large reception committee was gathering on the docks. Included were agents from the

Drug Enforcement Administration, US Customs, Immigration, Coast Guard, US Marshalls and the Internal Revenue Service.[17] Federal agents planned to serve Hubbard with a subpoena related to a civil tax case in Honolulu.[18] When a Scientologist onshore was blocked from entering the docks, he realised what was going on and the ship was alerted.[19]

Janis Gillham was with Hubbard when the news came through.

I was on watch with LRH when he was called down to the radio room, because Jane Kember was on the phone and he was like, what? Why is she calling? And here we are, we had just crossed into US waters and Jane is on the phone saying do not enter American waters, there's narcotics agents and the IRS on the docks waiting for you to come in.[20]

Hubbard argued the toss with his wife about whether they should go ashore. Hubbard was full of bravado; Mary Sue feared he would be arrested.[21] 'Everyone could hear them screaming at each other for about two hours,' recalled Hana Eltringham. 'She was adamant that we should not go ashore. She said he would be indicted 10 or 15 times and it would be the end of him and she wasn't going have it.'[22]

With the *Apollo* around 8 km[23] offshore, the ship turned around and headed towards the Bahamas. It was a deflating moment for the crew. They had been looking forward to returning to the US and now they faced the prospect of cruising the high seas indefinitely in a ship that had become overcrowded. 'It was like the black hole of Calcutta,' says Mike Rinder. 'The bunks were six high in an 8-foot bulkhead. To fit everyone in people were sleeping outside in the lifeboats.'[24]

The mood was not helped by the punishment regime that Hubbard had instituted earlier that year. In January, Hubbard issued Flag Order 3434, creating the Rehabilitation Project Force (RPF).[25] Sea Org members entered the RPF if they were discovered to have 'evil intentions' against Hubbard or his technology, displayed poor personality indicators, were caught up in 'trouble making', or had not met satisfactory production levels.[26]

The punishments on the RPF were harsh. Those undergoing rehabilitation were forced to wear black boiler suits, given leftovers for dinner and ordered to run everywhere. They had no free time and were segregated from the rest of the Sea Org. Once put on the RPF, Sea Org members were not allowed to initiate conversations and were forced to do the worst jobs, such as cleaning out the ship's bilges.[27] Gerry Armstrong recalls being forced to sleep in 'a roach-infested, filthy and unventilated cargo hold'.[28] Sea Org members could be sent to the RPF for real or imagined indiscretions.[29] As a result, the RPF created a culture of fear and unchallenged obedience to Hubbard. At one point, around a third of the ship was undergoing rehabilitation.[30]

Janis Gillham was witness to the conversation that led to the creation of the RPF. Hubbard was talking to his public relations aide Laurel Sullivan and to Ken Urquhart, a young musician who at the time had the title of LRH Personal Communicator.

> *I remember standing on the deck with Ken Urquhart, Laurel Sullivan and LRH and he was talking to Ken about setting up a rehabilitation force and Laurel and Ken were throwing in different ideas and I'm standing there thinking this is nuts! And that's how it came about. Ken went away and wrote up the order and it was implemented right away.*[31]

By the end of 1975, Hubbard made the decision to move the Sea Org ashore. Scientologists from the *Apollo* were sent to the US to scope out a place ripe for a Scientology takeover.[32] They found a seaside town in Florida with the perfect name: Clearwater. The small city was a virtual retirement village with over a third of its 100,000 residents over the age of 65.[33] Buildings in the town centre were run down and up for sale. In October 1975, Southern Land Sales and Development Corporation bought the 11-storey Fort Harrison Hotel for US$2.3 million in cash.[34] A few days later, the same company bought the old Bank of Clearwater building down the road for US$550,000.[35]

Local reporters began scrutinising the land deals. It turned out Southern Land Sales and Development Corporation, a company no-one had heard of, was leasing the buildings to the United Churches of Florida, a religious group no-one had heard of. Both were front groups for Scientology.

While the purchases were done undercover, the renovations were not. The sight of a group of serious-looking young men and women in naval uniforms scrubbing old buildings raised the suspicions of local mayor, Gabriel Cazares. 'I am discomfited by the increasing visibility of security personnel, armed with billy clubs and mace, employed by the United Churches of Florida,' he said in a public statement. 'I am unable to understand why this degree of security is required by a religious organization.'[36]

Gabriel Cazares was a man who never shirked a fight. The son of Mexican immigrants, he was a record-breaking middle-distance runner before joining the Air Army Forces. After making the rank of Lieutenant Colonel, he retired from the military, becoming a stockbroker and moving to Clearwater. As a Democrat in a Republican city, Cazares was schooled in political hand-to-hand combat. He would call on every bit of that resilience in his battles with Scientology.

After Mayor Cazares claimed Clearwater was being taken over by Scientologists, the church filed a US$1 million suit against him for libel, slander and violation of civil rights.[37] Scientologists began trawling through public records in an attempt to dig up dirt on Cazares.[38] When that failed to uncover anything, the Guardian's Office cooked up a bizarre fake hit-and-run accident.

When Gabriel Cazares attended a Mayor's Conference in Washington, DC, a Scientologist posing as a journalist asked him for an interview. Cazares agreed. After the interview, a friend of the 'journalist' offered to show the Mayor the sights of the capital. The 'friend', Sharon Thomas, happened to be an agent from the Guardian's Office. As she was driving the Mayor through the streets of the nation's capital, Thomas ran into a pedestrian. The 'pedestrian' was Michael Meisner, a fellow agent with the Guardian's Office. Thomas drove away without stopping.[39]

The Scientologists were sure this incident would implicate Cazares and finish his political career. Dick Weigand, a senior agent with the Guardian's Office, filed a report the following day that stated: 'I should think that the Mayor's political days are at an end.'[40] But Mayor Cazares survived the attempted framing unscathed. When his political opponent Bill Young was offered the potentially compromising information on Cazares, he refused to use it.[41] The failed scheme was a part of a trend of increasingly wacky behaviour coming out of the Guardian's Office. Michael Meisner, the 'victim' of the fake hit-and-run, was at the centre of a reckless operation that would see Mary Sue Hubbard end up in jail.

On 28 April 1973, Hubbard issued a secret order titled 'Snow White Program'. At the time, he was concerned about the growing number of countries who were denying him entry.[42] Hubbard believed he was a victim of false intelligence reports spread by American and English authorities and issued an order that he wanted 'all false and secret files of the nations of operating areas brought to view and legally expunged'.[43] It wasn't long before illegal means were used to expunge secret files. Hubbard tasked the Guardian's Office, under the stewardship of his wife Mary Sue, to achieve his order.

In the US, the Guardian's Office infiltrated an extraordinary range of government departments, foreign embassies, private companies, media organisations and medical associations. The Justice, Treasury and Labor Departments were all targeted, as was the Drug Enforcement Administration.[44] But the agency penetrated to the highest degree was the Internal Revenue Service, the department responsible for tax collection and tax law enforcement.

Michael Meisner was in his third year of a degree at the University of Illinois when a friend introduced him to Scientology.[45] Within months he'd dropped out of college and joined the staff at the Urbana Church of Scientology in Illinois. He trained as an auditor and course supervisor before being recruited to the Guardian's Office in May 1973.[46] Meisner was placed in the intelligence bureau in Washington, DC. He was told his role would include locating, removing and rendering harmless all enemies of Scientology and that this would require infiltration, covert operations and the theft of documents.[47]

In mid-1974, Meisner was instructed to recruit a loyal Scientologist to be placed undercover at the Internal Revenue Service (IRS) in Washington, DC. The recruitment process proved futile, so one of Meisner's superiors, Cindy Raymond, sent Gerald Wolfe, codenamed 'Silver', to do the job. Wolfe successfully infiltrated the IRS on 18 November 1974, when he was employed as a clerk and typist.[48]

Wolfe's strike rate was extraordinary. In the first five months of 1975, he stole and copied around 30,000 pages of documents,[49] a pile of information that stretched ten feet high.[50] The more he stole, the more the Guardian's Office wanted. In May 1975, under instruction from Meisner, Wolfe infiltrated the Tax Division Offices of the Department of Justice over a period of three weekends, pilfering 12 files' worth of notes from departmental attorneys dealing with the trial and pre-trial strategies for upcoming Scientology court cases.

In June, Meisner kickstarted 'Project Beetle Clean-up', an operation designed to obtain all of the IRS files in the Washington, DC office relating to Scientology and Hubbard. The IRS was about to audit the Church of Scientology of California. Wolfe, who had added lock-picking and break-in artist to his duties of clerk/typist, managed to ransack the office of the Chief Counsel of the IRS and steal his files and notes.

The brazen break-ins continued. Charles Zuravin, the IRS attorney who was defending Freedom of Information (FOI) cases against the Scientologists, also had his office looted by Wolfe. Zuravin had already provided Scientology lawyers with a list of IRS documents that were exempt from FOI. This list was passed on to Wolfe, who used it as a form guide for what to steal from Zuravin's office.[51]

The extraordinary success of Wolfe and Meisner's mass theft of secret government documents led to an expansion of the operation. There were plans for up to 5000 Scientologists to infiltrate 136 government agencies across the world.[52] Snow White Operating Targets, or SWOTs, had been drawn up for a range of countries.[53] Project Shoes targeted Algeria, Project Bashful was aimed at Belgium. Project Dopey sought to seize government files in Italy. While in the UK, where the Aliens Act prohibited non-British residents from studying or working for Scientology, Projects Witch and Stepmother were invoked.[54]

In Australia, The Guardian's Office launched Project Dig. This operation wasn't just about destroying government documents. Its more bizarre aims included prosecuting critics under the UN Genocide Convention and smearing conservative politicians. Hubbard was still smarting from the Anderson Inquiry and the bans that followed. The Guardian's Office was ordered to draw up a list of critics, 'including Anderson, psychiatrists, reporters, etc.' and then petition the Attorney-General to invoke the Genocide Convention against them.[55]

The Guardian's Office was ordered to help get the Whitlam Labor government re-elected. Scientologists were concerned the Opposition could reverse Lionel Murphy's changes to the Marriage Act, and that the ban on Scientology in Victoria could be reactivated. The 'genocide plan' is described in the order as 'an invitation for them to pull a Watergate on the opposition – which is to say, label them as criminals'.[56]

The 'genocide plan' was too ludicrous to ever be carried out. But Snow White–style tactics were being implemented in government departments. On 10 April 1975, Victor Kirby pleaded guilty in a Sydney court to fraudulently obtaining a confidential government file on Scientology.[57] Kirby, operating under the stage name of Peter O'Toole, had picked up the file from the NSW Premier's Department under the pretence he was taking it to the Under-Secretary of the Department. When Kirby returned the file the following day he was caught, arrested and charged.

In court, Kirby claimed he had been innocently having a sandwich in Martin Plaza, when a stranger offered him $10 to pick up the file. He denied in a police interview that he had any affiliation with Scientology, despite evidence he had attended 40 or 50 meetings of the cult. Kirby described himself as a salesman from Harris Street, Ultimo,[58] the same street where the Guardian's Office was located at the time.

It's highly likely that Kirby was working out of the Guardian's Office (GO). The GO was separate from other Scientology buildings and part of a highly secretive operation. Agents had to employ cloak-and-dagger tactics to even get inside the building. To enter they had to make a call from a nearby public phone, mention a password or phrase, and then wait for an agent to come down and let them in. The covert operation of simply entering the building could only be done after dark.[59]

One agent within the intelligence wing of the Guardian's Office in Sydney was put through a journalism course at university to help him carry out undercover operations. Under the guise of being a working journalist, Peter Marsh, who requested I give him a pseudonym due to the undercover nature of his work back then, interviewed politicians, attended mental health meetings and turned up at protests. Marsh occasionally wrote articles in the newspaper *Nation Review* and Labor publications under various pseudonyms.

In one article, Marsh launched an attack on NSW Liberal MP Tim Moore. The member for Gordon was considered a threat to Scientology because he had tried to initiate a parliamentary inquiry into the Children of God cult. 'The research we did on him was extensive,' says Marsh. 'It was huge. We interviewed his friends from university, we got photos of him from his university years, including a picture of him dressed as a woman and calling himself the "Paspalum Princess". It was part of a University prank at the time.' After that, Moore's political opponents used the 'Paspalum Princess' title to mock him in parliament.

Part of Marsh's role was to secure files from different sources to find out what information other organisations had on Scientology. Posing as a freelance journalist, Marsh was able to get his way into all the offices of Sydney's main newspapers and photocopy their files on Scientology. He even charmed his way into the archives of the Catholic and Anglican churches, spending hours going through their files on Scientology. Marsh estimates he copied several thousand pages from various sources. But in a classic case of Scientology overreach, he pushed it too far.

At the time, the Church of Scientology was obsessed by Australia's domestic security intelligence service, ASIO. It believed agents were acting beyond ASIO's charter and had played a major role in spreading false information that had led to Scientology being banned in three states.[60] Marsh was sent off to the ASIO offices in Kirribilli to see if he could access the agency's files on Scientology. Not surprisingly, his mission was unsuccessful. But the visit did help ASIO gain more information about Marsh. He had foolishly parked his car near the front of the ASIO building's security cameras. Soon after, Marsh got a knock on the door of his home at 4 am from officials claiming to be from the Attorney-General's department, asking him what he was up to.

The Scientologists did work out the nature of at least some of the information being held in ASIO files. On 29 August 1974, Michael Graham, the President of the Church of the New Faith, wrote to the Director-General of ASIO, Peter Barbour:

> *It has come to our notice that your dossier system contains*
> *information disseminated in Victoria by the late Phillip*
> *Bennett Wearne and others. Such data remaining on your file*
> *is a source of false, defamatory and damaging statements in*
> *respect of our Church and its Australian membership.*[61]

Graham asked that a legal representative be able to view ASIO's
Scientology files and offer correction to any 'false statements'. Barbour
declined the request, responding in classic spook speak:

> *I am not prepared to disclose to you whether or not any*
> *information concerning your Church or its membership is in*
> *the possession of my Organization; and I am not prepared to*
> *comply with the request in the penultimate paragraph of your*
> *letter that a legal representative of your Church be permitted*
> *to examine records of my Organization.*[62]

This was not the last ASIO would hear from Michael Graham.
When the Whitlam government established the Royal Commission
on Intelligence and Security in 1974, Graham fired off a 27-page
submission to the inquiry, accusing ASIO of conspiring with the
CIA in a 'well co-ordinated, covert intelligence operation'[63] which
targeted Scientology. The church submitted that 'it has clear evidence
that indicates that the Australian security services played a hidden
but direct role in the events which led to the improper banning of
a religious movement in Victoria, Western Australia and South
Australia'.[64]

The 27-page document was littered with hearsay, supposition
and inaccuracies. ASIO described it as, 'Though well presented, [it]
appears to be a farrago of little fact, vivid imagination and false
conclusions.'[65] The CIA/ASIO conspiracy is based on claims made by
Wearne that he had close contact with a CIA employee, and ongoing
contact with ASIO to such a high level that he was given a code name.[66]
Declassified ASIO files from the time show Wearne did make regular
contact with the agency, but he was not considered a reliable source.
ASIO's Assistant Director-General at the time described his office as
being 'pestered' by Wearne,[67] 'peddling his claim that Scientology is

a Communist plot'.[68] Wearne was assessed as 'unstable and obsessed about security work' and the Assistant Director-General of ASIO had begun the process of blacklisting him when he died in 1970.[69]

Michael Graham also claimed in his submission to the Royal Commission that Kevin Anderson did not write all of *The Anderson Report*, and was helped by Labor MP Jack Galbally and others. Graham went on to argue that Galbally had connections with ASIO and therefore must've been part of a cover-up. While providing no evidence of Galbally's so-called connections with ASIO, Graham ignores the fact that the longstanding Labor MP disagreed with some of Anderson's key findings, and voted against the bill that banned Scientology, considering it to be a 'direct assault on freedom of speech, thought and ideas'.[70]

Michael Graham saw spies and conspirators wherever he looked, including in the parliament, the judiciary and the newspapers. Justice Kevin Anderson QC was considered to be in on the plot because he'd served in naval intelligence during World War II.[71] Scientology's submission also fingered Sol Chandler from *Truth* as being a British spy, and *Truth*'s campaign against the Scientologists as part of the conspiracy. 'Wearne swears that Chandler told him he worked for MI6,' wrote Graham.

Whether Chandler, who dedicated his life to exposing secrets, was also into keeping them, is unproven; all we have to go on are the claims made by Wearne. In patching together another piece of his conspiracy, Graham was patently wrong. He described Chandler as 'the editor of *Truth* in Melbourne prior to and during the Inquiry'. According to former *Truth* reporter Evan Whitton, Chandler became editorial adviser of *Truth* in late 1965.[72] The inquiry sat from December 1963 to April 1965. *Truth*'s 'Bunkumology' series of articles began in 1961.

ASIO made it clear in its response to the Royal Commission that it was not that interested in the activity of Scientologists.

The Church of Scientology has been of marginal interest to ASIO in a security context. ASIO has not investigated the Church but some of its publicised activities have been recorded. Routine inquiries of (redacted) substantiated ASIO's assessment that the organization should not be regarded as

subversive ... ASIO was not involved in the Victorian inquiry
into that organization or with any alleged police action
against it.[73]

It was not to be the end of the matter. The Church of Scientology would eventually issue a writ against ASIO for smearing and harassing its members, taking it all the way to the High Court.[74] But back in the US, it was Scientology's own intelligence agency that was playing a dangerous game. While it was accusing ASIO and the CIA of conspiracies and cover-ups, the Guardian's Office was knee deep in dirty tricks and criminal behaviour that would soon blow up in its face.

BY THE END OF 1975, L. Ron Hubbard was becoming more and more concerned that he could be implicated in the illegal activities conducted in the name of Operation Snow White. On 5 December, 'Guardian's Program Order 158 – Early Warning System' was issued. It was designed to give notice of any potential legal action against Hubbard and his wife Mary Sue.[75] The order directed agents be placed in the US Attorney's Offices in Washington, DC and Los Angeles, the IRS Office of International Operations, and that agents already in the DEA, IRS and the Coast Guard monitor the situation closely. The newly placed agent in the IRS Office of International Operations was ordered to steal any files on the Hubbards as it was thought a tax evasion case was being prepared.

Over the next few months the break-ins continued across the Justice Department and the IRS. Even the Interpol Liaison Office was raided, with important files stolen concerning terrorism and Interpol's history. The agents from the Guardian's Office were becoming increasingly audacious. They burgled the Office of the Deputy Attorney-General of the United States, Harold Tyler, a former judge who had put away former Tammany Hall leader and onetime Democratic kingmaker Carmine DeSapio.[76]

The Scientologists had a particular loathing for Nathan Dodell, an assistant US Attorney who had represented the government in a number of Scientology cases. He was the target of Operation Big Mouth, a plan to discredit him and get him fired from his job.[77]

On 14 April 1976, when Dodell mentioned during a case hearing that he was open to the possibility of taking sworn evidence from L. Ron Hubbard, the Guardian's Office decided it was time to strike. Meisner and Wolfe by this time had made their own forged IRS identity passes. They used their fake IDs to get into the United States Courthouse building where Dodell's office was located. After one fruitless attempt to break into his office, Wolfe discovered a set of keys left on a secretary's desk. He copied them and the pair returned to the Courthouse building on 21 May under the guise of doing research in the nearby Bar Association library. Over two nights they copied around 3000 pages from Dodell's files.[78] But Operation Snow White was about to come unstuck, courtesy of a fastidious librarian.

As Meisner and Wolfe returned to Dodell's office through the library, to replace the photocopied files, Charles Johnson stopped them. The night librarian asked them whether they had signed in. When Meisner and Wolfe said they hadn't, Johnson told them not to return without specific authorisation from the regular librarian. Johnson notified the US Attorney's office and contacted the FBI. When Meisner and Wolfe returned two weeks later with a letter of authorisation, Johnson once again called the FBI. Special Agents Christine Hansen and Dan Hodges arrived and confronted the two Scientologists at one of the library's back tables. After being questioned for 15 minutes, Wolfe and Meisner were allowed to leave.

After 18 months of covert operations, infiltrating US government departments, breaking into the offices of high-ranking government officials and stealing tens of thousands of documents, the criminal activities of the Church of Scientology had finally been halted by a diligent librarian. Wolfe was arrested at his desk at the IRS. Meisner was harder to track down. On 30 August 1976, two Special Agents with the FBI arrived at the Church of Scientology in Washington, DC with a warrant for his arrest. For the next nine months the Guardian's Office hid Meisner, changing his identity, and at various times holding him against his will. At one point, two Scientology bodyguards removed Meisner from his hideaway by handcuffing him, gagging him and dragging him out of the building.[79]

In June 1977, Meisner escaped, surrendered himself to the FBI and confessed. The following month, over 150 FBI agents, armed with warrants and sledgehammers, raided Church of Scientology buildings in Washington, DC and Los Angeles, seizing over 100,000 pages of documents.[80] Hubbard went into hiding leaving Mary Sue to face the music. Hubbard's wife and ten other officials from the Guardian's Office would eventually be imprisoned in relation to stealing documents, breaking and entering, forging government credentials and bugging at least one government meeting.

Among the documents seized by the FBI were the Guardian's Office plans for Operation Freakout, a conspiracy to frame journalist and Scientology critic Paulette Cooper for bomb threats against Arab consulates, and threats against US President Gerald Ford and US Secretary of State Henry Kissinger.

Janis Gillham, who was one of the Commodore's Messengers at the time Operation Snow White was devised, believes Hubbard was intimately involved in the criminal operations that saw Mary Sue Hubbard go to jail while he remained free. 'Oh, he was in on it,' says Gillham. 'Definitely. Mary Sue would not have done that on her own. He was definitely in on it. I overheard him talking to her about it. He talked to her a lot about Snow White. He was also in on the Paulette Cooper stuff. He knew exactly what was going on with that.'[81]

CHAPTER 14

DEEP SLEEP

BARRY HART WOKE UP from a deep sleep in agony and distress. He was vomiting blood and unable to move his arms or legs. Each breath he took caused paralysing chest pain. He had no idea where he was or what was wrong with him. Hart was close to death. He was suffering from double pneumonia, deep vein thrombosis, pleurisy, a pulmonary embolus and anoxic brain damage. No-one was by his side to ease his torment.

Ten days earlier, the 37-year-old gym owner and part-time model and actor had arrived at Chelmsford Private Hospital in peak physical conditional. At 188 cm and a muscular 90 kg, Hart was fit and in demand, having acted in advertisements for Bonds singlets, Jockey underpants and Magic Tan. Now he was lying naked and nearly lifeless on a trolley, with rubber tubes up his nose and an overwhelming feeling that his head was exploding with white light.[1]

When he tried to alleviate the pain by moving his arms, Hart realised he was shackled. 'Get these things off!' he screamed. He could not understand what was going on, or what version of hell he had descended into.

ON A STICKY FEBRUARY afternoon in 1973, Hart had taken a long cab ride from his gym in the beach-side Sydney suburb of Coogee to Pennant Hills in Sydney's north-west to see psychiatrist Dr John Herron at Chelmsford Private Hospital. His shirt clung to his muscular torso with sweat from the heat and the apprehension. Hart was suffering from anxiety brought on by botched plastic surgery. The surgeon had removed herniated fat from under his eyelids, but had taken away too much tissue, leaving him permanently bug-eyed. He was in a state of great distress. He believed his face was deformed and that his acting and modelling career was over.

A tall, dark-haired woman at the hospital reception asked Hart to sign a form. As he scanned the sheet of paper he noticed a disclaimer giving permission to perform electric shock treatment. Hart recoiled in horror. 'I'm not signing that!' he said. He already knew something about shock treatment from the film *Fear Strikes Out* and wanted nothing to do with it. He was simply there to see a psychiatrist about his anxiety. A nurse asked him if he was nervous. When he admitted he was, the nurse gave him a pill to help calm his nerves. That was the last thing he remembered before he woke up shackled and near death.

For ten days Barry Hart was sedated with near-fatal doses of barbiturates, and while in a drug-induced coma, was given electric shock treatment on six occasions without his consent. His respiratory rate rose from 16 breaths per minute to 150. His temperature peaked at 39.9°C. He became incontinent, cyanosed and went into shock.

Hart was a victim of gross medical negligence and abuse, but he was lucky to be alive. Between 1963 and 1979 over 1000 patients were subjected to deep sleep therapy at Chelmsford.[2] Of those patients, 24 died at the hospital,[3] and another 24 committed suicide within a year of their release, although it's hard to pinpoint how many of these suicides related to pre-existing mental health conditions.[4] The Church of Scientology played a major role in exposing the atrocities committed at Chelmsford, a rare instance where the Scientologists used their undercover operations as a force for public good.

Dr Harry Bailey was responsible for introducing deep sleep therapy to Chelmsford Private Hospital. The psychiatrist had initially worked in the public health system. In 1959, at the age of 37, he had been appointed to the position of Superintendent of Callan Park Mental Hospital by the NSW Labor government. In 1961, he blew the whistle on mismanagement and mistreatment at the hospital, triggering a Royal Commission. But he had bitten the hand that fed him, and the government retaliated by forcing him to resign. He had no option but to go into private practice, opening an office in Macquarie Street.

Bailey had long been interested in the potential of psychosurgery, electroconvulsive therapy (ECT), and deep sedation to treat psychiatric ills. He had learned more about these techniques while travelling on a 15-month World Health Organization fellowship in the mid-1950s.[5] Upon his return he had convinced the NSW government to set up the Cerebral Surgery and Research Unit at Broughton Hall in the grounds of Callan Park. When he moved into private practice, Bailey was able to try out these techniques away from the scrutiny of the public hospital system.

Bailey's experiments with deep sleep therapy at Chelmsford Hospital began in 1963. Working in a ten-bed sedation ward, he put his patients into a coma with barbiturates, often keeping them in a state of narcosis for weeks at a time. Bailey believed the procedure helped shut down a patient's brain, allowing them to be reprogrammed and cleared of mental disorders. While sedated, many patients were subjected to ECT, commonly known as shock treatment.

Bailey used deep sleep therapy to treat a range of disorders, including anxiety, depression, anorexia, post-natal depression, alcoholism and drug addiction. He claimed an 85 per cent success rate for his treatment without ever producing a single piece of credible evidence to back up his claim.

Other psychiatrists had rejected Bailey's theories. A trial of deep sleep therapy at Parramatta Psychiatric Hospital had been discontinued in 1957 after it was deemed too dangerous and unproductive.[6] In 1959, the *American Handbook of Psychiatry* warned that the mortality rate for 'continuous or prolonged sleep treatment' was on average 1 to 3 per cent.[7]

The handbook listed a range of potential complications, including cardiovascular collapse, bronchopneumonia and respiratory depression. Even William Sargant, the British psychiatrist who inspired Bailey's treatment, had warned that 'continuous narcosis has remained the most problematic of all methods of physical treatment in psychiatry, as its results are the least predictable'.[8] Sargant outlined a number of safeguards to minimise the risks of prolonged narcosis, but Bailey ignored them.

These advance warnings from significant figures in the medical profession did not deter Bailey and his fellow Chelmsford doctors,

John Herron, John Gill and Ian Gardiner. Nor did the death toll mounting before their eyes. Twenty-six year old Miriam Podio was admitted for depression and died 16 days later after going into cardiac arrest.[9] Antonios Xigis, a 28-year-old Greek seaman, passed away three days after he was hospitalised with post-traumatic depression.[10] Peter Clarke, a 31-year-old policeman and father of two, died less than half an hour after Herron gave him ECT.[11] Eleven of the 21 people who died were under the age of 40.[12] Young people were dying old people's deaths, from pneumonia, coronary occlusions and cerebral vascular accidents.[13]

Chelmsford Hospital operated like secretive cult. The doctors and psychiatrists were operating in an era and environment where their authority was rarely questioned. Death certificates were falsified.[14] Family members were regularly denied visitation rights and routinely lied to about how seriously ill their loved ones were. The nurses, many of whom were underqualified[15] and desperate for work, didn't dare speak out for fear of losing their jobs; others blindly trusted the doctors.

Barry Hart, however, was determined to get out of Chelmsford and let the world know what was going on. After he had emerged from an enforced 10-day coma, a nurse told him, 'If I were you, I would get out of here – you're sick, you won't get treated for what's wrong with you in here. Get your parents to have you transferred to a public hospital.'[16] But Hart's parents had difficulties visiting him, let alone getting him out. After Barry called them, they arranged for Dr Francis, from nearby Hornsby Hospital, to visit Chelmsford and assess their son. After he examined Barry, Dr Francis called an ambulance, turned to him and said, 'Don't worry. You will live.'[17]

When Hart got out of hospital he realised his life had changed forever. His brain was damaged, his anxiety was far worse, and he was suffering from post-traumatic stress. An overachiever who was used to running his own business and remembering all his lines for theatre productions, he now struggled to recognise friends or remember where he left his house keys. He could no longer sleep in the dark. The bedside light was permanently switched on at night.[18]

Hart was determined to seek justice, but found it difficult to find a competent lawyer willing to take on his case. Finally, two years after he had nearly died at Chelmsford, a solicitor got access to his medical records. When they arrived, what was missing was just as critical as what was there: there was no signed consent form for shock treatment, and the bottom part of the admission slip had been cut off.[19]

The files reinforced what Barry knew was the truth; he had not consented to being sedated and given shock treatment. He showed the documents to Frank Taylor from the *Sydney Morning Herald*, who led with the front-page scoop on 11 November 1975. The headline said it all. 'Shock treatment protest, given against my will, says actor'.[20]

The *Herald* had been planning to run a series on the abuse of mental health patients, but the sacking of the Whitlam government that afternoon buried Hart's story and the series.[21] Herron and his colleagues at Chelmsford had dodged another bullet. A *Herald* series would surely have brought out more victims of Chelmsford and put pressure on the government to act. It may have even prevented more deaths.

Around the same time of the *Herald* revelations, Rosa Nicholson was planning her own exposé.[22] Dark-haired, chubby and in her mid-30s, Nicholson worked shifts at various hospitals and nursing homes around Sydney. Caring and bright, Rosa was popular with colleagues and the people she nursed. 'She was very sweet,' says former Chelmsford matron Marcia Fawdry. 'She was lovely with the patients.'[23]

Rosa Nicholson became the central figure in exposing the truth about the dozens of deaths caused by medical malpractice inside Chelmsford Hospital, but she did not do it alone. The Church of Scientology was deeply involved, but the truth about its role has remained a deep secret for over 35 years. Although it was to be Scientology's finest hour in Australia, the organisation has never come clean about its true role in the covert operations that led to the exposé.

Rosa Nicholson had an affinity for the vulnerable and mistreated. The eldest of four children, she was raised by a mother who rejected her from birth. 'Her mother was a harridan,' a relative told me. 'The way she treated Rosa made a mess of her life.'[24] Determined to treat others with the love and care she had missed out on, Rosa became a de facto mother for her three younger siblings and cared deeply for her patients. But her upbringing also made her emotionally fragile and vulnerable to the flattery and false promises of the Church of Scientology.

The way Rosa told her story, she first came across the horrors of Chelmsford Hospital on 8 November 1972 as a trainee psychiatric nurse sent by her agency to fill a shift at the hospital.[25] She said she was horrified by the high doses of drugs being administered by nurses and the lack of supervision by doctors.[26] The experience made a lasting impression on her:[27]

> *When I lifted the sheets off each patient, they were a mix of men and women in the same room. There was no partitioning. I noticed some were bleeding – at least two were bleeding from the mouth. They were all wet, and a couple had had faeces – they had emptied their bowels – and one had vomited.*[28]

Rosa Nicholson didn't do another shift at Chelmsford for over four years. When she returned as an undercover agent, she copied and removed medical records that became key pieces of evidence exposing a horror show of sustained medical malpractice and abuse.

Rosa claimed she tried to blow the whistle on Chelmsford from the earliest moment possible by writing to the Nurses Association and the Health Department to tell them what was going on at the private hospital. She said the complaint went nowhere and that she was consumed by guilt for not taking it further when a friend, the artist Arnold St Clair, died at Chelmsford in 1974. She spoke to her brother-in-law, who was a journalist, but he told her eyewitness reports were not enough, she needed documentary evidence to blow the whole thing open.[29]

The turning point came when she met a nurse called Brieda while working in an emergency ward in 1974. The two had an instant connection.[30] 'She said as a matter of fact, I'm doing Scientology,' Rosa recalled, 'and I turned around and said, "you're joking?" And she kind of looked at me for a moment, and I said, "My aunt's clear."'[31]

The conversation turned to shock treatment. Brieda told Rosa how Scientology campaigned against psychiatric abuses: 'She said, "We have got a guy in there you know who fights ECT," and I said, "You're joking. In the church?" And she said, "In the Guardian's

Office. So all he does is fight and expose ECT and other abuses," and
I said, "I want to meet him."'[32] The man Rosa Nicholson wanted to
meet was Ron Segal, a Scientologist and the President of the Citizen's
Commission for Human Rights (CCHR).

The CCHR was formed in 1969 by the Guardian's Office[33]
and is, in its own words, 'dedicated to investigating and exposing
psychiatric violations of human rights'.[34] In the years leading up to
the CCHR's formation, Hubbard launched an attack on psychiatry.
In a confidential directive labelled Project Psychiatry he ordered that
private investigators be hired to dig up dirt on psychiatrists in the
UK. 'We want at least one bad mark on every psychiatrist in England,
a murder, an assault, or a rape or more than one,' it read. 'This is
Project Psychiatry. We will remove them.'[35]

Hubbard blamed psychiatrists for the attacks on Scientology
in the US, UK and Australia.[36] In a confidential memo written for
Mary Sue in the year the CCHR was set up, Hubbard announced that
Scientology's ultimate goal of 'clearing the planet' had been replaced by
something far more sinister – destroying psychiatry and other mental
health practices. Under the heading 'The War', the secret memo lists
the new priority as: 'To take over absolutely the field of mental healing
on this planet in all forms … Our total victory will come when we run
his organisations, perform his functions and obtain his financing and
appropriations.[37]

Hubbard was not just gunning for contemporary mental health
practitioners; he claimed that 75 million years ago, psychiatrists
helped carry out genocide in the Galactic Confederacy.[38] In a 1970
memo, he claimed psychiatrists and psychologists 'opened the door
to death camps in Hitler's Germany' and 'gave Hitler to the world
as their puppet'.[39] To this day, the CCHR argues psychiatrists were
responsible for the Holocaust.[40]

In the mid-1970s, the Australian chapter of the CCHR set its
sights on shutting down psychosurgery and ECT. But its President,
Ron Segal, a pharmacist from Sydney's southern suburbs, did not share
Hubbard's rabid hatred of psychiatry as a whole. As a pharmacist
he understood the benefits of pharmaceutical drugs and did not
believe that all psychiatrists were dangerous. Although a dedicated
Scientologist, he was happy to work with non-believers to expose

abuses within the mental health sector. Many of his campaigns relied on information leaked from doctors, nurses and even psychiatrists.

As a pharmacist, Segal was used to dealing with people from all walks of life. Peter Marsh (a pseudonym), an undercover agent with the Guardian's Office, remembers that he was well connected with community groups and that he bore an uncanny resemblance to Scientology's founder. 'He looked like Hubbard, and people in the Sydney Org would say, "Hi, Ron!" and it would freak the newbies out.'[41] Segal's grandparents emigrated from Lithuania to escape the pogroms, but many of his relatives perished in the Holocaust. His family history instilled in him a lifelong commitment to standing up for the persecuted, the voiceless and exposing human rights abuses.

Rosa Nicholson insisted she first met Ron Segal in 1975 at the office the CCHR shared with the Church of Scientology, near Sydney's Central Railway Station, and it was then that she put forward a plan to go undercover at Chelmsford.[42] She later testified that she had told Ron Segal, 'I've got a brilliant idea. I'm going to go back there and get evidence and I'll give it to you because it looks like you can do something about it.'[43] Rosa boasted that she could get a camera into Chelmsford to take photographs of Harry Bailey, and sneak files out of the hospital to have them photocopied.[44]

Rosa Nicholson eventually returned to work at Chelmsford Hospital on 28 February 1977, carrying a list of files she and Ron Segal had decided they needed copies of.[45] 'He (Segal) would have complaints from patients or relatives,' Rosa recalled, 'and I would supply whatever he needed as well.'[46]

In what must have been a nerve-racking operation, Rosa would sneak into the matron's office and look through the filing cabinets. After consulting her 'homework list' she would remove the relevant files and place them under a cushion on a chair near the door. Eventually she would take the files out to her car, which was parked near the front door of the hospital.[47]

Rosa hoovered up documents with all the courage and efficiency of Meisner and Woolfe in Operation Snow White. She photocopied the daily nursing notes and removed blank drug sheets that had been pre-signed by Bailey and Herron. After each shift she compiled her own notes, documenting who had been admitted and how they were treated. Rosa also took six of the 'red books', ledgers containing daily reports and information that proved critical for subsequent court cases and inquiries, and salvaged a number of ECT books from the rubbish bin, which showed doctors defrauding the patient's health funds.[48]

Rosa Nicholson removed and copied critical files from Chelmsford Hospital for over a year. Marcia Fawdry, the Matron of Nursing whose office Rosa had ransacked, had no inkling of what was going on. 'I was shocked when I found out,' she says. 'We had no idea what she had been up to.'[49] Rosa was living a double life, acting as a confidante to Fawdry and helping to pick up her children after school, then raiding her office at night. Fawdry is still amazed that Nicholson was able to execute her undercover operation while continuing to be so diligent with her patients. 'She was very warm and caring,' she says. 'The patients loved her.'[50]

Nicholson was appalled at what she witnessed inside Chelmsford. The patients who survived deep sleep therapy woke up heavily traumatised. 'They would be hallucinating,' she recalled. 'They would be flailing – some would flail their arms around and they would be frightened, terribly frightened. They would be seeing things, hearing things.'[51] Many were given deep sleep therapy without their consent, and, when they regained consciousness, were 'delirious and frightened, unable to walk, unable to move their bowels because the bulk waste had settled in their bowels'.[52]

Rosa Nicholson was particularly damning about the cavalier attitude of the doctors. Although Bailey was making hundreds of thousands of dollars out of his patients, he was rarely there and Rosa had been back at Chelmsford for three weeks before she even saw him.[53] When nurses contacted Bailey during emergencies, he was often dismissive or abusive. According to Rosa, the nurses who dared to ring Bailey 'would come in feeling rattled and nervous because he'd just given them a barrage of abuse over the phone for being so ignorant and stupid as to ring him when they should be working it out themselves'.[54]

But Bailey was the one who was about to feel rattled. Rosa did her last shift at Chelmsford Hospital in April 1978.[55] By then she had photocopied over 100 files comprising a catalogue of psychiatric abuse and malpractice.[56] Now she was safely out, Ron Segal was able to go public with what they had found. He compiled a dossier of key documents and arranged a meeting with Frank Walker, the New South Wales Attorney-General. It helped that Segal operated outside of the Scientology bubble. Married with two children, he was an active member of the Labor Party and he and Walker knew each other from local branch meetings. The Attorney was aware of Segal's Scientology connections, but took the claims seriously, especially when confronted with the evidence. Walker was disturbed by what he was confronted with and handed over Ron Segal's dossier to a policy analyst in his department for further investigation.[57]

The contrast between Operation Snow White and Segal's operation could not have been starker. Whereas Scientologists in the US had burgled the Office of the Deputy Attorney-General, in Sydney a key Scientologist attended party meetings with the state Attorney-General and gave him a private briefing.

Meanwhile, Harry Bailey was beginning to feel the heat. The CCHR ramped up the pressure through letter-writing campaigns and public protests. They held a rally outside the Attorney-General's office demanding that the inquest into the suicide death of Sharon Hamilton be reopened. In a letter to the Attorney-General, the CCHR had pointed out that Hamilton was not only Bailey's patient, but also his lover, and that the psychiatrist had become the executor and sole beneficiary of her will.[58] The media reported on the rally, and the publicity gave Chelmsford victims and staff the courage to contact the CCHR – although at least one withdrew her statement when she discovered the CCHR was a Scientology front.[59]

The Hamilton protest coincided with the increased involvement of Jan Eastgate, a dogged 24-year-old campaigner who would eventually become the International President of the CCHR. Segal had left his post at the CCHR to give more time to his family and his business. Within months, Jan Eastgate had taken over his role. While Segal was not anti-psychiatry, considering himself instead to be opposed to psychiatric abuses, she took a more hardline stance.

Eastgate had two compelling reasons to crusade against psychiatry in all its forms. As a teenager in Melbourne, she was given shock treatment for depression. At one point she had run away from psychiatrists, now she was in the mood to confront them head-on.

'When I ran away from the private hospital because I didn't want any further ECT,' she told Susan Geason, the author of *Dark Trance*, a retelling of the Chelmsford story, 'a psychiatrist came after me and threatened me with committal to a state psychiatric institution for life. When I returned to the hospital, he promptly discharged me. He just wanted the upper hand.'[60]

In 1977, Eastgate moved to Sydney and was introduced to the Church of Scientology by a friend,[61] but there were limitations placed on which Scientology services she could access because she was a former psychiatric patient. 'She was what they call in Scientology an illegal PC,' says Peter Marsh, who shared a house with Eastgate. 'In other words, she could not be audited – because of her psychiatric history.'[62]

Eastgate was ambitious, but her personal history was blocking her progress. According to Marsh she had only two options: 'As an illegal PC there's a couple of routes you can go forward in Scientology. One is to get trained up as an auditor and demonstrate a production record in delivering Scientology. The other way is to do something extraordinarily brave and courageous in terms of defending Scientology or attacking the enemy. Jan went that route.'[63]

Eastgate, who described herself as a human rights fighter,[64] joined the CCHR in January 1978[65] and by the end of the year she was President of Scientology's anti-psychiatry lobby group in Australia.[66] Peter Marsh, who lived with her at the time, says he never saw a more committed campaigner. 'She was quite relentless in pursuing the scientological goal of "eradicating psychiatry", she just never let up. I'd describe her anti-psych demeanour as being like someone who was on a "Mission from Ron". She seemed 100 per cent committed to taking down the psychs.'[67]

In October, Attorney-General Frank Walker wrote to the Health Minister Kevin Stewart, enclosing Ron Segal's CCHR dossier, which included blank treatment sheets signed in advance by Bailey,[68] and asked him to investigate Chelmsford.[69] The same month the newspaper *Sunday* told its readers that three patients had died from deep sleep therapy practised in a 'zombie room' in a Sydney hospital. The article was based on information disseminated by the CCHR at a public meeting.[70]

Under Eastgate's stewardship the CCHR continued to lobby politicians and the media. While previous claims made by Scientologists were dismissed as part of an elaborate conspiracy theory, this time they had proof, thanks to the dossier compiled by Ron Segal using the documents obtained by Rosa Nicholson.

But in the crusade to get justice for the victims of Chelmsford, the involvement of the Scientologists proved both a blessing and a curse. Kevin Stewart did not trust the evidence the Attorney-General had sent to him because it had been obtained and passed on by the CCHR.[71] As Shadow Minister for Health he'd had what he later described as 'a very unpleasant and nasty experience' with the CCHR.[72] They had been behind a letter he had received at his electorate office in Campsie enclosing a statutory declaration from a former patient at Rozelle Psychiatric Hospital, alleging 'maltreatment, forced treatment, treatment without consent, brutality, nearly everything you could allege about psychiatric treatment'.[73]

Stewart passed the letter onto the then Minister for Health, asking him to investigate the matter. But a fortnight later, he received a letter from the former mental health patient withdrawing the allegations, saying they were untrue and made up under duress from the CCHR.[74] Stewart then had to write to the Minister withdrawing his demands for an investigation. He felt he had been duped.

When a CCHR representative visited Stewart's office to find out what was going on, a heated exchange took place. Stewart could not remember the woman's name, but around 15 years later he testified that she was angry with him for withdrawing his calls for an investigation:

She said, 'How dare you do that. We thought we could depend on you, the opposition spokesman to help us in this matter. We have been trying for a long time to get evidence and declarations to embarrass the government, to force the government into a Royal Commission into mental health in New South Wales.'[75]

Stewart told the woman he would no longer accept representations from her organisation.[76] Now, as Minister for Health, Stewart did not trust the Scientologists. Nonetheless, he promised Walker he would look into the allegations and handed over responsibility to Dr Sydney Hing, the head of the Private Hospitals Branch of the Health Commission, and a close friend of his.[77]

Hing was not the ideal man to launch a thorough investigation. He had already refused to look into allegations made by Barry Hart in 1975,[78] and when he visited Chelmsford Hospital in October 1978 he could find nothing wrong. Hing did not look very hard: he failed to visit the sedation ward; interview the nursing staff; or review any of the patients' records.[79] He took no notes and took no records of the names of patients or nurses who used to work there.[80]

Dr Hing did not even make a written report about his inspection, leaving it to a nurse who accompanied him.[81] He failed to direct anyone to return to Chelmsford for a follow-up inspection. Kevin Stewart had promised Frank Walker that the Department of Health would conduct a full investigation,[82] but he delivered nothing of the sort. Hing's bungled investigation would not be the end of the matter.

In February 1980, seven years after he was given shock treatment without his consent, Barry Hart got his day in court. The former gym owner sued Dr John Herron and the company that ran Chelmsford Hospital in the NSW Supreme Court. However, Hart had no reason to feel confident, as no ex-psychiatric patient in Australian history had successfully sued a psychiatrist for unlawful treatment.

Representing Barry was Edward St John QC, an establishment man who didn't mind upsetting the establishment. As a barrister he had defended *Oz* magazine in their first obscenity trial, and in his one event-filled term in parliament had upset two Prime Ministers from his own side of politics, Harold Holt by forcing a second inquiry into the sinking of the *Voyager*, and John Gorton by making allegations of impropriety.

Three days before the trial, Barry Hart was in St John's Chambers in Sydney, when the silk received a phone call from Tom Hughes QC, who was representing the defendants.[83] Hughes told his old Liberal parliamentary colleague he would be calling a surprise witness, a male nurse who would argue that Hart had given verbal consent to be treated at Chelmsford.

Recalling that the 'zombie room' exposé in *Sunday* two years earlier had mentioned the CCHR, Hart rang the organisation to see if they had any information on Brian Dilworth, the nurse who was going to testify against him. They invited him to their office to review their files. What he saw when he got there astonished him – the CCHR had the red day-books from Chelmsford Hospital: 'They had a pile of them, about half a metre high,' he said.[84]

Barry Hart could not find anything on Dilworth, nor his own admission form. But he struck gold when he noticed that an identification sheet from another patient contained a 'signed consent' form at the bottom. His solicitor had sent him a copy of his own sheet three years earlier, and there was no consent form on the bottom. After Hart's original clinical notes were subpoenaed, his lawyers discovered the original identification sheet was shorter than the rest of the document. The consent form for shock treatment had been cut off.[85]

The stolen files provided by the Scientologists helped Barry Hart win his case. The jury of 11 found unanimously that Hart had been falsely imprisoned and found on a 9–2 majority in favour of his claim of assault and battery against Herron.[86] But Hart was only awarded $60,000 in damages, nearly half of which went in legal expenses. The payout was so miserly that Hart had to go on the disability pension. Justice Fisher withdrew any possibility of punitive damages against the defendants, which could have resulted in a much larger payout, because he believed that Hart had not suffered long-term damage, was fit for work and only deserved a minimal payout.

Legal academic Brian Bromberger, who observed the trial, told Susan Geason that he felt Justice Fisher was not impressed with the role the Scientologists played in the case. 'My suspicion is that Fisher was appalled at the involvement of Jan Eastgate. I remember Barry being asked on a number of occasions whether he was a Scientologist or had attended Scientology meetings ... Sperling [counsel for the defence] made it look as though Jan Eastgate was pulling the strings in an attempt to discredit psychiatry in general as well as Herron.'[87]

When Scientology promotional material was found in the jury room during the trial, Dr Herron's lawyers tried to argue the Scientologists were trying to influence the jury. Hal Sperling unsuccessfully applied to have the jury dismissed and it was Eastgate's belief that someone had planted the literature to cause a mistrial.[88] Despite all of this, by securing documentary evidence, the Scientologists did help Hart win his court case.

Emboldened by Hart's victory, the CCHR took copies of the Chelmsford medical files to Channel Nine's *60 Minutes* program. Jan Eastgate met with Anthony McClellan, a young producer on the program. 'Jan was blonde, charming but intense,' he recalled. 'She knew how to work the media. I'm sure I knew the CCHR was a front organisation, but they had the documents, which was all that mattered.'[89]

'The Chelmsford File', presented by Ray Martin, revealed that at least seven people had died during or after deep sleep therapy between 1974 and 1977.[90] Martin had gathered compelling testimonies from Barry Hart, Denise Clarke, the widow of policeman Peter Clarke, and Vera Francis, whose sister Audrey had died while a patient of Dr Herron.

The program won a Logie award for Outstanding Public Affairs Report. McClellan has no doubt it would never have aired without the help of the Scientologists. 'We couldn't have done it without the documents,' he says. 'There was no way of proving what the doctors were doing without them, and I doubt the lawyers would have let us run the story.'[91]

The *60 Minutes* program shocked the public. Voters rang and wrote to their local MPs demanding an investigation into deep sleep therapy. Many demanded a Royal Commission, but the NSW government stalled. Police investigations and Health Commission inquiries were launched, but with the investigations caught up in legal and bureaucratic red tape, the Chelmsford doctors continued to avoid accountability for their actions. In 1983, the victims finally had a win when deep sleep therapy was outlawed under the Mental Health Act.

However, it was not until 1985 that the justice system started to catch up with Harry Bailey. A former patient, Patricia Vaughan, who had suffered brain damage from deep sleep therapy in 1977, took civil action in the Supreme Court. Bailey's lawyers told him it was unlikely he would win the case and that he could face a lifetime of litigation.[92]

On the day before the Vaughan case was due to begin, Bailey's legal team held a conference. They had bad news. They had contacted William Sargant, the doctor who had inspired Bailey's treatment methods, but Sargant told them that if he were called to give evidence, he would have to support the prosecution rather than the defence.[93]

Harry Bailey returned to his home in Haberfield and told Helen MacArthur, his secretary and girlfriend, that 'it's not worth going on'.[94] He left their home without speaking another word. He drove up the F3 to the Central Coast of NSW, pulled off the freeway and took an isolated dirt track near Mount White. After parking his car, he pulled out a handful of capsules of Tuinal, the drug he had used to sedate his patients at Chelmsford and swigged them down with a bottle of Heineken. Bailey's body was found slumped over his steering wheel by a highway patrolman at 1 pm the following day.

Bailey left a suicide note that said in part:

I apologise to my patients for deserting them after so long. Let it be known that the Scientologists and the forces of madness have won.

People should be warned that such cults are a danger to our society, and they should be crushed.

Drs like Ellard and Wade and Holland and Smith are equally to be abhorred. They are egocentric crazies almost as bad as the Scientologists.[95]

In the years following Bailey's death, the CCHR continued their campaign for a Royal Commission, but the victims were losing hope. Labor MP Pat Rogan made a number of speeches to parliament, repeatedly calling for a judicial inquiry while helping to set up the Chelmsford Victims' Action Group. Invariably, after speeches to parliament, Rogan's chief of staff, Margaret Como, would be bombarded with phone calls from victims and their families.

Como, a mother in her 30s, was smart, media savvy and a relentless campaigner. She had to be. No-one was keen to pick up the story. 'Every door we knocked on was closing. It was really, really hard,' she says.[96] The victims' stories touched her deeply. She knew those stories were the key to gaining support for a Royal Commission. In 1988, Como took around 50 victims and family members to meet *Sydney Morning Herald* journalists Robert Haupt and John O'Neill at the Fairfax building at Broadway.

A theatrette in the building was booked, and as the Chelmsford victims piled in, Como approached Haupt. 'I said, "You know you are their last hope",' recalls the former Labor staffer.[97] As the victims got up one by one and bravely told their stories, Haupt and O'Neill knew they were onto something big. For two weeks across July and August the *Sydney Morning Herald* ran a hard-hitting series that exposed the impact of the medical abuses of Chelmsford Hospital on dozens of victims and their families.

Margaret Como mobilised the electronic media to follow up on the *Herald*'s campaign, and the calls for a judicial investigation grew louder. On 6 August, the *Herald* ran an editorial titled 'Time for a Royal Commission'. Later that day, the Greiner government announced there would be an inquiry.[98]

The Royal Commission ran for close to two years. Nearly 300 witnesses gave evidence, including patients, nurses, the surviving Chelmsford doctors, senior bureaucrats and former Ministers.

The final report ran close to two million words. It revealed that at least 24 deep sleep therapy patients had died at Chelmsford Hospital between 1963 and 1979, with another 24 committing suicide within a year of being released. The commission found that Bailey falsified as many as 17 death certificates[99] and that many patients received treatment without their consent.[100] The Department of Health was criticised for neglecting to carry out proper checks at the hospital and for failing to investigate the deaths.[101]

While the report exposed the truth about deep sleep therapy and how it was practised at Chelmsford, it never quite got to the bottom of the role the Church of Scientology played in exposing it.

In his summary Justice Slattery wrote:

After Miss Nicholson resigned from Chelmsford in April 1978, she became a member of the Church of Scientology, remaining so until 1983. There was considerable reference in the evidence to this ... So far as my terms of reference are concerned the only relevance that the Church of Scientology bears is that Mr Segal in his capacity of the CCHR delivered various Chelmsford records to the then Attorney General Mr Walker in 1978.[102]

Justice Slattery chose not to challenge Rosa Nicholson's story. Anyone with an understanding of Scientology history would cast a sceptical eye over Rosa's version of events. From the time I first heard of her heroic undercover exploits, I had assumed the Church of Scientology had planted her inside Chelmsford Hospital.

For decades, Hubbard had been waging a war against psychiatry, and Scientology had a long history of using undercover agents. At the same time Rosa was said to be planning her covert operation at Chelmsford, Scientologists in the US were infiltrating the Justice Department and the Internal Revenue Service, stealing tens of thousands of documents as part of Operation Snow White. Project Dig, the Australian arm of Snow White, had advocated targeting psychiatrists.[103] Peter Marsh (a pseudonym), a former undercover spy for the Guardian's Office, confirmed my suspicions, telling me, 'I have no doubts whatsoever that Rosa was recruited to spy for the Guardian's Office; that's just standard operating procedure.'[104]

As we learned from Operation Snow White, Scientologists would often adopt what they refer to as a 'shore story', a well-rehearsed, plausible story that would, if they were caught, explain who they were and what they were doing, without implicating the Church of Scientology.

The story that Rosa had given to explain her undercover work at Chelmsford was detailed: that first night shift; the unanswered complaints; Arnold St Clair's death; the meeting with the Scientologist Brieda; the introduction to Ron Segal at the CCHR; and her plan to go into Chelmsford undercover to get evidence. Could it be that this was a classic Scientology 'shore story'?

As I made my way through the Royal Commission transcripts, holes in Rosa Nicholson's story became apparent. There was no record of the complaint she had made to the Health Department in 1972.[105] Her aunt, who was meant to be a Scientologist, was not really her aunt.[106] She testified that she did not know that former CCHR President Ron Segal was a Guardian, even though she had previously told journalist Toni Eatts that he was.[107]

At the Royal Commission, Rosa was particularly cagey about anything to do with Scientology. Under cross-examination she said she could not remember who her auditor was.[108] At one stage she admitted she used to attend Scientology's weekly religious service, but could not remember what day it was on.[109] (It is known universally as the Sunday Service.) She testified that she joined the Church of Scientology straight after leaving Chelmsford Hospital in 1978, a claim that would allow the church plausible deniability in relation to her actions. It was as if she was trying to distance herself from the Church of Scientology and protect them from claims they had planted her in Chelmsford to remove medical files.

Some of the most contentious evidence given at the Royal Commission came from Rosa. She claimed she was at a key meeting of senior Chelmsford staff where they had discussed how they could alter Barry Hart's admission form so it looked like he had consented to ECT. Rosa had previously made this claim to Toni Eatts, repeated it to police and now had put it on oath at the Royal Commission. Marcia Fawdry said Nicholson was not there. The former matron is still stunned that Rosa would make the claim. 'I don't know why she said that,' says Fawdry. 'She was a nursing assistant. It was a meeting of the executive.'[110] Justice Slattery generously described Rosa's version of events as 'mistaken'.[111]

It is highly likely that Marcia Fawdry told Rosa about what happened at the meeting, and that information was passed on to the journalist Toni Eatts. If Rosa placed herself at the meeting, Eatts could report it as first-hand testimony rather than hearsay. Dr Herron's counsel at the Royal Commission, John Sackar QC, accused Nicholson of lying. 'You are making this story up,' he said, 'and you have continued to make this story up over the years.'[112]

The Sydney silk grilled the whistleblower nurse relentlessly, asking her why she had not even contacted Barry Hart when he was taking legal action against Herron. After all, this was an explosive piece of evidence that would have exposed a conspiracy to falsify Hart's medical records. Rosa told the commission she did not pass the evidence on to Hart because 'I had not met him'.[113]

Sackar continued to press Nicholson. The barrister asked if she had even followed the progress of Hart's court case in the newspapers. 'No, I didn't,' said Nicholson under oath.[114] This was inconceivable. How could a nurse who had dedicated herself to working undercover for 14 months to expose the Chelmsford doctors not even follow the first court case taken by the hospital's most high-profile victim against one of the doctors?

When I met journalist Susan Geason, who had meticulously researched the story for her unpublished book *Dark Trance*, I found out she had worked on the assumption that Rosa had all along been a spy for the Scientologists, and had uncovered further parts of Rosa's story that did not make sense. Geason had managed to track down a relative of Rosa's who confirmed there was no Scientologist aunt, either biological or honorary, and that it was 'highly improbable that Rosa would have been friends with Arnold St Clair, as she did not move in arty circles'.[115] When I spoke with another relative, that person cast further doubt on the story that she had joined the Church of Scientology in 1978. 'In my mind,' the relative told me, 'I've always thought she was into Scientology and under their influence before she took that fateful casual shift as a night nurse.'[116]

Susan Geason had concluded that Ron Segal sent Rosa in as a spy:

> *Segal was an experienced organiser – he had led the Scientologists' campaign against psychosurgery – and as a Guardian ... would have had the backing of the church hierarchy. If this is the case, Rosa's stories about the sleuthing operation being her own idea were designed to protect the church.*[117]

Rosa's relative, who had spoken to Geason under the condition they remained anonymous, thought the author's theory made sense. 'She wouldn't have known how to go about it by herself. Rosa was the classic target for the Scientologists. She had a difficult upbringing and was a bit adrift. She was looking to belong.'[118]

Geason was unable to track down Ron Segal to test her theory. He was not in the phone book, and public company records listed businesses that had long closed down. All of my Scientology contacts drew a blank; they had not heard of Segal for years. I was about to knock on the doors of a few old addresses I had gleaned from electoral rolls and company records, when a contact told me they had found an email address. My heart sank when she told me it was an OzEmail account, an old email provider from the Internet's stone age. My hunch was that Segal was dead and that I would never get to the bottom of what happened. Rosa Nicholson could not give her version of events. She had suffered a stroke in 2002 and could no longer speak.

I punched out an email to Ron Segal's OzEmail account, resigned to the fact I would get no response. A few days later, to misappropriate a Scientology term, Ron came back. He called me at home moments before I was due to leave to go to the NRL Grand Final. I told him I wanted to talk about Chelmsford and asked if we could meet the following day. He agreed.

The next day, Ron welcomed me into the apartment he shares with his wife. In his late 70s, he was sharp of mind and happy to talk about the extraordinary events surrounding the Chelmsford operation. Segal had kept his files from over 35 years ago, which include newspaper clippings, legal opinions, the dossier he prepared for Frank Walker and copies of Harry Bailey's pre-signed drug treatment forms. He remains proud of the role he played in exposing the medical abuses of Bailey and his fellow Chelmsford doctors.

Within minutes of my arrival, Segal confirmed that he was the mastermind behind the operation. It was he who decided to put Rosa into Chelmsford undercover. 'She was attracted to the CCHR because she was concerned about violations of human rights,' he said. 'She had a lot of integrity and she wanted to do something. I said to her would you be prepared to work at Chelmsford and she was. I told her what I was looking for and she got it. She did a very good job.'[119]

Before Rosa came on the scene, Segal had already been planning a covert operation. The CCHR had placed advertisements in newspapers calling on people who had been victims of psychiatric abuses to contact them. Dozens of Chelmsford victims and family members rang his office. Segal knew that victims' testimonies would not be enough; he had to get evidence from the inside. 'I knew what to do but I didn't have anyone to do it,' says Segal, 'and then Rosa comes along and we became a team.'[120]

The operation was very much a team effort. Ron needed Rosa's courage and commitment; she needed his encouragement and advice. 'I don't want to anyway reduce the importance of Rosa in this because she is a heroine to me,' says Segal, 'but she would never have done it on her own. She needed someone like me.'[121]

Segal convinced Rosa that they were morally right to engage in an undercover operation and that copying and removing medical records was not illegal. He pointed out to Rosa that under the law, one of the key elements of theft was an intention to permanently deprive the owner of their property. 'If what we did was theft,' says Segal, 'then the Attorney-General was guilty of receiving stolen goods.'[122]

As a young man, Segal had gained a rare insight into the kind of strategic planning required for successful undercover operations. His neighbour worked in the NSW Police Force's infamous 21 Division and shared his stories of various operations, including how they were able to shut down SP bookmakers in country towns. Segal learned all about covert operations, the importance of planning and keeping secrets. 'They considered the local constabulary in the country towns to be part of the criminal network,' he said. 'My neighbour taught me about the importance of working in isolation and not letting other people know what's going on.'[123] Segal applied what he had learned from his neighbour to the Chelmsford operation.

While many former Scientologists I had spoken to were sure that Rosa's undercover operation must have been run out of the Guardian's Office, Segal kept Scientology's agents completely in the dark. He treated B1, the intelligence wing of the Guardian's Office, with the same contempt the 21 Division had for country coppers during their SP bookmaker raids. After the disaster of Operation Snow White, Segal did not want them anywhere near his operation. 'I reckon they are the biggest bunch of dickheads the world has seen,' he says. 'I thought the GO's ideas of covert ops were idiotic, and that's why I wouldn't let them know what I was up to.'[124] Segal did not reveal the details of the Chelmsford operation to other Scientologists until he handed over his dossier to the Attorney-General.[125]

Ron Segal says he was not even aware of Project Dig, the Australian arm of Operation Snow White, which the Guardian's Office was meant to implement, and included targeting psychiatrists. 'I've never heard of it,' he told me. The pharmacist was opposed to psychiatric abuses, but saw no point in going after the whole profession. 'I had psychiatrists inside the system helping me and giving me information,' he says: 'If I was anti-psychiatry, I'd be anti-the people helping me and providing the information I needed.'[126]

So was Rosa Nicholson a Scientologist when she was working inside Chelmsford? Under oath at the Royal Commission, she said she joined the Church of Scientology in 1978 after she finished working at the hospital.[127] This was misleading according to Segal. 'I believe a more truthful interpretation would be to say she was a Scientologist back then, but that she was not a staff Scientologist,' he told me.[128]

According to Segal, Rosa was not involved in church procedures or rituals while working undercover, because he did not want her to be exposed. 'Put it this way, if they had known she was a Scientologist she would not have got the job, and she would have lost the job if they found out that she was a Scientologist.'[129]

Although that might explain why she was not able to publicly identify as a Scientologist while working at Chelmsford, it doesn't explain why the Church of Scientology didn't want to tell the world about their triumph once the operation was over. The exposure of psychiatric abuses inside Chelmsford is arguably Scientology's finest moment in Australia. A large part of their mission is to recruit more and more people to Scientology, to help 'clear the planet' and rid the world of insanity. Rosa Nicholson could have been paraded as a Scientologist and a hero, and used as a recruitment tool to draw idealistic young people who wanted to make the world a better place into Scientology.

But Segal had other plans for Rosa. 'I told her to disappear,' he says. 'I said don't talk to me, don't go near me, go and get a job at Wollongong, Broken Hill, sell newspapers in Brisbane, I don't care, but just go away, because I didn't want her to be exposed.'[130]

Segal hoped Rosa would vanish for six months, slink under the radar and then help him with his plans for a new undercover operation at the Neuropsychiatric Institute (NPI) at the Prince of Wales Hospital in Sydney, whose practices he believed need exposing. But that covert operation never happened, Segal left his post at the CCHR to concentrate on supporting his young family, while Rosa became a staff member at the Church of Scientology, thereby blowing her cover.

If Ron Segal is telling the truth, why did Rosa insist at the Royal Commission that she had not joined the Church of Scientology until after she left her job at the hospital? Why did she try to distance herself from Scientology? Why would she claim it was her 'brilliant idea' and not Ron Segal's? By 1989, the opportunity to go undercover again had long passed.

Rosa did admit under oath that she had spoken at length to Jan Eastgate a number of times about her testimony.[131] It seems that somebody overheard one of these conversations outside the court and passed the information onto the doctors' lawyers. John Sackar QC asked Rosa:

'Did you ask Miss Eastgate if she thought you were sounding believable?'

'No,' Rosa said. She had asked Eastgate outside, 'How do you think I'm going? Do you think it looks all right? Is it going okay?'[132]

Rosa had good reason to feel nervous. 'I always understood that they didn't want her to say anything that would implicate them,' one of Rosa's relatives told me. 'She was very afraid to give evidence against them fearing what may happen to her.'[133]

Ron Segal believes a number of Scientology staff worked on Rosa to convince her that what she did was illegal. He says that both he and Rosa were victims of a black propaganda campaign within Scientology to portray their actions as unlawful. Segal himself was the subject of a Knowledge Report asserting that he was part of an illegal operation (a Knowledge Report is a part of Scientology's surveillance and snitching culture where one person submits a write-up of another individual's so-called crimes). Segal disputes any claims their actions were illegal. 'If there was evidence that either I or Ms Nicholson has acted illegally then why was no police investigation conducted nor charges laid against either of us?'[134]

Segal speculated that Rosa may have been coached on how to best give evidence that would minimise the damage to Scientology. 'There were staff members who were misleading people,' he told me, 'and making people do things that were wrong under the false premise of protecting the mother church.'[135]

While Ron Segal did not name names, in a story I put to air on ABC TV's *Lateline* in 2010, Jan Eastgate was accused of coaching an 11-year-old girl, Carmen Rainer, to lie to police and community services in 1985 about the sexual abuse she had suffered at the hands of her stepfather, Robert Kerr, an ordained Scientology minister. Jan Eastgate denied the claim, describing it as 'egregiously false'.[136]

However, two witnesses, Carmen's mother, Phoebe Rainer, and a former Scientology staff member, Carmel Underwood, backed up the allegations.[137] In 2011, Eastgate was arrested and charged with perverting the course of justice over the matter, but the Director of Public Prosecutions withdrew the charges the following year on the grounds there was no reasonable prospect of conviction. Eastgate never sued for defamation in relation to the allegations contained in my story, which she had previously described as 'egregiously false'.

There were good reasons why the Scientologists would want to distance themselves from Rosa Nicholson and her undercover operation. At the Royal Commission, the Chelmsford doctors' counsel tried to make the argument that principals of the Church of Scientology were involved in criminal activities in relation to the removal of medical files from the hospital.[138] The Church of Scientology is obsessed with good public relations. Scientologists would have been working furiously behind the scenes to ensure claims like this did not stick and that the organisation suffered no reputational damage from the Royal Commission. Hubbard once said, 'We do not find critics of Scientology who do not have a criminal past.'[139] If his followers had to own up to acts that could be labelled criminal, it would make it harder to accuse its critics of the same.

Perjuring yourself, or asking others to perjure themselves, is a high-risk strategy at a Royal Commission, but the Church of Scientology's 'ethics' system carries a built-in incentive for Scientologists to lie to police, the courts and public inquiries. It is a high crime, the worst crime of all within Scientology's internal justice system, to make 'public statements against Scientology or Scientologists'. It is also a high crime to testify 'hostilely before state or public inquiries into Scientology to suppress it'. Hubbard referred disparagingly to the outside world's legal system as 'wog justice'. Many 'high crimes' within Scientology relate to preserving the organisation's reputation.[140]

Despite repeated attempts, Jan Eastgate would not respond directly to my phone calls or emails. Her Sydney lawyer Kevin Rodgers told me via email 'there is no factual basis for the question as to whether Ms Eastgate "coached" Ms Nicholson and there was no finding of any such conduct made by the Royal Commission'.[141] Lawyer Pat Griffin, who represented both the CCHR and Rosa before the Royal Commission, says, 'I didn't think she was coaching her, but I knew they had a lot of contact.'[142]

There is little doubt that Jan Eastgate did give questionable evidence at the Royal Commission that masked her true motivations. At the commission, Eastgate was asked, 'From your point of view you would regard it as a worthwhile social objective to do away with psychiatry as we know it in the community today?' She responded, 'No. I think what I pointed out before is that I feel there are a lot of abuses within the psychiatric system.'[143]

This was a very different message from the one Eastgate was pushing in the International Association of Scientologists' magazine *Impact* the following year. In an eight-page spread that documented how 'a small group of Scientologists decided to rid their country of one of its biggest evils – psychiatry',[144] Eastgate wrote about Scientology's role in exposing Chelmsford and boasted of 'the persistence and dedication of CCHR in wiping out psychiatry in Australia'.[145] When alerted to these two very different versions of the truth, her lawyer Kevin Rodgers responded, 'Ms Eastgate maintains that the testimony she gave was truthful at the time that she gave it.'[146]

This persistence and dedication led to Jan Eastgate becoming the international head of the CCHR. In 1988, she was awarded Scientology's highest honour, the Freedom Medal. Pat Griffin, the lawyer who represented the CCHR at the Royal Commission, and the journalist Toni Eatts,[147] who helped get the message out about Chelmsford, were both flown to the US to receive CCHR International Human Rights Awards.[148] Singer Isaac Hayes gave Griffin his award. Eatts was photographed with celebrity Scientologist Nancy Cartwright as she was awarded her prize at the Bonaventure Hotel in Los Angeles.[149]

It is true that Jan Eastgate's commitment and drive were critical in keeping the abuses of Chelmsford Hospital on the public agenda through the 1980s, helping to trigger a Royal Commission, but the committed Scientologist who was the mastermind behind the exposé, and the nurse who carried it off, received no such international recognition.[150]

Ron Segal and Rosa Nicholson were never flown to the US to be feted; instead they received certificates from the Sydney chapter of the CCHR. Segal does not understand why Rosa's role was downplayed. 'The granting of an award such as the Freedom Medal if not to the whole team should go to the individual who made the greatest contribution,' says Segal. 'In this case, the person who made it all happen, the one whose actions made all the difference, the one who gave meaning to all the others' actions is solely and exclusively Rosa Nicholson.'[151] (Eastgate's lawyer says his client received the Freedom Medal, not just for Chelmsford, but also for ten years of 'mental health reform work'.)[152]

Ron Segal is right to give credit to Rosa Nicholson for pulling off the daring covert operation, but it's hard to see how it would have occurred without him. It was Segal's pragmatism and contacts outside Scientology that allowed him to plan and execute the Chelmsford operation. Mental health workers, including psychiatrists, gave him tip-offs, a policeman taught him about covert operations, a politician he engaged with in his local community allowed him to get the allegations taken seriously at a ministerial level.

Segal has been a Scientologist for over 50 years. He says he is grateful that he and Rosa were able to bring the scandal of Chelmsford to an end, and credits the policy and the facilities provided by the Church of Scientology as being critical to achieving that goal. That may be so, but his distance from Scientology groupthink was also important. While Jan Eastgate was determined to 'wipe out psychiatry' as per Hubbard's policy, Segal was far more moderate. As he puts it, 'If you're going to wipe out psychiatry, you better have something to take its place. Who's going to look after people who have a mental illness? Does the Church of Scientology deal with mental patients?'[153]

The lives of the three Scientologists who did the most to expose Chelmsford took very different paths. Jan Eastgate went on to high office in the Church of Scientology in the US, Ron Segal returned to work as a pharmacist and brought up his family in Sydney's south, but Rosa Nicholson's life after Chelmsford was not so blessed. 'Rosa was crucified when it was exposed what she had done,' says Segal. 'No-one would employ her. There was no professional gain, only hardship and pain. But she knew she had done the right thing.'[154]

Two of Rosa's relatives, who spoke to me on the condition I protected their identity, claim the Church of Scientology made her life a misery after she left Chelmsford Hospital. The hero of arguably Scientology's finest moment in Australia was not given the hero treatment. 'They promised her a trip to the US, so she sold up everything and prepared for the trip,' one relative told me. 'Needless to say, the trip never eventuated and she was left penniless and homeless.'[155] Jan Eastgate's lawyer Kevin Rodgers described the claim of the offered trip as 'far-fetched'.[156]

Short of money, Rosa moved into a boarding house. According to her relative, the pressure to hand over money to the Church of Scientology was relentless. At one point she turned up at a relative's workplace in tears. She did not have the money to pay the rent. 'She was about to be thrown out of her house,' the relative told me. 'I asked are you still in Scientology? And she said yes. I gave her a cheque for the next month's rent.'[157]

In 2002, Rosa had a stroke. She moved from her boarding house to hospital, before being sent on to a nursing hostel, then a nursing home, and another nursing home. She had no private phone and only her family was meant to know where she was, but this did not keep her safe from the Scientologists. 'Jan Eastgate was able to track her down to each new place and hound her, posing as a visiting family member,' a relative told me, 'until I asked the last home not to allow her to visit. I think they finally realised that Rosa had lost cognitive ability to do them any harm anymore so they finally gave up.'[158]

Jan Eastgate's lawyer Kevin Rodgers told me via email, 'There is no reasonable basis for this allegation.' He said that Eastgate had met Rosa only three times after she moved to the US in 1993. He said the visits were primarily 'social calls' that occurred in 2007 and 2008 with the initial visit related to 'proposed TV and film productions about Chelmsford'.[159] Rodgers says by the time of the last visit Rosa was at another nursing home and she let 'the nursing staff know that she was a friend from years earlier'.[160]

Rosa Nicholson could not shed any light on this or any of the new revelations about the role the Church of Scientology played in exposing the abuses at Chelmsford Hospital. I could not ask her if she gave a truthful testimony before the Royal Commission. In her final years, Rosa lost her capacity to talk and her memory failed. On the afternoon of 4 May 2015, she died in her nursing home in Sydney aged 73. The newspapers carried no obituaries and there was no hero's farewell, no acknowledgement of her risky 14-month-long undercover operation and what it achieved. The woman who had done more than anyone else to expose the dark secrets of Chelmsford Hospital passed away in silence, forgotten by the society who had benefited from her courage.

CHAPTER 15

THE GREATEST GAME OF ALL

A HUGE ROAR FROM across the road startled Joe Reaiche as he tried to get to sleep. 'What in the hell was that noise?'[1] he called out to his younger brother Tony, with whom he shared a room in his family's Redfern terrace. Joe got no response. His brother had already passed out. There was only one way to find out what was going on. Joe peeled back his cotton sheets and leaped out of bed.

As the eight-year-old peered out the window of the third-floor attic at 68 Redfern Street, he could see floodlights shining in the distance. The oval he mucked around on after school, playing scratch games with his mates, had been transformed into an arena full of people, energy and noise.

Young Joe changed out of his pyjamas and crept down the stairs, sneaking past the rooms his parents leased out to itinerant men for ten bucks a week. He slowly opened the front door, making sure his father knew nothing of his escape. He crossed the street and raced through the park. The sprawling Moreton Bay fig trees, the ancient Canary Island palms and assorted flooded gums of Redfern Park swayed over him as he sprinted through the park urged on by the roar of the crowd. He soon arrived at the source of all that noise, a tribal gathering that would change his life forever.

Redfern Oval was home to the champion rugby league side the South Sydney Rabbitohs. In 1908, a rugby league competition formed in Sydney as a breakaway from the amateur sport of rugby union. Players were disillusioned that the governing body would not pay compniensation for injuries and lost wages. A professional competition was set up and South Sydney was one of its foundation clubs.

Rugby league became Sydney's most popular and most brutal winter sport. Its clubs were built around tightly knit working-class communities like Redfern. The players were made up of tough uncompromising men drawn from the docks, the mines, the building sites and other blue-collar industries. The Rabbitohs got their nickname from footballers who earned extra money on a Saturday morning walking the streets of Redfern and Surry Hills, skinning and selling rabbits to the large impoverished families crammed into rows of terraces and workers' cottages.

On the hot February night when Joe Reaiche broke out of his bedroom and raced across the road to Redfern Oval, the Rabbitohs were at the peak of their powers. They had already won 16 premierships, and would claim another four titles in the next five years. Souths were playing the Balmain Tigers in the first game of the 1967 Preseason Cup. Joe did not have the five cents needed to get through the turnstiles, but that did not matter. He peered through a hole in the fence, catching a glimpse of the Rabbitohs team that contained legends such as Eric Simms, Bob McCarthy, Ron Coote and John Sattler. Young Joe was mesmerised.

When his nerve gave out and he headed for home, Joe found his father waiting outside the front door. 'Where in the bloody hell were you?'[2] his father yelled. Kabalan Reaiche had migrated to Australia from Beirut in the early 1950s, and worked in the local Reschs brewery. He was a strict disciplinarian and Joe knew what he was in for. His father pulled off his belt and gave Joe a hiding. That night, as he lay in bed crying, the roars of the crowd distracted Joe from the pain of the welts swelling on his legs. He went to sleep dreaming of running with the ball in front of a screaming crowd.

Eleven years later, Joe Reaiche found out what it was like to hear the roar of the crowd from the middle of a football field. On 30 April 1978, he made his first-grade debut in front of over 13,000 fans at the Sydney Sports Ground.[3] Reaiche wasn't playing for the Rabbitohs. He had been graded with their arch enemies the Eastern Suburbs Roosters. His team included Ron Coote, the former Souths star he had seen make charging runs as he peered through the fence at Redfern

Oval. 'It was crazy,' says Reaiche. 'I watched Ron Coote as a kid when I was eight years of age, and now 11 years later I'm playing with him.'[4]

The Roosters side was stacked full of some of the game's greats. Arthur Beetson, Bob Fulton and Coote would all eventually be selected in the competition's team of the century. The side contained other premiership winning stars such as Russell Fairfax, Mark Harris, and Bob 'The Bear' O'Reilly. Reaiche had just turned 20. As he looked around the dressing room before the match, he could hardly believe these superstars were now his teammates.

A fast and elusive runner, Reaiche played most of his football at fullback but made his first-grade debut on the wing. 'He was an incredible talent,' remembers John Quayle, Easts' reserve-grade coach at the time. 'We all thought that. He was a natural.'[5]

Rugby league in Sydney in the 1970s was a blood sport. Games would descend into all-in brawls; players were regularly knocked out in head-high tackles. Joe Reaiche's first game in the top grade was a typically ferocious affair. Parramatta's barrel-chested prop Bob Jay was sent off for a high tackle on Bob Fulton. Bob O'Reilly was dumped on his head in a dangerous spear tackle. Reaiche's hero Ron Coote broke his collarbone. The Roosters hit the lead with just six minutes to go, courtesy of a goal from Bob Fulton. After their durable halfback Kevin Hastings scored a try with just two minutes to go, Easts held on to win 19–13.[6]

As Reaiche celebrated the hard-earned victory with his teammates, he could not believe his luck. The Redfern local junior was not your average first-grade footballer of the day. His Lebanese heritage stood out in a team of Anglo-Celts. Like his teammates, his upbringing was working class, but what made him different was not just his heritage, he had just a few years earlier returned to Sydney from a war zone.

'I missed the shagging and panel vans of 1970s Sydney,' says Reaiche. 'I was dodging sniper bullets, artillery shelling and Israeli jets dropping bombs in Beirut.'[7] In July 1972, Kabalan Reaiche told his family he was taking them back to Beirut. Joe, who had just turned 14, was devastated. 'I almost hit the roof,' he says. 'Why would I want to go back to a third-world country? I was captain of my football team, playing representative football for Eastern Suburbs District; that was my life.'[8]

Kabalan Reaiche's quest to take his family back to his homeland was marred by unfortunate timing. Lebanon was becoming an increasingly dangerous country. The Palestinian Liberation Organisation had relocated to Beirut in the early 1970s following the civil war in Jordan. Tensions grew between the country's Christian and Muslim populations. Militia groups formed and fighting broke out. The capital was divided into Christian East Beirut and Muslim West Beirut. By 1975, the country had descended into civil war.

If Joe Reaiche had stayed in Sydney he would have been a target for recruitment by rugby league talent scouts. In Beirut, he and his friends were targets for recruitment by the local militias. Sensing that his eldest son was in danger, Kabalan Reaiche organised for Joe to return to Australia.

Despite missing three years of junior football, Reaiche returned to playing the game he loved as if he had never been away. He starred for Christian Brothers Lewisham in the Metropolitan Catholic Colleges competition and attracted the attention of scouts from Eastern Suburbs. 'I distinctly remember Arthur Beetson and I going to watch that tournament,' remembers John Quayle. 'We had a brother at Marcellin College who kept an eye out for players and he said you should have a look at this kid.'[9]

The following year, Joe Reaiche made his first-grade debut, playing seven out of the next nine games in the top grade, and keeping the club's then highest ever try scorer, Bill Mullins, in reserve grade.[10] However, in July, that promising first season came to a premature end. Running in a sprint race at Leichhardt Oval against the likes of Larry Corowa and Steve Gearin to find the fastest man in rugby league, Reaiche badly tore his groin muscle. With the 20-year-old sidelined, the Roosters' star-studded line-up bombed out of the competition, failing to make the semi-finals by just two points.

In the off-season Reaiche worked hard on his rehabilitation. He'd got a taste of first-grade football and was determined to regain his place the following season. The young Rooster built up the muscles surrounding his groin, and sought treatment to get his injury right. One afternoon, after visiting an acupuncturist, Reaiche paused to get a drink while waiting for a bus at Railway Square. As he bent over the water fountain a young woman named Joey Lawrence approached him and began asking questions. Joe Reaiche's life was about to change forever.

Joey Lawrence was a body-router with the Church of Scientology. Her role was simple, to get what L. Ron Hubbard referred to as 'raw meat'[11] off the street and into the organisation. From there the raw meat was given a personality test, which hopefully led to them signing up for a course. As Hubbard said, 'It is a maxim that unless you have bodies you have no income. So on any pretext get bodies in the place, and provide ingress to the Registrar when they're there.'[12]

On the street at Railway Square, Joey asked Joe what were the three things in life he most wanted to have. Reaiche answered, 'Love, happiness and money.' The young footballer was intrigued to find out how the young Scientologist could help him find any of the above. The body-router did her job. Reaiche followed her 50 metres around the corner and into the Church of Scientology.

As he walked through the doors, Joe Reaiche did not appear to be in any danger of parting with his money. 'The first thing I saw was the Scientology cross on the wall and I thought that was pretty fucked up,' he says.[13] He was taken into a room with a young Scientology Registrar, Sue Bloomberg, who told him about L. Ron Hubbard and *Dianetics*.

Bloomberg tried to sell Reaiche a copy of *Dianetics*. 'I'm not going to read that!' he said. 'It's too long, it's got very small print, it's too technical and I'm not interested.'[14] He was asked if he wanted to do the Oxford Capacity Analysis, the famous Scientology personality test that has no association with Oxford University. Reaiche saw no harm in a doing a free test and was soon answering questions such as, 'Do you often feel depressed? Do some noises set your teeth on edge? Do you often make tactless blunders?'[15]

After he'd answered 200 of these questions, Reaiche was given the results in the form of a graph. Bloomberg analysed the results. 'She told me I was high on the communications level, a bit low on the personal side and she asked me if there was anything bothering me,' Reaiche says.[16] He didn't know it at the time, but Joe was about to be delivered Scientology's sucker punch, a bait and switch that would end up costing him hundreds of thousands of dollars.[17]

Scientologists are taught to 'find the ruin'[18] of potential new recruits. As *A Scientologist Guide to Dissemination* puts it, 'What you're looking for is the thing that is ruining a person's life ... the major complaint he's got about his life; the one dynamic that is pulling down all the rest of his dynamics.'[19]

Joe Reaiche's 'ruin' was the torn groin muscle that had taken so long to heal. It was a source of immense frustration to the young player. 'He was really on the verge of establishing himself at the time,' says John Quayle. 'We weren't really up to date with modern medicine. We didn't know how to properly fix a groin muscle back then.'[20] The Scientologists, however, claimed they had all the answers to all physical ailments. 'They said it was mental,' says Reaiche. 'They said they could fix it and I thought, okay I'll give it a shot.'[21]

When Joe Reaiche told Sue Bloomberg he played for the Roosters, the reaction was immediate. 'Her jaw dropped and she said, "Could you wait here for a second?"' says Reaiche. 'And she went upstairs and said to Steve Stevens, "You're not going to believe who I've got downstairs," and all of a sudden there was five Sea Org members downstairs and talking to me. They were all mad Easts supporters.'[22]

Steve Stevens was one of Scientology's best and brightest salesmen. His official title was the Commanding Officer of the Tours Registration Org. He toured Australia and New Zealand convincing Scientologists to come to Sydney and do more advanced and expensive courses.[23] Stevens was a rare beast in Scientology. He was a Sea Org member who did not live in poverty.[24] He wore flash clothes and drove fast cars. As a 'Field Staff Member' he was able to make good money from Scientology, charging commissions of 10–15% on sales of books and E-Meters.[25]

The Church of Scientology had not only found Joe Reaiche's ruin, they had found their first celebrity recruit in Australia from a high-profile sport.[26] Rugby league was the most popular football code in Sydney at the time and Reaiche had the potential to become a valuable marketing tool. Steve Stevens became Reaiche's friend and point man, making sure things ran smoothly for the young footballer. 'He said to me, "What are your goals?" and I said to him, "To play first-grade football, to make $30,000 a year, to run the 100 metres in 10.7 seconds, and to be happy." He said, "they can all be achieved through Scientology, you just need to go OT."'[27]

Joe Reaiche did not have the time or the money to study Scientology courses like a regular recruit. According to Reaiche, going 'clear' through Dianetics would have cost him around $18,000 at the time. Stevens came up with a solution. 'He said to me I should train up as an auditor and get the professional auditing at 50 per cent off,' says Reaiche.[28] The young footballer was sold on the 'success stories' of other athletes who had gotten involved in Scientology in the US: including San Francisco 49ers quarterback John Brodie; LA Lakers basketballer Jim Brewer; and former Pittsburgh Steeler Bob Adams.

After a delayed start to the season, Reaiche returned to the top grade in 1979. Alternating between wing and fullback, he played 12 games in first grade, finishing the season as the Roosters' top scorer. By now his groin injury had healed, due to strength and conditioning work, according to Reaiche, rather than, as promised, the powers of Scientology.[29]

However, Reaiche was getting something out of Scientology. He felt like it was making him a better person, and he continued juggling Scientology course work with his football career and his studies at teachers' college. He soon went 'clear' at Scientology's new Sydney centre in Castlereagh Street.[30] The Scientologists had bought the five-storey building from the Public Service Association for $800,000, financing the purchase through cash brought in from a Luxembourg bank account.[31] Steve Stevens drove Reaiche up 'the Bridge' at Scientology's new centre in between driving him to football training.

Scientology's Bridge to Total Freedom, or 'the Bridge', provides a roadmap for Scientologists to achieve enlightenment through coursework and training. New recruits start at the bottom with auditing, and at the time Joe Reaiche was studying, could aspire to reach the highest rank of Operating Thetan Level VII (OT VII). The further you go up the bridge, the more expensive the courses.

Joe Reaiche was told he would acquire supernatural powers as he made it to the top of 'the Bridge'. Hubbard told his adherents that reaching the highest OT levels would allow them to control 'physical matter, energy, space and time'.[32] To a professional athlete, the idea that Scientology could make you somehow superhuman was an enticing prospect. But it did not quite work out that way for Reaiche. As he moved up 'the Bridge', his football career stalled.

In 1980, Roosters coach Bob Fulton did not pick him in the top grade. In the off-season Reaiche went to Los Angeles and stayed in the

Celebrity Centre Hotel while he completed Operating Thetan Level III (OT III). The following season, he transferred to the Canterbury Bulldogs, but struggled to dislodge established players such as Chris Anderson, Steve Gearin and Greg Brentnall, playing only one first-grade game that season.

In 1982, Reaiche moved to Souths, playing just two games in the top grade. At the end of the year he returned to Los Angeles to complete OT IV and OT V and then to Clearwater, Florida, for OT VI and OT VII. In the world of professional sport, at the age of just 24, Reaiche was a pioneer. 'I was the first professional playing athlete in the world on OT VII.'[33]

On a high, Reaiche returned to Australia in March 1983. He did not have a contract, but turned up at his old club Easts and begun playing lower grades. Reaiche took on a job at a gym in Earlwood, where he began an association with a footballer who would become Scientology's biggest-name convert, helping to open the door to recruiting players at one of rugby league's most famous clubs.

PAT JARVIS WAS A man used to putting his body on the line. As a Sydney policeman in the late 1970s and early 1980s, he patrolled the tough beat of Newtown, back in the days when the inner-city suburb was known more for its street crime than its street theatre. One of Jarvis's tasks was to corral local hoodlums into the boxing ring at the Newtown Police Boys Club. A young Jeff Fenech was one of those street toughs who benefited from training at the club. Under the mentorship of Johnny Lewis, Fenech went on to become a world boxing champion in three different weight divisions.

When he slipped out of his police uniform on the weekends, Pat Jarvis pulled on the red and white of St George. Tall, dark-haired and muscular, Jarvis played prop forward, a position reserved for the biggest and hardest of players. 'Pat was as tough as nails,' recalls his teammate Graeme Wynn. 'He had the body of a freak. Ripples everywhere.'[34] Michael O'Connor, who watched Jarvis tear into the opposition from the relative safety of the backline, remembers him as a fearless competitor. 'Pat had no respect for his body, he would run through a brick wall. He was a very resilient, disciplined athlete.'[35]

Pat Jarvis may have been notorious at St George for his ability to play through pain, but it was a case of the sniffles that triggered his interest in Scientology. When Joe Reaiche returned from doing Scientology's upper-level courses in Florida, he landed a job in the same gym where Jarvis did weight training. The pair bonded over rugby league and Reaiche soon introduced the big front rower to Scientology.

'One day I was having a chat with him,' says Reaiche, 'and he wasn't feeling too good, he had a sniffle and I said, "Pat would you like me to do a process on you?" and he said, "What's that?" I said, "Let me do it and see what you think." I did a "touch assist" on him for 30–40 minutes and he felt better.'[36]

According to Scientology doctrine, the purpose of a 'touch assist' is to 're-establish communication with injured or ill body parts'.[37] The person giving the touch assist issues the command 'feel my finger', then places moderate pressure on the appropriate areas with one digit. The theory is that by putting the person in 'communication' with their injured or ill body parts, this will somehow hasten their recovery.

After receiving his first touch assist, Jarvis asked his fellow league player what he had just done to him. 'It's a thing called Dianetics or Scientology,' Reaiche replied.[38] Jarvis was curious to find out more. Reaiche thought Scientology could help the St George prop forward in other ways.

While Joe Reaiche's ruin was his dodgy groin muscle, Pat Jarvis's weakness was his poor ball skills. A rugby league prop forward needs to be a hard man with soft hands. When Jarvis tried to catch the football during a game, it was as if his fingers were laced with lead. While universally admired for his toughness and resilience, Jarvis's poor handling was frustrating his coaches and preventing him from fulfilling his potential.

Like any ambitious footballer, Jarvis was willing to try just about anything to improve his game. Reaiche took the St George player down to a local park and started practising a Scientology drill on him called 'reach and withdraw'. 'It works by getting you to communicate with something,' says Reaiche. 'The commands are "reach and withdraw". For Pat it was about being asked to reach for that ball and once he was in complete contact with the ball, then I would ask him to withdraw from that ball.'[39] The commands were repeated back and forth until Jarvis felt comfortable with the football in his hands.

Joe took Pat under his wing. They would meet at the gym during the week where Jarvis would receive one-on-one tutoring in Scientology. The communication ball drills continued throughout the season, often at Kogarah Oval on game day when Reaiche had no commitments with Easts. Joe's goal was to help Pat get over his fears about his ball skills, improve his general confidence as a person and turn him into an in-form footballer.

It's unclear whether there was something special about the Scientology drill, or whether the simple act of practising more helped improve Jarvis's hands. Whatever it was, his teammates noticed a difference. 'Something helped him,' says Graeme Wynn. 'Pat had the worst hands in the world. Then he started catching balls and running hard and he had belief in himself.'[40] Halfway through the 1983 season, Jarvis's improved form was rewarded with his selection in the Australian team to play New Zealand.

While his sessions with Jarvis seemed to help the St George forward, Reaiche was struggling to get his own career back on track. The Roosters' fullback Marty Gurr had been selected to play in the NSW State of Origin team that season and was keeping the Scientologist in reserve grade. Reaiche believed his own form had never been better. 'I was playing my best football,' he says. 'I knew that somehow what I was doing spiritually was working in a weird way.'[41]

With Reaiche starring from fullback, the Roosters' second-grade team made a charge for the semi-finals. But the speedster was juggling divided loyalties. 'I was getting hounded with around 15–20 calls a week from the Director of Processing at Clearwater to go there and do a "special addition" with OT VII,' Reaiche recalls. 'She told me it was top secret and confidential and would make my life easier and greatly help my football career immediately.'[42]

The Roosters' fullback had been convinced he could fly out of Sydney on the Monday and be back in time to play the following weekend. 'Well guess what?' says Reaiche. 'I went there and all of the promises of getting me through in a half a day was all just a sales pitch and bullshit as it took me over a week to get through the course.

I was now stuck and couldn't come back in time to play. The team lost that weekend and lost the remaining two games and missed the play-offs. I felt like I let the team down big time.'[43]

Reaiche had been constantly sold on the idea that Scientology courses and doctrine would improve his football; now they were preventing him from even getting on the field. He never played top-grade rugby league again.

At the end of 1983, Pat Jarvis's informal dabbling with Scientology came to an end. Joe Reaiche took him into the organisation's Sydney headquarters and introduced him to Steve Stevens. The following season the front rower was selected to play in the NSW State of Origin team for all three games. Jarvis felt his game had benefited from Scientology, but he was not letting on to his fellow players. 'At that time Pat wasn't known as a Scientologist,' says his former St George teammate Chris Guider. 'He was keeping his participation in the group a secret. He was worried about the backlash from others. His wife Anne was upset about him doing Scientology, so he wasn't very open about it.'[44]

Chris Guider joined St George at the beginning of the 1984 season and made an immediate impact. At just 162 cm and weighing 75 kg, he was one of the smallest forwards to play the code at the highest level. His teammate Steve Rogers gave him the nickname 'Tattoo' after the character in the TV series *Fantasy Island*.[45] Guider was part of a new breed of hooker who was fast, agile and possessed the ball skills of a halfback.

In *Big League*, former Manly second rower Peter Peters described him as 'an amazing player'.[46] Despite his size, Guider had no problems felling the biggest of opponents. His coach Roy Masters said during his debut season, 'I haven't coached a hooker with his all-round qualities and while his attack is excellent, so is his defence.'[47]

The 22-year-old had grown up in the tough school of country rugby league. As a junior he played in Moss Vale and Tamworth, before signing to play with Maitland in the Newcastle competition. His premiership-winning coach in the Hunter, former St George centre Robert Finch, suggested he trial with his old club. Guider's first season at St George was a success. He played 14 games in the top grade, keeping former Queensland hooker John Dowling in reserves. But towards the end of the season, health problems began to emerge. 'He would come off after a game looking as red as a traffic light,' recalls Graeme Wynn.[48] Guider was suffering from high blood pressure and was struggling to recover after matches.

Eventually the young hooker went to see a specialist about his high blood pressure. The news was not good. 'The doctor told me I shouldn't play anymore,' says Guider. 'He found that one of my kidneys hadn't developed to its full size and that my other kidney had grown larger than normal to compensate. Between the two of them they functioned normally, but they said it's risky to keep playing.'[49]

Pat Jarvis was well aware of Guider's health issues. He had packed down alongside the talented rookie in 11 matches that season. At the end of the year, as Guider weighed up his future, he received a call from his teammate:

> It was a very odd phone call because it was very clandestine. Pat's not a great talker anyway, but he was very slow and quiet about what he was saying. He said he was going to connect me up with some sort of group that he had to be secretive about. I thought it was a bit of a joke. I just laughed and said, 'Look mate, if you don't have another kidney for me you're not going to help.'[50]

Soon after taking Jarvis's mysterious phone call, Guider accepted the doctor's advice and ended his rugby league career. It was a heartbreaking decision to make at the age of just 22. As a young boy he had dreamed of making it as a professional footballer, and in his first year in the big time, he had shown that he had what it took to be a star player. Disillusioned and distraught, Guider returned to Tamworth, dusted off his tools and took up a job as a carpenter.

While Chris Guider had given up on his dream of playing big time rugby league, the Scientologists had not given up on him. In early 1985, Steve Stevens called him in Tamworth and tried to convince him to give Scientology a try. When his approach over the phone failed, the smooth-talking recruiter drove 400 km up the New England Highway. 'He had hired a car and driven to Tamworth with the goal of getting me to come with him,' says Guider. 'He was saying that Scientology could help me, but again there was this air of secrecy which I did not like and I didn't go.'[51]

In the meantime, St George was on a roll. After 12 rounds of the 1985 competition, they were on top of the table and were emerging as favourites to win their first premiership in six years. Guider was watching their winning streak with envy from his lounge room. One cold Tamworth winter's night he hired *The Natural* from his local video store. The Robert Redford film told the story of Roy Hobbs, a baseball pitcher whose sporting career was derailed after a woman shot him in a hotel room. Sixteen years later, he finally made the big time after reinventing himself as a batter.

The Natural got under Guider's skin. He couldn't stop thinking about what he had given up by retiring from his own sporting career. Watching the movie was a catalyst for his comeback. 'I just decided I was going to go back,' says Guider. 'I was going to move mountains. There was nothing in Tamworth for me. I didn't want to stay there. I was going to make it happen.'[52]

The former Saint was prepared to do just about anything to return to top grade rugby league. If that meant contacting the Scientologists and seeing what they could do for him, then so be it. He rang Steve Stevens, who promised to set him up in an apartment in Kings Cross. Guider packed his footy boots, mouthguard and other essential items into his car and hit the road.

Three days after arriving back in Sydney, Chris met Pat Jarvis, Joe Reaiche and Steve Stevens at the Newtown Police Boys Club. Outside the gym the three footballers and the recruiter sat on a wall and discussed Scientology.

Guider was given the hard sell. Reaiche told him how Scientology had helped his rugby league career. Steve Stevens introduced him to the idea of a 'Suppressive Person', or SP – antisocial personalities who, according to Hubbard, could affect an individual's wellbeing. At the conclusion of their discussion, Guider agreed to undergo Scientology auditing.

Once again Scientology had found an individual's 'ruin'. Like the actors who were so successfully targeted by Scientology's Celebrity Centre, professional footballers are prone to suffering from a deep sense of insecurity. They perform in a cut-throat environment where only the best make it to the top. Their achievements and failures are subject to intense public scrutiny from fans and the media. They rely on self-confidence when they are often burdened with self-doubt. They live or die by their ability to compete under pressure on the big stage. If they do not play well, they can be dropped from the top team, or fail to have their contract renewed.

But rugby league players have to deal with a professional hazard that makes their livelihoods even more fragile than actors. If a player is lucky, their career at the top might last eight to ten years. But at any given time, that career can be ruined by injury.

'When you're injured as a league player you're like a leper,' says former St George and Australian representative Brian Johnston. 'You don't feel like you're a part of the team anymore. You're not part of the group mentality, you're not part of the emotion anymore when you win or lose and you'll do anything to get back in the team. You're very vulnerable to approaches from people who say they can solve your problem.'[53]

By now Pat Jarvis was being more open with his teammates about his Scientology beliefs. Michael O'Connor would occasionally give Jarvis a lift to the Church of Scientology after training. 'The building I used to drop him off at was a bit creepy,' says O'Connor. 'I was inquisitive about it and he explained to me about auditing and the different levels. I was very sceptical.'[54]

The classy St George centre was struck by Jarvis's dedication to Scientology. 'He was very committed to them,' says O'Connor. 'He was winning player of the match awards, and then donating the prizes to the Church of Scientology.'[55] Graeme Wynn remembers this causing tension between Pat and his then wife, Anne. 'He'd win televisions and donate them to the Church of Scientology and Anne wanted him to go back in and get them.'[56]

With Jarvis now more open about his beliefs, he and Stevens got to work trying to recruit other players. 'It was a real us against them idea,' says Guider, 'with Steve and Pat working to get more people to see the light and come into the fold with them.'[57] Brian Johnston was one of those targeted. 'Pat had approached me when I had an injured groin,' says Johnston. 'I said, "This is not for me." I was clear. I cut him off.'[58]

Graeme Wynn started to get unusual phone calls from Pat Jarvis, which he now believes were an attempt to recruit him:

> *Pat used to ring me up on a Saturday night before a game and I'd be trying to have a feed, and he'd be on the phone to me trying to talk 'positives and negatives' and I'd be at home with my wife trying to have dinner and he'd be on the phone for half an hour. Anyway, the third Saturday in a row the phone rang and I told my wife, 'If it's Pat tell him I'm blind down at the Allawah pub.'*[59]

No-one it seems was immune from the Scientologists' aggressive recruiting strategies. Even the coach Roy Masters was targeted. A former schoolteacher, Masters was an innovative coach who went on to became one of Australia's most respected sports journalists. At first he was given copies of Hubbard's books, and then given the hard sell to sign up to Scientology services. 'I am pretty certain that Steve and Pat felt they were on the brink of getting Roy to do some auditing,' says Guider. 'But Steve and Pat had inflated ideas, like all Scientologists do, about their influence and how Roy was responding to them. He never mentioned the subject to me and all his communications were about the team and how we could improve it. Nothing ever about Scientology, its books or any of its ideas.'[60]

It is highly unlikely that Masters even considered undergoing Scientology auditing. The St George coach had grown up in a large family known for their keen intellects and sceptical minds. His mother, Olga, was a novelist and journalist. Two of his siblings, Chris and Deb, built formidable reputations as investigative journalists at ABC TV's *Four Corners*. At his first senior coaching role at Wests, Masters had taken a team of battlers and turned them into one of the most feared teams in the competition. He was renowned for using psychological tactics on his players that got the best out of them in big matches. Masters was in his early 40s, streetwise and sure of himself. He was by no means easy prey for the recruiting tactics of the Scientologists.

Masters does not have fond memories of the time when the Church of Scientology tried to recruit his players from under his nose.

He declined to be interviewed for this book, stating: 'It caused me some aggravation at the time and I don't want to have any more.'[61]

While Masters resisted Scientology's recruitment strategy, Chris Guider was well and truly in. He underwent the 'Purification Rundown', a detoxification program involving intense exercise, lengthy stints in the sauna and high doses of niacin and other vitamins. Hubbard developed the course while on the *Apollo* as a means of dealing with Sea Org members who were suffering from acid flashbacks brought on by previous LSD use.

The young footballer felt the 'Purification Rundown', which has been heavily criticised by the medical establishment,[62] did help relieve his high blood pressure. But in the age before player managers and team counsellors, it was the sense of backing Guider received from Scientology that most helped him.

'It was basically a support group,' says Guider. 'To have people around you that want you to do well and would help you deal with things outside of the game, that to me was the best thing I got out of it. I had celebrity status and they were very interested in having me there, so I didn't have any bad connotations about Scientology at that time.'[63]

While Guider and Jarvis felt like they were benefiting from Scientology, some of their teammates were not happy with the growing influence of Steve Stevens. Guider and Jarvis were well liked and respected by their fellow players, and their beliefs were tolerated, but Stevens was an unwanted presence. 'We all treated Pat the same,' says Graeme Wynn, 'but that Scientology bloke hanging around Pat, we didn't like him.'[64]

It is no surprise that the likes of Graeme Wynn did not approve of Scientology's gun recruiter. Before games Stevens would isolate Pat Jarvis from his teammates and run Scientology drills with him in the grandstand. 'Rugby league is a very tribal sport,' says former St George centre Brian Johnston. 'By having Pat separate from the team before the game, it was quite divisive.'[65]

Before long Stevens started to encroach on the players' inner sanctum, turning up inside the dressing room after games. The move was not well received. 'Roy put a stop to that,' says Johnston. 'Roy's a sharp man and understood what he was up to. He was looking for a weakness or vulnerability in a player, offering friendship or support, and then advice. It was part of their hard-core recruiting.'[66]

The St George captain Craig Young was not impressed by Scientology. The burly front rower worked as a detective in the NSW Police's infamous armed hold-up squad and was alert to suspicious behaviour of any kind. Young offered to rescue Chris Guider from the cult. 'Craig told me, "Listen, if you need some help getting out of that group, you tell me." He offered to bust me out of there if I needed it. He was concerned about me.'[67]

Complaints were made about the Scientologists' recruiting methods to the sport's highest levels. John Quayle, General Manager of the New South Wales Rugby League at the time, remembers club officials expressing their anger and frustration to him. 'We were getting complaints from the clubs. St George came to us at one point and said, "They are trying to control our footballers. Can you get them to stop?" I said that's a decision for the players. It didn't become an issue for the league.'[68]

The influence of the Scientologists, which coach Roy Masters described as an 'aggravation',[69] did not appear to undermine the club's performance on the field. In 1985, St George made the grand final in all three grades, winning premierships in under 23s and reserves, before losing a gruelling contest 7–6 to Canterbury in the top grade. Saints had been favourites to win, but opposition coach Warren Ryan devised a set of tactics that starved St George of possession. The Bulldogs' halfback Steve Mortimer relentlessly bombed fullback Glenn Burgess in his in-goal area, forcing a series of line drop-outs and pinning the St George team in their own half. The following season, the rules were changed to prevent Ryan's tactics from being employed again.

On that day, Chris Guider entered rugby league folklore. He became the first and only footballer to play in all three grand finals. After playing a full game in under 23s, he came on as a replacement in both reserve and first grade. It is a record that is unlikely to ever be broken.

By the end of the 1985 season, Steve Stevens's interest in St George had evaporated. 'Steve was really pissed off with Roy after the end of '85,' says Guider, 'because Roy didn't want to have anything to do with him. I didn't have any support group in '86 because by then Steve had spat the dummy.'[70]

Stevens and other Scientologists in the Sydney organisation felt that St George had lost the 1985 grand final because Masters had failed to embrace Scientology. 'I know they were all blaming Roy for the fact that the team didn't win the premiership,' says Guider.[71]

Chris Guider became a key member of St George's first-grade team in 1986. But by then football was not his only focus. Soon after the beginning of the season he joined Scientology's Sea Org. The indefatigable hooker who had played three grand finals in one day was now combining the unthinkable twin roles of professional footballer and Sea Org member. He had signed a one-year contract with St George and a billion-year contract with L. Ron Hubbard.

'It was like living two lives, being both these things at the same time,' says Guider. 'In the Sea Org I was a full-time student and was able to leave and go to training anytime I needed to, and on match day I was just gone the whole day. I even remember taking a call from a radio station in the reception of the Sea Org facility. It was before we played Canterbury in a Monday night game at Belmore.'[72]

Guider played 23 games in first grade that season.[73] When Craig Young was injured towards the end of the season, the Sea Org member took over as captain. It was to be his last season as a professional footballer. The Scientologists, who encouraged him to return to the field in 1985, ended his career just over a year later. 'I was basically told by the head of the organisation that I was attached to at that time, that I had to give away the rugby league. No real reason, just I had to devote more time to the church.'[74] At the age of 24, with his best football in front of him, Guider's billion-year contract with Scientology trumped his contract with St George.

Eventually Guider moved to the US, where he rose to become Master at Arms at the Religious Technology Center, the most senior 'Ethics Officer' in the Church of Scientology in the world. Joe Reaiche had returned permanently to the US in 1985, signing up to the Sea Org in Clearwater, where he married Carol Masterson. Her two children from her previous marriage, Danny and Chris Masterson, later became TV stars, Danny in *That '70s Show* and Chris in *Malcolm in the Middle*. Joe and Carol had two children together, Jordan and

Alanna, who both followed in their step-brothers' footsteps. Alanna starred in *The Walking Dead* and Jordan became best known for his role in *The 40-Year-Old Virgin*.

Joe was in the Sea Org for two years and became Scientology's go-to man in Florida for solving disputes with disgruntled parishioners who were demanding their money back. Pat Jarvis continued his football career before he too joined the Sea Org. Another league player, Errol Hillier, a front rower with Cronulla and North Sydney, ended up a Scientology staff member in Sydney. No elite sporting competition in the world had delivered so many recruits to Scientology and the Sea Org at the one time as the Sydney rugby league competition in the 1980s.

Pat Jarvis remained committed to Scientology, but not St George. At the end of the 1986 season he signed to play for Canterbury, but his new club was not about to become a recruitment ground for Scientology. 'When Pat went to Canterbury,' a former St George official disclosed to me, 'he was told by Peter Moore we don't want to have anything to do with Scientology at this place.'[75]

Peter 'Bullfrog' Moore was the heart and soul of the Canterbury Bulldogs. A Catholic and father of nine, Moore was the Chief Executive of the club for 26 years. He died in 2000, having dedicated most of his adult life to making the club a success. Steve Mortimer, who was the Bulldogs captain at the time, says the story of Moore's intervention with Jarvis has the ring of truth to it. 'I don't know if he sat him down or not,' says Mortimer, 'but it makes sense that he would've told him to keep it to himself.'[76]

While Roy Masters found pressure from the Scientologists to be an 'aggravation', Jarvis's coach at the Bulldogs, Warren Ryan, had nothing to complain about. 'I didn't realise he was a Scientologist,' says Ryan. 'I just thought he was a good clean-living fella.'[77] Whether Peter Moore intervened or not, Scientology's experiment with actively targeting rugby league players was over.

Chris Guider and Joe Reaiche eventually left the Sea Org and Scientology. Showing the same courage they displayed on the football field, both blew the whistle on what they saw as the culture of abuse, lies and greed at the heart of the Church of Scientology.

When Joe Reaiche looks back at the time he was recruited as a young footballer he feels he was misled and duped about what Scientology was really selling and what it could really deliver:

> *I just had this idea that Scientology was the only answer and if you followed it 100 per cent and committed to it your goals would be realised. As a result, I had the misconception that my talent didn't need any more improvement and that I just needed to have a stronger mind to do metaphysical actions and that Scientology was the answer to that. I don't believe that anymore. Scientology is the greatest mind-fucking maze trap ever created via a religion on Earth.[78]*

In 2005, while still a member of Scientology, Joe was issued with a declaration order labelling him a 'Suppressive Person', expelling him from the church. When he got the order in the mail, he picked up the phone and tried to call his children, Jordan and Alanna. It was too late. They had already been told that the best thing for their spiritual freedom and happiness was to follow church doctrine and 'disconnect' from their father.

The organisation that had promised to improve Joe Reaiche as an individual and help him to attain superhuman powers and eternal life had now separated him from his own children. He has not heard from them in over a decade despite repeated phone calls and birthday cards. He says the indefinite separation from his children 'breaks his heart each and every day'.[79]

At the time of writing, Pat Jarvis was still a committed Scientologist. The durable front rower's toughness and stamina saw him play over 300 games across 16 seasons in rugby league's toughest competition, in its most physically demanding position.

Jarvis is still doing the hard yards for Scientology. When I first rang him to ask for an interview for this book, he said he would be happy to talk to me.[80] When I followed up to arrange a time, he had become cagey, finally responding to my request via email:

> *I am actually not interested in taking part in this assignment. I do not see the value in this as a worthwhile story. As a*

scientologist I am very focused on seeing others do well in their lives and help them change conditions towards an improved society. I do not believe your story is of such intention. I would like to see people gaining knowledge and information which will assist them live life better and be more successful.

We have some great life improvement courses for the public and also provide some vital education with The Truth About Drugs. This is an area which I see as a major stumbling block for our youth and adults. As a parent I know there is not a more concerning issue here today than the harmful effects of drugs.

Scientology has made me more aware of my responsibility to others, my family of course and the next-door neighbour. I wish you well but doubt that your venture would be of any value to my goals of achieving a better society.[81]

CHAPTER 16

THE GILLHAMS BLOW

TERRI GILLHAM GAMBOA[1] KNEW Scientology had changed forever when David Miscavige asked her to spit in the face of her Treasury Secretary, Homer Schomer. As a 13-year-old she had been one of Hubbard's original messengers on board the *Royal Scotman/Apollo*. In 1981, Hubbard made Terri, at the age of 26, head of Author Services Inc., a for-profit company staffed by Sea Org members. But the young Australian was no longer taking direct orders from Hubbard. She was now answerable to David Miscavige, the man who would soon take over Scientology.

Hubbard had been in and out of hiding in various locations for years. With the FBI raids of 1977 and Mary Sue's criminal conviction in 1979, Hubbard knew it was wise to make himself scarce. But by 1980, he had to deal with a whole new threat. Hubbard was under increasing pressure from disgruntled former Scientologists who were suing him. He was now facing 48 lawsuits and three grand jury subpoenas.[2]

In the second month of the new decade, Hubbard went into hiding for good. A white Dodge van with velvet curtains and a built-in bed whisked him away. The Dodge was then ditched, destroyed and replaced by an orange Ford, which was in turn replaced by another Dodge. Hubbard swapped his hideouts like his getaway cars.[3] He stayed first at Newport Beach in a one-bedroom apartment, before taking up residence in a Blue Bird motorhome that was driven to various locations in the Sierra Mountains.

Hubbard was angry about having to go into hiding and blamed everyone but himself. His parting words to his most senior executives were, 'To hell with you all, to hell with everybody.'[4] As his personal messenger on board the *Apollo*, Terri had seen Hubbard at his darkest. Her mother, Yvonne, who had set up the Celebrity Centre and worked closely with Hubbard, had also put up with his fits of fury, but the tirade he delivered before he left was one of his most ferocious. 'He was livid,' says Terri. 'Oh, my goodness, he was so mad, this was one of the worst.'[5]

According to Terri, who took on her married name Gamboa in 1979, many of the lawsuits were Hubbard's fault. 'He would make people stay up all night to get something done,' she says. 'There were some people who couldn't deal with that, there were elderly people and they got upset, left and filed lawsuits and that made him furious.'[6]

Just as he took no responsibility for Operation Snow White, instead letting his wife Mary Sue take the fall and go to prison, Hubbard was after a scapegoat for the lawsuits. 'He wanted an "all clear",' Terri says, 'and my job and Norman Starkey's job was to get an "all clear" and that meant no lawsuits, so that he was invincible and nobody could ever sue him.'[7]

Hubbard assigned Terri Gamboa to the newly formed 'All Clear Unit' and special lawyers were hired to kill off all litigation against him. It was an absurd assignment. 'Any attorney will tell you it's impossible,' says Terri. 'Anybody can sue anybody for anything!'[8] Hubbard was furious that his executives could not somehow inoculate him from the US justice system.

When Hubbard went into hiding, he was looked after by two of his messengers, Pat and Annie Broeker. Eventually the three of them settled on an old 160-acre horse ranch in Creston, California. Hubbard grew a beard, assumed the pseudonym of Jack Farnsworth and, by his own admission, took on the appearance of Colonel Sanders.[9] Angry and isolated, his only conduits to the outside world were Pat and Annie at the ranch, and his ambitious former cameraman and mission operator, David Miscavige, who was back at Scientology's International Base near Hemet, California.

Miscavige had grown up in Willingboro's Pennypacker Park neighbourhood in New Jersey in the 1960s and early '70s.[10] His father, Ronnie, a salesman and trumpet player, thought Scientology might help his son with his chronic asthma and allergies. According to Miscavige, he was in the midst of an asthma attack when his father took him to see a Scientologist. Father and son both said the auditing session stopped the attack and changed their lives forever. 'From that moment I knew this is it,' said David. 'I have the answer.'[11] [Miscavige continued to use asthma medication after becoming a Scientologist.] Soon after, Ronnie took his four children out of school and moved to the UK to be close to Hubbard's headquarters at Saint Hill in the Sussex countryside.

Miscavige became something of a child prodigy within Scientology. He learned how to audit by the age of 12. He went 'clear' by 15. When he and his family moved back to the US he dropped out of high school and joined the Sea Org. He became one of the Commodore's Messengers, working under the organisation's commanding officer, Terri Gillham. She remembers him as a hyper-ambitious, arrogant teenager. 'I think Miscavige was trying to get power from the day he came in at 16 years old,' she says.[12]

Soon after Miscavige arrived, Terri found out just how ruthless he could be. She had been sent to the Rehabilitation Project Force (RPF) for defending her then husband, Gerry Armstrong, who had been placed on the RPF. 'Miscavige was sent on a mission to oversee and handle the RPF,' she recalls. 'He'd come and stand with his arms crossed in his full uniform while I was scrubbing a wall and then he'd go and report to my seniors that I was slacking off. They'd tell me off and I'd start scrubbing harder and faster. He'd come back and cross his arms again while watching me work and then disappear again and my bosses would come back and say the Mission in Charge says you're not working fast enough. This happened three or four times. He wanted me in trouble.'[13]

Miscavige did not lack confidence. Even as a teenager he was not the type to bow down to senior Scientology executives like Terri. He soon caught Hubbard's eye through his mixture of energy, enthusiasm and sheer will. Scientology's founder assigned him to work as a cameraman on his training videos and around the same time appointed him to the position of Action Chief to oversee and manage the missions. At that young age Miscavige had already developed a reputation for arrogance and violence. Mike Rinder remembers him as an 'abrasive obnoxious teenager'.[14]

Of Hubbard's three conduits to the outside world, Miscavige was best placed to assert his authority. Pat and Annie Broeker were in isolation with Hubbard on the ranch. Pat would communicate with Miscavige via pagers and pay phones. Miscavige was able to control communications going to and from Hubbard. Senior Scientologists, including former messengers who had worked with Hubbard, became sidelined. No-one knew for sure if Hubbard's orders sent from the ranch were truly coming from Scientology's founder and no-one knew if the reports sent from the executives were reaching him.

Terri's brother, Peter Jnr, was deeply troubled by the power shift. In 1982, he became the first of the Gillhams to leave Scientology. 'I saw what was going on and the clique he was forming around him (Miscavige),' he says, 'and I thought this place is going down the frigging toilet. I saw that he had complete control of what Hubbard was told and he could alter what orders Hubbard gave.'[15] Peter Jnr left and got married later that year. On the morning of his wedding his father rang to apologise. He had just found out his son had been declared a 'Suppressive Person' and the Church of Scientology would not allow him to attend the wedding. Arthur Hubbard, who was supposed to be Peter Jnr's best man, also had to pull out.

With Miscavige controlling all the information going to and from the ranch at Creston, it made it easy for him to manipulate the truth about how well Scientology was travelling. 'I saw him change reports all the time,' says Terri. 'I'd read what he wrote and go, wow, he makes it sound really great when a situation was not that great. He had a real talent for making himself look good or making events sound way better than they really were.'[16]

Terri Gamboa was busy trying to manage her own important part of the Scientology empire. As Executive Director of Author Services, she was in charge of Hubbard's business management company. It was set up, as Terri puts it, 'as part of the corporate sort out so LRH could not be accused of inurement by the IRS'. Author Services was not just in charge of Hubbard's book royalties. As Terri says:

> We had to create a business management company that ran all
> of his personal affairs, that oversaw all his oil investments, stock
> market investments, money, bank accounts, book publishing,
> and all the artwork that we created from his fiction books.
> So Author Services was strictly LRH's business management
> company. We implied we were a Hollywood company for
> different authors, when really he was our only client.[17]

Author Services was not immune from Miscavige's meddling. According to Terri, Miscavige and Pat Broeker lost US$30 million of Hubbard's money after they decided they knew more about oil well investing than the specialists at Author Services. 'They invested and lost $30 million in oil wells, the biggest loss ever in the history of ASI or Scientology,' she says. Terri insists Miscavige would not take responsibility for the loss and did not want Hubbard to know about the debacle. 'He came to me and said you guys have to make up for the oil well loss, you guys have to sell these paintings we had from LRH's fiction books, you have to make up this $30 million loss because we can't have a problem with LRH finding out about this.'[18] Terri had to hire more sales staff and get more artwork made to cover for the investment losses.[19]

While Hubbard was well known for his temper tantrums, Miscavige began taking the fits of rage to another level. In October 1982, he ordered that Homer Schomer, the Treasury Secretary for Author Services, be given what Scientologists call a gang-bang security check.[20] Schomer was interrogated by a series of people in a small room inside the Author Services building on Sunset Boulevard while he was attached to the E-Meter. The security check lasted ten hours, from around 10 pm to 8 am the following morning.

Homer Schomer later testified that Miscavige wanted him to be interrogated because of a failed gold deal that lost Scientology hundreds of thousands of dollars, a transaction he said he had no knowledge of. Schomer was also in trouble for allowing a finance officer to audit Hubbard's accounts.[21] During his gang-bang security check, he was accused of being a CIA or FBI plant.

Later, under oath, Schomer told the Superior Court of California that Miscavige and his offsider, Norman Starkey, spat tobacco juice in his face during the security check. Terri Gamboa was asked to join in, but she considered spitting in her colleague's face to be beyond the pale.

> He (Miscavige) ordered all of us to go in there and spit on him. Everybody stand in line walk through spit on him and walk out the other door. Norman did it. Miscavige did it. I refused. When he saw that I wasn't there he came in my office and said, 'Terri why aren't you with everybody else?' I said, 'Dave I'm not going to spit on anybody. I'm not going to do that.'[22]

Miscavige glared at Terri and walked out. There was no immediate punishment, but Miscavige had already begun targeting others who had long associations with Hubbard. 'I knew then the writing was on the wall,' says Terri. 'One by one he worked to get rid of all the old-timers or bust them to menial tasks so they had no power or control.'[23]

Gale Irwin, who had been on board the *Apollo* with Terri when they were both teenagers, had risen to the leadership of the powerful Commodore's Messengers Organization (CMO). She had previously raised concerns about Miscavige's behaviour and ordered that he be security-checked because of his abusive behaviour and attitude. According to Irwin, when Miscavige received this news, he lost his temper and lashed out at Irwin, knocking her to the ground with a flying tackle.[24] (Miscavige denies all allegations of abuse.)

Irwin rang Hubbard's former chauffeur John Brousseau. She wanted immediate action. Irwin demanded a meeting be arranged with Pat Broeker. Brousseau drove her to a pay phone in San Bernardino used for emergencies when the Scientologists needed to contact Pat. As they waited for the call from Broeker, Miscavige arrived in a black van with five other men. According to Irwin, Miscavige pulled out a tyre jack from the back of the van and smashed the pay phone. She was ordered into the van and told soon after she was no longer head of the Commodore's Messengers Organization.[25]

While Miscavige was taking control, Hubbard was isolated in his hideout and unaware of what was going on. Those close to him on the outside were being purged. Miscavige forced Mary Sue to step down as Controller of the Guardian's Office and turfed Hubbard's children Arthur and Suzette off the property at the International Base for being 'security risks'.[26] In a further humiliation he appointed Suzette to be his personal maid. Hubbard's auditor and top technical executive David Mayo was found guilty of 'committing a problem' and sent to a remote camp where he was forced to run around a pole in the desert heat for hours on end.[27]

With Hubbard in hiding and those close to him being marginalised, speculation increased that he was no longer alive. His son Nibs filed for the trusteeship of his father's estate on the basis he was either dead or mentally incompetent.[28] The Church of Scientology provided a statement from Hubbard that said, 'I am not a missing person. I am in seclusion for my own choosing.' Each page of the statement included copies of his fingerprints.[29]

In his years living in seclusion Hubbard struggled with his health. His Operating Thetan abilities could not overcome chronic pancreatitis, the ageing process, or the effects of his near lifelong addiction to Kool cigarettes. On 16 January 1986 he suffered a serious stroke. Three days later, Flag Order 3879, titled 'The Sea Org & the Future', was issued in Hubbard's name. The order announced that Pat Broeker had been promoted to the new position of First Loyal Officer, and Annie Broeker to Second Loyal Officer.[30] If the order was truly the work of Hubbard, he seemed to be making it clear who should take over Scientology. Miscavige was not mentioned.

On the evening of 24 January 1986, Hubbard died in his Blue Bird motorhome after another stroke.[31] Alongside him were Pat Broeker, his auditor Ray Mithoff and his doctor Eugene Denk.[32] He was 74. Despite Hubbard's vehement opposition to psychiatric drugs, the coroner found traces of Vistaril, an anti-anxiety tranquilliser, in his blood sample.[33]

Between them, Pat Broeker and David Miscavige cooked up a plan about how to break the news. On the following Monday, around 2000 Scientologists squeezed in to the Hollywood Palladium for a special announcement. David Miscavige took to the stage. Despite the internal power plays, the 25-year-old was not well known to the audience. Miscavige announced that Hubbard had moved on to his next level of OT research, that he had chosen to discard his body:

*Thus, at 2000 hours, Friday 24 January 1986, L. Ron
Hubbard discarded the body he had used in this lifetime
for seventy-four years, ten months and eleven days. The
body he had used to facilitate his existence in this universe
had ceased to be useful and in fact had become an impediment
to the work he now must do outside its confines.*[34]

According to Miscavige's logic, Hubbard wasn't really dead; he
was simply doing research somewhere else.

Pat Broeker announced to the crowd that before Hubbard had
'discarded his body' he had completed new Operating Thetan levels –
going up to OT IX and OT X. It was a surprising revelation that
would come back to haunt him. Broeker claimed that Hubbard got up
to OT XV and that only he knew where the secret files were hidden.[35]
This was too much for Miscavige. A team of private investigators was
hired to monitor Broeker.[36]

Miscavige grew impatient about the lack of evidence surrounding
the higher OT levels. Eventually, he and a team of Scientology
lawyers turned up at the ranch and demanded Broeker hand over
any confidential OT materials. As they argued, a small squadron of
Scientology heavies led by Miscavige's lieutenant Marty Rathbun
hid in the bushes outside. Broeker was threatened that he could face
charges relating to US$1.8 million in funds that he could not account
for. Rathbun entered the house and took away the filing cabinets of
Hubbard's First Loyal Officer.

As Scientology operatives sifted through Broeker's files, no
evidence emerged of the higher OT levels. During a second raid, under
intense interrogation from Miscavige, Annie Broeker revealed the
location of a storage locker her husband kept in Paso Robles.[37] There
were more files, but no evidence of the higher OT levels. Broeker's
bluff had been called. In March 1987, Miscavige appointed himself
Chairman of the Board of the Religious Technology Center (RTC).[38]
In April the following year, he cancelled Hubbard's final order that
had anointed the Broekers to be his Loyal Officers. Soon after, Pat
left the country and Miscavige assumed complete control. He placed
Hubbard's First Loyal Officer under surveillance for the next 24 years
at a cost of over US$10 million.[39]

TERRI GAMBOA MAY HAVE been one of Scientology's most senior executives and one of Hubbard's most trusted and loyal veterans, but she was kept in the dark about the power struggle between Broeker and Miscavige. 'I didn't know he was kicking Pat out,' she says. 'He kept that very quiet because he knew I was fairly good friends with Pat.'[40] Terri and Pat shared a love of horses and knew each other from back in the *Apollo* days. Pat Broeker's first wife, Trudy Venter, was Terri's best friend. Terri had married her first husband, Gerry Armstrong, and Trudy married Pat as part of a double wedding on board the *Apollo*. 'Pat was very good to me and I think Miscavige knew there could be a concern if I knew too much, that I would stand up for Pat.'[41]

There may have been another reason why Miscavige kept Terri out of the loop. Hubbard had personally appointed her as one of three lifetime trustees to the Church of Spiritual Technology (CST) as part of the corporate restructure of Scientology in 1982.[42] The trustees were unaware their terms lasted for the whole of their lives. The CST was the highest level of the church that held all the trademarks and copyrights. According to its Articles of Incorporation, CST is meant to 'espouse, present, propagate, practice, ensure, and maintain the purity and integrity of the religion of Scientology'.[43]

Terri believes the lifetime trustees of the CST have the power to vote in and out Miscavige as the Chairman of the Board of the RTC, and that he withheld this critical information in order to shore up his position. Terri did not find out she was a lifetime trustee until over 20 years after she had left Scientology. 'He hid it [the corporate structure] away,' she told me. 'He locked it up, nobody got to see it. He took the power, but he knew on paper who had the power and he made sure he manipulated it to control every one of them.'[44]

The three lifetime trustees were Terri Gamboa, Greg Wilhere and Marion Pouw. Terri and Marion were Australian and close. They had been good friends growing up as children in Melbourne. The Gillham and Pouw families had formed a close bond when the Anderson Inquiry was being held in Victoria and the children of Scientologists were being shunned in the playground. By the 1980s, Marion had become one of Terri's executives at Author Services. Terri and Marion were also close friends with fellow trustee and Scientology executive

Greg Wilhere. All three were on the ship in the early days of the Sea Org before Miscavige had appeared on the scene. In Terri's mind, Miscavige would have seen them as a tight voting bloc who had the ability to undermine his takeover plans.

Others see the power of the CST lifetime trustees as being illusory. Denise Brennan, who oversaw Scientology's corporate restructure in the early 1980s, told journalist Tony Ortega the trustees held no real power. 'The people who think they're following the power of control by looking at the lists of directors for CST are falling for the sham we set up,' she said.[45] According to Brennan all power resides with the Sea Org and the person with the highest rank there is Miscavige. But Gamboa insists Hubbard intended for the corporate structure to take over after he was gone. 'He had specifically assigned the lifetime trustees for this purpose,' she says, 'along with assigning the Commodore's Messengers as the WatchDog Committee to oversee the entire management of the Scientology network worldwide.'[46]

In the early days of his transition to power, Miscavige did all he could to undermine Gamboa's power. Marion and Terri worked closely together at Author Services. In 1989, Miscavige split Terri and Marion up. 'She was one of my top executives,' Terri told me. 'He took her off post and made her his steward – his personal slave. I couldn't believe it, but now when I found out later that she and I were two of the CST lifetime trustees, it all makes sense, it was all part of his hijacking of the church for his personal benefit and power.'[47]

Removing Marion Pouw from Terri's executive team was just the first step. 'He took away my main execs and started stripping my org down,' says Terri, 'and then he started blaming me for the stats going down, and it was like, well yes, you take the main people out, the stats are going to go down.'[48]

After Author Services' sales figures declined, Miscavige punished Terri. She was put 'on the decks', a Scientology punishment that dates back to Hubbard's time on the *Apollo,* where he would demote Sea Org members to cleaning duties.

Terri was assigned to wash the cars and clean the offices at Miscavige's Religious Technology Center. To further humiliate her, Miscavige had her move a pile of rocks from one location to another in stifling heat with a security guard watching over her. 'There was no purpose in moving rocks,' she says. 'It was just Miscavige trying to get at me and I could see him up on the hill watching through binoculars – he loved to manipulate, degrade and humiliate people; it made him feel good. He has no compassion for others, he is a ruthless dictator and I knew I could no longer be a part of this.'[49]

As Gamboa moved rocks under the desert sun, she thought about what was coming next from Miscavige. 'I know him really well, having worked with him directly for ten years straight,' she says. 'So when I'm moving these rocks I'm thinking this is the end of the line for me. He's going to have me doing this until he can break me. I've seen him squash people like a bug. He'd bring some of the best people on the base up and make mincemeat out of them in front of everybody – they were just shrinking as beings. Scientology is meant to make people better, yet he used it to squash and demean people and he was extremely good at it. He would yell and scream until they disappeared, until they were crushed.'[50]

Terri had decided to leave. But getting out was not going to be easy. She had no car, no contact with her sister, Janis Grady, on the inside and no contact for her brother, Peter Gillham Jnr, on the outside. She hadn't even revealed her plans to her husband Fernando Gamboa, who was a drummer and recording engineer with the Sea Org band the Golden Era Musicians.

Inside Scientology there is an all-pervasive culture of surveillance and snitching. Sea Org members fear telling their partners about any plans they might have to leave because it's not unusual for partners, relatives and best friends to inform on each other through Scientology's internal justice system. This can result in their loved ones being security-checked on the E-Meter and then being assigned to intense physical labour or locked up. Many have fled the Sea Org without telling their spouses. It can take years to come to the realisation that it's time to bust out. To then convince their partner in a short amount of time can be a high-risk manoeuvre.

At the time Terri, Fernando and other Sea Org members were staying in temporary accommodation in an apartment block in Hemet. It was before the permanent residencies for Sea Org staff had been built in the fortified compound at the International Base. On a January night in 1990, Terri nervously waited at the apartment complex for Fernando to return home after recording in the studio with the Golden Era Musicians. She had decided she was going to tell her husband it was time to leave.

When Fernando arrived at the apartments at about 1 am, Terri had already been preparing her lines. 'This is crazy, let's leave,' she said. 'The treatment of staff is so bad, so degrading and debilitating.' Fernando had seen the abuse up close and was appalled by it, but he was not sure about leaving. Terri had to use all her powers of persuasion.

After a couple of hours, Terri had convinced Fernando she was right. But her sense of relief soon turned to despair. 'Okay,' Fernando said, after agreeing to leave, 'we'll let them know in the morning.' Terri knew this would not work. 'No, no, no,' she responded. 'We're not going to let anyone know. We're going to go out the window tonight, right now.'[51] Terri explained that if they did not leave that minute, Miscavige would make their lives hell. There would be security checks, they would be placed 'on the decks', they would be humiliated in front of the rest of the Sea Org until they changed their minds. 'There was no way I was going to go through all that and allow Miscavige the satisfaction,' she says.[52]

After another hour of talking, Fernando came round to Terri's point of view. 'You're right,' he told his wife, 'but do you realise the repercussions of this?' Having one of Hubbard's original messengers and one of Scientology's most senior executives escape in the dark of night would be a big deal. But the Sea Org veteran was adamant they had to leave. 'I know and I don't care,' she told her husband. 'I'm past all that now. We have to get out.'[53]

Fernando still had the keys to the musicians' vehicle. The black Dodge van that drove the band around, and had previously been Miscavige's private vehicle to take communications to and from Hubbard, now became their getaway car. The pair climbed out their first-floor window into the dark of night with a handful of belongings. They started up the van and headed for Los Angeles. But Terri and Fernando were not in the clear yet. Not by a long way.

While Fernando had been working at the base near Hemet, Terri's office was in Hollywood. As an executive who worked long hours for Author Services, she was provided with a room inside the Scientology complex in Los Angeles. Before she left the Sea Org, Terri wanted to go back to her room and retrieve some personal items. Fernando had to drive the musicians' van to Scientology's famous 'Big Blue' building in LA and hope they could get in and out without being seen. 'We had to get there, get everything loaded and get out by 8 am at the very latest,' says Terri, 'because the RPF starts coming out then. I didn't want anybody who knew I was on the decks up at Int [International Base] to see me and report on me as then they would come after us with security guards.'[54]

The Sea Org fugitives arrived at the Big Blue building after the sun came up. Terri took the stairs to avoid the early morning activity in the elevators. She gathered her most prized possessions and loaded up the van. The couple were closing in on their 8 am deadline and getting ready to make their final escape. But Terri knew she was leaving forever and insisted on getting one more load of personal belongings. Fernando was adamant it was time to go. 'No! No!' he yelled. 'Get in! Get in!'[55]

Terri insisted she had time for one more load. She headed up to her room for the last time, but on the way up the stairs ran into her brother-in-law, Paul Grady. 'He was surprised to see me,' says Terri, 'and I'm thinking oh no, he's going to report it because everybody reports everything.' Terri and Fernando got lucky. Paul said nothing. She went back into her room and using a trolley and some bungee cords secured her final load before making her way back down the stairs. They were almost in the clear.

As she headed out the back door Terri saw the RPF pouring into the garden to work on landscaping right next to the stairs she had used to get to the van.

As she made her way towards Fernando, the bungee cord detached and her belongings spilled everywhere. There, staring her in the eye, was the last person she wanted to see – the Bosun, the head of the RPF, with a platoon of Sea Org members scurrying around him. Fernando watched on from the van. They were desperate to avoid the RPF. Despite his protests, Terri had gone back for one last load. Now it seemed as if that one small trip would cost them their freedom and that they would soon be joining the RPF on landscaping duties.

As Fernando watched from the van, he could not quite believe what he saw. Suddenly the RPF swung into action and started helping Terri.

The Bosun didn't know I was busted and on the decks. And he said, 'Sir, can we help you?' And I quickly said, 'Yes, please.' So we had five RPF members loading up my stuff – and they say, 'Where would you like it, Sir?' I said, 'Right there in the van' and they loaded it up. I said, 'Thanks, guys,' and acted as if everything was normal and as if I was still the head executive at Author Services.'[56]

Terri hopped in the front passenger seat and slammed the door shut. She urged Fernando to put his foot on the accelerator and get the hell out of Hollywood. 'We took off and Fernando was like, "What the hell were you doing going back again?"' says Terri. Once the adrenaline stopped pumping they were able to laugh about what had just happened. The RPF had helped them escape from the Sea Org.

Fernando and Terri had two immediate problems to solve. They had get rid of the van and pick up two horses. The first task proved easy enough. They rented a vehicle and drove to a suburb near Chick Corea's studio, parked the musicians' van on the side of the street and put the keys in the mail. As an executive for Hubbard's business management company, Terri had been paid fairly well in Sea Org terms. She had enough money in the bank to buy a replacement vehicle – half with cash and half on credit card. Dealing with the horses proved more complicated.

Back when Pat Broeker was in a position of power, Terri had been allowed to keep a horse at the corral at International Base along with a couple of other Sea Org members who also had a horse. Terri and Pat shared a deep love of horses. Eventually Terri bought another horse, Dasher – a Thoroughbred/Quarter Horse cross-bred on the ranch at Creston. She kept Dasher in private stables at Los Angeles. As soon as Terri escaped from the Sea Org, the Scientologists placed two guards outside the stables 24 hours a day, waiting for her to come and reclaim her horse.

Terri not only had to get Dasher out, she had promised a Sea Org friend she would sell her the horse, as she was still stuck at International Base and could no longer care for it. Fernando and Terri snuck in to the stables through a back entrance. 'We got the horses and led them out the back way down the side of a big wash basin so they couldn't see us,' she says. 'We got the horses out and put them at the stables next door without them knowing.'[57] From there they were able to sneak them out the back and have them transported interstate.

The Scientologists didn't realise the horses had been collected, and continued their 24-hour watch outside the stables. The security guards were spooking Terri's riding instructor. 'She told me they are scaring away my clients, can you please call them off,' she says.[58] Terri rang Greg Wilhere, who at the time was Inspector General of the RTC, second in charge to Miscavige. She told him the horses were gone and he should remove the guards. Wilhere said he would only do that if Terri agreed to meet with him.

The pair met at a hotel near the Californian city of Burbank. Terri pulled no punches about why she had left. 'I spent three hours telling him about my disagreements with Miscavige,' Terri recalls. 'His evil treatment of staff, his craziness, the bad management, his stat pushing, his false stats, his lying to staff and I could tell I got to Greg. I could see it by the end when he said to me, "You know, Terri, despite all this, you know the Sea Org will always be around, whether it's with Miscavige or whatever." In other words, he was trying to say this will pass one day.'[59]

While Greg tried to convince Terri to return to the Sea Org, Fernando was chewing the fat with his old band mate Ronnie Miscavige, the father of Scientology's leader. 'Greg brought him with him so he could try and handle Fernando while Greg tried to handle me to try and get us to come back,' says Terri.[60] Fernando had a genuine connection with Ronnie. He loved his sense of humour and the two talked intimately about why Fernando had left.

Despite their close relationship, Ronnie was not the ideal man to try and haul Fernando back in. 'He asked what is it like being out?' says Terri. 'He was all enamoured by the fact that we were out, because he had wanted to leave years before and DM [his son] talked him out of it. He said to Ronnie that he would never see his family again if he left and that he would make sure of that.'[61] It would be another 22 years before Ronnie finally acted on his instincts and escaped from the Sea Org.

The following morning, Terri and Fernando packed up and left. They would never return to the Sea Org. The pair had decided to head for Florida where Fernando's family were based. Through their lawyers, the Church of Scientology arranged for private investigators to tail them. It would be a long drive from California to Florida.

When Terri and Fernando made it to Colorado a few days later, they started having problems with their car. As their SUV made its way up the mountains, it began spluttering. Fernando called the car dealer in Los Angeles, who explained that it was just the high altitude. The car dealer had some further information for him. 'You know you are being followed?' he said. 'Three guys came in here right after you bought the vehicle and said they were the police, they wouldn't show us any ID, and they wanted to know where you guys were going.'[62]

Terri believes Scientology's Office of Special Affairs (OSA) got the car dealership address from her credit card transaction. 'OSA is notorious for obtaining credit card information and tracking down departed staff and bringing them back,' she says. 'They have everybody's social security card numbers and are able to run credit reports and obtain all bank and credit card accounts. They then call up the bank as if they are the card holder and request an account statement.'[63]

The car dealer refused to give up the pair's destination, but it didn't matter. Terri and Fernando were soon being followed. At one point they drove off the road to try and shake the person tailing them when they suddenly saw the tail car switch with a second car that took over following them. They decided to follow the first car and see where he went. He stopped soon after at a 7/11. 'He came out with a newspaper and a cup of coffee because he's off duty so I said, "Hey, who is paying you to follow us?"' Terri says. 'And he said, "I don't know what you're talking about."' The man lowered his head and scurried away, pretending he was getting into a truck across the parking lot. Terri and Fernando lingered while the private investigator kept peeking at them through the windows of the other side of the truck hoping they would leave.[64]

As they drove across the country tailed by private investigators, Terri continued to check in with Greg Wilhere. He had made her promise she would call him along the way. Terri thought it might minimise the harassment if she co-operated. As they closed in on Florida, Greg insisted they meet once more in Nashville. Terri and

Fernando headed to Tennessee's capital in the hope it would keep relations smooth with the church.

THE HOME OF COUNTRY music was an appropriate place for Marty Rathbun to turn up in. In the late 1970s, Rathbun had been chosen to work at one of Hubbard's secret locations at La Quinta. Marty's real name was Mark. As Steve 'Sarge' Pfauth drove him there, Rathbun was told he'd need an undercover name. The old Marty Robbins country and western hit *El Paso* came on the radio station they were listening to. 'How does Marty sound?' Rathbun asked. Sarge looked at the radio and grinned. 'Perfect,' he said.[65]

Rathbun had impressed Hubbard's executives by displaying extraordinary courage in defending a young Scientologist named Diane Colletto. Rathbun agreed to ride home with the 25-year-old after she had received a threatening call from her husband John who had just escaped from the RPF. As they approached the Scientology complex in Los Angeles, a Volvo driven by Diane's husband sideswiped her car. John Colletto leaped out of the car and shot her in the leg.

Rathbun could have done a runner, but instead he tried to protect Diane. He ran towards the gunman and got him in a headlock, but then blacked out after he was smashed over the head and neck repeatedly with the gun barrel. When he regained consciousness, Rathbun renewed the struggle, narrowly avoiding being shot as he wrestled the 100-kg man to the ground. Eventually John Colletto freed himself and shot his wife dead.

Rathbun was lauded for his bravery and considered worthy of promotion. Soon after, he went to work for Scientology at La Quinta where Hubbard was living at the time. Later on, when Terri Gamboa and Norman Starkey left the 'All Clear Unit', Marty was promoted to take it over. He later became the Inspector General for Ethics in Miscavige's RTC.[66] By the time Terri and Fernando decided to leave in 1990, Rathbun had become Miscavige's most trusted and effective enforcer over both the Ethics and Intelligence arms of Scientology.

When Terri arrived in Nashville, she thought the meeting with Greg would be just like the little chat they had had in Burbank – another harmless attempt at getting her and Fernando to come back to the Sea Org. But Terri soon realised that something else was up. Into the meeting walked Wilhere and four more of Scientology's most senior executives – Marty Rathbun, Norman Starkey, Marc Yager and Ray Mithoff. Terri saw it as an act of intimidation. According to Terri, the only one missing was David Miscavige. 'He always sends others to do his dirty work,' she says. 'He likes to have somebody else to blame things on.'[67]

Scientology's top executives went to work on Terri and Fernando, putting the hard word on them to return to the Sea Org, but the couple were adamant they would be not be coming back. The conversation lasted for over an hour and became heated. Terri and Fernando were accused of being 'criminals', 'liars' and 'out ethics' – the usual claims made against people trying to leave. When Marty Rathbun excused himself, saying he needed to take a break, Terri became suspicious. 'I waited a minute till he went outside and I got up to follow him,' she says.[68] Norman Starkey tried to stop Terri, but Fernando intervened, throwing down his coat as a signal he was willing to fight Starkey if he did not let his wife go.

When Terri left the room she spied Marty in the hotel corridor with the private investigator she had previously seen at the 7/11. The investigator had been walking towards Marty carrying a slim jim, a strip of metal used for breaking into cars. When he recognised Terri he tried to hide the slim jim behind his leg , and turned away from Marty and continued down the hallway as if there was nothing happening.

Terri turned to Marty and said, 'Hey, what's going on, what are you up to?' When she didn't get a straight answer, Terri went downstairs to check on their car and then their room. 'They had neatly removed everything from the glove box of the car, gone through it and left it on the floor of the car,' she says. 'They had gone through all of our suitcases and belongings in both the room and the car. They weren't even careful about it and didn't put things back in the right place. I went back up to the room and I said to Fernando, "They went through our stuff, let's get out of here." So we left.'[69]

Years later Terri was told what the Scientology executives were looking for. 'Miscavige told them to go through all our stuff because I might have had the combination for the safe where all of LRH's estate papers and valuable documents are and I might have taken something important. In actual fact Miscavige wanted to make sure I didn't have anything to use against him or the church.'[70]

Terri Gamboa believes Miscavige wanted to make sure she did not have any documents that showed she was a top executive in the church or anything embarrassing she could use against him. 'He didn't know if I had bad intentions,' she says. 'He didn't know if I had taken anything that I could blackmail him with or use against him or the church. He didn't want me to have any ammunition that I could use to weaken his position or power. Tom Cruise was already becoming an important person to the church and knew me well as the head of Author Services; he wouldn't want me to have anything that could harm that relationship with Tom. I didn't take anything, but he had to make sure of that to keep his position secure.'[71]

Marty Rathbun agrees that Miscavige had grave fears about the kind of information Terri could have revealed. 'She probably had more potentially damaging information than anybody else who had left the church up to that point besides Pat Broeker,' Rathbun told me. 'She knew a lot about what was going on with Broeker and Hubbard and his last days and all the coups that occurred to get Broeker out of the road.'[72]

Terri didn't just know the truth about Miscavige's abusive past. As a former Executive Director of Author Services, she knew better than anyone how Hubbard's business management company worked at a time when they were trying desperately to convince the IRS they should be given tax-exempt status. She also knew the truth about Hubbard, both the good and the bad. Terri had seen the culture of abuse up close on the *Apollo*, and she knew how appallingly the Church of Scientology could treat its followers, including its best and brightest, like her mother.

Terri's parents, Yvonne and Peter Gillham, had been two of the most successful disseminators of Scientology in its history, both while they were married and in the years after they went their separate ways. 'People would follow them in droves because they truly were the essence of what we all believed Scientology to be,' says Terri. 'Their charisma, their deep devotion to both LRH and Scientology, their application of the Scientology technology that made people feel better, feel lifted, feel larger than life as a spiritual being.'[73]

Yvonne, with her charm, energy and hard work, had secured many influential followers for Hubbard. Yet at various stages she had been treated woefully. She was separated from her children, declared 'suppressive' and sexually harassed by Hubbard. Somehow she kept bouncing back and remained faithful to Scientology. In 1969, Yvonne had set up the Celebrity Centre in Los Angeles and it had flourished under her leadership, recruiting marketable stars like John Travolta and becoming the largest single Scientology organisation in the world.[74]

Despite its success, Hubbard had ordered an evaluation of Celebrity Centre (CC) in early 1977. The Guardian's Office (GO) had contempt for the way Yvonne had connected with writers and performers through her concerts, tie-dye classes and candlelit poetry readings. The GO made sure they dropped negative reports about Yvonne into the evaluation. After the report was handed down she was dismissed from the organisation she had conceived, founded and run so successfully. She was reassigned to set up the PR organisation without adequate funding or support. Later, as punishment, she was made to clean the pool at Scientology's base in Florida. By the time Yvonne returned to Los Angeles in June that year, her health had deteriorated. She was suffering from intense headaches and her sight was failing.

Tragically, Yvonne did not get the medical treatment she needed until it was too late. When she finally saw a doctor she was told she had a brain tumour. 'They said it was inoperable,' says Spanky Taylor, who was her personal public relations officer at the time.[75] Yvonne's lack of treatment was not unusual. 'Nobody got medical help in Scientology,' recalls Nancy Many, who worked with Yvonne. 'We were taught it was your overts – if you were sick, it was your fault, you pulled it in.'[76] Yvonne's daughter Janis says sick people in Scientology were considered a liability. 'It was not a matter of singling her out, it's a matter of the culture. If you get sick you are considered "downstat", you're not contributing.'[77]

The appalling treatment of one of Scientology's most successful disseminators continued. When Yvonne requested to go to Flag base at Clearwater to get the auditing she thought would help her, Spanky Taylor asked one of Scientology's finance executives if they could pay for an airline ticket. 'I was told if Yvonne wants to get to Flag, she can take a fucking Greyhound bus,' says Taylor.[78]

Yvonne's children were not even told she was dying. Spanky Taylor remembers how devastating that was for the mother of three. 'She wanted her kids so bad,' she tells me in tears, nearly 40 years later. 'We talked a lot about how much she wanted to be with her kids and she was not permitted.'[79] Hubbard had callously separated Yvonne from her children when they very young. Now his organisation and its warped policies were denying her access to her children once more, as she lay in bed dying from the effects of a tumour and a stroke that had gone undiagnosed and had not been treated properly.

When Yvonne first became ill, none of her three children were told. Terri found out through an anonymous phone call. When she picked up the phone, a woman said, 'Your mother is very ill and nobody is going to tell you.' The caller hung up straight away. Terri jumped in her car and drove to the Wilcox berthing building where her mother lived with her then husband, Heber Jentzsch.

Terri arrived to find her mother in a delirious state with the door wide open and no-one attending to her. 'It was the strangest thing,' says Terri. 'It was like the *Twilight Zone*; nobody was there.'[80] Terri called an ambulance and got her mother to the hospital where doctors discovered a large inoperable tumour in her brain.

Yvonne's eldest daughter was not allowed to stay and look after her. 'I was forced back to work,' says Terri. 'I was told others were caring for her, that she was getting auditing and that would handle her illness and that she was improving.'[81] Terri was lied to. Yvonne was not getting better. A few months later Terri received a letter from her mother that had been handwritten by someone else. 'I knew it was her way of telling me something was very wrong,' she says.[82]

Terri borrowed money for an airfare and flew straight to Clearwater without telling her superiors. She was faced with an awful dilemma; she knew she had to go and see her mother, but didn't feel like she could tell her brother, Peter, or sister, Janis. 'If I tell them and they ask permission to go, nobody's going to let all three of us go. They'll stop all of us from going. So I had to do it secretly. I had no choice.'[83]

When Terri landed at Tampa airport she called Yvonne to tell her she was on her way. 'She was slurring her words, she could hardly speak,' says Terri. 'I could tell it was a bad situation. I said, "Hang on, hang on I'll be there soon."[84] When Terri arrived she found her mother in a room by herself, with no-one there to comfort her. 'Tezzie, I'm so glad you're here,' Yvonne told her eldest daughter. 'She repeated it over and over as I hugged her and she hugged me,' says Terri, 'and then she faded away and never came to and died two to three days later.'[85]

After Yvonne died in January 1978, Hubbard ordered that the Celebrity Centre become a shrine to her.[86] For a while her old office at the building in Los Angeles was set aside as a tribute to Yvonne and her work, but it didn't last long. 'It was demolished,' says Nancy Many, a former head of the Celebrity Centre. 'It's now the President of CC's office with no mention of Yvonne.'[87] Terri says she heard David Miscavige personally order that it be removed in its entirety. 'He never wanted anyone to receive any credit for anything unless it was himself,' she says.[88]

IN AUGUST 1990, JANIS Grady became the third of the Gillham children to break out of the Sea Org. David Miscavige's extreme behaviour was once again a driving force behind the decision. Like Terri, Janis had made the successful transition from being one of Hubbard's first messengers into a Scientology executive. In 1988, she led the team that prepared Scientology's cruise ship the *Freewinds* for its first voyage. From 1987 to 1990, she was in charge of Scientology's international management team.[89]

In the summer of 1990, Sea Org members at Scientology's International Base (also known as Int or Gold) had been working overtime preparing for the arrival of Nicole Kidman and Tom Cruise. As part of the base's overhaul, the villas, also known as the G units, were being renovated for Scientology's star couple. For weeks Sea Org members had been working day and night to get the accommodation up to Hollywood standards.[90] Then Mother Nature intervened and turned all of Miscavige's best-laid plans to mud.

Flooding rains ravaged the nearby town of Hemet and Scientology's base did not escape the damage. Roads were closed due to mudslides, trees were uprooted, water flooded into buildings. Former Sea Org member Marc Headley estimated the rain caused several million dollars' worth of damage. 'The villas were flooded,' he said. 'The mountain above the G Units turned to mud and flowed over the highway and straight into the Gs.'[91]

The staff on the base were drenched, exhausted and covered in mud. They had done all they could to try and save the villas from being destroyed by mudslides. 'I saw the Gold crew risking their lives to prevent property being ruined,' says Janis Grady.[92] But their efforts were not appreciated. Miscavige blamed the Sea Org for the damage.

Miscavige called for a compulsory muster of all staff in the base's dining hall.[93] A podium was set up at the front of the room. The crew, in their hundreds, stood to attention while they waited for their leader to arrive. Miscavige thundered into the room and started screaming at the staff, berating those who had risked their lives to save the villas from being damaged.

Miscavige described the workers assembled in front of him as 'scum' and assigned the entire base to the condition of 'Confusion' meaning 15-minute meal breaks and no other liberties.[94] Janis Grady, like many others, was shocked by the tirade. 'DM [Miscavige] got up there in front of everybody ranting and raving about how the Gold crew were doing nothing about dealing with the storm and I was standing there and I'm thinking this guy has flipped! And that's when I made my decision – I'm done.'[95]

Janis had permission to go to Los Angeles for three days to catch up with her Australian aunt and uncle who were visiting the US. Her husband Paul did not have a leave pass, so she pretended she was dropping him back at the apartment complex before heading to LA.

Instead, Janis and Paul headed straight to the airport where they picked up Janis's aunt and uncle before heading to her father's place. Peter Gillham Snr was still a Scientologist but he was not in the Sea Org. They told him they were not returning to Hemet and asked for a number and address for Janis's brother.

Peter Gillham Jnr had been out of the Sea Org for eight years and lived in the rural Californian community of Upper Ojai. Janis tried calling him, but he did not answer. She decided to turn up unannounced. 'We found his house but he wasn't home but there was someone from down the road in his house watching TV,' Janis recalls, laughing. 'And she said, "Oh, your brother is camping down at the beach at Point Mugu."'[96] Janis and Paul headed for the coast.

Janis had been in the Sea Org since she was 11. At the age of 34, she was about to spend her first night as a free woman. It was a joyous occasion. 'We camped out on the beach, our first night of freedom,' she says. 'And I got to meet my nieces and my nephew. Because my brother was declared "suppressive" I'd never seen the kids!'[97] Soon after, Janis got confirmation that she was pregnant. She would now, like her brother, be able to have her own family, something she could never have done inside the Sea Org.

Eventually Janis called her sister, Terri, in Florida to let her know she had escaped. Then she called the International Base and told them she was not coming back. When Janis tried to retrieve personal items she had in storage at the U-Haul at Hemet, she discovered that someone had already been through her belongings. 'They had already broken in to the storage room and they took all my photographs of me, my mother and any crew members, or me in uniform. They took all my birthday cards that were signed by LRH [Hubbard]. They took anything that was Scientology or LRH connected.'[98]

By the end of the year Janis and Terri were reunited. They decided to set up a business in Las Vegas. Terri had spent time there in the 1980s visiting Caesar's Palace casino with Tom Cruise, Nicole Kidman and Miscavige when Tom flew them there in his private airplane for Terri's birthday. After leaving the Sea Org she got an offer that took her back to the desert city. 'I got a call from somebody who knew my mother in the early '70s,' she says, 'and he said come to Vegas, it's boomtown USA, come and help me start a mortgage company. I'll teach you the mortgage business and you manage the company for me.'[99]

The sisters and their husbands moved in to a two-bedroom apartment in the Polo Club on Decatur Boulevard. Mark Fisher, a former Sea Org colleague who left the same night as Janis, joined the business as well and was sleeping on the sofa in their apartment until he could afford his own place. After a few months, their company, City Mortgage, needed a new agent. Terri interviewed a friendly young man from out of town named Dave Lubow. She hired him soon after as a loan officer.

Lubow got very close to Terri and Janis, their husbands, and Mark Fisher. He moved in to the same apartment block as them, played racquetball with Fernando and hung out with the former Sea Org members after hours. He started asking personal questions about their time in Scientology and why they all decided to leave. Fernando asked him if he worked for the Church of Scientology. He denied it.

Dave Lubow didn't close too many sales in those early months, but he didn't really need to. He had another source of income he could rely on. The Church of Scientology, through its lawyers, had paid him to infiltrate City Mortgage and spy on the former Scientologists. He would send regular reports to the Office of Special Affairs (OSA) in Los Angeles. Miscavige wanted as much information as he could get on Terri and Janis.

Marty Rathbun was Miscavige's right hand man at the time. He says he was told to arrange for someone to infiltrate and spy on the Las Vegas group. Rathbun told OSA-Intel head Linda Hamel to find the right person for the job. Lubow was hired soon after.[100]

The intelligence flowed freely back to Scientology headquarters and to Miscavige. 'Quite frankly, the more reporting he did, the more obsessed Miscavige became,' recalled Rathbun. 'Those people all pinned their gripes about their experiences in Scientology to their personal experiences with Miscavige.'[101] According to Rathbun, Scientology's leader became 'intensely obsessed with that Las Vegas crowd.'[102] Just how obsessed was highlighted by the undercover operation that was coming.

Dave Lubow had given Fernando a telephone as a Christmas present. The phone was used to call David Mayo, Hubbard's former auditor, who had been treated so brutally by Miscavige. Terri had been trying to track down Mayo for years and had finally found a phone number for him. She now believes the phone was bugged and that phone call triggered the extraordinary operation that was about to unfold.

Terri Gamboa was used to working late from her time as head of Author Services. At City Mortgage, she continued the habit to get ahead of the game for the following day. One night at around 9 pm the phone rang. It was Ian Markham-Smith, a Brit who said he was from an international public relations firm and wanted to have lunch and talk about investing with them in the mortgage company. After their initial meeting he indicated that he liked them so much he had a further opportunity for them.

Markham-Smith was a former Fleet Street journalist who would later publish books about Jerry Springer and Nicolas Cage. He took Terri and Fernando to Caesar's Palace where he wined and dined them and outlined his proposal. He wanted them to go to Australia and set up and run a horse property. They would host international clients, take them riding in the countryside, escort them to the opera and high-end restaurants and be paid good money for their troubles.

For someone like Terri, who loved riding horses, it was an irresistible offer. 'We were definitely suspicious at first,' she says. 'It was too good to be true, but what the hell, what are we going to do? Not do it because you are suspicious it's the church?'[103]

TERRI AND FERNANDO SIGNED on for the deal. They were paid $84,000 a year for just three days work each month as well as being on call whenever needed. It was excellent money for 1991, with expenses thrown in on top. The rest of the time they could ride horses and enjoy themselves. The property was north of Melbourne. In the two years they were there only two or three clients were sent out. With their living expenses covered, they were able to bank their wages and reinvest them into the mortgage business back in Las Vegas when they returned.

Dave Lubow, the loan officer who could not close a sale in Las Vegas, found the money to visit them in Australia a number of times. After the first year, when Terri and Fernando were thinking of leaving, he tried to convince them to stay and set up a Bed and Breakfast with him. 'He was like, "No, no, this will be great." He tried everything,' says Terri.[104] It all seemed very suspicious. Ian Markham-Smith gave Terri and Fernando a mobile phone and insisted they must be available to answer it at all times, even though there were was virtually no demand for clients.

Back in Las Vegas, Lubow blew his cover while drinking with a friend. On one occasion he brought a broker named Jack into City Mortgage. Janis started doing private deals with him. 'One day,' recalls Janis, 'I ask Jack, "Is Dave bringing you deals? Because he's not closing anything with me." He says, "Oh, no. Dave's not here as a loan officer, that's just a cover. He's a private investigator and he's on a case."'[105]

Janis switched to private investigator mode on Lubow. She asked Jack how he knew his friend was working undercover. He admitted that, after a night of drinking, he was invited back to Dave's apartment, which was full of equipment used for bugging telephones. It was then that Dave explained what he really did for money. 'I'm not a loan officer,' he told Jack. 'That's just my cover. I'm actually a private investigator and I'm on a case.'[106]

According to Janis, Lubow showed Jack his private investigator badge, his gun and his bugging equipment. 'Jack was innocently spilling the beans to me on Dave,' says Janis, 'and he had no clue.'[107] Janis and Terri now knew that Lubow was a spy, but they did not let on. If they had exposed him, the Church of Scientology would have simply hired another operative.

After two years of being paid good money to ride horses in Australia, Terri and Fernando returned to Las Vegas in late 1993, despite protests from Lubow and Ian Markham-Smith, who had urged them to stay. Both Marty Rathbun and Mike Rinder, two of Scientology's most senior executives at the time, have confirmed that the church financed the operation to get the pair out of the country. According to Rathbun, the reason was clear. He says Miscavige was concerned that Terri could have undermined their negotiations with the Internal Revenue Service (IRS) to gain tax-exempt status.[108]

At the time, Scientology's greatest priority was to regain the tax exemption it had lost in 1967, when the IRS had decided it was a commercial operation run for the benefit of Hubbard. In 1973, Hubbard decided the church should not pay its back taxes. Within 20 years, the Church of Scientology owed US$1 billion to the IRS, a debt that threatened its livelihood.[109] The church continued to fight the decision, bombarding the IRS with lawsuits, with over 200 cases on behalf of the church, and over 2000 on behalf of individual Scientologists.

When the Scientology entity the Church of Spiritual Technology (CST) sued the United States government over its denial of tax-exempt status in 1992, court documents listed Terri as a trustee of CST and a Director, President, and shareholder of Author Services. This was two years after she had left the Sea Org.

Terri believes Miscavige wanted her out of the country because he feared that she could have undermined either the litigation or the negotiations with the IRS. 'If the IRS called me and said you're a lifetime trustee, I would've said I left years ago,' she says. 'That would have undermined it right there, because they filed that I was a lifetime trustee. So they lied. Either way they would've been in trouble.'[110]

If the IRS had contacted Terri, it would have blown Miscavige's cover. 'I think Miscavige also didn't want me to find out that I was a lifetime trustee and that I had power over him,' she says. 'I'm sure to this day Marion Pouw and Greg Wilhere have no idea that they are lifetime trustees of CST and that they have power over Miscavige.'[111]

The two-year period when Terri was out of the way in Australia was a time when the IRS was asking a lot of questions of Miscavige. The US tax agency was conducting an extensive review of the Church of Scientology's affairs. The review came about after the Scientologists had bombarded the IRS with litigation and freedom of information requests, had put their staff under surveillance and made personal attacks in their magazine *Freedom*. When Miscavige and Rathbun told the IRS commissioner Fred Goldberg the attacks and litigation would cease if they got an unqualified tax exemption for all of their activities, the IRS agreed to review their tax-exempt status.[112]

Over the following two years, the Church of Scientology gave the IRS everything they wanted. Miscavige and Rathbun would visit Washington, DC virtually every week to answer questions and deliver documents. Two hundred Scientologists had been commandeered to internally review the organisation's financial records.[113] During their two-year review the IRS failed to interview the lifetime trustee Terri Gamboa who was named in key documents. If they had tracked her down, Scientology's history could have been very different.

On 8 October 1993, Miscavige announced before a crowd of over 1000 Scientologists, 'The war is over!' The IRS had settled. It agreed to grant exemption for all of the church's 150 entities, including the publishing house that produced Hubbard's books. The irony is that while the Church of Scientology was trying to argue in the courts and to the IRS that it was not a commercial enterprise, it was trying to remove a potential critic, who just happened to be the head of its former for-profit company, by paying them good money to leave the country for an isolated property in Australia.

Neither Marty Rathbun nor Mike Rinder know how much the operation cost. Terri Gamboa estimates it could have cost millions of dollars once you take into consideration salaries and expenses, the cost of renting the farm, buying horses, paying Ian Markham-Smith and his business partner to run the operation and keeping the private investigator Dave Lubow on a retainer. Terri says no expense was spared. 'They flew us to Hong Kong at least twice,' she says. 'They would take us to the fanciest places, they wined and dined us, they once paid $1400 for a five-course dinner for just four people, and it was all church money. No expense was spared when Miscavige's power was at stake.'[114]

I FIRST MET TERRI Gamboa (née Gillham) in June 2015. Twenty-five years after she left the Sea Org she was still wary about being followed while talking to a journalist. Our meeting place was a secret. I was told to ring her when I was ready to be picked up. When I called, the instructions were direct. She would pick me up on the third floor of the car park of the low-rent Las Vegas casino I was staying at. 'Make sure you're not tailed,' she told me. When I got in the car she took me to a Cheesecake Factory outlet in a nearby shopping plaza. We talked for hours about her amazing life inside Scientology.

It was the first time Terri had agreed to be interviewed by a journalist since she fled the Sea Org. In 1991, legendary news anchor Ted Koppel had tracked her down and asked if she wanted to go on *Nightline* and debate David Miscavige. It would have made for explosive television, but Terri declined the offer. 'I had just escaped from a very dangerous prison and was in no frame of mind to do that.'[115] Twenty-five years later Terri was ready to talk.

In a subsequent conversation Terri made an extraordinary revelation. Up until the week before we met she was weighing up whether she would be part of a Scientology takeover bid. Former Sea Org members were urging her to go back in, use her status as a lifetime trustee and try and kick Miscavige out. 'I had this vision that I would go in, clean it all up and make it into the good we all thought it was supposed to be,' she told me. 'We thought we could change it for the good and make it a great movement that really helped people, not the insidious controlling and overpowering entity that it has become.'[116]

There were people around the edges of Scientology, disenfranchised believers in Hubbard, who felt Miscavige had perverted his ideas, and wanted to see Terri lead a takeover. Terri thought long and hard about the ramifications. Even if she were successful in knocking off Miscavige, who was a master at both seizing and keeping power, she would inherit a nightmare scenario. Any reformation of Scientology would require a reconciliation process that would involve admitting to previous abuses and providing compensation.

Terri believes that process, while necessary, would paralyse the Church of Scientology. 'It would be a domino effect,' she says. 'As soon as Miscavige was gone many would want to have a refund. We would give everybody a refund that wanted one and deserved one, but once you start doing that it would be a nightmare. With the mess that Miscavige has created and the number of people he has ripped off there might be nothing left. It could bankrupt the church and take years to clean up this mess and figure it all out.'[117]

In 1990, Terri had left the Sea Org because of the culture of abuse that she saw up close on the inside. Now, she wanted to speak up about what she could see from the outside – the damage and destruction that the policy of disconnection had caused by tearing families apart and preventing those suffering from abuse on the inside from escaping for fear of never seeing their family members again.

Instead of getting involved in a takeover bid, Terri pursued another plan. She tried to contact Miscavige to see if a peaceful resolution could be brought about through cancelling the policy of disconnection. Terri wanted to propose a general amnesty where all former Sea Org members who had left and been declared 'suppressive' would be allowed to see family members on the inside. She made several attempts at trying to organise a meeting with Miscavige and spoke with his lawyer Monique Yingling.

For Terri the policy of disconnection is the biggest issue that Scientology must deal with. 'Families need to be able to reunite and those who want Scientology can have it and those who don't should be left alone. There's something wrong when you have to abuse people, lock them up, manipulate and control them in order to make them believe in a faith, and they can't speak out or they will be declared a "Suppressive Person" and forced to disconnect from their family and friends. This is America, the land of the free, it's shocking that this goes on in this country and they get away with it.'[118]

Miscavige would not respond to Terri's approaches. 'Of course cancelling disconnection would only damage his power,' says Terri, 'as disconnection is his sole protection from those inside finding out about the truth on the outside. Once disconnection was gone it would tear down his wall of protection and security. It is his only insurance policy for maintaining complete power and control over the church and every person in there.'[119]

Terri is concerned that by speaking out after all this time she is making herself a target. After all, the Church of Scientology had a private investigator infiltrate her business in the years when she remained silent. 'He will now come after me and will have OSA publish all kinds of bad statements about me to try and discredit me,' she says. 'This is their routine, they will try to harm my business, my income, my livelihood and my wellbeing. I am saying it now so that if anything happens to me you can follow the trail and you will find them behind it.'[120]

While Terri considered being involved in an attempt to reclaim Scientology from Miscavige, she decided she was not the person to lead it. For starters her husband, Fernando, did not want her to do it. 'He feels it's too late for reform and that the church is doomed,' she says.[121] Further to that, Terri questioned whether she had the desire to go through with it. 'I'm 60 years old,' she said. 'I don't want to take on something like that at my age. I have worked hard all my life. I was a slave as a kid. I've worked my butt off my whole life. I want to start relaxing a bit and I would never be able to do that if I took this on, and for what? Who's going to appreciate it? You'd be in the crossfire – there's so much animosity and hatred on both sides.'[122]

We will never know if Terri Gamboa, as a lifetime trustee, would have had the legal authority, or the internal support, to dethrone David Miscavige. That moment has now passed. One thing is for sure, if Miscavige did not have the legal authority to remain in control, he would have used every dirty trick imaginable to hang on to power. Terri is comfortable she made the right decision in 2015 to stay out, just as she made the right decision in 1990 to get out.

CHAPTER 17

JULIAN ASSANGE'S NOISY INVESTIGATION

OVER A DECADE BEFORE Mike Huckabee wanted him executed, and Sarah Palin thought he should be 'pursued with the same urgency we pursue al Qaeda and Taliban leaders',[1] Julian Assange had a different bunch of enraged Americans on his case. At the time, Assange did not need any more trouble. He had just avoided a jail sentence after pleading guilty to 25 hacking charges, and was in the middle of an acrimonious custody battle over his son. Then he found himself under investigation from the Church of Scientology.

On a spring day in Melbourne in 1997, Assange was at home in the two-bedroom brick house he shared with his young son, Daniel, when the phone rang. On the line was Roger Middleton, a private investigator working for the Scientologists. The former Australian Federal Police agent had got hold of Assange's unlisted number and started pumping the 26-year-old for information. Middleton was conducting what Hubbard referred to as a Noisy Investigation.

Assange had been ignoring legal threats from Scientology lawyers in California and needed to be taught a lesson. 'The way Scientology works,' Assange told me, 'is it does sub-surface investigations where the targets do not know they are being investigated, and it does investigations where the targets do know and the investigations are deliberately noisy. Their purpose is not to gain intelligence, their purpose is to create fear – to create a specific deterrence and a general deterrence – this was a noisy investigation – the private investigator said he was working for Scientology.'[2]

As was the case with WikiLeaks over a decade later, Assange was in trouble for publishing secrets. At the time, he was running Suburbia.net, a non-profit Internet Service Provider (ISP) staffed by volunteers. 'We were the free speech ISP in Australia,' he says.[3]

Suburbia was hosting an anti-Scientology website run by university student David Gerard. The site had published secret Scientology literature including excerpts from confidential course materials for Operating Thetan Level VII (OT VII). The Church of Scientology guarded these secrets closely. It cost hundreds of thousands of dollars to go up 'the Bridge'. If some computer geek in Melbourne published parts of the course online, it removed some of the mystique surrounding Scientology's upper levels and undermined their ability to make money from them.[4]

Helena Kobrin, a Scientology lawyer in California, who specialised in the cease and desist letter, sent a series of legal threats to Assange. Kobrin accused Suburbia of violating copyright law in Australia and the US. The Scientology lawyer warned Assange: 'We are currently involved in litigation over the same and similar materials in several lawsuits.'[5] Kobrin claimed her client had already been awarded damages and that in one case in San Jose, in which Netcom was the defendant, 'the court ruled an access provider which is informed that infringement is occurring through its system and does nothing to stop it can be liable for contributory infringement'.[6]

At the time, Netcom boasted that it was the largest ISP in the world. If the Church of Scientology was willing to take them to court, what hope was there for a small non-profit run by volunteers in Melbourne?

As US officials would come to learn in later years, Assange was not easily intimidated. The hacking charges he had pleaded guilty to related to an operation that had embarrassed the US military. Assange and two colleagues, who formed a collective known as the International Subversives, had hacked into what the author of *Underground*, Suelette Dreyfus, described as 'the Who's Who of the American military-industrial complex',[7] including the Pentagon, NASA and the Naval Surface Warfare Center in Virginia.

Julian Assange was not about to be steamrolled by the Church of Scientology. Not only did he possess the crazy/brave attitude required to hack into the Pentagon, he and his peers had strong beliefs in the importance of fighting for freedom of speech in cyberspace. 'As people involved in building an Internet to bring knowledge to the people – to bring ideas from one part of the world to another,' Assange told me, 'we saw this interference by Scientology as an attack on all the things we had been building and dreaming for. These were not just isolated attacks. Scientology was setting adverse precedents in some of its legal suits which went on to be used by other corporations trying to silence speech on the Internet.'[8]

Assange ignored the legal threats and refused to pass on information about the website's founder, David Gerard, to Scientology's private investigator. 'The guy's got balls of titanium,' says Gerard.[9] The two met online in 1995 when the Victoria University of Technology (VUT) caved to pressure from the Church of Scientology and locked Gerard's student computer account after he made critical posts online about Scientology. Assange provided Gerard with an alternative account and a platform to set up an anti-Scientology website.

From the outside, the Scientology lawyers might have considered the pair soft targets – a couple of impoverished 20-somethings with no corporate or legal backing. But Assange and Gerard had other things going for them. They were smart, had spare time and shared a love of troublemaking. 'He is an inveterate shit-stirrer,' says Gerard.[10] The pair were fuelled by a surplus of outrage. Having no money bought them even more freedom. They acted like men who had nothing to lose.

An editor with the student newspaper *No Name*, and a member of the VUT Student Representative Council, David Gerard became interested in Scientology through his love of William S. Burroughs. The beat writer had a complicated relationship with Scientology. In 1968, he went 'clear' while on a course at Saint Hill, writing that 'Scientology can do more in ten hours than psychoanalysis can do in ten years'.[11] Yet Burroughs also railed against Scientology's founder, criticising Hubbard's 'fascist utterances'[12] and Scientology's 'control system ... with its own courts, police, rewards and penalties'.[13] Gerard had a curious mind and wanted to find out more. In the early days of the Internet, Usenet newsgroups sprung up. A precursor to online forums, they were basically discussion groups formed around a common interest. A conversation would start around a certain topic and members could then respond. Newsgroups formed around a diverse range of subcultures such as hackers, astrophysicists, muscle car enthusiasts and fans of *The Simpsons*.

One of the most popular newsgroups in the 1990s was alt. religion.scientology. Started in 1991 by Scott Goehring, another renegade 20-something, partly as a joke and partly as he described it 'because I felt Usenet needed a place to disseminate the truth about this half-assed religion'.[14] To initiate the group Goehring used a forged message, signing in as *miscaviage@flag.sea.org*, a made-up email address based around a misspelling of the name of Scientology's leader.

Back in Melbourne, David Gerard started engaging with others on alt.religion.scientology. His curiosity about William S. Burroughs led him headlong into the first big freedom of speech battle in cyberspace, in what became known as Scientology v the Internet. The Church of Scientology had just triumphed in its long-running conflict with the taxman, but it was about to become engaged in a guerrilla war with an enemy it would find impossible to defeat.

In the first two years of its operation, posters to alt.religion. scientology could generally be split into three categories. Critics, supporters and members of the Freezone – Independent Scientologists who embraced Hubbard's technology but rejected the way the Church of Scientology was being run.[15] The newsgroup hosted arguments about the E-Meter, the purification rundown and other aspects of Hubbard's technology. It was a fairly niche operation. But that small newsgroup began to reach a much larger audience once the Church of Scientology tried to control it.

In 1994, Elaine Siegel from the Office of Special Affairs released an internal Scientology memo titled, 'Briefing to all Scientologists on the Internet.'[16] The letter began:

> *Dear Scientologist,*
> *As you know, there has been quite a bit of false and*
> *derogatory information going out over the Internet by a few*

detractors, squirrels etc ... We have a plan of action that
we are taking, to simply outcreate the entheta [upsetting
information] on these newsgroups.[17]

Elaine Siegel's plan was to encourage Scientologists to bombard
alt.religion.scientology with positive messages. 'If you imagine 40–
50 Scientologists posting on the Internet every few days, we'll just
run the SP's [Suppressive Persons] right off the system. It will be quite
simple, actually.'[18]

It was not as simple as Siegel made out. The letter soon leaked onto
alt.religion.scientology and spread like wildfire. As Wendy Grossman,
the author of *Net.Wars* wrote: 'Its widespread circulation heated the
debate to yet another degree, bringing a new constituency into the
newsgroup: people who wanted to defend the Net against what they
saw as a threat to their freedom. Many of them knew nothing about
Scientology except for that letter, and they were incensed.'[19]

Just before Christmas 1994, messages posted to alt.religion.
scientology started being removed by a cancelbot – a program that
sends messages to Usenet groups to remove certain postings. In most
cases, the posts targeted involved discussions about Scientology's
'Advanced Technology' secrets.[20] These tactics further enraged the
free speech advocates, but the Scientologists were only just getting
started.

In January 1995, Scientology lawyer Helena Kobrin tried to get
alt.religion.scientology shut down. Kobrin posted a 'remove group'
message on Usenet that read:

We request that you remove the alt.religion.scientology
newsgroup from your site. The reasons for requesting its
removal are: (1) It was started with a forged message; (2) not
discussed on alt.config; (3) it has the name 'scientology' in
its title which is a trademark and is misleading, as a.r.s [alt.
religion.scientology] is mainly used for flamers to attack
the Scientology religion; (4) it has been and continues to be
heavily abused with copyright and trade secret violations
and serves no purpose other than condoning these illegal
practices.[21]

The system administrators knocked back the lawyer's plea to shut down the newsgroup. Instead of restricting debate, Kobrin's intervention made alt.religion.scientology a haven for online activism, attracting sceptics and free speech advocates who piled in to the debate. The newsgroup became bigger and nastier. It morphed into what Wendy Grossman described as 'one of the most contentious, roisterous, fiery, and vicious newsgroups ever'.[22] The Church of Scientology was never going to take it lying down. Heeding the words of its founder, it attacked all of its critics. The war being waged in cyberspace had become toxic and it was about to move offline.

At 7.30 am on 13 February 1995, a man wearing a suit and carrying papers repeatedly rung on Dennis Erlich's doorbell. On the porch and driveway outside Erlich's home in Glendale, California, around 25 people had gathered. The crowd was waiting to get inside and search for information relating to posts the former Scientologist had made on alt.religion.scientology. Erlich had been a staff member at Scientology headquarters in Clearwater, where he worked as the 'chief cramming officer', or, as he preferred to put it, 'the quality control engineer at the brainwashing plant'.[23]

When Erlich refused to answer the door he received a call from off-duty policeman Ed Eccles, who was waiting outside on the porch. Sergeant Eccles warned Erlich that he had a writ of seizure that allowed him to enter his home by force. The former Scientologist told Sergeant Eccles he did not want so many people coming into his home. After a brief negotiation Eccles and six others entered Erlich's home on the condition the policeman would not identify the other men until after the raid was over.[24]

The search party included Warren McShane from Scientology's Religious Technology Center (RTC), Thomas Small, a lawyer for the RTC, and Paul Wilmhurst, one of Scientology's top computer experts. Also present were on-duty Glendale police officer Steve Eggert, off-duty Inglewood police officer Mark Fronterotta, and Robert Shovlin, a private investigator hired by lawyers for the RTC.

The raid lasted around seven hours. Personal papers, books, financial records and over 300 floppy discs were confiscated. Files from Erlich's hard disk were copied and then erased. As Erlich wrote at the time: 'Potentially they copied all my personal correspondence, mailing lists, financial records and personal notes.'[25] As the material was seized, Erlich was only aware of the identity of Sergeant Eccles. The representatives from the Church of Scientology were not identified until after the raid was over.

Dennis Erlich's home had been turned over because of posts he made on alt.religion.scientology. The Church of Scientology claimed these posts breached its copyright. From August 1994, Erlich had been an active critic of Scientology on the newsgroup. As one of the most senior defectors to be active on the site, Erlich was often asked questions relating to Scientology policy. His responses would include quotations from policies or scriptures. Scientology lawyers argued this was a violation of copyright law. Northern California District Judge Ron Whyte approved the writ of seizure, and Erlich's home was raided.

In the coming months, other critics got the same treatment. On a Saturday morning in August, Arnie Lerma was nursing a coffee in his living room when federal marshals knocked on his door. Holding a warrant, and accompanied by computer technicians, cameramen and Scientology lawyers, including Helena Kobrin, the marshals barged in.[26] Lerma was a former Scientologist and a director of FACTnet, an online anti-cult information service. Lerma had published what was known as the Fishman affidavit on alt.religion.scientology. The documents came from a 1993 court case where Steven Fishman revealed in evidence course materials from various Operating Thetan levels, including the highly secretive Xenu myth.

The Church of Scientology had gone to extraordinary lengths to keep the Fishman affidavit out of the public domain. As a result of the court case, the documents had to be kept in a Los Angeles court file for two years, where members of the public could borrow them. But Scientologists monopolised access to the documents by 'alternately checking out the files each day and retaining them until the clerk's office closed'.[27]

Having his home raided traumatised Lerma. His computer, and his disks, with critical information stored on them like client lists and phone numbers, were all removed. 'I'm one of those guys who keeps everything – my whole life – on the computer,' Lerma told the *Washington Post*, 'and now they have it all.'[28] The Church of

Scientology was unrepentant, arguing it had a right to protect what it called, unusually for a church, its 'trade secrets'. 'We take very forceful and elaborate steps to maintain the confidentiality,' said Scientology spokesman Kurt Weiland. 'This is not a free-speech issue. It's a copyright issue.'[29]

The Church of Scientology continued its show of force in a series of raids and lawsuits around the world. Lerma's colleague on the board of FACTnet, Larry Wollersheim, and a former director, Bob Penny, both had their homes searched. Julf Helsingius, the operator of the anonymous remailer *anon.penet.fi* had his home raided in Finland. Scientology critic Zenon Panoussis had hard drives and disks seized from his apartment in Sweden. In the Netherlands, journalist Karen Spaink had her home searched for two and half hours by local police. Lawsuits often followed the raids. The Church of Scientology sued the *Washington Post* over the publication of its copyrighted scriptures in its reporting of the Lerma raid, and took legal action against ISPs such as Netcom and XS4ALL.

By the mid-1990s, the Church of Scientology had, to a large degree, been able to silence the mainstream media. The US$416 million lawsuit against *TIME* magazine had a chilling effect on critical reporting. However, the free-spirited netizens on alt.religion. scientology were not so easily muzzled. The raids and the court cases were covered in-depth on the newsgroup. Members who received legal threats from Helena Kobrin seemed unfazed, publishing them online to the newsgroup.

Despite all the raids and the legal threats, the Church of Scientology was losing the battle to control the information flow from defectors and the courts. Secret scriptures, court documents and testimonies were being published instantly online. The Internet was ushering in a revolution in publishing and Scientology, an organisation built around copyright and control, was caught in the crosshairs. As former Scientology spokesman Robert Vaughn Young told Wendy Grossman at the time, 'I am thankful I'm not having to face the Net. It's going to be to Scientology what Vietnam was to the US. Their only choice is to withdraw. They cannot win.'[30]

In the month before Arnie Lerma's home in Arlington was raided, David Gerard received his first legal letter from Helena Kobrin. Like

Lerma, the Melbourne-based computer science student was accused of publishing confidential OT materials to alt.religion.scientology. Gerard had posted what he describes as 'six stupid lines from OT VII'.[31]

> OT7-48
> *1. Find some plants, trees, etc., and communicate to them individually until you know they received your communication.*
> *2. Go to a zoo or a place with many types of life and communicate with each of them until you know the communication is received and, if possible, returned.*

While Gerard argued that under fair use provisions of copyright law it was completely legitimate to quote a portion of the OT materials, the Church of Scientology thought otherwise, and Helena Kobrin threatened the student with a lawsuit. 'These actions constitute violations of applicable copyright laws and trade secret misappropriation,' Kobrin wrote, 'entitling our client to damages and an injunction.'[32]

Gerard had been following the Erlich case and like other members of the newsgroup was outraged by the Church of Scientology's actions. 'People on the Net back then took this whole thing very seriously,' says Gerard. 'We were very doctrinaire about it, as only young, educated, privileged geeks could be!'[33]

The computer science student fired off a response to Kobrin, picking apart her legal letter with all the smartarsery an undergraduate student could muster. Gerard described Kobrin's legal arguments as 'utter bilge' and 'legal harassment'. He accused her of quoting the copyright registration number for OT II when she meant OT VII, and argued that the OT levels could not be considered trade secrets when they had already been read into publicly available court records.[34]

Helena Kobrin did not end up taking David Gerard to court. But the Scientologists tried another avenue to silence the outspoken critic. According to Gerard's account, published on alt.religion. scientology at the time, representatives from the Australian arm of the Church of Scientology made a formal complaint to Haddon Storey, the Minister for Tertiary Education in Victoria, that Gerard's posts to the newsgroup were not part of academic usage and should be prohibited. Twenty years later, Haddon Storey told me he did not recall the complaint.[35] A Freedom of Information request found that any documentation from that period would have been destroyed.[36]

Fifteen days later Gerard received a letter from the IT department of the university notifying him that his account had been locked until further notice at the direction of the Deputy Vice Chancellor. Eventually the account was unlocked, but Gerard was outraged that his freedom of speech could be trampled on at a university – an environment that was meant to foster freedom of thought and expression. The computer science student was determined to fight back, and, like Arnie Lerma, set up a website that would document all he wanted to say about Scientology.

Setting up a website in Australia at the time was easier said than done. There was no real marketplace for cheap website hosting. Gerard had heard that the non-profit Suburbia had solid freedom of speech credentials. He got in contact with its systems administrator, Julian Assange. Gerard told him he wanted to build a webpage that was critical of Scientology and that 'it was certain to attract a considerable amount of trouble'.[37] Assange did not need his arm twisted. 'That sounds like fun,' he said.[38]

David Gerard began building what became known as The Australian Critics of Scientology Resource Collection. The website still exists today and includes Australian newspaper reports on Scientology going back to the 1950s and information for journalists on how to deal with the cult. Gerard published personal testimonies of ex-Scientologists and maps and photos of all the Scientology organisations operating in Australia. He had a special section that documented all protests against Scientology in Australia and exposed how the Scientologists were using private investigators to harass critics. Pulling together the website was a painstaking process. 'With the old newspaper reports, I typed in every one of them, from a folder of smudgy photocopies and microfilm scans,' says Gerard.[39]

Julian Assange had started running Suburbia when its founder, Mark Dorset, moved to Sydney. That meant he was now in the firing line as the man who was responsible for hosting Gerard's website. 'Helena Kobrin started to attack us and several of our upstreams and

Telstra, trying to cut us off,' recalls Assange. 'They were not successful in doing that. I had given a commitment to publish that material and proceeded to do so.'[40]

Assange was far more than just a sympathetic host of an anti-Scientology website. He started reading up about Hubbard and his OT levels and soon found himself campaigning against the cult. 'Julian is a person who deeply investigates a topic,' says Suelette Dreyfus, who was collaborating with Assange on the book *Underground* at the time. 'He would say you can tell a lot about someone's character from what they said early on in their life.'[41] Assange thought Hubbard's comments that 'the easiest way to make money would be to start a religion'[42] said it all about Scientology.

Through alt.religion.scientology, Assange gained further knowledge about the Scientology raids going on at the time. 'He was deeply offended by the dirty tricks campaigns they would use to try to repress any critics,' says Suelette Dreyfus. 'I remember Julian reading articles about the raids in the US and him being outraged about what was in effect the privatisation of a public police force for Scientology's gain.'[43]

The raids may have outraged Assange, but they also underlined the risks he was taking in hosting David Gerard's anti-Scientology website. Not only were all his files and computers at risk, he would not have wanted to have his young son exposed to police raids. But in his mind, the risks were worth it. Instead of retreating, he began agitating against Scientology and turning up at protests organised by David Gerard.

Assange distilled his thoughts about Hubbard and Scientology into a call to arms he sent out to the Cypherpunks email list on 15 March 1996. He urged his fellow free speech advocates to attend a rally outside the Church of Scientology in Melbourne the following morning:

> *The Church of Scientology was founded by the late L. Ron Hubbard in the United States some 30 years ago. To followers, Hubbard is their profit [sic], and his prolific writings are the sacred word. The Church's hierarchy and financial viability revolve around Hubburd's [sic] verbose scriptures. Each new level gained by a church follower brings to them, among other*

rights and privileges access to a new and previously verboten set of the works of Ron. But to the Church it brings something else. Revenue. A very sizeable revenue. Ron's works are a required element in order for the follower to progress through the many of successive levels the Church has – and they cost hundreds or thousands of dollars each.

In fact, by the time a devote of the Church has realized the highest OT level, the Church has usually had them for over five figures. But revenue isn't the only reason for keeping the works of Ron occulted away. A common technique used by cults to brainwash their followers is gradual immersion in cult mythology and philosophy. To put it bluntly, it is often advisable to keep the more wacko beliefs and practices out of your new recruit's faces until they are sufficiently wacko themselves.

Now, the problem for the Church of Scientology is that on the wacko scale the higher level works of Ron hover somewhere near the figure 10. To an outsider it is an immediate farse [sic]. But to a follower who has become psychologically dependent on the Church's philosophy & society and invested thousands and thousands of dollars in doing so, it is just another step on the road to mental subservience.

What you have then is a Church based on brainwashing yuppies and other people with more money than sense. This may not concern you. If Nicole Kiddman [sic], Kate Cerbrano [sic], John Travolta, Burce [sic] Willis, Demi Moor [sic] and Tom Cruise want to spend their fortunes on learning that the earth is in reality the destroyed prison colony of aliens from out of space then so be it.

However, money brings power and attracts the currupt [sic]. Money is something the Church has a lot of. Not all of the Church's beliefs and practices are so out of it as to be completely as irrelevant as the previous example. Some are quite insidious. For instance, L. Ron Hubbard devised a range of methods that could be used against critics and other 'enemies of the Church'. Among the list was manipulation *of the legal/court system. To the Church the battle isn't won in the court room. It is won at the very moment the legal process starts unfolding, creating fear and expense in those the Church opposes.*

Their worst critic at the moment is not a person, or an organisation but a medium – the Internet. The Internet is, by its very nature a censorship free zone. Censorship, concealment and revelation (for a fee) is the Church's raison d'etre. The Church, via its manipulation of the legal system has had computer systems seized, system operators forced to reveal their users personal details, university accounts suspended and radio stations, such as RRR cut their programs.

It has sued ex-cult members, newspapers, and many others for copyright infringements, loss of earnings and trade secret violation. Trade secret violation? Yes, the Church of Scientology claims its religious works are trade secrets. The fight against the Church is far more than the Net vs a bunch of wackos with too much money. It is about corporate suppression of the Internet and free speech. It is about intellectual property and the big and rich versus the small and smart. The precedents the Church sets today the weapons of corporate tirany [sic] tomorrow.[44]

Julian Assange saw the battle against Scientology as being much bigger than taking on one cult that was trying to harass and silence its critics. As essayist Robert Manne put it, 'Assange's main political preoccupation seems to have been the extraordinary democratic possibilities of the information-sharing virtual communities across the globe created by the Internet, and the threat to its freedom and flourishing posed by censorious states, greedy corporations and repressive laws.'[45] Assange knew this battle would set important precedents for Internet freedom.

In the end Assange was not sued by the Church of Scientology, his home was not raided by the police like other free speech advocates around the world. But the experience of taking on Scientology proved formative. He would later claim that Suburbia acted as the prototype for WikiLeaks more than any other project he had been a part of.[46]

In March 2008, 15 months after WikiLeaks published its first leaked document, and over a decade after his first skirmish with Scientology's lawyers, Assange published a 208-page file relating to a former intelligence agent in the Office of Special Affairs (OSA), Frank Oliver.

Included in the documents were the former OSA operative's billion-year contract and a whole range of Scientology policy documents relating to black propaganda, how to attack enemies and how to choose appropriate Scientologists for covert operations. The leak also included the policy on how to conduct a 'noisy investigation', something Assange had been subjected to in 1997.[47] Scientology's secrets about how it conducted surveillance programs were online for all to see.

Two weeks later, Assange had an even bigger scoop. WikiLeaks published a 612-page manual that included course materials for all eight OT levels. The documents included handwritten notes from Hubbard laying out his OT research. Given that Scientology lawyers sent legal threats to David Gerard for repeating just six lines from OT VII on a fledgling newsgroup, the publication of 612 pages' worth of OT secrets must have sent Scientology's Religious Technology Center into a state of apoplexy.

The following day, a legal letter from Ava Paquette of Moxon and Kobrin lawyers arrived in the WikiLeaks inbox. It asked the whistleblowing website to remove its copyrighted materials and preserve any documents relating to the matter including 'logs, data entry sheets, applications – electronic or otherwise, registrations forms, billings statements or invoices, computer print-outs, disks hard drives, etc'.[48] The Church of Scientology not only wanted the documents taken down, they wanted to find out who had leaked them.

As he did over a decade earlier, Julian Assange ignored Scientology's lawyer's requests. A statement appeared on the WikiLeaks website, which said: 'WikiLeaks will not comply with legally abusive requests from Scientology any more than WikiLeaks has complied with similar demands from Swiss banks, Russian off-shore stem cell centers, former African Kleptocrats, or the Pentagon.'[49]

Andy Greenberg, author of *This Machine Kills Secrets*, called it 'the most gratifying moment of WikiLeaks ascension'. Assange promised that several thousand additional Scientology materials would be leaked the following week. In the WikiLeaks statement

Assange made sure to highlight the Church of Scientology's history of censorship:

> *After reviewing documentation of Scientology's endless*
> *assaults on journalists from* TIME *magazine and CNN, which*
> *spent over $3 million defending against just one of their suits,*
> *to investigative freelancers who have had publishers pulp*
> *their books rather than facing litigation costs, we have come*
> *to the conclusion that Scientology is not only an abusive cult,*
> *but that it aids and abets a general climate of Western media*
> *self-censorship.*
>
> *If the west can not defend its cultural values of free speech*
> *and press freedoms against a criminal cult like Scientology,*
> *it can hardly lecture China and other state abusers of these*
> *same values. Such states are quick to proclaim their censorship*
> *regime is no mere matter of protecting cult profits, but rather*
> *of national security.*[50]

The Church of the Scientology did not end up suing WikiLeaks. The secret documents remain online in perpetuity. It was another battle lost in Scientology's war with the Internet. As Robert Vaughn Young predicted in 1995, the Internet was becoming Scientology's Vietnam and 'their only choice is to withdraw'.[51]

However, the Scientologists could not easily withdraw from the battle. Hubbard's policy dictated that all critics must be attacked and destroyed. Retreat was never really an option. Hubbard was the Source of Scientology and his word was considered the incontrovertible truth. His pronouncements from the pre-Internet age about how to deal with critics boxed the Scientologists into a corner that would prevent them from adapting and moving with the times.

Scientology's war with the Internet was a self-destructive act of colossal overreach committed by an inflexible organisation incapable of learning from its mistakes. Their lawyers threatened David Gerard and he set up a website. They raided Arnie Lerma and he became a permanent thorn in their side. They antagonised Julian Assange over six lines from OT VII and he ended up releasing 612 pages' worth of all the OT levels.

In the same year Assange published thousands of pages of secret Scientology documents, an internal video of Tom Cruise praising the benefits of Scientology leaked onto the Internet. What did the Church of Scientology end up doing? It tried to enforce copyright laws and demanded that the clip be removed from YouTube. The action then triggered a force field of criticism, protest and troublemaking from the online activist group Anonymous, who like Assange and the members of the alt.religion.scientology community believe the Internet is a sacred place where freedom of expression should triumph.

In the end more people saw the Tom Cruise video because they wanted to know why Scientology wanted to censor it. Then the protest moved offline, with monthly rallies attracting thousands of protestors across the globe converging on Scientology organisations in major cities.

But would it have mattered whether they had fought the war online or simply had withdrawn as Robert Vaughn Young suggested? The Church of Scientology is essentially a cold war organisation based on command and control. As it collided with the anarchy of the Internet and communities of free speech advocates who would not cower to legal threats, it had no hope of keeping its secrets intact. Those secrets, if aired publicly, had the potential to cause reputational damage and undermine Scientology's ability to recruit new members.

The secret OT levels, once published, were held up to ridicule in the media and popular culture, most prominently on the TV show *South Park*. Once Hubbard's various claims about his war record, education and adventures were scrutinised, it undermined his and Scientology's credibility. The horror stories of abuse and the tales of surveillance, black ops and enforced separations, once exposed, caused irreparable damage. But unlike an old newspaper report, these stories did not become tomorrow's fish and chip wrappers. On the Internet they stayed there forever. If a potential new recruit googled Scientology they would be bombarded by the kinds of stories that Scientology used to be able to suppress. Would they really then have the nerve to take the leap of faith and sign up for Scientology's initial course?

An American Religious Identification Survey from 1990 estimated there were 45,000 Scientologists in the US. By 2008, that figure had dropped to 25,000.[52] Just like newspapers, the Church of Scientology had its business model carved up by the Internet. In October 1993, David Miscavige told the International Association of Scientologists that, 'The war is over!' The war with the taxman may have been done with, but Scientology's war with the Internet was just beginning. It was a war Scientology hasn't recovered from.

CHAPTER 18

CRUISE AND KIDMAN

IT STARTED WITH THE kind of excess that only Sea Org slave labour can provide. When David Miscavige heard that Tom Cruise had an unfulfilled fantasy of running through a field of wildflowers with Nicole Kidman, Scientology's leader decided to make it happen.

It was the American summer of 1990. A few months earlier, Kidman and Cruise had hooked up on *Days of Thunder*. Things can move fast when you're on the set of a film about a stock car racer. Cruise began the shoot married to Mimi Rogers and ended it in the arms of his young co-star. In the delirious early weeks of their relationship Kidman agreed to shack up with Cruise in one of the strangest places imaginable.

At the base of the San Jacinto Mountains in California lies Scientology's secretive 500-acre compound known as International Base. Referred to more commonly as 'Gold' or 'Int' it houses hundreds of Sea Org members. Around 20 of them were assigned to work through one crazy night to make the movie star's field of flowers fantasy come true.

As harsh rain pelted down, a platoon of commandeered Sea Org members tore up a large section of the compound's highly manicured lawn. The grass was carefully cut and rolled up before being transplanted onto pallets. Drenched to the bone, the workers pushed through till dawn, ploughing the field by spotlight to have it ready to be fertilised and seeded over the weekend.

Sea Org member and ex-marine Andre Tabayoyon estimated the project cost tens of thousands of dollars.[1] It was money ploughed into the dust. The wildflowers did not blossom in the way Miscavige anticipated. Some shot up as tall green stalks, others wilted in the harsh desert sun. Weeds sprang up and overtook what was left of the wildflowers. 'Miscavige inspected the project and didn't like it,' said Tabayoyon. 'So the whole meadow was ploughed up, destroyed, reploughed and sown with plain grass.'[2] Cruise and Kidman never got to run through that field of flowers.

What began with dreams of fields of flowers would end with wiretaps and marital sabotage. Nicole Kidman would find out what it was like to be both the beneficiary and the victim of David Miscavige's obsession with Tom Cruise. In the beginning Scientology's leader had actively encouraged their relationship, but before long the Australian actress came to be seen as the greatest threat to Scientology's greatest asset.

At the beginning of 1990, Nicole Kidman proved useful to the Church of Scientology. Miscavige had a problem with Cruise's wife Mimi Rogers and the brand of Scientology that she preached. Rogers had introduced Cruise to Scientology in 1986.[3] Her father, Phil Spickler, had worked with L. Ron Hubbard at the Founding Church of Scientology in Washington, DC, and set up a Scientology mission in the Bay area of San Francisco.

Up until 1982, around a hundred Scientology missions operated in the US.[4] In October that year, David Miscavige called all the franchise owners into a meeting at the San Francisco Hilton. From 9 pm to 2 am the mission holders were lectured and harangued by Miscavige and his other young Sea Org cohorts. They were accused of withholding money from the Church of Scientology and, according to then mission holder Bent Corydon, were lined up and had their photos taken mugshot style while being forced to confess to 'crimes'.[5]

Phil Spickler and other mission holders left Scientology around this time, disillusioned by the direction the organisation was heading. While Miscavige was thrilled when Spickler's son-in-law first came to Int Base in 1989, there were concerns about his connections. At that time, in Scientology terms, Spickler was considered a 'squirrel', someone who practised Scientology outside of its formal structure and it was assumed his daughter followed suit. Cruise received his first auditing at the Enhancement Center in Sherman Oaks, a mission set up by Mimi Rogers and her former husband, Jim.[6] The pair sold it when they divorced, but Mimi continued to visit with her friend Kirstie Alley. Cruise needed to be separated from the squirrels.

Tom Cruise first saw Nicole Kidman on the big screen in her breakthrough film *Dead Calm*. Kidman played the role of Rae Ingram, the young wife of a navy officer who is trapped on a yacht in the middle of the Pacific Ocean with a sociopath played by Billy Zane. Kidman's character fights off her attacker with a combination of prescription drugs and a harpoon gun. The young actress shone in the role. The *Washington Post*'s movie critic Rita Kempley described her character as an 'Amazon for the '90s'.[7]

Tom Cruise was mesmerised by Kidman's performance. The actor was preparing to shoot *Days of Thunder* and convinced the producers to cast the 21-year-old in the role of Dr Claire Lewicki, a neurosurgeon who falls in love with Cruise's character, an up-and-coming stock car driver named Cole Trickle.

On the set, Kidman and Cruise fell in love.[8] David Miscavige had by now assigned Greg Wilhere to be Cruise's auditor and point man. Wilhere was the same Scientology executive who had tried to get Terri Gamboa back into the fold. According to Marty Rathbun, Miscavige used Wilhere to encourage Cruise to cheat on his Scientologist wife. 'It just shows you how twisted and corrupted Scientology is,' Rathbun told journalist Tony Ortega. 'Why would Scientology want to promote Tom's promiscuity? Because Mimi was connected to her father, Phil Spickler, and Miscavige wanted to own Tom outright.'[9]

After *Days of Thunder* wrapped in May 1990, Mimi Rogers demanded she be given access to Scientology's version of marriage counselling. The process took around a week, but went nowhere. With Miscavige determined to undermine the marriage of his new star recruit, the sessions were doomed to fail.

Mimi Rogers got confirmation her marriage was over when Marty Rathbun paid her a visit. Accompanied by Sherman Lenske, a former personal lawyer to L. Ron Hubbard, Rathbun arrived carrying divorce papers. The involvement of both men was significant.

Like Harvey Keitel's character 'The Wolf' in *Pulp Fiction*, Marty Rathbun solved intractable problems at short notice. He would hunt down Scientologists who had escaped, crush critics through intimidation, and break the most formidable of foes. He played a key role in Scientology's most famous victory – getting the Internal Revenue Service to roll over and grant the Church of Scientology tax-free status. Rathbun used any means at his disposal including lawsuits, multiple Freedom of Information requests and by putting tax officials under surveillance.

Rathbun and Lenske's visit to Mimi Rogers was designed to intimidate. The actress already knew just how ruthless Miscavige could be through his attack on the Scientology mission holders. It was clear to Rogers what she had to do. She signed the divorce papers and quit the Church of Scientology soon after.

By meddling in Cruise's private life, Miscavige had solved one problem, but created another. Scientology's golden boy was now making plans to marry Kidman. The Australian actress was the daughter of the prominent Sydney psychologist and author Dr Antony Kidman. In Scientology, psychologists are considered 'Suppressive Persons' – what Scientologists consider to be anti-social personalities who will cause harm to the organisation. As the daughter of a psychologist, Kidman was what Hubbard called a 'Potential Trouble Source'.

According to Marty Rathbun, Miscavige asked Greg Wilhere to try and undermine Cruise's new relationship in his next auditing session. Rathbun says Miscavige screamed at Wilhere, 'He thinks this Nicole thing is for real! You son of a bitch, you better start planting a seed!'[10]

Wilhere carried out orders, but the move backfired. Cruise was besotted with Kidman and angrily reported back to Miscavige what Wilhere had done. In an act of confected outrage, Miscavige demoted Wilhere from his position as Inspector General of the Religious Technology Center – a role that was effectively second in command in Scientology's hierarchy. 'Miscavige was bragging to Tom that he'd busted him down,' says Rathbun.[11] Miscavige would now have to bend over backwards to please Tom *and* Nicole.

John Brousseau had a unique vantage point from which to witness the campaign to lock Hollywood's hottest couple into Miscavige's brand of Scientology. A former personal chauffeur to L. Ron Hubbard, Brousseau had got to know Miscavige when the pair worked as cameramen on training films for Hubbard in the late 1970s.

The men became brothers-in-law when Miscavige married Shelly Barnett, the sister of Brousseau's first wife, Clarisse. After Cruise got into Scientology, Miscavige assigned Brousseau to help lay out the red carpet for his star recruit.

Brousseau spent 32 years in the Sea Org working predominantly at International Base. He was one of those guys who could turn his hand to anything. He worked as an automotive technician, a cabinetmaker and a construction manager overseeing many of Miscavige's personal building projects. When impressing Tom Cruise became Miscavige's most important project, Brousseau was at the ready. 'I was the guy who did all the fancy stuff for Tom,' he says, 'whether it was painting his motorcycles, building limousines or million-dollar motorhomes, and helping make his aircraft hangar in Burbank look better than anybody else's.'[12]

Tom and Nicole were moving into Int Base so they could both study Scientology full-time. This meant Scientology's international headquarters would soon harbour a 'Potential Trouble Source' and its gun new recruit would soon have a 'Suppressive Person' as his father-in-law. Brousseau says Miscavige had to do whatever it took to please Cruise. 'You can imagine the dynamic drive Tom has about his newfound woman,' he says. 'You just can't get in between the two of them, you've gotta go with the flow and let's see if we can get her on our side too. Nicole was part of the whole TC package.'[13]

Brousseau was a key part of the team overseeing the preparation for Tom and Nicole's arrival at Int Base. 'A huge amount of work was done,' he says. 'Probably millions of man hours went into it. I am talking hundreds of staff working 12–16 hour days, renovating buildings, painting, laying sods, getting ready for their arrival.'[14]

A VIP bungalow was custom built for Cruise near the golf course on the base.[15] A private gymnasium was fitted out so he and Miscavige could pump iron together. A tennis court was laid out with a special form of rubber coating.[16] There was a private rose garden, Sea Org valets on call and a personal chef at the ready to prepare whatever meal Tom and Nicole felt like. A special course room was set up to help fast-track the pair through Scientology's upper-level courses.

It was an incongruous scene. As Miscavige made sure the Hollywood treatment was laid out for Tom and Nicole, the Sea Org staff surrounding them were doing 16-hour days in the desert heat, for just US$50 a week. Sinar Parman, who was assigned to be the couple's personal chef, remembers sudden outbreaks of conspicuous consumption amid the extreme austerity of Sea Org life. 'A silver Mercedes 500SL convertible was delivered to the Int Base as a present to Nicole,' Parman says. 'The Motorpool guys then had to take care of it, keeping it spotless in their garage facilities.'[17]

Motorbikes were bought for Cruise and Kidman so they could ride around the base.[18] 'She would hang on in the back of the seat with her long hair flying,' recalls Parman. 'Cruise used the bike to get from his VIP suite to the Star of California (pool and entertainment area) where he would hang around and eat and lounge around, making phone calls etc. in between his auditing and courses.'[19]

According to Marty Rathbun the couple stayed at Int Base for around two to three months.[20] In that time Nicole Kidman had a meteoric rise up Scientology's bridge, going higher than some Scientologists do in a lifetime. Kidman rose to Operating Thetan Level II (OT II). She was now just one level away from learning about the evil galactic overlord Xenu, his spacecraft and the exploding volcanoes.

As Scientology's worldwide quality control man for auditing at the time, Bruce Hines was responsible for evaluating Kidman's sessions. 'She was given kid glove one-on-one treatment all the way,' says Hines. 'No-one, during the time I was involved, has ever got the service – the extra perks and everything that Tom and Nicole got when they were there. There were several Sea Org members, almost full-time getting them through all the steps.'[21]

Kidman, the 'Potential Trouble Source', was about to be well and truly welcomed into the Scientology family. On Christmas Eve 1990, Tom and Nicole were married in a rented cabin outside the resort town of Telluride, Colorado. It was the full Scientology extravaganza. Cruise's auditor Ray Mithoff officiated, Miscavige was the best man and the Sea Org supplied free labour. Italian pastry chef Pinuccio Tisi made the wedding cake, his Sea Org colleague Sinar Parman cooked for the wedding party.

Cruise and Kidman were the beneficiaries of Sea Org servitude at the expense of the hundreds of workers toiling away inside

Scientology's desert compound. With Parman away, immense pressure was put on those working inside the kitchen. 'This left only 3 cooks at Gold (Int Base) to cook for 800 people three times a day,' said Andre Tabayoyon.[22]

Sinar Parman had to reach into his own pocket for the privilege of catering the wedding. He says the Church of Scientology backed down on a promise to pay him extra for feeding the wedding guests. In the end Parman was only paid his US$50-a-week Sea Org wage. When he tried to claim wedding-related expenses he had put on his credit card he was told he would have to pay them off himself.[23] In a statement, Scientology's lawyer Patrick George said, 'The allegations attributed to Sinar Parman are denied.'[24]

As 1990 came to a close, David Miscavige must have felt on top of the world. Aged 30, he had been Scientology's leader for close to five years. He'd just been best man at the Scientology wedding of Hollywood's hottest couple. The film industry's most marketable star was about to make Scientology the world's most marketable new religion. But within six months a public relations disaster would engulf Scientology and help trigger Cruise's drift away from Miscavige's orbit.

IN MAY 1991, *TIME* magazine published a searing exposé on Scientology, 'The Thriving Cult of Greed and Power'. Its author, investigative journalist Richard Behar, had stumbled onto Scientology by accident. Working at *Forbes* magazine in 1985, he and the editorial team had worked out that Hubbard belonged on the Forbes 400 list of America's wealthiest individuals. 'I was intrigued by it,' says Behar, 'and I dug deeper.'[25] The result was an investigation titled 'The prophet and profits of scientology' that was published by *Forbes* the following year. From his research Behar estimated that Hubbard's empire was worth US$400 million.[26]

Five years later Behar conducted another investigation into Scientology. His eight-page cover story for *TIME* was built on 150 interviews as well as hundreds of court records and internal Scientology documents. Behar came to the conclusion that Scientology was a 'hugely profitable global racket that survives by intimidating members and critics in a Mafia-like manner'.[27] He published allegations that close to half a billion dollars of Scientology money was buried in offshore accounts and aired claims that John Travolta feared his sex life would be exposed if he left Scientology. Behar wrote that critics found themselves 'engulfed in litigation, stalked by private eyes, framed for fictional crimes, beaten up or threatened with death'.[28]

Helping Behar to prove his point, the Church of Scientology served up the journalist his own dose of punishment. TIME magazine and Behar were sued (unsuccessfully) for US$416 million. The case dragged on for a decade. Behar was followed by private investigators for months before and after publication. Investigators illegally obtained copies of his credit report and his phone records.[29] Friends, neighbours and former classmates were contacted and asked for information about Behar's finances, health and whether he had ever taken illicit drugs.

In 1991, TIME was one of the most influential publications in the world with over four million readers each week.[30] In response to the article, Scientology went into overdrive, launching an aggressive public relations campaign to try and counter the damage caused by Behar's article. It spent millions of dollars on full-page advertisements in the national broadsheet USA Today that ran for 12 weeks.[31] The advertising campaign tried to suggest that TIME in the 1930s and '40s had been sympathetic to Hitler and Mussolini and that its coverage of the illicit drug LSD was responsible for many deaths.[32]

The TIME article led to Miscavige going on live television for the first and last time.[33] He was interviewed on [the American] ABC TV's Nightline program by legendary news anchor Ted Koppel nine months after the publication of Behar's article. The interview was preceded by a two-part story, which included accusations that Scientology tore families apart, ripped off its members and put its critics, including Behar, under surveillance.

Miscavige had war-gamed the interview for months beforehand with Marty Rathbun and Mike Rinder. 'We would have to sit through hours and hours and hours of him role playing and figuring out how he was going to answer questions,' says Rinder. 'It was almost like an obsession. It was like all day this shit would go on and we would be forced to sit there and either take the role of Ted Koppel asking questions or let Miscavige try and pretend to be Ted Koppel and ask us questions and see if he could trip us up.'[34]

When Miscavige arrived with his entourage at the ABC News studios in Washington, DC on 14 February 1992, he was confident things were under control. 'Miscavige thought the set-up story would be like a puff piece intro to him,' says Rinder. 'He had gone and met Ted in his office in Washington, DC and thought he had him totally under his thumb. He thought Koppel thought he was this great guy.'[35]

As Miscavige settled into the green room, one of *Nightline*'s producers began to brief him on how the program would work. According to Rinder, they were told there would be two reports, with Miscavige's interview with Koppel sandwiched in between the two tape items. 'When he found this out, Miscavige blew a gasket,' says Rinder. 'He said, "You're trying to trick me. I won't know how to respond to the second piece because I won't have seen it." It got very heated. He pushed the guy up against the wall and started screaming in his face. The compromise was to show both pieces at the top of the show.'[36]

The interview went for close to an hour. Miscavige made a series of bewildering claims. He portrayed himself as a victim of harassment, said the *TIME* piece was done at the behest of Eli Lilly, the drug company who made Prozac, and claimed that Richard Behar 'was on record on two occasions attempting to get Scientologists kidnapped'.[37]

Behar had done no such thing. Koppel pressed Miscavige on this allegation and asked if it were true, why hadn't charges been laid? Miscavige misleadingly said it was because 'he didn't succeed' with the kidnapping. The veteran news anchor pointed out attempted kidnapping was also a crime. Miscavige had gone into the interview underestimating Koppel. 'Miscavige thought he was much smarter than Ted Koppel, but Koppel really played him,' says Rinder. 'He was way, way, way over-matched for Miscavige. I was just thankful I wasn't the one in the hot seat.'[38]

Afterwards, Miscavige was in no mood to hang around the ABC studios. 'He walked into the green room and said let's get the fuck out of here,' says Rinder.[39] Miscavige and his aides went out the back of the studios for a smoke. When Miscavige asked how he went, Rinder and fellow Scientology executive Norman Starkey lavished praise on Scientology's leader. They had little choice. If Miscavige had delivered a poor performance, it would have been their fault for not briefing him properly.

Ted Koppel won an Emmy for the interview. His probing questions got under the skin of Scientology's leader. 'I don't think Miscavige completely bought that everything was fabulous,' says Rinder. 'I think he got rattled by some of Koppel's questions and realised it could get a lot worse. I mean, what if someone asked him about OT III?'[40] Miscavige never appeared on live television again.

The *Nightline* interview had given the world a small insight into the abrasive personality of Scientology's secretive leader. Nicole Kidman was only 25 at the time but she knew enough already to form her own character assessment. The young actress was becoming increasingly irritated by Miscavige's behaviour and the influence it was having on her husband. 'Her biggest beef was that Tom was becoming increasingly like Dave,' says Marty Rathbun.[41] 'She smelled a rat. Him being all about power and image and wealth, and his obsession with Tom. She was onto him.'[42] Something had to give.

Nicole Kidman was from a well-read family with a keen interest in politics and international affairs. Her parents campaigned against the Vietnam War. Her mother, Janelle, was a member of the Women's Electoral Lobby, a feminist group aimed at increasing women's political power and representation. As a child Nicole would hand out how-to-vote cards for the Labor Party on election day.[43] Dinner table discussions were dominated by talk of politics, injustice and human rights. When confronted by both Miscavige's personal behaviour and the revelations contained in the *TIME* exposé, she was never going to let it slide. It was time to withdraw from Scientology and take Tom with her.

'The *TIME* magazine article had a big influence on Nicole,' says Rathbun. 'She was already pushing him away from Scientology. Tom started acting like Miscavige, like a little zealot and Nicole abhorred it. She could see what she didn't like about Miscavige and the church and the *TIME* article exacerbated it. The *TIME* article gave her a wedge to stop Tom's involvement and it worked.'[44]

Rathbun says Kidman and Cruise drifted from Scientology from around 1992.[45]

The *TIME* article and Miscavige's behaviour weren't the only reasons Kidman was turning away from Scientology. By now she had also been exposed to its teachings on her father's profession. Marty

Rathbun had taken Kidman through the Potential Trouble Source/ Suppressive Person (PTS/SP) course. 'I was assigned to get her to understand the evils of psychology and psychiatry,' says Rathbun, 'and to come to the correct conclusion about her father.'[46] The session did not go down well with Kidman. 'It was a dismal disaster,' says Rathbun. 'It just backfired.'[47]

Rathbun says initially Kidman was drawn to certain aspects of Scientology. 'In reality there's a lot of neat little things that Scientology does,' he says, 'and she thought they were pretty neat.' But Kidman's attitude noticeably changed when Scientology's teachings on the mental health profession were laid out before her. 'When it got to that point,' says Rathbun, 'where she needed to be read the riot act, or she needed to come to the realisation that her connection to her psychologist father was a negative, I think that was probably the first thing that sent red flags up for her.'[48]

After Kidman and Cruise left Int Base, the actress stopped taking Scientology courses. 'She hadn't officially said that she didn't want to continue,' says Bruce Hines, 'but she showed no interest. She was sort of resisting going back to the international headquarters where she could do OT III.'[49] Hines was assigned to haul Kidman back in and get her on track. He had previously had success turning around opera singer Julia McGinnis who had been planning to leave Scientology. 'That went well,' says Hines, 'so I had a feather in my cap. When something came up with the big names, I became the guy of choice.'[50]

Hines had audited a range of celebrities and big names such as Kirstie Alley, Chick Corea and Mary Sue Hubbard. He didn't know it at the time, but Scientology's network of spies had informed Miscavige that Kidman was the one responsible for getting Cruise to drift from Scientology. If Nicole could be convinced to get back on the Bridge, the logic was that Tom would follow.

Hines received his written instructions at Int Base. He was to conduct an auditing session with Kidman at the Celebrity Centre in Los Angeles. He was to ask her whether she had any problems, or if there was anything she was concerned about. Hines was meant to determine whether she was withholding any information that could account for her loss of interest in Scientology auditing.

Hines hopped into a borrowed Honda Civic with Ray Mithoff, the man who had officiated at Cruise and Kidman's wedding in Colorado. The pair drove 150 km from Int Base to Los Angeles where they met Kidman. The actress had taken time off from her busy filming schedule. Armed with her preclear folder, full of the intimate secrets she had disclosed during previous auditing sessions, Hines got to work.

Kidman held on to the cans of the E-Meter as Hines asked his pre-ordained questions. 'It was an auditing session,' says Hines, 'and so it was very formal. You have written instructions ahead of time and you're not allowed to vary from those instructions.'[51] Hines asked his questions, but didn't get the answers Scientology was hoping for. 'The session didn't last very long,' he says. 'She seemed pretty happy about everything, happy about her life. She said, "No, I'm not upset about anything."'[52] Whatever she was thinking, Kidman resisted criticising either Miscavige or Scientology. According to Hubbard's doctrine, if Kidman had been lying or withholding information it would have shown up on the E-Meter.

Looking back, Hines believes Kidman was going through the motions. 'She acted as if she was very willing to do it,' says Hines, 'but in retrospect she's a great actress and I don't know what she really, really thought. I think she was doing it to be polite and she was willing to go through with it, but at the same time I don't think she was willing to talk about all the details of her life. I would say that probably she had sort of moved on by then and she wasn't bothered about Scientology, she seemed sort of past it.'[53] A former Kidman staffer agrees with Hines's assessment. 'She got tired of it, she was done with it,' he says. 'It was sucking up her time and she'd rather read a film script than more Scientology books.'[54]

That Kidman had moved beyond Scientology was easy to understand, that she had taken Cruise with her, might seem harder to fathom. This is the man Miscavige would later describe publicly as 'the most dedicated Scientologist I know', while presenting him with a specially struck 'Freedom Medal of Valor'.[55]

Former staffers to both Cruise and Kidman gave me rare insights into what was going on behind the scenes in their relationship and how Scientology had meddled in their marriage. These ex-employees were able to shine a light on how Kidman was able to get Cruise to drift from Scientology and what happened when Cruise decided to return to the fold. They spoke to me anonymously but at great personal risk. Both Cruise and Kidman make their staff sign strict confidentiality agreements. The former staffers I spoke to believed there was a strong public interest in exposing how Scientology had got its claws into Kidman and Cruise's relationship and helped end their marriage.

One former member of Cruise's staff told me the actor stopped getting audited and attending Scientology events because he was besotted with his new wife. 'He was absolutely obsessed with Nicole from the moment he met her,' the former employee told me. 'If she said jump, he would say how high. I'm not kidding you. So if she didn't want to be involved in Scientology anymore, he wouldn't be involved anymore. Even though it was his life and blood and he thought it was the greatest thing and it was going to save mankind, it doesn't matter. If Nicole was into it, he was into it, if not, he wasn't.'[56]

Cruise's obsession with Kidman was obvious to all those around the couple. One former staffer described it as 'suffocating'.[57] Others found it endearing. His infatuation with his wife was on display each time his driver took him back to the pair's Los Angeles mansion after a day's filming. 'He would be dropped off at the front lawn which was maybe 25 yards from the front door,' a former staffer told me, 'and he would sprint to the front of the house and open the door and yell, "Nic! Nic!" and run to wherever she was.'[58]

Within Scientology's elite circles Cruise's sudden lack of enthusiasm for Scientology was being noticed. According to Marty Rathbun, in 1993 Cruise and Kidman left halfway through the annual gala for the International Association of Scientologists, a move that upset Miscavige.[59] Nora Crest, who worked at the Celebrity Centre in Los Angeles, says it was obvious by the mid-1990s that Cruise was no longer turning up. 'He used to come to Celebrity Centre frequently; we used to get parts of the building locked down at least once a month or so when he turned up. Then when he was drifting from Scientology he wasn't there at all. He'd come to the gala once a year and that was it.'[60]

Kidman may have gotten Cruise to drift from Scientology, but the Scientologists never drifted far from Cruise. He continued to employ a number of Scientologists who worked with him on movie sets, flew him around on his Gulfstream jet, managed his affairs and ran his household. The most significant of these was his personal assistant, Michael Doven. Cruise referred to him as 'The Dovenator'. Doven knew everything Cruise was up to. Kidman may have thought she got Scientology out of her relationship, but she never quite got it out of her house.

Michael Doven was hired to work for Tom Cruise around the time they were shooting *Far and Away*, Ron Howard's 1992 feature, which starred Kidman and Cruise as a pair of Irish immigrants trying to make a new start in the US in the 1890s. According to Marty Rathbun, Doven was chosen for the job, not by Cruise, but by the Church of Scientology. 'Doven was approved by Miscavige,' says Rathbun, 'after he ordered all sorts of people with administrative experience, who were OTs or very advanced Scientologists, to be searched to find the ideal personal assistant for Cruise.'[61]

A native of Colorado, with an interest in extreme sports and photography, Doven was a devout Scientologist. Eventually he would lay claim to being the first person to complete and be tested on Scientology's 'Golden Age of Knowledge for All Eternity'. This involved watching around 1500 hours' worth of Hubbard's lectures and reading thousands of Hubbard's essays and bulletins.[62] 'He was a robot of Scientology,' a former co-worker told me. 'He knew everything there was to know about the study tech and all that bullshit.'[63]

Doven may have been paid by Cruise, but there was little doubt within Scientology's executive where his loyalties lay. 'He was briefed from the outset that his senior was Miscavige, not Tom Cruise,' says Rathbun. 'His job was to facilitate Tom Cruise's career but he had a separate brief to keep him on board and loyal to Miscavige.'[64] Rathbun says that Doven, for over two decades, was a 'card carrying, deep cover mole into the life and family of Tom Cruise'.[65] Mike Rinder, who attended top-level meetings with Doven when the pair were trying to get the infamous *South Park* episode pulled off air, agrees with Rathbun. 'It was very clear that Doven's loyalties were first to Miscavige and second to Tom Cruise,' says Rinder.[66]

According to one former Cruise staffer, Doven was the perfect man for the job. 'I never knew Doven was spying on them,' he told me, 'but it would've been so easy to do because he knew everything about

Tom. He knew every call he made. He knew everything he was doing from the time he woke up till the time he went to bed. Doven knew everything.'[67] When I rang Michael Doven to ask him to comment on his role with Tom Cruise he hung up on me. He did not respond to any of the allegations I put to him via email.

A loyal Scientologist, Doven put up with tirades of verbal abuse from Cruise for the greater good of his mission. After one humiliating episode of screaming and ranting from Cruise, a muscular security guard said he would hold his boss down so Doven could give him a beating. Doven declined the offer. 'He said don't ever interfere,' an ex-Cruise staffer told me. 'That's the kind of Scientology robot he was.'[68]

When Kidman got Cruise to drift from Scientology, Doven's role became even more important. He was ordered to report regularly about exactly what was happening inside their relationship. 'Doven reported on every significant event in Cruise's personal life directly to David Miscavige,' says Rathbun, 'right on down to arguments with his then-wife, Nicole, down to problems with his kids, down to every origination made by Tom in confidence to his personal assistant.'[69] Former Scientology executive Claire Headley was exposed to the secret operation when she worked with Rathbun. 'I was a party to the conversations that Doven was supposed to be, you know, feeding us information and getting Tom back on lines,' she told journalist Tony Ortega.[70]

It infuriated Miscavige that Kidman and Cruise had moved away from his orbit. The couple were shooting more films outside of the US and spending more time in Australia. In 1995, they bought a $4.2 million villa in the exclusive Sydney suburb of Darling Point.[71]

The drift away from Scientology was not harming their careers. Kidman won a Golden Globe in 1995 for her role as a pathologically ambitious TV reporter in *To Die For*. In 1996, Cruise won a Golden Globe and was nominated for an Academy Award for his role as the hyperactive sports agent in *Jerry Maguire*. The same year he released the first of his blockbuster *Mission Impossible* series. It was his first film credit as a producer in own right. The film was a runaway success, grossing over US$450 million.[72]

In 1996, Cruise made a one-off return to Scientology services. With Doven keeping communication lines open with Scientology,

Cruise agreed to be audited by Marty Rathbun in Los Angeles.[73] But according to Rathbun the session went nowhere and he did not return to Scientology services again that year. In the autumn Cruise and Kidman moved further away from Miscavige when they flew to London to begin work on Stanley Kubrick's final film, *Eyes Wide Shut*.[74]

Kubrick was a notorious perfectionist and on *Eyes Wide Shut* it was 15 months before he yelled, 'Cut!' for the final time. The film broke a Guinness World Record for the longest continual film shoot. Kubrick wasn't just driving the cast and crew mad, he helped to infuriate Scientology's leader. 'They were away for more than a year shooting *Eyes Wide Shut* in the UK,' says Mike Rinder, 'and Cruise was not in touch with Miscavige and this drove Miscavige crazy!'[75]

While in London, Kidman was interviewed by Anne Summers for the *Sydney Morning Herald*. For the first time, Kidman publicly declared that she was no longer a Scientologist. She did not mention that her husband had also stopped receiving Scientology services. Anne Summers wrote about the parallels between Kidman and her mother and how she had temporarily embraced Catholicism:

> *In the past, Kidman has said she is a Scientologist but now she seems to have left that behind her: 'I wouldn't classify myself as a Scientologist, but my husband is.' She is, she says, her own woman: 'I am who I am and I don't credit anybody except my parents with helping me.' Janelle Kidman observes that it's a bit like when she first married Antony and tried to become a Catholic like him; she took it very seriously 'in the first blush of everything' but her heart was never in it. She's now an agnostic.*[76]

The following year on *Desert Island Discs* on BBC Radio, Kidman was asked whether Scientology would help her if she were ever stranded on an island. 'No,' she responded. When pressed she admitted that it was 'Catholicism which will keep me going. I'm a Catholic girl. It will always stay with you.'[77] In March 1999, Kidman made similar comments to legendary New York gossip columnist Liz Smith. When asked if she was still a practising Scientologist, Kidman did not answer the question directly, but admitted she'd sought solace in St Patrick's Cathedral following the death of Stanley Kubrick. 'I suppose once a Catholic always a Catholic,' she said.[78]

With Kidman out in the open as an ex-Scientologist, and Cruise out of the country and out of contact, Michael Doven continued to feed Miscavige inside information. 'Doven is an unsung hero to David Miscavige and Scientology for keeping a lifeline to Tom,' says Marty Rathbun. 'There was never a period when he wasn't reporting in – if things went dark for too long and we weren't hearing anything, Doven would get hauled in and it was like "Hey, what's going on man?"'[79]

Michael Doven wasn't just reporting in on Cruise and Kidman. He was a key part of the operation to get Cruise back in to Scientology. Two years after his one-off auditing session with Marty Rathbun, Cruise returned to be audited in October 1998. The sessions lasted a week and were done in secret in the Guaranty Building on Hollywood Boulevard, away from the scrutiny of the Celebrity Centre. Cruise entered via a private car park and a back door that led to a hallway in the basement. He then caught the lift up to level 11, where Miscavige and Rathbun both had their private offices.

While Greg Wilhere's attempt to undermine Cruise and Kidman's relationship back in 1990 had failed, this time Miscavige was determined that the job would be done properly. Rathbun says the instructions to Doven were clear:

> *Miscavige said Nicole was the problem and you want*
> *to reinforce that with Tom as subtly as you can without*
> *making it sound like you are trying to break them up. That's*
> *how it started in '98 and all the while from '98 to 2000*
> *I'm constantly being told to reinforce with Doven, who is*
> *reporting to me probably on a weekly basis on everything*
> *that is going on with Tom, to keep planting the seed to*
> *drive a wedge because she's been determined by Miscavige*
> *to be what's keeping Tom separated from Dave, keeping*
> *Tom separated from Scientology.*[80]

Miscavige was desperate for Cruise to return to Scientology. But it would take a few years before Michael Doven's hard work paid off. In January 2001, Rathbun took a call from Cruise's personal assistant.

According to Rathbun, Doven relayed the message that Cruise needed help, that his life was a shambles, he needed auditing and he wanted a divorce.[81] Rathbun swung into action. Part of his role was to facilitate the hiring of private investigators to spy on Kidman. 'Tom wanted to know exactly who she was talking to, he wanted to tap her phone,' Rathbun said in the film *Going Clear.* 'When I reported that to David Miscavige I reported it like, "I mean he wants to tap her phone." He said, "Goddamn it get it done!"'[82]

Rathbun arranged through a Scientology lawyer to get a private investigator on the case to wiretap the phone in the couple's mansion in Los Angeles. Kidman soon knew about it. The actress was already distraught about the prospect of a divorce, now she was dealing with the paranoia that comes with having private investigators monitoring your conversations. 'She said I just know they are tapping my line,' a former Kidman staffer told me. 'I think what would happen is Tom would get the information and blast her. She'd be like, "How in the hell did he get that? He must be listening to my lines."'[83]

Kidman paid thousands of dollars to have surveillance experts come in and check her home for listening devices. But the private investigators hired at arm's length by the Church of Scientology were able to avoid detection. 'There was no bug in the house,' says the former staffer. 'The lines were being tapped at the main phone company. We found that out later.'[84]

In that era, one prominent Hollywood private investigator successfully ran wiretaps through the local phone exchange. His name was Anthony Pellicano. In 2008, Pellicano was sentenced to 15 years in prison for illegal wiretapping and running a criminal enterprise. When the FBI raided his office, they found wiretap transcripts, hand grenades and military grade plastic explosives.[85] Pellicano had successfully tapped lines of big-name Hollywood stars through the phone exchange, with Southwestern Bell telephone technician Ray Turner also doing time for his role in the private investigator's illegal operations.

Tom Cruise's lawyer Bert Fields knew Pellicano well. A number of his clients used the private investigator, though Fields maintains he had no knowledge of Pellicano's illegal activities. In 1992, Fields praised Pellicano's ability to get results. 'Time after time, Anthony comes up with the witness I'm looking for,' he told a journalist. 'He gets me results, so I stick with him.'[86]

A former Kidman staffer told me he was sure Pellicano was involved in the operation to wiretap the actress. 'I thought it was Pellicano the whole time,' he said. 'Bert Fields used Pellicano, so why wouldn't he use him for Nicole?'[87] The ex-staffer also recalls Kidman being interviewed by the FBI at the time of their Pellicano investigation: 'Why would they ask to meet her unless Pellicano bugged her?' he said.[88] In 2006, *Vanity Fair* reported that sources had claimed FBI agents had also questioned Tom Cruise.[89]

But Marty Rathbun maintains the Church of Scientology wanted nothing to do with Pellicano and that he intervened to make sure he wasn't used.

> *Bert Fields kept advising Tom to get Pellicano onto her. He never said to wiretap her. He said get Pellicano onto her and I kept telling Tom no, because I kept informed about what was going on in the investigative community and I knew this guy was bad news and had been subject to investigation over and over again. I actually had to go see Bert Fields to tell him that what we can do through our contacts we can do just as much as Pellicano and better and he finally backed off.[90]*

So did Bert Fields ignore Marty Rathbun's advice and hire Pellicano? Or were there two operations? One with Pellicano, and one without? Was it possible that Pellicano was employed before the Scientology-sponsored operation and that he acquired information from earlier wiretaps that prompted Tom to walk out the door?

Bert Fields is adamant that Pellicano was not used to tap Nicole Kidman's phone. 'Prior to the Kidman divorce, Anthony Pellicano had a dispute with Tom Cruise's accountant,' Fields told me, 'which led Tom to instruct us not to use Pellicano on any of Tom's cases – and we did not. Pellicano was *not* retained for Tom on any part or aspect of the Kidman divorce.'[91]

Cruise's lawyer also disputes Marty Rathbun's version of events. 'At no time did I tell Marty Rathbun that I wanted to hire Pellicano for Tom on the Kidman matter,' Fields says. 'I was well aware of Tom's instruction not to use Pellicano on his cases. At no time did Rathbun and I discuss anyone tapping Kidman's phone.'[92]

Tom Cruise would not respond to any of the allegations I put to him via his lawyer. But Bert Fields says Cruise had nothing to do with any phone tapping operation. 'Tom did not seek or want to tap Kidman's phone at any time and did not ask Rathbun or anyone else to do any such thing.' He sees his client as a victim of a smear campaign. 'Tom Cruise is a decent, honest man, who has caused no harm whatsoever to Rathbun or his fellow anti-Scientologists,' he said. 'Their continuing attempt to smear him with lies is despicable.'[93] In a statement, Scientology's lawyer Patrick George said, 'The Church denies the allegations concerning Nicole Kidman.'[94]

On 6 February 2001 it was announced that Kidman and Cruise were splitting. A press release put out by Cruise's then publicist Pat Kingsley stated the couple had regretfully decided to separate, 'Citing the difficulties inherent in divergent careers which constantly keep them apart, they concluded that an amicable separation seemed best for both of them at this time.'[95]

Kidman was shocked when Cruise suddenly wanted to end their marriage. So, too, were those close to her. Kidman's staff saw how infatuated Tom was with her. It simply didn't make sense. At the time it was reported that Tom had explained the sudden divorce by saying, 'Ask Nicole. She knows.'[96] One ex-staffer said to me, 'I would like to know from the Scientologists the real reason that Tom walked out the door – what was it? Was there something explosive in those recordings?'[97] It's a question I could not get an answer to. The tapes have never been made public and no-one close to these events would reveal to me what was on those recordings.

The Scientology-sponsored wiretapping of Nicole Kidman's phone went on for around a month.[98] Kidman was not the only target. According to Marty Rathbun, Cruise wanted to find out more about the conversations she was having with her long-term friend Russell Crowe. 'I'm not sure who else,' Rathbun told me, 'but I definitely knew he came up because we got in a big background number on Crowe. We went and investigated him to find out everything about him right down to the doctor who delivered him.'[99]

Crowe's star was on the rise in Hollywood. He had just won the Academy Award for Best Actor for his role as Maximus in Ridley Scott's film *Gladiator.* Two years earlier Cruise had been photographed sitting next to Crowe as his football team, the South Sydney Rabbitohs, played the Auckland Warriors. Now the Church of Scientology was compiling a file on Crowe as part of a surveillance operation organised on behalf of Cruise.

Rathbun says there was no evidence that Crowe was being anything other than a good friend at a time of deep personal despair for Nicole. 'I was privy to all these calls,' he says. 'I had to be briefed on them and I had to understand them because I had to relay them to Miscavige. In my personal opinion there was nothing to warrant any concern based on the substance and content of those calls.'[100]

Once the surveillance stopped and the divorce was finalised, the Church of Scientology did not leave Nicole Kidman alone. According to former senior Scientologists, its next step was to turn Kidman's children against her. Marty Rathbun claims Scientology official Tommy Davis was indoctrinating Isabella (Bella) and Connor Cruise. 'Tommy told them over and over again their mother was a sociopath, and after a while they believed him,' Rathbun told the *Hollywood Reporter.* 'They had daily sessions with Tommy. I was there. I saw it.'[101]

Back when Tommy Davis was still an active Scientologist he denied the claim. In a written statement in 2012 he said, 'Marty Rathbun never witnessed conversations between me and Isabella and Connor Cruise about their mother because no such conversations ever occurred. I have never spoken with Isabella or Connor about their mother and never would as it is none of my business.'[102]

John Brousseau, the former Sea Org member who built limousines and motorhomes for Cruise and renovated his airport hangar, believes someone was indoctrinating the children by telling them that their mother was what Scientology calls a 'Suppressive Person', or SP. After the divorce the children spent time in his care while Tom was being recruited back in to Scientology:

I sort of became the guy to keep them occupied, to keep them out of the way so that Miscavige could deal with Tom without the kids. So I hung out with them took them around to ride

ATVs (all-terrain vehicles), took them fishing and all kinds of things on the Int Base and got to know them quite well. I was sort of like Uncle JB to them.[103]

Brousseau says the Cruise children confided in him and would talk candidly about their mother. 'I knew they were getting some kind of training on the PTS/SP course,' he says, 'and they probably on half-a-dozen occasions would make derogatory comments about Nicole. On one occasion Connor and Bella were both telling me how they had recognised that she's an SP and I remember thinking at the time, Wow, they were coerced into this thinking.'[104]

TV star and former Scientologist Leah Remini says she heard similar terms used by Bella Cruise when she was a teenager. After the 2006 wedding of Tom Cruise and Katie Holmes, Remini shared a ride with Connor and Bella to the airport. The star of *The King of Queens* asked the siblings, 'How's your mom? Do you see her a lot?' According to Remini, Bella shot back, 'Not if I have a choice. Our mom is a fucking SP.'[105] A former Kidman staffer says after the divorce Nicole remained scared of the Church of Scientology. 'She knew they were powerful,' he says. 'She knew they were dirty.'[106]

Scientology got Tom Cruise back in to the fold and secured his children at the same time. But the surveillance culture used against Nicole would soon be turned against Tom. According to several former Sea Org members, Cruise's auditing sessions with Marty Rathbun were videotaped and his personal confessions became fodder for Miscavige's warped sense of humour.[107]

Former Scientology executive Tom DeVocht says Miscavige would watch tapes of Cruise's confidential auditing sessions before sharing personal details about his sex life with close colleagues. 'I would sit there every night with a Scotch and watch and listen to Miscavige comment about Cruise's sex life and how perverted he was,' recalled DeVocht.[108]

Privately Miscavige might have belittled Scientology's star recruit but publicly and in person Miscavige was full of praise for Cruise, suggesting that he, like him, had superhuman powers. 'Miscavige convinced Cruise that he and Tom were two of only a handful of truly "big beings" on the planet,' recalled Rathbun. 'He instructed

Cruise that LRH [Hubbard] was relying upon them to unite with the few others of their ilk on earth to make it on to "Target Two" – some unspecified galactic locale where they would meet up with Hubbard in the afterlife.'[109]

Cruise's renewed dedication to Scientology came with benefits to Miscavige. He was used to lobby foreign leaders and US ambassadors to help defend Scientology. He asked President Clinton to try and convince Tony Blair to give Scientology tax-deductible charity status in the UK. He met with Deputy Secretary of State Richard Armitage to see what he could do about the hostility towards Scientology in Germany.[110]

Miscavige rewarded Cruise for his efforts. At the International Association of Scientologists' 20th anniversary gala in 2004, he was presented with a special award struck in his honour, the Freedom Medal of Valor. As he hung the diamond-encrusted medal around Cruise's neck, Miscavige described him as 'the most dedicated Scientologist I know'. It was a deeply offensive comment to all those Sea Org members who had dedicated their lives to the cause, slaving away for just US$50 a week. This was the man who had gone missing during the *TIME* magazine controversy, and the battle to win tax-free status with the IRS.

As Cruise received his award, saluted Miscavige and then hugged him, there in the front row applauding was James Packer – the son of Australia's richest man. Unbeknownst to most of the Scientologists in the room, the recruitment of James Packer became Miscavige's next big priority. The man who delivered the young mogul to Scientology was, of course, Tom Cruise.

CHAPTER 19

THE PACKER ACQUISITION

PETER BARNES HAD BEEN stalking James Packer for weeks. The freelance paparazzo had been hired by Sydney gossip columnist Annette Sharp to get the photographic evidence she was so desperate for – confirmation that the son of Australia's richest man had been recruited into Scientology. Barnsey, as he was known in the game, hovered around the corner of the Glebe laneway where Scientology's 'Advanced Organisation' in Sydney was located. With his long lens camera hidden in his backpack, he patiently waited for Packer to enter or leave the building.[1]

Inside the 'Advanced Org' Eric Kleitsch had already discovered that James Packer was Scientology's latest big name recruit. Kleitsch, along with around 30 other Sea Org members, had been commandeered to scrub the car park in preparation for the businessman's arrival. 'We were told an important VIP was arriving and we all had to do a white glove clean-up of the garage,' he says. Kleitsch was shocked when he caught a glimpse of Packer getting out of his black Mercedes. 'I thought to myself, shit how the hell did they get him?' Kleitsch says. 'And what the hell would his father say?'[2]

While Peter Barnes waited for his money shot and Eric Kleitsch polished the car park floor with rags and an all-purpose cleaner, 12,000 km away in Los Angeles, Marty Rathbun was in charge of the in-depth operation to recruit the son of Australia's richest man. David Miscavige took the project so seriously he had the second most senior Scientologist in the world running it. Rathbun was to oversee every level of the operation. As he describes it:

*[In the US] I was his auditor. I was his contact. When he was
back in Australia we went through this whole process that
I had to supervise directly to take all of the greatest newly
trained completely loyal top-flight Australian auditors and brief
them and get them all set up to go service him. I had to set up
the whole thing at the Advanced Organisation there and they
were sending me submissions on the security there and how we
would go in the back way and sneak in there and the tabloids
could never see him and there would be no connection. I set
that whole thing up. I supervised the entire thing.*[3]

Marty Rathbun achieved many famous victories in his time as
Inspector-General of Scientology's Religious Technology Center. The
biggest was convincing the US Internal Revenue Service to grant
Scientology tax-free status. But outfoxing Peter Barnes and Annette
Sharp, a paparazzo and a tabloid journalist with a mutual love of the
stakeout, proved a tough assignment.

In 2002, James Packer was in desperate need of help. Friends
feared he was in danger of taking his own life.[4] In a TV interview
over a decade later he would admit that during this period, 'I became
depressed and I was emotionally exhausted ... I felt isolated, I felt
like a failure, you know, it was not a great time in my life.'[5] His wife
Jodhi Meares had moved out of their luxury Bondi apartment and a
disastrous business deal had eroded his self-confidence and strained his
relationship with his father, Kerry, who at that stage was Australia's
wealthiest man, worth $6 billion.[6]

A few years earlier, the world was at James Packer's feet. In 1995,
he invested $250,000 in One.Tel, a telecommunications company
run by fellow Cranbrook old boy Jodee Rich. Soon those shares
were worth $5 million.[7] Packer was grateful to Rich for making him
independently wealthy and giving him the opportunity to move out
of the shadow of his formidable father. But in desperation to prove
himself to Kerry and gain financial independence from him, James
was blinded by Rich's bluff and bluster.

Jodee Rich had a history of dazzling then disappointing investors.
In the 1980s, the rapid expansion of his software retailing business,
Imagineering, led him to be called 'The youngest and richest self-

made millionaire this side of the Indian Ocean.'[8] But it all ended in tears. By the end of the decade, shareholders had lost over $100 million and the company's fortunes had collapsed under the weight of its own debt. The experience did little to temper Rich's taste for taking risks with other people's money. In 1998, he decided One.Tel should build its own telephone network, a project that would require a capital injection of at least $1 billion.

In the beginning, James Packer convinced his father that the family company, Consolidated Press Holdings, should invest $47 million in One.Tel. He then worked on Lachlan Murdoch, suggesting he try and get his father, Rupert, on board. By February 1999, the Packer and Murdoch families had decided to plunge $710 million into One.Tel, acquiring 40 per cent of the company's shares.[9] It was a disastrous investment.

Just over a year later, the dot.com bubble burst on Wall Street. By May 2000, One.Tel had lost a third of its value on the stock market. By the end of June it had lost $291 million for the financial year and spent $775 million in cash. In January 2001, as he recovered from a life-saving kidney transplant, Kerry Packer called in James and Jodee Rich for a meeting. The pair were harangued for three hours. 'You ran out of cash at Imagineering,' Kerry said to Jodee, 'and you're going to do it again. I was right and now the markets are telling me I was right. You blokes never listen to me.'[10]

One.Tel continued to haemorrhage money. A few months later, with Kerry back in hospital and too sick to attend a key meeting, he asked one of his lieutenants to tell Rich the whole debacle would cost him 'his right testicle'.[11] That month an emergency board meeting was held and Jodee Rich was forced to resign from One.Tel. James Packer and Lachlan Murdoch killed off the business. Kerry blamed James for losing $400 million of the family company's money. James had lost his financial independence and his father's respect. Kerry was not the kind of man who would let him forget it.

If you want an illustration of how tough Packer men can be on their sons, look no further than how Kerry's father, Frank, treated him. As a child Kerry had been sent interstate to board at Geelong Grammar School. One summer holiday he returned to the family home in Bellevue Hill after a long train trip from Victoria. Instead of being welcomed with open arms, Kerry was chastised for forgetting his tennis racquet. To teach him a lesson Frank put the young boy on the train back to Geelong. The round trip was over 2000 km. It was days before young Kerry returned home for his family holiday with tennis racquet in hand.[12]

When James was at his lowest point after the One.Tel debacle, Kerry was hardly sympathetic. In 2001, when the family company made its first ever loss, James was the one who had to announce it to the public and apologise to shareholders. One of Kerry's trusted former lieutenants told biographer Paul Barry that Kerry 'left him hanging out to dry'.[13] James withdrew from running the company, even though he was executive chairman. 'James was completely fucked,' a Packer company executive told journalist Richard Guilliatt. 'He went from one of the most confident executives in the world to a complete mess.'[14] It took a year for Kerry to realise his son had even had a breakdown.[15]

Into the void left by his father stepped Hollywood superstar Tom Cruise. Following his divorce from Nicole Kidman, Cruise was back in the game as an enthusiastic proselytiser for Scientology. He took the young businessman under his wing and suggested he try some of Hubbard's techniques. As James told TV journalist Mike Willesee over a decade later:

Tom Cruise reached out to me and it was a surreal thing.
I'd met him once or twice, only once or twice, and he was
in Australia and we got together. I think he could tell that
I was in pain ... and he invited me to his house to go skiing
with him at Christmas – probably in Christmas, 2001, so six
months after One.Tel went broke – and we spent a couple
of weeks together and subsequently, he was just an amazing
friend to me.[16]

While James Packer is eternally grateful to Tom Cruise for his support at a time when others were missing in action, the mission may not have been entirely altruistic. Marty Rathbun, who was in charge of the operation to recruit and keep James in Scientology, told me that it was all a part of a grander plan. Locking in James was the first step in a bid to recruit Lachlan Murdoch, son of Rupert, the media magnate whom Scientology blamed for triggering the Anderson Inquiry in Victoria in the 1960s. As Marty Rathbun told me:

> *Tom and myself and Miscavige all were impressed with the idea that he was very tight close friends with one of Rupert Murdoch's sons and so the idea was, in Tom's concept and Dave fully endorsed it, and so did I, was to win Jamie over and ultimately get our claws into News Corp. It would be the greatest coup of all time because it was perceived by Scientology, in our files, which were extensive, that Murdoch was an incredibly important player because of his involvement or perceived involvement with the Inquiry.*[17]

Marty Rathbun knew intimately how obsessed Scientology was with Rupert Murdoch. In 1981, he had been seconded to join an elite, secretive Scientology team known as the Special Project. Rathbun's first task on that operation was to get across the details of all the law suits filed against Hubbard and to help gather evidence that the FBI had infiltrated the intelligence wing of the Guardian's Office and convinced its agents to commit crimes.[18] This meant meticulously making his way through the organisation's secret files.

Rathbun ultimately found out there was no FBI conspiracy, but he did discover a whole lot more about the organisation as he sifted his way through hundreds of filing cabinets at the Guardian's Office in Los Angeles. Included in the files were dossiers in which Rupert Murdoch featured prominently:

> *One of the first things I did in 1981 was to read the big conspiracy folders and everything L. Ron Hubbard said about it, and Rupert Murdoch was right up there with the heads of banking and the heads of the pharmaceutical industries as the sort of James Bondian Mr X villains.*[19]

It is drilled into Scientology's followers, and in particular its leadership, that its critics are never forgiven nor forgotten. As Hubbard wrote in 1959 in his *Manual of Justice*: 'People attack Scientology, I never forget it, always even the score. People attack auditors, or staff, or organisations, or me. I never forget until the slate is clear.'[20] When it came to Rupert Murdoch, the slate was far from clear.

In the early 1960s, in the years leading up the Anderson Inquiry in Victoria, Murdoch's Melbourne tabloid *Truth* crusaded relentlessly against Scientology. It held Hubbard up to ridicule referring to his creation as Bunkumology. While delivering the AN Smith Lecture in Journalism in 1972, Murdoch boasted that 'as a result of *Truth* campaigns the practice of Scientology has been legislated against'.[21] It was one thing that the Scientologists and Murdoch agreed upon, that his newspaper had been responsible for triggering the first ban on Scientology in the world.

According to Rathbun, this was at the front of their minds when Cruise told him and Miscavige that he was in close contact with James Packer. 'You can understand what it was like when Tom goes, "Hey, Jamie Packer is best friends with Lachlan Murdoch." It was like man! We were actively talking about this, that this would be the coup of all coups to get the son of Rupert Murdoch! We thought he was potentially the guy who was going to help take over the evil genius Murdoch's empire.'[22]

Tom Cruise did not respond to any of the allegations made by Marty Rathbun about James Packer's recruitment. His long-time lawyer Bert Fields told me via email: 'His not responding should not be taken as an indication that any of the allegations are true.'[23] The Church of Scientology via their Sydney lawyer Patrick George stated in an email: 'The Church denies the allegation that it attempted to use James Packer to recruit Lachlan Murdoch, together with the other allegations concerning Mr Packer.'[24]

In the early 1990s, Tom Cruise had been silent when Scientology needed him most. When *TIME* magazine published its damaging exposé, *The Thriving Cult of Greed and Power*, Cruise was nowhere to be seen. Scientology's aggressive public relations counter-attack was done without assistance from its most high profile member.

As Rathbun puts it, through targeting Packer and Murdoch, Cruise had an opportunity to make amends, 'He stood by while we were taking the *TIME* magazine shellacking and when we went and got the IRS exemption he wasn't part of any of that, so he was really keen to make up the damage,' says Rathbun. 'He was already friends with James and he knew the guy needed help and he sort of in his own way was kind of doing that as a friend, but he originated that this was an incredibly important, potentially influential, person.'[25]

The plan not only fitted in with Hubbard's policies in relation to seeking revenge on critics. It squared with another pronouncement made by Scientology's founder. In 1969, Hubbard issued a confidential policy titled 'Targets, Defense'.[26] The policy was designed to create a defense perimeter around Scientology insulating it from continual attacks. The policy stated that the targets on which they should invest most of their time should include 'taking over the control or allegiance of the heads or proprietors of all news media'.[27]

Targeting James Packer and getting to the Murdochs became the number one priority for Scientology. Rathbun, the second in command in Scientology's hierarchy, and the man who brought Cruise back into the fold just a year earlier, was assigned to be James Packer's auditor and point man:

Jamie would come to the Celebrity Centre and Tom was there. I was intensively auditing Tom, I had Penelope Cruz getting audited and we had the (Cruise/Kidman) kids getting indoctrinated on PTS/SP (Potential Trouble Source/ Suppressive Person) – but the big project that we were working on was Jamie and so Jamie would come by from time to time when he was in the States and we would after session go up to the President's suite – it's the penthouse suite at the Celebrity Centre – Tom had it reserved for that entire several month period.[28]

The Scientologists were desperate to impress Packer. They had their second in command play the role of James's auditor and key contact. They had their number one celebrity hang out with him in the exclusive President's suite at the Celebrity Centre. Back in Australia, they put their foot soldiers to work, with around 30 Sea Org members assigned to scrub the car park at the Advanced Org building in Sydney in preparation for his arrival.

ERIC KLEITSCH WAS SEVEN years into a 12-year stretch on the Sea Org's punishment camp, the Rehabilitation Project Force (RPF), when he was ordered to clean the basement car park in the Scientology building in Glebe. Kleitsch's RPF sentence is almost unsurpassed in Scientology history. 'I think there are only one or two people in America who have been on longer than me,' he says.[29]

Kleitsch was considered a troublemaker within Scientology circles. 'I was not a meek follower of Hubbard who did everything that his seniors told him,' he says. 'I questioned things.'[30] When two Scientologists who'd had mental breakdowns were detained in a caravan on an isolated property, Kleitsch kicked up a stink, threatening to take the story to the media. 'I was RPF'd to keep me quiet,' says Kleitsch. 'I was pissed off. I told them what they were doing was completely illegal.'[31]

When the operation to clean the car park began, Kleitsch was given a pile of rags, a mop and some all-purpose cleaner. The work was dirty and monotonous. He scrubbed the car park floor, wiped down walls, cleaned out the inside of the dumpster with bleach and removed any junk that had been stored in the basement. 'There were around 30 of us,' Kleitsch says. 'We worked all night and until lunchtime the next day.'[32]

Upstairs in Scientology's three-storey Advanced Org things were just as hectic. Orders had come in from Scientology headquarters in the US that everything had to be in top shape in preparation for a special visitor. Only a handful of people were briefed about who was coming.

Sea Org member Dean Detheridge was one of those in the loop. He had been called in urgently to help install hidden audio and visual recording devices in a special room upstairs. 'I was asked to install the equipment in one particular room that I was told would be used to do the Director of Processing (DoP) interviews on Packer,' says Detheridge.[33]

The former Scientologist says that at the time it was highly unusual for these kinds of personal conversations to be recorded. 'DoP interviews aren't usually recorded for the average Joe Blow,' says Detheridge, 'but Miscavige's RTC (Religious Technology Center) would have been all over Packer's actions – and would definitely want the interviews recorded.'[34] In a statement, Scientology's lawyer Patrick George said, 'The allegations attributed to Eric Kleitsch and Dean Detheridge are denied.'[35]

Down in the basement car park the cleaning crew was none the wiser as to who was going to be the beneficiary of all their hard labour. On the RPF you are forbidden from initiating conversations. 'We were just told an important VIP was arriving,' says Kleitsch.[36]

As a former undercover operative for the Guardian's Office, Eric Kleitsch was adept at uncovering secrets. Twenty years earlier, he had infiltrated the Labor Party in South Australia and gleaned important information about its plans to overturn the ban on Scientology. Now stuck on Scientology's chain gang, scrubbing dumpsters and sweeping floors, Kleitsch was about to find out just who that VIP was.

The plan was for James Packer to be able to drive straight into the basement car park and avoid detection from the tabloid media or any common grade Scientologists. But on one occasion Kleitsch caught a glimpse of the young mogul. His mind immediately turned to Kerry Packer and what he might think of his son dabbling in Scientology. 'From what I had read his father was not someone you would want to trifle with,' Kleitsch says. 'He was a very tough man who always got what he wanted.'[37]

By discovering Scientology's big secret, Kleitsch had landed himself in big trouble. He was soon given the Sea Org's ultimate punishment. 'I was sent to the RPF's RPF for being in the same space as Packer,' says Kleitsch. 'I was in there for a month.'[38]

When Kleitsch returned to the standard RPF, he was back on car park cleaning duties, making sure the basement garage passed the white glove test. The Church of Scientology describes the RPF as a 'voluntary program of spiritual rehabilitation'.[39] But Kleitsch says it was nothing of the sort. 'On the RPF we were treated like animals,' he says. 'Like slaves, really.'[40]

If the RPF really is a spiritual retreat, where Sea Org members are meant to 'restore one's condition to an optimal spiritual state',[41] the Church of Scientology seemed keen to shelter James from its members as they scrubbed the car park for his benefit. According to Kleitsch, on one occasion Packer arrived early, causing a massive problem for the Scientologists as they tried to hide around 30 RPF crew:

> *We were all bundled into a closet and I had to go to the toilet,*
> *and it was either piss my pants or go to the toilet. So I thought*
> *I would go to the toilet but then the bosun [person in charge*
> *of the RPF] pulled me back and nearly tore my shirt off and*
> *screamed at me. I was given a bottle to piss in. We were in*
> *that closet for hours – it could have been four or five hours –*
> *we had to wait until Packer was finished upstairs and had left*
> *before we were let out.*[42]

If Annette Sharp had been able to get to Eric Kleitsch she could have confirmed the rumours she had picked up from her contacts inside Sydney's stockbroking belt, that James Packer had become a Scientologist.

Instead the *Sun-Herald* gossip columnist had to start from scratch. 'I had spent a bit of time doing my own stakeout work because I didn't know where Packer was being audited,' Sharp recalls. 'I spent a week at their grounds in Dundas speaking primarily to Australian Asian students of Scientology who were coming and going.'[43]

Sharp didn't spot James Packer, but she soon worked out that auditing was done at the Advanced Org in Glebe. In November 2002, she convinced her bosses at Fairfax to employ freelance photographer Peter Barnes to hover outside the building to try and capture a shot of Packer entering or leaving the building.

Annette Sharp was sure that if anyone could get the shot, it was Peter Barnes. 'Barnsey and I had worked together on stakeouts before, and had discovered we shared a real passion for hard-to-get subjects,' says Sharp. 'At the time, there was none harder than James at the bosom of Scientology. The church were protecting him by letting him use undercover car parks and they were never going to confirm his attendance.'[44]

Peter Barnes spent weeks on the job, moving between the multi-storey shopping centre car park opposite the Advanced Org and a street corner down the road. Eventually he got the shots he needed – photographs of James driving in and out of the much polished basement car park, and pictures of him smoking outside the building.

Annette Sharp is still surprised that the Scientologists gave them the opening they were looking for. 'It seems no-one at Scientology

HQ had thought to locate for James an internal courtyard in which to smoke,' she says. 'It gave Barnsey his window. I can still remember his delight when he rang to tell me he had our picture.'[45]

Annette Sharp had her story and was well placed to cover it. She had an understanding of the intricacies of both the Packer family and the Church of Scientology. Sharp had worked for the Packers for seven years as a publicist at Channel Nine. As a 19-year-old cub reporter working on the *Illawarra Mercury* she had had an unusual introduction to Scientology. Sharp was assigned to interview singer Kate Ceberano. Kate was a third-generation Scientologist, and her mother, Cherie, came along to the interview. 'Cherie tried to recruit me,' says Sharp. 'She sent me a copy of *Dianetics* and rang me on a couple of occasions and asked, have I read it, what was I getting from it?'[46]

Sharp's own brief brush with Scientology, and her subsequent coverage of the Tom Cruise and Nicole Kidman marriage and divorce, meant she had an understanding of the difficulties of covering any story relating to the organisation. When she broke the story, neither the Church of Scientology nor the Packer family would confirm James was now a committed Scientologist.

The Packers were not happy with Sharp's reporting and what they saw as an intrusion into their personal affairs. In *Killing Fairfax*, journalist Pamela Williams revealed that Kerry sent the publishers of the *Sun-Herald* a pointed message: 'Kerry Packer had obtained a copy of the United Nations Human Rights Charter,' Williams wrote, 'and angrily sent it to the company's chief executive, Fred Hilmer, with a warning that he was violating the charter.'[47]

If Fairfax Media were violating James's rights, others soon joined in including the newspapers owned by his friends the Murdochs. The recruitment of James Packer to Scientology had become big news. News Limited's Sydney tabloid the *Daily Telegraph* reported that neighbours had heard him playing The Pretenders' hit 'Brass in Pocket' and Tina Arena's pop ballad 'Heaven Help My Heart' at full volume three times over before jumping into his Mercedes CL600 and heading for the Church of Scientology in Glebe.[48]

More and more details were being published by the Sydney newspapers. Richard Guilliatt of the *Sydney Morning Herald* reported that on Boxing Day of 2002, James Packer flew to Los Angeles to visit Tom Cruise and attend a Scientology end of year event:

> *For much of the flight, Packer focused intently on a*
> *fat paperback copy of* Dianetics, *Hubbard's rambling*
> *philosophical manifesto. Occasionally he would peruse*
> *other pamphlets from the church, or put on a set of*
> *headphones to listen to a Scientology CD on a portable*
> *player. As the hours passed on that long transpacific flight,*
> *Packer's attention rarely shifted from his Scientology*
> *studies – although he did order a succession of Paddle Pops,*
> *which he sucked on ruminatively. For a man who stands to*
> *inherit several billion dollars, he cut a rather forlorn figure.*[49]

James had come to rely more and more on Tom Cruise and Scientology to help him through his tough times. He later described Cruise as 'a very special person'.[50] The actor cast him as an extra in his film *The Last Samurai*.[51] In 2004, Packer was in the front row seated next to singer Isaac Hayes when David Miscavige presented Tom Cruise with the one-off diamond-studded Freedom Medal of Valor for being 'the most dedicated Scientologist'.[52]

While Marty Rathbun believes Cruise used James Packer to try and recruit Lachlan Murdoch, he does acknowledge that Cruise also wanted to help him. 'It was both,' says Rathbun, 'and I'm not going to start assigning evil motives at every turn. It was both and so he did want to help and I do truly believe we did help him.'[53]

Like Cruise, Packer started employing Scientologists at close quarters, with an Australian member of the church tasked with running his Bondi apartment. He also helped recruit new members, with his former schoolmate Chris Hancock and his actor wife, Dee Smart, soon signing up. James's new girlfriend, Erica Baxter, was also doing Scientology courses.

Getting his father on board was a very different proposition. While Pamela Williams reported in *Killing Fairfax* that Kerry had agreed to let Tom Cruise look after his son,[54] he remained sceptical about Scientology. Kerry organised a meeting with Mark O'Brien, one of Australia's leading media and litigation lawyers. O'Brien had defended Packer's TV station Channel Nine when the Church of Scientology sued the *60 Minutes* program over a critical story it did in 1992. The Scientologists eventually dropped the case when Packer's legal team dug in for a long fight and started requesting Scientology policy documents as part of the discovery phase of the trial.

Mark O'Brien was a fierce legal advocate who had received a crash course in Scientology courtesy of the defamation trial. He and *60 Minutes* producer Anthony McClellan had travelled to London, New York and Los Angeles to gather information, find potential witnesses and get legal advice in preparation for the trial.[55] 'They were playing hardball with us,' recalls McClellan, 'so we decided to play hardball back.'[56] (Ironically McClellan had relied on evidence gathered by Scientologists for his *60 Minutes* program exposing deaths at Chelmsford Hospital in 1980.)

O'Brien and McClellan spoke to a number of experts including one of the key American lawyers involved in defending the libel case for *TIME* magazine. After returning from the trip O'Brien gained first-hand experience of the kind of random surprises reserved for those who take on Scientology. He got a call from his accountant to tell him the Tax Office was investigating him. 'There had been an anonymous tip-off that I was not declaring my proper income,'[57] says O'Brien. The accusations were baseless and the tax department soon called off its investigation once the likely source of the complaint was revealed.

While the Scientologists eventually dropped the defamation case, Kerry Packer did not emerge unscathed. Mounting a legal defence would have cost him hundreds of thousands of dollars. When his son became involved with the same organisation that tried to sue him he called in Mark O'Brien for a briefing. In his usual formidable way, Packer wanted answers. 'I want to know what this organisation is about,' he said to O'Brien. His legal counsel responded, 'I will send you tapes of the two *60 Minutes* stories which show how they operate.'[58]

Reports later emerged that Kerry might have been concerned the Scientologists were after a slice of the Packer fortune.[59] 'I never heard Kerry say he was worried they would take all his money,' O'Brien told me.[60]

Kerry was not just suspicious of Scientology. He took a cynical view of any organisation promising eternal life. In 1990, the billionaire had a massive heart attack during a polo game. His heart stopped beating for seven minutes. Afterwards he told his friend Phillip Adams, 'I've been to the other side, and let me tell you, son, there's fucking nothing there.'⁶¹ It is likely Kerry would have been even more sceptical of a religion that pumped its parishioners so vigorously for donations. One former Packer executive doubts the Scientologists were ever in danger of getting much out of Kerry or James. 'You find a religion that can take away the Packers' money,' Brian Powers said to Paul Barry, 'and I'm going to convert.'⁶²

In the end Kerry acknowledged that Scientology was good for his son. 'Kerry ultimately had the view it helped James,' says Mark O'Brien. 'Something helped him, he was a lot better after being involved with them.'⁶³ Marty Rathbun agrees. 'I saw it,' he says. 'I knew what was going on in his life. I saw him improve as a person, be more in the present, more analytical, more happy.'⁶⁴

As James pulled himself back into shape, his father's health continued to decline. Kerry was now too sick to play polo, or even golf, or follow any of the thrill-seeking pursuits he'd once enjoyed.⁶⁵ The drugs he was taking to help his body accept his new kidney also made him vulnerable to infection. He was spending more time in hospital and taking on the appearance of a frail old man. His body was rejecting the kidney that had been so generously donated to him by his helicopter pilot Nick Ross.

On Boxing Day 2005, Kerry Packer died at his home in Bellevue Hill. A state-funded memorial service was held at the Sydney Opera House seven weeks later. Tom Cruise and his new wife, Katie Holmes, flew to Australia on their private jet to attend the service. If Kerry had any concerns about the Scientologists getting at his money, it was not reflected in the will. The family empire was now in James's hands.⁶⁶

In November 2006, 11 months after his father had died, James spoke publicly for the first time about Scientology. As part of an expansive profile for the *Australian Financial Review*, journalist Pamela Williams asked him if he would spend an hour or so on Scientology every couple of days? 'Sometimes,' he responded. 'I could well spend that amount of time on it and I think it has been very good for me. It has been helpful. I have some friends in Scientology that have been very supportive. But I think it's just helped me have a better outlook on life.'[67]

Around the same time James Packer was talking about how beneficial Scientology had been for him, his absence from Scientology courses was causing a major meltdown inside the organisation's management offices on Hollywood Boulevard. According to one former insider, James was no longer an active Scientologist by the middle of 2006.

Lucy James served in many roles in her 30 years as a Scientology staffer. In 2006, she was working in Los Angeles as the 'management head' of all Advanced Organizations across the world. The Sydney office, where Packer had been receiving services, was under her jurisdiction. According to Lucy, Anne McCarthy, the Scientology 'management head' of Celebrity Centre International, gave her access to a top-secret file on the Australian billionaire.

> *The file showed that James Packer has been serviced by AOSH ANZO (Advanced Org in Sydney) but was no longer taking such services, no longer cooperating and Anne wanted me to handle AOSH ANZO to get James back in and taking Scientology services. Dave Petit, Executive Director of Celebrity Centre International, had come to the management building to meet with Anne and complain about the huge Scientology flap that was James Packer. In fact, Packer was considered so important to Scientology, Petit wanted the three top executives of AOSH ANZO in Sydney hauled before the Sea Org – equivalent of a court martial.*[68]

According to Lucy James, the file contained information about why James Packer had withdrawn from Scientology. 'It was simply that Packer was done with Scientology,' she says. 'He had gotten out of it what he wanted and was busy getting on with his life.'[69] James Packer had entered Scientology depressed and in a bad way and left it in much better shape. But this was not good enough for the Church of Scientology. The organisation wanted the billionaire on their books permanently.

Lucy James says there was immense pressure on her to find someone to punish for James Packer's retreat from Scientology. 'It was considered scandalous that I did not discipline AOSH ANZO (Sydney based) executives,' says the former Sea Org member, 'such was the pressure on the Celebrity Centre network staff to keep Packer in the fold.'[70] With Tom Cruise's involvement in the initial recruitment of James, coupled with Miscavige's demands that it be a top priority, the hunt was on to find a scapegoat.

The secret files revealed much more than a sense of panic over Packer's withdrawal from Scientology. According to Lucy James, the dossier included evidence that the Australian billionaire was being spied on by three of his staff members who were Scientologists. She says the intelligence gathered by these staffers was sent to senior US executives at the Celebrity Centre and the Religious Technology Center. If true, it is a move straight from Scientology's Tom Cruise playbook, where his personal assistant, the Scientologist Michael Doven, was in the words of Marty Rathbun, a 'card carrying, deep cover mole into the life and family of Tom Cruise'.[71]

As Lucy James told me, the operation was highly organised:

The file contained a number of reports from James Packer's own staff. These three staff were handpicked Scientologists, all recruited and screened by Celebrity Centre International (CCInt) to work for James. Essentially they were spies, reporting on Packer's movements and actions. One report covered the fact that James was sleeping in until 11.00 am every morning, which for some reason was considered a really big deal by Scientology executives. All three of James Packer's staff were being disciplined by special CCInt staff sent all the way to Australia to handle them, but of the three it was decided the girl (who seemed to carry out or coordinate household duties) should be removed and replaced as she had gone 'off the rails' and was 'compromised' because she was defending James Packer saying he was 'just living life'.[72]

James Packer would not talk to me for this book. He has never commented publicly on why he severed ties with Scientology. His defection did not become public knowledge until two years after Lucy

James saw the secret files that suggested he was no longer receiving Scientology services. In May 2008, the *Sydney Morning Herald*'s Andrew Hornery reported that he 'was no longer undertaking Scientology courses and had slowly moved away from the religion, telling his closest friends he no longer "needs it".'[73]

By this time Marty Rathbun was not around to retrieve James in the way he had got Tom Cruise back in. In January 2004, Rathbun was hauled into David Miscavige's office. 'He lambasted me,' Rathbun wrote in *Memoirs of a Scientology Warrior*, 'for having failed to beat a long-time, close associate of mine named Mike Rinder for his failure to confess to thought crimes to Miscavige's liking.'[74]

Marty Rathbun says Miscavige then smashed his head against a steel wall and sentenced him to time in 'The Hole', an office prison at International Base where Scientology executives were held, sometimes for years. (Miscavige denies all allegations of abuse made against him.) Rathbun, second in command to Miscavige, escaped the Church of Scientology the following month.

Because he had left Scientology by 2006, Rathbun is unsure why James Packer left Scientology. Years later he tried to reach out to him:

I sent an email to him and I don't know whether it arrived. It was several years ago, after I began to speak out and it was being speculated that he was done with Scientology. I really liked James Packer. I just think he is one of the sweetest people I have ever met in my life. Cruise became like Miscavige and wanted to be Miscavige and in many ways had parallel personalities. Jamie was not part of that. He did not fit that mould at all he is just a wonderful person and I have nothing but good things to say about him.[75]

James Packer may have been used by the Church of Scientology to get to Lachlan Murdoch, but many of those close to him believe he benefited from the experience. Yet in Scientology terms the mission was a failure. Scientology may have helped James Packer, but it did not hang on to him. The mission to recruit Lachlan Murdoch came to nothing. 'Essentially we got nowhere with him while I was there,' says Rathbun.[76]

Lachlan Murdoch would not talk to me for this book. In 2012, after Rupert Murdoch tweeted that Scientology was a 'very weird cult', *The Daily Beast* reported that Cruise had tried to recruit Lachlan, and that Rupert had staged an intervention to make sure he had nothing to do with them.[77]

Both Rupert and Lachlan denied the story of any intervention. In a statement to *The Daily Beast*, Lachlan Murdoch said:

> *I can confirm, on the record, that I have never considered becoming a Scientologist in any way or at any time. The premise of the story is entirely wrong. I probably come close to sharing my father's views about the religion, but I resist tweeting them.*[78]

For Eric Kleitsch, one of the Sea Org members tasked with cleaning the car park in preparation for James Packer's visits to the Advanced Org in Sydney, Scientology still gives him nightmares. Spending 12 consecutive years on the Sea Org's punishment camp the Rehabilitation Project Force (RPF) has left him physically broken.

According to Kleitsch, when he first arrived on the RPF he was forced to run barefoot on bitumen roads as a form of punishment. 'I destroyed my heels and the arches of my feet,' says Kleitsch, 'and basically I tore the ligaments out of my feet.'[79] The former Scientologist says he was forced to run on the road up to two hours a day for around a year. 'It was painful,' Kleitsch says. 'Your feet would wind up at the end of the day bleeding.'[80]

Kleitsch had arrived on the RPF with no money or no decent shoes. 'The only shoes I could afford to buy for $5 from the army surplus store were army overshoes with no heels or soles,' he says. The impact of his bare feet hitting bitumen is still being felt over 20 years later. 'I can't even wear shoes,' he says. 'I have to go barefoot or wear Crocs.'[81]

The punishments against Kleitsch grew increasingly bizarre and barbaric the longer he was on the RPF. He says at one point he was forced to live underneath a squash court on the premises of Scientology's headquarters in Dundas. 'It was beneath the building,' he says. 'It was mouldy, cold and damp. I was basically there from

6 am till midnight, and then if I was good I was allowed to sleep in the concrete passage hidden away from the rest of the RPF.'[82]

While he was on the RPF, Kleitsch was completely separated from his Scientologist wife, Liz. 'We could only communicate by writing letters and the letters were vetted,' Liz Kleitsch told me.[83] On one of Liz's birthdays, Eric stumbled across her. 'I happened to see her in the passage and gave her a quick peck on the cheek,' he says. 'It would only have taken a second, and then Liz's boss saw us and I was sent to the RPF's RPF for that.'[84]

In the end Eric Kleitsch's salvation came courtesy of the *Encyclopaedia Britannica*. 'I was reading about serfs in medieval England,' Kleitsch told me, 'and then realised I was a bloody slave.'[85] From that point on Kleitsch was antagonistic to his superiors, who eventually had enough of his insubordinate behaviour and gave him what was called an 'offload order'. He was no longer welcome in the Sea Org. After 12 long years on the RPF he was finally free.

Eric Kleitsch got out of the Sea Org in 2007. He had entered Scientology in 1970 as an idealistic young student with long hair and bell-bottomed trousers. He had been attracted by Scientology's underground status as a banned organisation, and by its promises that it was working to make the world a better place. Thirty-seven years later, Eric left Scientology a broken man. He'd escaped what he came to believe was a form of slavery. He was free, but he had no money to show for his hard labour, only physical ailments such as his butchered feet.

After interviewing him in his Melbourne flat I took Eric down the road to a nearby pub and bought him a few beers. It was the least I could do after he had relived so many traumatic memories with me. As I caught a tram back from his home, Eric texted me:

Thanks for everything Steve. That was the first time I've been to a pub in 43 years.[86]

Scientology may have helped James Packer but it's hard to see how it helped Eric Kleitsch.

CHAPTER 20

MIKE RINDER LEAVES THE BUILDING

'OPEN THE LETTER BOX!' The command comes so fast and with such authority, I do what I'm told. I am in Palm Harbor, Florida, arm dangling out the window of a black Acura RL, on the verge of doing my first mailbox raid. The driver barking the orders is Mike Rinder, the former head of the Church of Scientology's Office of Special Affairs. We are parked on his neighbour's lawn looking for evidence.

This doesn't feel right to me. I know it's illegal to open someone's mail, but is it okay to drive up on a kerb, with two wheels turning on the lawn and open their letterbox? I have to make a decision on the fly and I begin to rationalise. Rinder doesn't want to check the contents of his neighbour's mail; he just wants to read the name on the front of the envelope. I flip the mailbox open.

The situation I find myself in is partly my fault. I arrived that morning at Tampa International Airport bearing gifts. I had some top-notch inside information that suggested that one of Rinder's neighbours was a paid-up Scientology spy. Rinder, as the former head of Scientology's intelligence wing, knew the best way to find out what her real name was. When I opened up the letterbox, however, there was nothing inside.

From the time he left Scientology in 2007, Mike Rinder has been under constant surveillance. Spies cruise past his house on a regular basis, his rubbish is rifled through by private investigators, on one occasion seven Scientologists including his daughter, his former wife and his brother confronted him outside a doctor's surgery as Miscavige's executives yelled at him: 'You are a fucking SP!' 'Stop doing what you are doing!' 'You are going to die!' 'You are trying to destroy Scientology.'[1]

Just after I visited Rinder at his home in Palm Harbor he discovered a secret camera had been installed in a birdhouse on his neighbour's property. It was pointed towards his home, presumably so it could monitor who had been visiting him. Rinder climbed up a ladder, peered into the birdhouse and disconnected the hidden camera. He filmed the whole episode and posted it online.

While Rinder and his young family were being exposed to around-the-clock surveillance, I had managed to gather some intelligence on the intelligence gatherers. I was able to glean some inside information on a key part of the Church of Scientology's external spy network that shone a light on the lengths they would go to to pry into the personal life of Mike Rinder and his family.

One of the first things I obtained was a dossier compiled by one of the private investigation firms hired by Scientology's lawyers. Included in the file were photos to help their expansive team of investigators identify prominent former Scientologists such as Mike Rinder and his partner Christie Collbran, Haydn and Lucy James and Tom DeVocht. There were photos of their cars and licence plate numbers to help in any stakeout. The files even included photos of their children and grandchildren.

I also obtained key details about how the operation worked. Back when Rinder lived at his previous home, 15 minutes away in Tarpon Springs, a house was rented a few doors down and used as a spy base. The tenant monitored Rinder's home and reported back on who was coming and going. Private investigators were hired on different shifts to monitor Rinder around the clock. If there was a car parked near his house the licence plates would be photographed and run through an identity check. Another house in West Clearwater was used as a meeting place before each investigator's shift. They would park their cars at the property and pick up a rental car so Rinder could not trace them.

Mike Rinder was not just being watched at home. If he went to the grocery store, the local school, or the airport he was followed. At times he was tailed by as many as six private investigators with a further one or two monitoring activities from the house. Journalists who met with Mike were also followed. It was a campaign of intimidation designed to stop him speaking out about abuse inside the Church of Scientology. Rinder was not the only person they were trying to silence. The private investigators hired as part of the operation were forced to sign contracts that stipulated they would be fined tens of thousands of dollars if they disclosed details about the operation.

Not only did I get my hands on this key dossier, I also received a map and the location of the house that was used as the spy base. Another key piece of information came my way – that two cameras had been installed under the awning of the rental property, one by the front door, one down the side of the house. The two cameras had long lenses and were able to take photographs of who was coming and going from Mike's home. Photographs of local reporters Joe Childs and Thomas Tobin, who had published a number of ground-breaking exposés on Scientology in the *St. Petersburg Times*, were taken outside the house and used as 'evidence' that they were somehow biased against Scientology.

When Mike picked me up from Tampa airport I told him about the inside information I had acquired. After having breakfast at a local diner we headed to Tarpon Springs. We pulled in to the driveway of a cream-coloured bungalow in Anclote Drive and walked up to the front door. The cameras were no longer there because Rinder had moved out of the neighbourhood. But under the awnings, in the two locations I had been told to look for, were bolt holes that had been drilled either side of where the cameras were once fixed. We had been able to confirm what Mike and his partner Christie had long suspected – that a Scientology spy had moved in to their neighbourhood and befriended them as part of a covert surveillance operation.

The rental property at Anclote Drive had been the home of Heather McAdoo, a single mother with a four-year old son. Her child was the perfect age to befriend Christie's boy, who was just a year older. Christie and Heather had bumped into each other in the street a few times in January 2012. One day Heather knocked on Christie's door and told her she didn't know anybody in the neighbourhood. Heather invited Christie to a Pampered Chef party, a multi-level marketing sales gathering for kitchen products, not unlike a Tupperware party. Christie couldn't make it, but, like a good multi-level marketing woman, Heather did not let go.

Christie's new neighbour now had her mobile phone number and bombarded her with texts. In her messages she came across as lonely and in need of a friend. She was constantly offering to help Christie and to organise play dates with her son. Pregnant with her second child, Christie held a baby shower and invited Heather along. For a single mum with no visible means of support, Heather went overboard on the presents, bringing along three gifts.

When Heather found out Christie and Mike were looking to move to Palm Harbor, she offered to help them look for a new house. It didn't end there. She offered to go shopping with Christie at Home Goods, invited her to board game nights at her place and asked if her son wanted to register to play T-Ball with her boy.

Soon after they moved, Heather moved too, securing a place a few blocks away. Christie was by now completely creeped out. It didn't make sense that a single mother with one child would move in to a three-bedroom house in a neighbourhood known for its manicured lawns and backyard pools. Christie decided to stop seeing Heather, but felt tinges of guilt. What if she wasn't a spy? Had Scientology and its culture of surveillance polluted their minds and made them excessively paranoid?

By telling Mike about the cameras in the rental property at Tarpon Springs I had been able to confirm that Christie's hunch was right. It also showed the depths to which the Church of Scientology would sink to place the likes of Mike Rinder and Christie Collbran under surveillance. They would be happy to pay for an operation that saw a single mother use her four-year-old child as bait to create a fake friendship and infiltrate the lives of a family who had left Scientology.

Armed with this new evidence, Christie confronted Heather about working for the Church of Scientology. She suggested she do some research about the organisation, texting a link to an article where videographer Bert Leahy had blown the whistle on Scientology's squirrel buster campaign, an operation designed to harass former Scientologist Marty Rathbun outside his home in Texas. McAdoo responded by text, 'Sorry for whatever happened to your family, but

I really don't know what you are talking about.' (Heather McAdoo denies she was a spy, but did admit to me her then boyfriend was a private investigator.)[2] Within two weeks Heather had moved out of her Palm Harbor home. Mike and Christie never heard from her again.

It's an extraordinary tale, but for those with an intimate knowledge of Scientology operations, it comes as no real surprise. This is the way it has been for Mike Rinder since he left Scientology in 2007. Just after I visited him he not only discovered the camera in his neighbour's fake birdhouse, he also captured vision of a short tubby man in brown pants and a pony-tail stealing his garbage and placing it in his maroon Camaro.[3]

These rubbish raids have been going on for years and were a standard Scientology tactic. A local waste management worker had confessed to Rinder that he was part of the operation. 'The garbage man in Tarpon came and knocked on our door one day and said, "Look I feel really bad but they are paying me money to give them your garbage,"' says Rinder.[4]

Later on it was proven in court that Rinder had been subjected to even more dirty tricks. In 2015, Eric Saldarriaga, a private investigator from Queens, was sent to jail for hacking into emails. One of the people he had targeted was Mike Rinder. It can't be confirmed whether the private investigator was operating on behalf of the Church of Scientology. The judge said he had no power to compel Saldarriaga to reveal who he was working for.[5] But Tony Ortega, the New York journalist who writes about Scientology on a daily basis, was also targeted in the same hacking operation and the *New York Times* reported that, 'The client is said to be someone who has done investigations on behalf of Scientology.'[6]

Back when I first met Rinder in Florida I asked him how he felt about being targeted by Scientology's Office of Special Affairs (OSA), given he was once the head of OSA, and was issuing the orders for various surveillance operations. He responded:

I guess it's poetic justice in some ways and in others it sort of motivates me to keep doing what I'm doing to put an end to it. It's really just like water off a duck's back to me. I really don't care. I'll turn around and figure out how to fuck with them

*more than they are ever able to fuck with me. It just doesn't
have any effect on me, but it bothers me that they do it to
other people.*[7]

Scientology still hadn't learned from its mistakes. It was continuing
to rile its critics in ways that made them even more determined to
continue speaking out. Just like Paulette Cooper, Julian Assange
and the netizens in Anonymous, Mike Rinder was not about to be
intimidated into silence.

IN THE LATE 1970s and early 1980s, Mike Rinder, along with Marty
Rathbun and David Miscavige, were part of the young guard who
took over Scientology. After surviving the chaos of the Portuguese
Rock concert of 1974 and two years on board the *Apollo*, Rinder
moved to Clearwater, Florida, in December 1975 when Hubbard set
up Scientology's land base there.

During the move, Rinder was working in external communications.
He handled telexes, and picked up the mail and freight that was flown
in from Los Angeles as the Scientologists got established in Clearwater.

When the Guardian's Office was dissolved following the disaster
of Operation Snow White and the jailing of Mary Sue Hubbard, the
Office of Special Affairs replaced it. Mike Rinder was one of the
young operatives tasked with reforming Scientology's intelligence and
legal affairs wing.

At the time, the Church of Scientology and Hubbard were under
siege from lawsuits. The new Office of Special Affairs wanted to end
the litigation and prevent further lawsuits. Rinder and his colleagues
decided to clean out the bad people and the bad practices of the old
Guardian's Office. He says the disclosure of Operation Freakout
documents from the FBI raids made Scientology vulnerable to lawsuits:

*It gave a really good foundation for people to come in with
civil suits and say look at these people, they are like the
lunatic fringe and it doesn't matter how outrageous they make
their claims, it couldn't be more outrageous than what they
admitted they did. So it was important to get rid of anybody
that had been involved in any of those things.*[8]

The old Guardian's Office acted autonomously from the Church of Scientology. It operated in secret and was accountable only to itself. Mike Rinder says when the Office of Special Affairs (OSA) was set up things changed. The church hierarchy made sure it closely monitored OSA's activities and there was a basic rule for any new operation:

> It was do not do anything illegal. Don't engage in illegal activities. Don't do anything without lawyer signoff and authorisation. Don't go trying to frame people for stupid shit – hit and runs and that kind of nutty stuff – honestly at that point I was aghast. I was stunned I couldn't believe that anybody would do that stuff, it was beyond comprehension to me.[9]

The new dictates didn't mean the Church of Scientology stopped putting people under surveillance. That could still be justified by the church hierarchy. 'Spying isn't illegal,' Rinder told journalist Tony Ortega. 'It's not done by *churches*, I understand that, but it's done by corporations all the time. It's not very savory, but it's not illegal.'[10]

Shortly after being involved in the cleanout of the Guardian's Office, Rinder became the head of the new Office of Special Affairs. It was a position he would hold for close to 20 years. Eventually he would combine that role with the position of Scientology's international spokesman. With David Miscavige avoiding TV interviews following his experience with Ted Koppel on *Nightline*, Rinder stepped up to the plate.

It was a hell of a tough gig. As Scientology started to face more scrutiny, Mike had to deal with more and more difficult questions. He was grilled about Scientology's handling of Lisa McPherson, a young woman who'd had a mental breakdown and died on Scientology's watch. He had to deflect questions about Xenu and Hubbard's infamous myth involving spacecraft, aliens and volcanoes, which had leaked out during a court case. In 2007, he had to deal with one of the toughest questions of all. During an interview with the BBC's John Sweeney, he was forced to deny allegations that David Miscavige had assaulted him. It was this interview that became the catalyst for Rinder leaving Scientology forever.

The BBC *Panorama* program 'Scientology and Me' became famous for the footage of reporter John Sweeney losing his rag with Scientology spokesman Tommy Davis. After being taken through the brainwashing section of the Los Angeles Scientology museum, *Psychiatry: An Industry of Death,* Sweeney screamed manically at Davis, 'You were not there at the beginning of the interview! You were not there! You did not hear or record all the interview!' Sweeney was referring to an interview he had done with a Scientology critic.

During the filming of the program, Mike Rinder had been assigned to help Tommy Davis handle John Sweeney. In the documentary, Rinder looks gaunt and shell-shocked. He had just been released from 'The Hole', the prison for Sea Org executives where he had been detained for almost two years.

By early 2004, Mike Rinder had fallen out of favour with Scientology's leader. According to Rinder, Miscavige was upset at how he and other Scientology executives handled a special New Year's event. 'He's like, "Fuck you all, you're all a bunch of cock sucking arseholes. Security, take them back to the base and lock them up in OGH."'[11]

Eventually OGH, otherwise known as Old Gilman House, was overflowing with Scientology executives and they had to be moved to what became known as 'The Hole', a set of double-wide trailers inside Scientology's International Base. At times there were over a hundred of the most senior Scientologists in the world working and sleeping in the ant-infested offices.[12] To prevent them from escaping, bars were placed on the doors and security guards controlled the only exit.[13]

Conditions inside 'The Hole' were oppressive. Former Scientology executive Debbie Cook would later testify that senior Sea Org members slept on the floors, ate slops and screamed at each other during bizarre confessionals. At one stage Cook was made to stand in a rubbish bin for 12 hours while fellow executives poured water over her, yelled at her and draped a sign over her declaring she was a lesbian. The punishment came about after she objected to the treatment of her fellow executives Marc Yager and Guillaume Lesevre. Cook later testified that Miscavige wanted the pair to confess to having a homosexual affair and were beaten until they made forced admissions.[14]

At one stage, when Mike Rinder was accused of withholding a confession from the group, he was taken outside and beaten up.[15] No-one escaped the perverse punishments. During one hot summer Miscavige had the electricity turned off in the trailers so the executives could sweat it out without air conditioning as temperatures soared over 40°C.[16] John Brousseau witnessed the pale and lifeless executives shuffling to and from the showers in the garage. He described them as looking like 'prisoners of war'.[17]

'The Hole' was the scene of the infamous game of musical chairs depicted in Alex Gibney's award-winning documentary *Going Clear*. Miscavige had arrived one evening at around 8 pm and demanded that the conference table be removed and replaced by around 70 chairs. Miscavige explained that in this version of musical chairs they would be competing to stay *in* 'The Hole'. While the last person standing would get to stay, everyone else would be sent off to various far-flung places. Mike Rinder was threatened with being sent to 'the furthest outreach of Western Australia'.[18] Those with spouses outside 'The Hole' would be forced to divorce them.[19]

As 'Bohemian Rhapsody' played out over the ghetto blaster, Scientology executives fought and scrambled for the remaining chairs. As players dropped out, Miscavige had airline tickets printed out to prepare them for their imminent departure. Trucks waited outside ready to haul their personal belongings away. It was a game of mental and physical torture. Finally, at 4 am, Lisa Schroer secured the final chair. But nothing happened. It was all a game. Miscavige never carried out his promise to send the others to Scientology's outposts.

As one of Scientology's most senior executives, Mike Rinder had over the years delivered his fair share of unpalatable orders. This made him a target inside 'The Hole', in an environment where executives were being bullied by their colleagues and forced into confessions. One night Marty Rathbun grabbed him in a headlock and threw him to the ground. With Rathbun sitting on top of him Rinder whispered to his long-time friend and colleague: 'Marty I'm not playing this game no more.'[20]

Over the two years he was stuck in 'The Hole', Rinder was released periodically to attend press conferences, appear at Scientology galas and to work on editing new versions of Hubbard's old books. He was released from 'The Hole' for the final time in 2007 to help handle BBC reporter John Sweeney and to report back to Miscavige about how Tommy Davis was dealing with the documentary crew.[21]

Tommy Davis had replaced Rinder as chief spokesman for the Church of Scientology while the Australian was stuck in 'The Hole'. The son of *Fatal Attraction* star Anne Archer and wealthy real estate developer William Davis, Tommy had joined the Sea Org after dropping out of Columbia University.[22] His first assignment as spokesman was to deal with the veteran BBC reporter Sweeney.

Tommy and Mike became key figures in the BBC documentary. Davis goaded Sweeney on camera, and the reporter took the bait, screaming at the Sea Org member in an unhinged fashion. At one stage during filming for the program, Sweeney door-stopped Rinder outside a Scientology building in London and asked him if he had been beaten up by Miscavige. Rinder denied it. 'Those allegations are absolute utter rubbish,' he said.[23] The exchange did not make it to air in that program. Rinder threatened to sue and the BBC's lawyers backed down. But Sweeney's question changed Rinder's life forever.

Former Scientology marketing executive Jeff Hawkins had told Sweeney that Miscavige had beaten Rinder up and thrown a chair at him. 'John's shorthand name for that program became "The Thumping Pope of Scientology",' says Rinder.[24] But the BBC's lawyers were nervous that they did not have enough evidence at that time to back up the allegations against Miscavige. The stories of violence would have to wait for another program.

Rinder's intervention may have kept the allegations of violence out of the BBC program, but Sweeney's question had cut to the core of Rinder. He was used to fudging answers or telling lies based on the justification that it was for the greater good of Scientology. It was much harder to justify covering for someone he felt deep down was poisoning the well of the organisation he had dedicated his life to. 'That really got to me,' says Rinder, 'because as much as I was willing to defend Scientology from someone that I thought was out to do it harm, the fact that I was blatantly denying something that was absolutely true. That was hard to take.'[25]

Miscavige helped Rinder to make the decision to leave the Sea Org forever. Instead of being grateful that his spokesman had managed to prevent the allegations of violence against him from being aired on the BBC, Miscavige ordered he be sent to the English countryside to dig ditches.[26] Soon after, Rinder left the Scientology office in Fitzroy Street in central London, turned off his two BlackBerries and vanished. 'I was 52 years old, with no resumé, with no money, no car, nothing. I walked out of the Church of Scientology in London with this briefcase with basically nothing in it,' says Rinder.[27]

London is Rinder's favourite city in the world. For three to four days he walked its old streets and visited its finest art galleries. He stayed in cheap rooming houses and planned his next move. Rinder had no money, but relied on an American Express card he'd acquired through his parents. After a few days Rinder rang former Scientology executive Tom DeVocht at his home in Orlando and asked him if he could come and stay. DeVocht agreed. Rinder hopped on the tube to Heathrow airport. To avoid detection from Scientology spies he booked a flight at the last minute to Washington, DC, where he got a connecting flight to Orlando.

Rinder knew there would be severe repercussions. He faced disconnection from his wife, his son, his daughter, his mother, his brother and his sister. After arriving back in the US he wrote to Cathy, his wife of 31 years, asking if he could see her. According to Rinder, he received a handwritten note that said: 'Fuck you. I should have put your ethics in long ago. The divorce papers will be sent and I will tell the kids.'[28]

After settling temporarily in Virginia, Rinder moved to Denver where he worked as a car salesman in a Toyota dealership. It was there that a producer from the BBC's Panorama program tracked him down. Rinder agreed to be interviewed by John Sweeney for his follow-up program 'The Secrets of Scientology'. Sweeney would finally be able to run his program about the 'Thumping Pope of Scientology'.

'Is it true that David Miscavige hit you?' Sweeney asked the former head of the Office of Special Affairs on camera.

'Yes.'

'And you denied it?'

'Yes. That was a lie.'

'How many times did he hit you?'

'Fifty.'[29]

Marty Rathbun later confirmed that 'Mike Rinder was beat on the order of 50 times by David Miscavige'.[30] The Church of Scientology denies all allegations of abuse made against its leader. Rinder may have taken his fair share of beatings, but now he was landing a series of telling blows against Miscavige and the Church of Scientology.

Over the next five years, Rinder became a thorn in the backside of Scientology. Not only did he give a revealing interview to John Sweeney, he did a series of TV interviews around the world, contributed significant details to the ongoing and highly influential reporting of Joe Childs and Thomas Tobin at the *St. Petersburg Times* and featured heavily in the book and documentary *Going Clear.* He set up a blog, was regularly quoted by Tony Ortega in his daily reporting on Scientology and was available for legal advice for ex-members involved in litigation with the church.

In July 2010, Mike flew home to Australia to be interviewed by television journalist Bryan Seymour. As part of the trip he drove to Melbourne to try and visit his mother, Barbara. Mike had been able to write to his mother up until 2009 when he agreed to be interviewed for the *St. Petersburg Times*'s 'Truth Rundown' series. Soon after publication, the Church of Scientology gave Barbara an invidious choice. She would have to choose which son she wanted to stay in contact with. If she did not disconnect from Mike she could no longer see her other son, Andrew, and his children who lived nearby in Melbourne.

From that point on Mike was unable to contact his mother. When he visited Australia in 2010, private investigators followed him and Christie around, filming them for much of their trip. When he tried to visit Barbara in her nursing home, they were told she had gone away for nine days. Mike believes the Church of Scientology made sure she moved out of town when he visited.

Mike's father, Ian, had died in a car accident almost 20 years earlier. Barbara was driving at the time. With his mother grief stricken, injured and alone in a country hospital, Mike was unable to leave International Base and see her. 'It is one of the biggest regrets of my life that I didn't just abandon my post and get on a plane to join her when she really needed me the most,' says Rinder. 'I didn't understand the insanity of my callous lack of concern for her until nearly 20 years later after I had well and truly broken free from the brainwashing. This was the single thing I most wanted to tell her, face to face, when I tried to visit her in Melbourne, along with a simple "I love you Mum, and always will."[31]

Back in the country of his birth, Rinder was able to see first-hand the pressure Scientology was under in Australia. A few months earlier, ABC TV's *Four Corners* had dedicated a 45-minute program to documenting abuses inside the organisation, including the first TV interview with former first-grade rugby league player and Sea Org member Joe Reaiche. Over at Channel Seven, Bryan Seymour was well into a run of what would grow into over 80 stories on Scientology for *Today Tonight* and *Seven News*. At *Lateline*, I had just completed my first two stories on the organisation – including allegations that Scientology executive Jan Eastgate had covered up child sexual abuse, and an interview with Scarlett Hanna, the daughter of the head of the church in Australia, who described it as a toxic organisation that tore families apart.

According to Mike Rinder, the reporting coming out of Australia at the time had an influence on how the US media started to cover Scientology. While Thomas Tobin and Joe Childs at the *St Petersburg Times* and Tony Ortega at the *Village Voice* were ahead of the pack in their brave and bold reporting, the broadcast media in the US had been unusually timid.

> *I believe that the press in Australia and in particular the TV reporters paved the way for a lot of other people to recognise that they don't need to sit cowering in fear of threats from the Church of Scientology. The stuff you have done and the stuff that Bryan did and the original* Four Corners *were pretty serious allegations made by individuals and you took those allegations and said, 'Okay, we're going to run what they say.' In the US, the church had managed to persuade a bunch of journalists that they shouldn't do that because we have 27 people who say in affidavits that they're a liar.*[32]

Much of that reporting in Australia was generated by the advocacy of Nick Xenophon, the Independent Senator for South Australia. On

17 November 2009, Senator Xenophon shocked the parliament and the country by accusing the organisation of widespread criminal conduct. 'Scientology is not a religious organisation,' he told the Senate. 'It is a criminal organisation that hides behind its so-called religious beliefs.'[33]

Xenophon's interest in Scientology had been triggered by a simple question from journalist Bryan Seymour about tax exemption for groups like the Church of Scientology. By this stage Seymour had already done over 20 stories on the organisation. After Xenophon's comments were broadcast on *Today Tonight*, his office was inundated with letters and emails from former Scientologists alleging widespread abuse and criminal activity and asking if he could do something to help.

Xenophon was elected to the Senate in 2007, but his first taste of public office came in 1997 when he was voted into the South Australian parliament on an anti-poker machine platform. As a personal injury lawyer working in a suburban legal practice in the 1990s, he had been exposed to the damage gaming machines caused to individuals and families. As an advocate for victims' rights, he found it hard to turn away from the personal stories of abuse relayed by former Scientologists.

Senator Xenophon sat down with his senior adviser Rohan Wenn and discussed what they should do. Wenn already knew his way around Scientology – as a former TV journalist he had reported on abuses inside the organisation. His first encounter was back in his university days when he wrote a piece about the aggressive recruiting tactics of the Scientologists on campus at the University of Queensland. Soon after publication someone broke into his apartment and rearranged his furniture. Wenn had no proof who did it, but he saw it as a warning to stop investigating the organisation. Wenn was not deterred: he ended up doing a series of stories on Scientology for both Channel Nine and Channel Seven.

Taking on Scientology was not at the forefront of Nick Xenophon's mind in 2009. He is one of the busiest politicians in Australia. As an independent senator he does not have the party infrastructure or staffing levels that many members of parliament are able to rely on. He gets personally involved in a range of causes and policy areas and finds it hard to say no to an individual or group who he thinks needs help. Back in 2009, he shared the balance of power in the Senate with the Greens and Family First. He took it upon himself to carefully look through every piece of legislation that passed through the parliament. It was a gruelling time for him and his three full-time staff.

Becoming embroiled in a battle with one of the most litigious and vindictive organisations in the world was the last thing Xenophon needed at the time, but he felt like he had no choice. Xenophon and his advisers met face to face with former Scientologists and heard dozens of horrifying testimonies. 'We were all deeply affected by the stories we heard,' he says. 'These were decent people who hadn't had a voice up until that time. There was something systemic and pathological about the way the church treated them – the way they could crush people, split families apart and cause so much destruction. I thought it was unconscionable and that they needed to be held to account.'[34]

Rohan Wenn drafted a speech for Xenophon laying out the litany of abuse that had been relayed to his office by the witnesses who had come forward. The senior adviser was concerned his boss would not be prepared to go as far as he hoped for when it came to condemning the organisation. He was in for a surprise. 'Nick said we should go harder,' says Wenn. 'He wanted to go in boots and all.'[35]

On the evening of 17 November 2009, there was a sense of anticipation inside Parliament House. Journalists had been tipped off that Xenophon was going to deliver something big in the Senate. Rumours were bouncing around the house about what explosive allegations were about to be aired under parliamentary privilege. 'We were nervous,' says Wenn. 'There was this feeling in the office that we were about to drop a bomb.'[36]

At 8.09 pm, Senator Xenophon rose to speak on what he called 'an issue of utmost seriousness that I believe deserves a great deal of scrutiny by law enforcement agencies and by this parliament'.[37] The Church of Scientology, which had for so long been able to control the information flow about what went on inside their organisation, did not know what was coming. Xenophon did not mince his words:

> *What we are seeing is a worldwide pattern of abuse and criminality. On the body of evidence this is not happening by accident; it is happening by design. Scientology is not a*

religious organisation. It is a criminal organisation that hides
behind its so-called religious beliefs. What you believe does
not mean you are not accountable for how you behave.

The letters received by me which were written by former
followers in Australia contain extensive allegations of crimes
and abuses that are truly shocking – crimes against them and
crimes they say they were coerced into committing. There
are allegations of false imprisonment, coerced abortions,
embezzlement of church funds, physical violence, intimidation,
blackmail and the widespread and deliberate abuse of
information obtained by the organisation. It is alleged that
information about suspicious deaths and child abuse has been
destroyed, and one follower has admitted he was coerced by
the organisation into perjuring himself during investigations
into the deaths of his two daughters.[38]

'It was a momentous speech,' says Rohan Wenn. 'No-one has said the kind of things Nick said in such a formal setting like parliament. He delivered it in a beautifully understated way and it was treated seriously because Nick is considered a truth teller.'[39] Wenn believes the speech had a global impact. 'It was a game changer,' he says. 'Everyone suddenly got brave. It was like we can now call them a criminal organisation because a respected senator had done just that.'[40]

Tony Ortega, who has been writing about Scientology in the US for over 20 years, agrees with Wenn's assessment. 'Those words had such a strong effect on people here, where the rise of Anonymous had made the public more aware of Scientology than ever before,' he says. 'Xenophon was saying exactly the things that church critics had been saying for many years, but it was stunning to hear it from a federal senator.'[41]

The Scientologists were stunned as well. The following day, they released a statement describing Xenophon's speech as 'an outrageous abuse of Parliamentary privilege'.[42] The statement did not deal with the individual allegations laid out by Xenophon in his speech and the 53 pages' worth of letters he tabled to the Senate. Instead the Church of Scientology described the senator as 'obviously being pressured by disgruntled former members who use hate speech and distorted accounts of their experiences in the Church'.[43]

Senator Xenophon called for a Senate inquiry into Scientology's tax-exempt status. Out of nowhere, Scientology was suddenly on the national agenda. The following day, Prime Minister Kevin Rudd responded to Xenophon's speech. 'Many people in Australia have real concerns about Scientology,' he said. 'I share some of those concerns. But let us proceed carefully, and look carefully at the material which he has provided, before we make a decision on further Parliamentary action.'[44]

Neither Labor nor the Liberals had any appetite for an inquiry into an organisation that the High Court had declared a religion in 1983. The Prime Minister's office passed the issue on to Chris Evans, the leader of the government in the Senate. A month later, Senator Evans's office told the Scientologists the government did not support Xenophon's push for an inquiry because it was 'inappropriate to conduct an inquiry into a private and, in this case, religious organisation'.[45]

According to Wenn, who was lobbying senators behind the scenes, Labor and Liberal MPs were concerned the spotlight could soon shift to their own religious beliefs. 'There were too many people on both sides who were asking where would it end?' he says. 'They thought it would start with Scientology, but were concerned the Catholic Church might be next. They simply didn't want to go there.'[46]

As Xenophon continued to lobby for a Senate inquiry, more powerful testimonies of abuse were revealed in the media. Canberra woman Janette Lang gave an emotional press conference outside Parliament House, urging politicians to act. She said she had been a Scientologist for 13 years and in that time had been coerced into having two abortions. The first time, she said, occurred at the age of 20 after her boss pressured her to have a termination. 'We fought for a week,' she said. 'I was devastated, I felt abused, I was lost and eventually I gave in. It was my baby, my body and my choice, and all of that was taken away from me by Scientology.'[47]

In the end former Scientologists did get to testify before the Senate. Xenophon managed to instigate a Senate inquiry into the tax-exempt status of charities and religions. The inquiry was not all about Scientology, but led to a framework where there was greater transparency in the non-profit sector. Xenophon's plan for a public benefit test on religions went nowhere. The proposal was based on the UK model, where institutions who received tax exemption had to prove they worked for the benefit of the community as a whole. The measure was voted down in the Senate with both major parties rejecting it.

While Xenophon didn't quite get the inquiry he wanted, or his public interest test, his 2009 speech in parliament proved an ongoing public relations disaster for Scientology. His speech triggered the *Four Corners* program 'The Ex-Files'. The *Four Corners* program was the catalyst for an investigation by the Fair Work Ombudsman into abusive work practices and for my reporting on Scientology for *Lateline*. Xenophon's office had access to a range of former Scientologists who had horrific tales of abuse and was able to help victims get in contact with journalists.

The Independent Senator for South Australia, who sees himself as a self-deprecating pessimist, does acknowledge his intervention made a difference. 'While we didn't get the law changed, Scientology was taken out of the shadows, a light was shone on them, which I think meant there was a check on some of their excesses. I think it also would've meant people who might have been thinking of getting involved in Scientology didn't do so, or stepped back. I think it would've effected their recruitment.'[48]

In the aftermath of Xenophon's speech, the Scientology brand in Australia became so toxic it came to rely on Taiwan as the main recruiting ground for local staff. In 2010, Scientology spokesman Tommy Davis told *Four Corners* there were 'tens, if not hundreds of thousands' of Scientologists in Australia.[49] The 2011 census found that just 2163 Australians called themselves Scientologists, a decrease of 13.7 per cent from the 2006 census. The organisation that called itself the fastest growing religion in the world was going backwards fast in Australia.

FROM THE TIME I first met Mike Rinder, on the day he asked me to open a Scientology spy's letterbox, his attitude to Hubbard and Scientology has evolved. In 2012, he still called himself an Independent Scientologist. That basically meant he still believed in Hubbard's philosophies and 'technology' but rejected the way David Miscavige was implementing his policies. Rinder no longer calls himself a

Scientologist of any kind. 'There is absolutely no chance at all that I would sit down and study a Scientology course or engage in auditing,' he told me, 'but do I think that everything about Scientology is wrong? No. I don't. I'm not of the view the whole subject is evil and should be eradicated from the face of the earth. But on the other hand I wouldn't say there was a lot of it that is of any real benefit.'[50]

The transition from dedicated Scientologist to non-believer can be a complex process. When you grow up with a religion or a belief, it becomes ingrained in you in the deepest of ways. To completely eradicate all traces of that belief can sometimes prove impossible. For Rinder, writing his blog has sharpened his critical thinking and helped deprogram himself from Scientology dogma. 'When you write a blog every day,' he says, 'by reason of doing it you are looking at something and discussing it, or explaining it, or presenting it, or taking some form of position on it: it forces you to analyse things.'[51]

Reading *Bare-Faced Messiah*, Russell Miller's biography of Hubbard, challenged his views on Scientology's founder. Lauren Wolf, one of the researchers on *Going Clear*, asked him questions during the fact-checking process that triggered self-reflection and further analysis. 'It was a bit transformative for me,' says Rinder. 'She was a very non-judgemental person, she was exceedingly intelligent and it was interesting explaining or answering things for her and having her always challenge them. I spent a lot of time with Lauren. I think that had a role to play and I think as you become less convinced about the efficacy of Scientology as a subject it tends to change your opinion of Hubbard as a person.'[52]

For those who have left Scientology, one of the hardest things to come to terms with is the feeling that they have wasted large chunks of their life. Former members often feel deep remorse and even shame about being hooked in by a scam that cost them money, relationships and personal freedom. Mike Rinder is not the type to dwell on what might have been. 'I don't think that serves any purpose to live your life in a state of regret,' he says. Besides, despite the beatings, the abuse and the trauma of 'The Hole', Rinder did have a front row seat to some pretty extraordinary events. 'I had a lot of experiences. I did a lot of things, met a lot of people. I went a lot of places, I learned a lot. I've had a pretty interesting life,' he says.[53]

However, Rinder does have one lingering regret, not about himself, but about what he has done to his estranged children by bringing them up in the Sea Org. 'They were given no choice,' he says. 'They were indoctrinated into Scientology and today are zealots, fundamentalists by reason of their upbringing and I feel a regret about that and a sense of responsibility and sort of a sadness that I did not experience really raising them like I am now experiencing raising Jack [his son with Christie].'[54]

Rinder is still separated from his children from his first marriage, who remain in the Sea Org. When his son Benjamin was diagnosed with cancer he was not even told. When he found out through the media, he went to the Fort Harrison Hotel in Clearwater to see if he could visit him. When Rinder arrived, he was met by six security guards, six private investigators on foot holding video cameras, and another two private eyes in cars circling the scene. Security called the local police and complained that Rinder was trespassing.[55] He was told his cancer-stricken son did not want to see him. It is unlikely that he will ever see him again, unless Benjamin decides to leave the Sea Org.

GLOSSARY OF TERMS

ABS Australian Bureau of Statistics

ALP Australian Labor Party

ANZO Australia/New Zealand/Oceania region

AOSH Advanced Organization and Saint Hill – the place where Scientologists pay for advanced Scientology services such as auditing and training.

ASI Author Services, Inc. – a literary agency that represents the works published by L. Ron Hubbard.

ASIO Australian Security Intelligence Organisation – Australia's domestic intelligence agency.

BMA British Medical Association of Victoria – the peak doctors' group in Victoria in the 1960s.

CC Celebrity Centre – established in 1969 by Yvonne Gillham, the Celebrity Centre trains and recruits celebrities and marketable stars.

CCHR Citizen's Commission for Human Rights – formed in 1969 by the Guardian's Office. The CCHR is, in its own words, 'dedicated to investigating and exposing psychiatric violations of human rights'.

CCInt Celebrity Centre International

CMO Commodore's Messengers Organization – initially created to deliver L. Ron Hubbard's messages to Sea Org members on board his ships and look after his personal needs, the CMO evolved into an organisation that manages the operations of the Sea Org.

CST Church of Spiritual Technology – the highest level organisation in the church hierarchy, whose role is to 'espouse, present, propagate, practice, ensure and maintain the purity and integrity of the religion of Scientology'.

DEA Drug Enforcement Administration – the US drug law enforcement agency, which operates under the Department of Justice.

DoP Director of Processing

ECT Electroconvulsive therapy – commonly known as shock treatment.

FECRIS European Federation of Centres of Research and Information on Sectarianism

FOI Freedom of Information

GO Guardian's Office – established in 1966 as Scientology's legal and public relations unit, the Guardian's Office also operated to a large degree as an intelligence gathering operation. It was renamed the Office of Special Affairs (OSA) in the 1980s, after 11 of its operatives were jailed for their role in Operation Snow White.

HAS Hubbard Association of Scientologists

HASI Hubbard Association of Scientologists International – the Victorian HASI was registered in Australia as a foreign company on 15 June 1955, with a head office based in Phoenix, Arizona.

HCO Hubbard Communications Office – circulates bulletins and office policy letters, as well as articles, journals, speeches and internal letters. Also, the division in every Scientology organisation that recruits staff members and administers Scientology's ethics and justice system.

IAS International Association of Scientologists – established in Cyprus in 1984 as a means of accumulating funds outside US Internal Revenue Service jurisdiction, to be the ultimate legal defence fund for the church. The IAS has developed into a much bigger operation, relentlessly soliciting for donations, with a cash reserve estimated in excess of US$2 billion.

IASA International Association of Scientologists Administrations – solicits and banks donations for the International Association of Scientologists (IAS).

IRS Internal Revenue Service – the revenue agency of the US federal government.

LRH short for L. Ron Hubbard

MFA Movimento das Forcas Armadas – a group of left-wing military officers who pulled off a coup and restored democracy in Portugal in 1974.

OGH Old Gilman House – a building on Scientology's International Base that became the original prison for Sea Org executives. When Old Gilman House filled up, people were moved to 'The Hole', a set of double-wide trailers nearby.

OSA Office of Special Affairs – the current legal, public relations and intelligence wing of Scientology, which replaced the Guardian's Office in the 1980s.

PC Preclear – in early days of Scientology, 'preclear' meant someone who had not yet gone 'clear'. Now, it refers more generally to someone receiving auditing.

POB 'Pope on a Box' – a disparaging nickname given to Scientology's current leader, David Miscavige.

PTS/SP Course Potential Trouble Source/Suppressive Person Course – a Scientology course dealing with how to handle a suppressive person (SP) or a potential trouble source (PTS), someone who's in contact with a suppressive person (SP).

RAAF Royal Australian Air Force

RPF Rehabilitation Project Force – a punishment program for Sea Org members who have upset their superiors. Former Scientologists refer to them as prison camps; the Church of Scientology refers to it as a voluntary religious retreat.

RTC Religious Technology Center – headquartered at International Base, the Religious Technology Center owns Scientology's trademarks and copyrights, and is responsible for the orthodoxy of Scientology practices. David Miscavige is Chairman of the RTC board.

Sea Org Sea Organization – an elite unit of Scientologists established in 1967 by Hubbard. The church refers to the Sea Org as a religious order; critics describe it as the paramilitary wing of Scientology. To hold any senior position in Scientology, a person has to be a member of the Sea Org.

SP Suppressive Person – often applied to critics or perceived enemies of Scientology. Hubbard described SP's as anti-social personalities.

SWOTs Snow White Operating Targets – programs for the implementation of Operation Snow White in different areas. For example, in Australia it was called Project Dig.

TRs Training Routine drills – a key part of the Communications Course, TRs are supposed to help a new inductee communicate better. Critics say they use a form of hypnosis. Practices included in TRs are staring at another person, repeating words and shouting at an ashtray.

VUT Victorian University of Technology – now known as Victoria University.

ENDNOTES

Chapter 1

1. José Navarro account comes from interviews with the author.
2. From entry in José Navarro's diary.
3. Senator Nick Xenophon speech to the Australian Senate, 17 November 2009.
4. Virginia Stewart, *730 Report*, ABC TV, 18 November 2009.
5. John Braniff, *Cradle to Canonisation – A Short History of St Patrick's Marist College*, St Patrick's Marist College, Dundas, 2001, p. 88.
6. Brian Etherington, 'Early years of Champagnat College, Dundas', *Champagnat*, vol. 11, no. 2, August 2009, pp. 83–90.
7. Stephen Kent, *Brainwashing in Scientology's Rehabilitation Project Force (RPF)*, Revised and Expanded Version of a Presentation at the Society for the Scientific Study of Religion, San Diego, 7 November 1997. Published by Hamburg Interior Ministry, 13 September 2000.
8. For the schedule of the RPF at Dundas I relied on interviews with Chris Guider, Valeska Paris and José Navarro.
9. Eric Kleitsch interview with author.
10. Policy on 'twins' explained to the author by Valeska Paris, former Sea Org member.
11. Confirmed by Valeska Paris, José Navarro and another former Sea Org member.
12. Mark 'Marty' Rathbun interview with author.
13. For example, Valeska Paris.
14. For information on the Desimones I spoke to a former Scientology executive who requested anonymity.
15. Mark 'Marty' Rathbun, *The Scientology Reformation*, CreateSpace Independent Publising Platform, 2012, p. 39.
16. A former IASA executive told me this.
17. Mark 'Marty' Rathbun, op. cit., p. 38.
18. ibid., p. 50.
19. Mike Rinder statement to Tony Ortega: http://tonyortega.org/2014/04/07/shock-dox-scientologys-book-value-for-just-two-of-its-entities-is-1-2-billion/
20. Lawrence Wright, *Going Clear: Scientology, Hollywood & the Prison of Belief*, Alfred A. Knopf, New York, 2013, p. 278.
21. www.tampabay.com/news/scientology/scientology-amped-up-donation-requests-to-save-the-earth-starting-in-2001/1201989
22. ibid.
23. Mike Rinder More on the Vulture Culture, 15 November 2011: https://markrathbun.wordpress.com/2011/11/15/
24. Mark 'Marty' Rathbun, op. cit., p. 50 and http://markrathbun.wordpress.com/2010/12/10/the-hijacking-of-international-association-of-scientologists/
25. http://markrathbun.wordpress.com/2010/12/10/the-hijacking-of-international-association-of-scientologists/
26. ibid.
27. *Tampa Bay Times*, 12 January 2013.
28. Former Scientology Executive Debbie Cook testified as reported by Joe Childs and Thomas Tobin in *Tampa Bay Times*, 9 February 2012.
29. Mike Rinder's Texas Declaration: www.mikerindersblog.org/mike-rinder-texas-declaration/
30. Joe Childs and Thomas Tobin, op. cit.
31. Robert Jay Lifton, *Thought Reform and the Psychology of Totalism*, The University of North Carolina Press, Chapel Hill, 1989.
32. Valeska Paris interview with author.
33. José Navarro interview with author.
34. ibid.
35. ibid.
36. Valeska Paris who was on the *Freewinds* told me she heard a Sea Org member talk about auditing Karleen and how she was surprised she was so upset about having the abortion. Valeska audited José in Sydney and his preclear folder mentioned the pregnancy and how they didn't want José to know about it.
37. Patrick George, lawyer with Kennedys, email to author.

38. Confirmed by Chris Guider.
39. Chris Guider interview with author.
40. Patrick George, lawyer with Kennedys, email to author.
41. Valeska Paris interview with author.
42. Chris Guider interview with author.
43. Valeska Paris interview with author.
44. Ramana Dienes-Browning interview with author.
45. ibid.
46. Marc Headley, *Blown for Good: Behind the Iron Curtain of Scientology*, BFG Books, Burbank, 2009, p. 314.
47. José Navarro interview with author.
48. ibid.

Chapter 2
1. Hubbard arrived in Brisbane on 11 January 1942. His arrival documented at: www.lermanet. com/L_Ron_Hubbard/mr271.htm. The temperature reached 31.4°C in Brisbane that day according to the Bureau of Meteorology.
2. David Malouf, *Johnno*, University of Queensland Press, St Lucia, 1998, p. 189.
3. Peter A Thompson and Robert Macklin, *The Battle of Brisbane*, ABC Books, Sydney, 2000, p. 2.
4. Russell Miller, *Bare-Faced Messiah*, Henry Holt and Company, New York, 1987, p. 93.
5. ibid.
6. Testimony of Thomas S Moulton, Church of Scientology v Armstrong, 21 May 1984.
7. ibid.
8. Kima Douglas in vol. 25, p. 4459 court transcript of Church of Scientology of California v Gerald Armstrong, Superior Court for the County of Los Angeles, case no. C 420153. Kima was asked by the Judge if Hubbard had any bullet wounds in his back. Her reply was, 'No, sir.'
9. Hubbard's 'The Game of Life' Lecture, London, 7 February 1956: www.carolineletkeman.org/ archives/10417
10. Report by L. Ron Hubbard, 5 February 1942: www.cs.cmu.edu/~dst/Cowen/warhero/navalint. htm
11. Memorandum from US Naval Attaché to Australia, 14 February 1942: www.cs.cmu.edu/~dst/ Cowen/warhero/1942/420214.gif
12. ibid.
13. Cable from US Naval Attaché to Australia, 17 February 1942: www.cs.cmu.edu/~dst/Cowen/ warhero/1942/420217.gif
14. Chris Owen, *Ron the War Hero*: www.cs.cmu.edu/~dst/Cowen/warhero/navalint.htm
15. L. Ron Hubbard, HCO Executive Letter, 6 October 1965.
16. Jon Atack, *Let's Sell These People a Piece of Blue Sky* (2nd edn), Richard Woods, Worthing, 2013, pp. 81–86.
17. Letter from Fletcher Prouty to Michael Joseph Ltd, 4 October 1987.
18. Jon Atack, 'Religion or Intelligence Agency', paper delivered at the Dialog Centre International conference in Berlin, October 1995: www.religio.de/atack/intelli.html
19. Flag Operations Liaison Memo, 28 May 1974.
20. L. Ron Hubbard, 'My Philosophy', as quoted in Jon Atack's *Let's Sell These People a Piece of Blue Sky* (2nd edn), Richard Woods, Worthing, 2013, p. 89.
21. Chris Owen, *Ron the War Hero*: www.cs.cmu.edu/~dst/Cowen/warhero/crippled.htm
22. George Pendle, *Strange Angel: The Otherworldly Life of Rocket Scientist John Whiteside Parsons*, Harcourt, 2005, p. 32.
23. ibid., p. 214.
24. For details go to John Whiteside Parsons, *The Book of Babalon*: http://hermetic.com/parsons/ the-book-of-babalon.html For more context, see Lawrence Wright, op. cit., pp. 45–47.
25. Alexander Mitchell, 'The Odd Beginning of Ron Hubbard's Career', *Sunday Times*, 5 October 1969.
26. Jon Atack, personal communication with author.
27. Alexander Mitchell, loc. cit. See also Jon Atack, *Let's Sell These People a Piece of Blue Sky* (2nd edn), Richard Woods, Worthing, 2013, p. 105. Also Atack's paper 'Hubbard and the Occult': www.spaink.net/cos/essays/atack_occult.html. Atack had access to the complete OTO correspondence.
28. Russell Miller, op. cit., p. 112.
29. Jon Atack, *Let's Sell These People a Piece of Blue Sky* (2nd edn), Richard Woods, Worthing, 2013, p. 97.
30. Russell Miller, op. cit., p. 116.
31. ibid., p. 118.
32. George Pendle, op. cit., p. 267.
33. Russell Miller, op. cit., p. 120.
34. Jon Atack, op. cit., p. 106.

35.   Russell Miller, op. cit., p. 126.
36.   ibid., p. 127.
37.   ibid.
38.   ibid., p. 129.
39.   ibid., p. 134.
40.   Lawrence Wright, *Going Clear: Scientology, Hollywood & the Prison of Belief*, Alfred A.
       Knopf, New York, 2013, p. 49.
41.   ibid.
42.   Letter from L. Ron Hubbard to Veterans Administration, 15 October 1947.
43.   Russell Miller, op. cit., p. 139.
44.   ibid., p. 142. These fingerprints were used to authenticate his body when he died.
45.   *What is Scientology?* – compiled by the staff of the Church of Scientology, Bridge Publications,
       Los Angeles, 1998, p. 122.
46.   In Gerry Armstrong's trial a letter was supplied that showed Hubbard requested his
       disability pension cheques be sent to another address in 1958. Ken Urquhart, former Personal
       Communicator to Hubbard, said he was responsible for looking after his pension cheques up
       until approximately 1972. www.clearing.org/cgi/archive.cgi?/bluesky/part2.txt
47.   According to Hugh Urban, religious scholar and author of *The Church of Scientology: A
       History of a New Religion*: http://blogs.villagevoice.com/runninscared/2012/02/scientology_
       and_4.php
48.   For a list of Hubbard's 'affirmations', called 'admissions' by some, go to: www.gerryarmstrong.
       org/50grand/writings/ars/ars-2000-03-11.html
49.   ibid.
50.   Decision of Judge Paul G Breckenridge Jnr, Church of Scientology of California v Gerald
       Armstrong, Superior Court of the State of California, 1984.
51.   Martin Gardner, *Fads and Fallacies in the Name of Science*, Dover Publications, New York,
       1957, p. 263.

Chapter 3
1.   Author interview with Dylan Gill, who helped build some of Scientology's vaults while
       working for the Church of Spiritual Technology.
2.   L. Ron Hubbard, Christmas message, *Communication*, Church of Scientology, December
       1963.
3.   Sea Org Flag Information Letter 67, October 1977.
4.   Letter from L. Ron Hubbard to Robert Heinlein, 8 March 1949.
5.   *Savannah Morning News*, 28 April 2002.
6.   Letter from L. Ron Hubbard to Robert Heinlein, 3 March 1949.
7.   ibid., 24 November 1948.
8.   'A Note on Excalibur': www.ronthephilosopher.org/phlspher/page06.htm
9.   www.whatisscientology.org/html/Part01/Chp03/pg0114.html
10.   ibid.
11.   Forrest Ackerman in Russell Miller, *Bare-Faced Messiah*, Henry Holt and Company,
       New York, 1987, p. 135.
12.   ibid., p. 136.
13.   Gerry Armstrong, *The Secret Life of L. Ron Hubbard*, 3BM, Channel 4, UK, 1997.
14.   'A Note on Excalibur': www.ronthephilosopher.org/phlspher/page06.htm
15.   Taken from the now-defunct weblink: www.lronhubbard.org.au/the_discovery/
16.   Arthur J Burks, 'Yes There Was a Book Called *Excalibur* by L. Ron Hubbard', *The Aberee*,
       December 1961.
17.   Letter from L. Ron Hubbard to his wife Polly, 1938, known as 'The Skipper Letter' and
       registered for copyright by Hubbard's agency, ASI.
18.   Arthur J Burks, loc. cit.
19.   Skipper letter, loc. cit.
20.   ibid.
21.   Letter from L. Ron Hubbard to Forrest Ackerman, 13 January 1949.
22.   Letter from L. Ron Hubbard to Robert Heinlein, 8 March 1949.
23.   ibid.
24.   ibid., 31 March 1949.
25.   John Campbell in Lawrence Wright, *Going Clear: Scientology, Hollywood & the Prison
       of Belief*, Alfred A. Knopf, New York, 2013, p. 59.
26.   *Astounding Science Fiction*, December 1949.
27.   ibid., March 1950.
28.   ibid., May 1950.
29.   Russell Miller, op. cit., p. 155.
30.   L. Ron Hubbard, *Dianetics: The Modern Science of Mental Health*, Bridge Publications,
       Los Angeles, 1985, p. 69.
31.   ibid., pp. 74–75.

32. ibid., p. 12.
33. ibid. pp. 102–121.
34. ibid., p. viii.
35. ibid., p. 173.
36. ibid., p. 145.
37. L. Ron Hubbard, *Dianetics: The Modern Science of Mental Health*, Hermitage House, 1950, p. 158.
38. Lawrence Wright, op. cit., pp. 67–68.
39. L. Ron Hubbard Jnr, 'Inside the Church of Scientology – an exclusive interview with L. Ron Hubbard, Jr', *Penthouse*, June 1983.
40. Barbara Klowden interview with Russell Miller.
41. Isaac Isidor Rabi, 'Dianetics: The Modern Science of Mental Health, by L. Ron Hubbard', *Scientific American*, January 1951.
42. ibid.
43. 'Psychologists Act Against Dianetics', *New York Times*, 9 September 1950.
44. *Journal of Clinical Medicine*, March 1951, editorial by Frederick R Stearns.
45. Russell Miller, op. cit., p. 150.
46. ibid., p. 169 and Jon Atack, *Let's Sell These People a Piece of Blue Sky* (2nd edn), Richard Woods, Worthing, 2013, p. 126.
47. Jon Atack, *Let's Sell These People a Piece of Blue Sky* (2nd edn), Richard Woods, Worthing, 2013, p. 123.
48. Russell Miller, op. cit., p. 159.
49. Helen O'Brien, *Dianetics in Limbo*, Whitmore Publishing Company, Pittsburgh, 1966, p. vi.
50. Jon Atack, op. cit., p. 125.
51. ibid., p. 123.
52. Bent Corydon and L. Ron Hubbard Jnr, *Messiah or Madman?*, 1987, p. 287: www.xenu.net/archive/books/mom/Messiah_or_Madman.txt
53. Helen O'Brien, op. cit., p. 27.
54. Russell Miller, op. cit., p. 165.
55. ibid.
56. ibid.
57. ibid., p. 166.

Chapter 4

1. RW Chalmers, *The Annals of Essendon*, vol. 2, 1998, p. 309.
2. ibid., p. 304.
3. *The Moonee Valley Thematic Environment History*, City of Moonee Valley, 2012, p. 101.
4. *Australian Dictionary of Biography* – Frank McEncroe.
5. For example, Honolulu passenger and crew list, 11 March 1933, 9 April 1938, 28 January 1939.
6. Frances B Cogan, *Captured: The Japanese Internment of American Civilians in the Philippines, 1941–1945*, University of Georgia Press, Athens, 2000, p. 1.
7. Extract from D'Arcy Hunt's diary: www.cnac.org/emilscott/darcyhunt01.htm
8. D'Arcy Hunt, Anderson Inquiry transcript, p. 5406.
9. ibid.
10. ibid.
11. ibid., p. 5407.
12. ibid., p. 5409.
13. ibid.
14. ibid., p. 5410.
15. ibid., p. 5413.
16. Don Greenlees, 'Dianeticism – the new science that could change our lives?' *The Argus*, 12 November 1951.
17. Treasure Southen, Anderson Inquiry Transcript, p. 4840.
18. ibid., p. 4841.
19. ibid., p. 4843.
20. Advertisement in *The Argus*, 7 May 1952: DIANETICS Forum. Meeting. Room 109, VRI Bldg., Flinders St. Station. 8 p.m. Fri. May 9.
21. D'Arcy Hunt, op. cit., p. 5410.
22. Edgar Oswald Haes, *The Release of Psychic Energy: Psychoanalysis for Ordinary People*, Australian Psychology Centre, Sydney, 1949.
23. Advertisement in the *Sydney Morning Herald*, 5 May 1951: DIANETICS latest literature from USA now available AUSTRALIAN PSYCHOLOGY CENTRE, 296 Pitt Street, 2pm 5pm
24. Advertisement in the *Sydney Morning Herald*, 12 November 1952: DIANETICS – the 'New' Psychology 3 wkly lectures by EO Haes, com Wed., 19 Nov., 7 30 p.m. Fee 3/Australian Psychology Centre – 296 Pitt St., 1st floor.
25. Sara Northrup Hubbard affidavit, 23 April 1951: www.spaink.net/cos/LRH-bio/sara.htm

26. ibid.
27. ibid.
28. ibid.
29. L. Ron Hubbard letter to Robert Heinlein, 28 March 1950.
30. ibid.
31. 'Wife accuses mental health expert of torturing her', *The Times Herald*, 24 April 1951.
32. Lawrence Wright, *Going Clear: Scientology, Hollywood & the Prison of Belief*, Alfred A. Knopf, New York, 2013, p. 71.
33. ibid.
34. ibid., p. 72.
35. Russell Miller, *Bare-Faced Messiah*, Henry Holt and Company, New York, 1987, p. 182 and correspondence with Jon Atack.
36. Sara Northrup Hubbard affidavit, 23 April 1951.
37. 'Hiding of baby charged to dianetics author', *Los Angeles Times*, 11 April 1951.
38. Sara Northrup Hubbard affidavit 23 April 1951.
39. ibid.
40. *The Courier-Mail*, 25 April 1951.
41. 'The Scientology story', *Los Angeles Times*, 24 June 1990.
42. Russell Miller, op. cit., p. 180.
43. Hubbard letter to the Attorney-General, 14 May 1951.
44. Jon Atack, *Let's Sell These People a Piece of Blue Sky* (2nd edn), Richard Woods, Worthing, 2013, p. 139.
45. Russell Miller, op. cit., p. 185.
46. ibid.
47. Jon Atack, loc. cit.
48. Russell Miller interview with Barbara Klowden.
49. Sara Hubbard statement 11 June 1951.
50. Russell Miller, *Bare-Faced Messiah*, p. 193.
51. Bent Corydon and L. Ron Hubbard Jnr, *Messiah or Madman?*, 1987, p. 285: www.xenu.net/archive/books/mom/Messiah_or_Madman.txt
52. Russell Miller, op. cit., p. 195.
53. ibid.
54. ibid., p. 197.
55. ibid.
56. ibid., p. 200.
57. ibid.
58. Jon Atack: http://tonyortega.org/2014/02/01/jon-atack-takes-apart-the-scientology-emeter/
59. Simon Singh and Edzard Ernst, *Trick or Treatment*, W. W. Norton & Company, New York, 2008, p. 164.
60. Russell Miller, op. cit., p. 201.
61. Marc Headley, author of *Blown for Good: Behind the Iron Curtain of Scientology*, BFG Books, Burbank, 2009, says one type E-Meter cost $40 per machine to build. The same one sells for $6000.
62. Hugh Urban, *The Church of Scientology – A History of a New Religion*, Princeton University Press, New Jersey, 2011, p. 71.
63. Russell Miller, op. cit., p. 204.
64. ibid., p. 205.
65. Jon Atack, loc. cit., p. 145.
66. Jon Atack, *Never Believe a Hypnotist*, 1994, www.lermanet.com/exit/parsons.htm
67. Jim Dincalci interview given to UK Channel 4 program 'Secret Lives – L. Ron Hubbard', 1997.
68. D'Arcy Hunt, Anderson Inquiry transcript, p. 5420.
69. Treasure Southen, Anderson Inquiry transcript, p. 4843.
70. ibid.
71. *The Journal of Scientology*, Issue 38G, 1954.
72. *The Journal of Scientology*, Issue 40G, 1954.
73. Department of Immigration memo, 25 February 1955, and undated memo no. 55/10765.
74. Undated Department of Immigration memo no. 55/10765.
75. Treasure Southen, Anderson Inquiry transcript, p. 4844.
76. Doug Moon, Anderson Inquiry testimony.
77. ASIO Minute for Senior Field Officer – Hubbard Association of Scientologists International – 30 July 1956.
78. ibid.
79. Roger Meadmore interview with author.
80. David Cooke correspondence with author.
81. *The Argus*, 26 March 1955.
82. *The Argus*, 30 December 1955.
83. Doug Moon, Anderson Inquiry transcript p. 2179.

84. Hubbard, *The Scientologist: a Manual on the Dissemination of Material*. This article first appeared in *Ability, the Magazine of DIANETICS and SCIENTOLOGY*, Major Issue 1, March 1955.
85. George Maltby, Anderson Inquiry transcript, p. 4657.

Chapter 5
1.   Letter from Hubbard to Helen O'Brien, 10 April 1953, submitted as evidence in Church of Scientology of California v Gerald Armstrong.
2.   ibid.
3.   Roy Wallis, *The Road to Total Freedom : A Sociological analysis of Scientology,* Columbia University Press, New York, 1977, p. 128.
4.   Nieson Himmel, as quoted in Russell Miller, *Bared-Faced Messiah*, Henry Holt and Company, New York, 1987, p. 117.
5.   Sam Moskowitz affidavit: www.xenu-directory.net/mirrors/www.whyaretheydead.net/krasel/aff_sm_930414.html. Lloyd Arthur Eshbach, *Over My Shoulder: Reflections on a Science Fiction Era*, Oswald Train, Philadelphia, 1983, pp. 125–126. For more witnesses and Sturgeon's comments, see: www.donlindsayarchive.org/scientology/start.a.religion.html
6.   According to Gallup polls, 1955 and 1958 had the highest churchgoing rates in US history.
7.   Robert S Ellwood, *The Fifties Spiritual Marketplace: American Religion in a Decade of Conflict*, Rutgers University Press, Brunswick, 1997, p. 1.
8.   'Dear Skipper …' letter from L. Ron Hubbard to his then wife Polly, 1938.
9.   'The Shrinking World of L. Ron Hubbard', *World in Action*, Granada Television, July 1968. Transcript at: www.lermanet.com/scientology/transcripts/shrinking.htm
10. Telex, 1979, provided to author by former Sea Org member Nancy Many.
11. Charlie Nairn interview with author.
12. ibid.
13. ibid.
14. ibid. Hana Eltringham says it could have been as many as 300–350 on board at the time.
15. Charlie Nairn interview with author.
16. Charlie Nairn email to author.
17. ibid.
18. Charlie Nairn interview with author.
19. Charlie Nairn email to author.
20. Charlie Nairn interview with author.
21. ibid.
22. ibid.
23. Peter Cox, *On the Box: Great Moments in Australian Television 1956–2006*, Powerhouse Publishing, Haymarket, 2006, p. 8.
24. Doug Moon, Anderson Inquiry transcript, p. 2078.
25. Phillip Wearne, Anderson Inquiry transcript, p. 4785.
26. Roger Boswarva interview with author.
27. The author can vouch for this, having trained as a surf lifesaver there!
28. Roger Boswarva interview with author.
29. Forbes Carlile interview with author.
30. Roger Boswarva email to author.
31. Steven Hassan interview with author.
32. Roger Meadmore, Anderson Inquiry transcript, p. 6393.
33. Roger Meadmore interview with author.
34. ibid.
35. Race Mathews interview with author.
36. ibid.
37. For example, Melbourne HASI Schedule of Training, April 1958.
38. ASIO Minute, 7 July 1958, Hubbard Association of Scientologists International, Victorian Office.
39. ibid.
40. Average weekly wages – Australian Bureau of Statistics, *Year Book Australia* 1960, Chapter 12, p. 426.
41. *The Anderson Report*, State of Victoria, p. 35.
42. ibid.
43. ibid., p. 26.
44. Testimony of John Campbell, an officer of the Victorian State Audit Office, Anderson Inquiry.
45. For more on company structure of Melbourne HASI at the time see *The Anderson Report*, p. 27.
46. Testimony of John Campbell, an officer of the Victorian State Audit Office, Anderson Inquiry.
47. *The Anderson Report*, pp. 32–33.
48. Letter from Malcolm Allen to Max and Jenny Anderson, 30 May 1963.
49. *The Anderson Report*, pp. 37–38.

50. Peter Crundall, Anderson Inquiry transcript, p. 854.
51. ibid.
52. Department of Immigration memo, Rev. and Mrs Farrell – permanent stay – written by WK Brown, 9 April 1956.
53. Pat Krenik – correspondence with author (a memo from the Department of Immigraton on 22 March 1956 says the Farrells were on a joint salary of £10 per week, plus rent, electricity and gas).
54. Letter from Harold Holt to the Secretary of the Department of Immigration, 21 February 1956.
55. ibid., 15 March 1956.
56. Letter from the Secretary of the Department of Immigration to Harold Holt Immigration, 17 April 1956.
57. File note 10 April 1956, Department of Immigration memo, Rev. and Mrs Farrell – permanent stay.
58. AL Nutt (Department of Immigration Acting Secretary) letter to Australian Embassy in Washington, 8 August 1957.
59. Department of Immigration memo, Rev. and Mrs Farrell – permanent stay – written by WK Brown, 9 April 1956.
60. Department of Immigration File No. n57/4119 – they were on aircraft N1028V from Sydney.
61. Photo of Scientology Centre in the Sydney *Truth*, 21 August 1955, shows the HASI banner.
62. Marcus Tooley, Anderson Inquiry transcript, p. 7354a.
63. ibid., p. 7355.
64. ibid., p. 7398.
65. 'Dux of the quacks', Sydney *Truth*, 21 August 1955.
66. Marcus Tooley, op. cit., p. 7356.
67. ibid.
68. Peter Gillham interview with author.
69. Roger Boswarva correspondence with author.
70. Marcus Tooley, op. cit., p. 7354.
71. ibid., p. 7365.
72. Letter from Rhona Swinburne to Marcus Tooley, 3 March 1959.
73. Letter from Elizabeth Williams to Rhona Swinburne, 19 February 1959.
74. Letter from Rhona Swinburne to Marcus Tooley, 3 March 1959.
75. For list of franchises see *Communication*, Church of Scientology, February 1960.
76. Roger Meadmore interview with author.
77. ibid.
78. ibid.
79. ibid.
80. Phillip Wearne, Anderson Inquiry transcript, p. 1680.
81. Doug Moon, Anderson Inquiry transcript, p. 2113.
82. L. Ron Hubbard, Welcome Address Melbourne Congress, 7 November 1959.
83. ibid.
84. ibid.
85. Russell Miller, *Bare-Faced Messiah*, Henry Holt and Company, New York, 1987, p. 236.
86. Church of Scientology: www.bridgepub.com/store/catalog/melbourne-congress-lectures.html
87. David Miscavige at the opening of the Ideal Scientology Church in Melbourne, 29 January 2011, as reported in *Freedom Magazine*, vol. 12, no. 1, 2011.
88. Church of Scientology: www.bridgepub.com/store/catalog/melbourne-congress-lectures.html
89. Doug Moon, Anderson Inquiry transcript, pp. 2114–2115.
90. ibid., p. 2115.
91. Phillip Wearne, undated note to L. Ron Hubbard – exhibit 291, Anderson Inquiry.
92. Phillip Wearne, letter to L. Ron Hubbard, 20 November 1959, Exhibit 292, Anderson Inquiry.

Chapter 6
1. Rupert Murdoch tweet, 1 July 2012.
2. ibid., 2 July 2012.
3. *Business Wire*, 16 July 1996.
4. *Associated Press*, Washington, 1 October 2001.
5. Sandra Hall, *Tabloid Man: The Life and Times of Ezra Norton*, Fourth Estate, Sydney, 2008, p. 178.
6. George Munster, *A Paper Prince*, Penguin, Ringwood, 1987.
7. Cyril Pearl, *Wild Men of Sydney*, W. H. Allen, London, 1958, p. 130.
8. *Sydney Morning Herald*, 1 October 1898.
9. Mark Day email correspondence with author.
10. Rupert Murdoch, 1972 Arthur Norman Smith Memorial Lecture in Journalism.
11. ibid.
12. Owen McKenna email correspondence with author.
13. Owen McKenna interview with author.

14. Melbourne *Truth*, 2 December 1961.
15. ibid.
16. Alan Gill, *The Turbulent Years of Doctor Rumble*: http://compassreview.org/autumn12/4.pdf
17. *Australian Dictionary of Biography* – Leslie Audoen Rumble.
18. ibid.
19. P O'N of Bexley questions and Rumble's answer republished in *The Tribune* on 27 October 1960, and also *The Anderson Report*, Chapter 28.
20. *The Tribune*, 27 October 1960.
21. HCO *Manual of Justice*, HCO, London, 1959.
22. ibid.
23. Peter Williams letter to Dr Rumble, 29 September 1960 – Exhibit 92, Anderson Inquiry.
24. Letter to *The Tribune* from Melbourne HASI, 3 November 1960.
25. Melbourne *Truth*, 2 December 1961.
26. Special Project Australia, HCO Bulletin, 24 July 1960.
27. ibid.
28. ibid.
29. *The Anderson Report*, Chapter 22.
30. Melbourne *Truth*, 11 June 1960.
31. *The Geelong Advertiser*, 7 June 1960.
32. ibid.
33. Geelong population – 1961 Australian Bureau of Statistics Data.
34. Letter from L. Ron Hubbard to Inspector Bent, 29 June 1960.
35. ibid.
36. Hubbard's Naval record of stations: www.spaink.net/cos/LRH-bio/servrcrd.htm
37. Rupert Murdoch, 1972 Arthur Norman Smith Memorial Lecture in Journalism.

Chapter 7
1. KD Gott, 'Mr Wearne's Legions of Space', *Nation*, 1 July 1961.
2. *The Truth*, 8 May 1955.
3. *The Sun,* 7 March 1955.
4. Phillip Wearne, Anderson Inquiry transcript, 1987–1987a.
5. ASIO report from Victorian Regional Director on *Probe* magazine, 30 January 1962.
6. National Archives of Australia – war record of Phillip Bennett Wearne.
7. Daniel Best, *The Strange, Strange Story of Phillip Wearne*: http://ohdannyboy.blogspot.com.au/
8. ibid.
9. Phillip Wearne, Anderson Inquiry transcript, p. 1638.
10. ibid., p. 1639.
11. ibid., p. 1640.
12. ibid.
13. ibid., p. 5272.
14. ibid., p. 1646.
15. Paulette Cooper, *The Scandal of Scientology*, Chapter 17: www.xenu.net/archive/books/tsos/sos-17.html
16. Phillip Wearne, op. cit., p. 1645.
17. Jon Atack, *The Total Freedom Trap: Scientology, Dianetics and L. Ron Hubbard*, Chapter 13: www.xenu.net/archive/techniques/
18. Margery Wakefield, *Understanding Scientology: The Demon Cult*, LuLu, Raleigh, p. 128: www.cs.cmu.edu/~dst/Library/Shelf/wakefield/us.html
19. Phillip Wearne, op. cit., p. 1646.
20. ibid., p. 1648.
21. ibid.
22. ibid., p. 1649.
23. ibid., p. 1674.
24. ibid., p. 1673.
25. KD Gott, 'Mr Wearne's Legions of Space', *Nation*, 1 July 1961.
26. ibid.
27. Australian Bureau of Statistics, *Year Book Australia* 2001.
28. Letter from Doug Moon to L. Ron Hubbard, Exhibit 199, Anderson Inquiry.
29. ibid.
30. Roger Meadmore interview with author.
31. *Communication*, Church of Scientology, June 1960, vol. 2, No. 6.
32. The special zone plan: the Scientologist's role in life, HCO Bulletin, 23 June 1960.
33. HCO Policy Letter, 15 August 1960, Dept. of Govt. Affairs.
34. ibid.
35. ibid.
36. Anderson Inquiry transcript, pp. 4475–4476.

37. *The Anderson Report*, Chapter 28.
38. *Reality*, April 1961. p. 25.
39. *Probe*, vol. 1, no. 1, 1961.
40. Anderson Inquiry transcript, p. 4790.
41. Phillip Wearne letter to Richard King, 28 July 1961, Exhibit 289, Anderson Inquiry.
42. Phillip Wearne, Anderson Inquiry transcript, p. 4472.
43. ibid., p. 4750.
44. Undated letter from Doug Moon to L. Ron Hubbard, Exhibit 199, Anderson Inquiry.
45. Phillip Wearne, op. cit., p. 1985.
46. ibid., p. 4472.
47. ibid., p. 1707.
48. ibid., p. 1710.
49. ibid.
50. Russell Miller, *Bare-Faced Messiah*, Henry Holt and Company, New York, 1987, p. 247.
51. ibid., pp. 247–248.
52. Jon Atack, *Let's Sell These People a Piece of Blue Sky* (2nd edn), Richard Woods, Worthing, 2013, p. 172.
53. Russell Miller, loc. cit.
54. Stop Press – 11 January 1963 from HCO Melbourne, The Anderson Inquiry, Exhibit 301.
55. This term was used in the local journal *Communication* in November 1960 and April 1961.
56. Letter from Elizabeth Williams to Charles Spry, received by ASIO on 20 June 1960.
57. See all 1963 editions of *Communication*.
58. *Communication*, Church of Scientology, June 1963.
59. Phillip Wearne testimony, Anderson Inquiry.
60. Earliest example I could find was on 9 May 1962. Phillip Wearne wrote to Elizabeth Williams: 'I am still awaiting a reply regarding the refund of processing fees.' He also asks about a refund in a letter to Peter Williams, 6 June 1962, copied to Hubbard this series of letters, Exhibit 308, Anderson Inquiry.
61. Phillip Wearne letter to the HASI Registrar, 8 April 1962.
62. Phillip Wearne letter to Peter Williams, copied to Hubbard, 6 June 1962.
63. ibid.
64. Phillip Wearne, Anderson Inquiry transcript, p. 1964.
65. Phillip Wearne telegram to L. Ron Hubbard, 14 April 1963, Anderson Inquiry transcript, p. 1733.
66. Letter from L. Ron Hubbard to Phillip Wearne, 26 April 1963, Anderson Inquiry transcript, p. 1734.
67. In a letter from Doug Moon to Hubbard on 5 Nov. 1963, he reminds Hubbard: 'I advised you some months ago to give Wearne his money back ... had you listened to me in the first place instead of the idiot advisers you employ in this part of the world the parliamentary attack would probably not have occurred.'
68. Letter from Phillip Wearne to L. Ron Hubbard, 16 May 1963, Anderson Inquiry transcript, pp. 1734–1735.
69. *Reality*, vol. 7, no. 1, 1966.
70. ASIO Headquarters memorandum to all regional offices no. 7813, 22 June 1962.
71. Department of Supply – Security Branch memorandum for ASIO, 16 April 1956.
72. According to ASIO Minute paper 23 January 1969.
73. Report by LF Dunn compiled by Victorian Police for the Department of Immigration.
74. 'Writ against Scientology association', *The Age*, 8 August 1963.
75. Terms of Phillip Wearne's settlement tendered at the Anderson Inquiry, p. 4453.
76. Phillip Wearne later admitted this at both the Anderson Inquiry and in his publication *Reality*.
77. *Australian Dictionary of Biography* – Jack Galbally.
78. Victorian Legislative Council Hansard, 19 November 1963, p. 2127.
79. Comments from a statement issued by Peter Williams, Denny Gogerly and the staff of HASI, Melbourne, 20 November 1963.
80. ibid.
81. *The Anderson Report*, Chapter 1.
82. Undated Doug Moon letter to L. Ron Hubbard written some time between 26 November and 10 December 1963.
83. 'Labor Scientology Bill in council – govt to oppose it', *The Age*, 27 November 1963.
84. *Kangaroo Court*, Hubbard College of Scientology, Church of Scientology of California, 1967, p. 3.
85. Telegrams sent to Arthur Rylah Chief Secretary and Rupert Hamer Assistant Chief Secretary (and future Premier of Victoria) on 22 November 1963.
86. *Enquiry Rumour UK*, Office of L. Ron Hubbard, 9 February 1966.
87. Letter from Mary Sue Hubbard to Yvonne and Peter Gillham, 17 February 1964.
88. Peter Gillham Snr interview with author.
89. ibid.

Chapter 8
1. Author interview with Janis Grady (née Gillham).
2. *The Anderson Report*, State of Victoria, 1965, Chapter 1.
3. Peter Gillham Snr interview with author.
4. 'Joined Sect; Stayed Bald', *Sunday Truth*, 22 March 1964.
5. *The Anderson Report*, loc. cit.
6. ibid.
7. ibid.
8. ASIO minute on the Committee for Mental Health and National Security paper, 26 January 1966.
9. Phillip Wearne, Anderson Inquiry transcript, pp. 4457–4458.
10. ibid., p. 4457.
11. ASIO report, Regional Director Victoria, 4 May 1964.
12. Letter from Doug Moon to L. Ron Hubbard, 9 July 1963.
13. ibid., 5 November 1963.
14. Undated Doug Moon letter to L. Ron Hubbard sent some time between when the inquiry was announced on 26 November 1963 and before Hubbard responded on 10 December 1963.
15. Doug Moon, Anderson Inquiry transcript, pp. 2134–2135, 2138.
16. ibid., p. 2123.
17. ibid., p. 2140.
18. ibid., pp 2124, 2126 and *Kangaroo Court*, Hubbard College of Scientology, Church of Scientology of California, 1967, p. 11.
19. Doug Moon, op. cit., p. 2306.
20. ibid., p. 2159.
21. ibid.
22. ibid., p. 2162.
23. ibid., p. 2325.
24. Richard King, Anderson Inquiry transcript, pp. 6837–6841.
25. Terms of witness Doug Moon making statutory declaration unfavourable to Phillip Wearne Exhibit 256, Anderson Inquiry.
26. Undated Doug Moon letter to L. Ron Hubbard sent some time between when the Inquiry was announced on 26 November 1963 and before Hubbard responded on 10 December 1963.
27. Richard King, op. cit., p. 6843.
28. Doug Moon, Anderson Inquiry transcript, p. 2323a.
29. ibid., p. 2347.
30. Roger Boswarva interview with author and see Anderson Inquiry transcript p. 4900.
31. Letter from Max Anderson to the Secretary of the Board of Anderson Inquiry, 2 December 1963, Exhibit 305.
32. ibid., 12 February 1964, Exhibit 305.
33. Max Anderson, Anderson Inquiry transcript, p. 4727.
34. ibid., p. 4903.
35. ibid., p. 4902.
36. For example, John Simpkin – Max Anderson, Anderson Inquiry transcript, p. 4903.
37. Max Anderson, Anderson Inquiry transcript, p. 4728.
38. ibid., and pp. 4904–4905.
39. Roger Boswarva interview with author.
40. Roger Boswarva, *Conjunction of Stars*, unpublished manuscript.
41. ibid.
42. Roger Boswarva interview with author.
43. Roger Boswarva, *Conjunction of Stars*, unpublished manuscript.
44. ibid.
45. Professor Malcolm Macmillan email to author.
46. ibid.
47. Simon Cooke, *A Meeting of Minds: The Australian Psychological Society and Australian Psychologists 1944–1994*, Australian Psychological Society, Carlton South, VIC, 2000, p. 106.
48. Professor Malcolm Macmillan's notes provided to author.
49. *The Anderson Report*.
50. *The Age*, 3 June 1964.
51. Letter from Peter Williams to L. Ron Hubbard, 26 June 1964, Exhibit 294, Anderson Inquiry.
52. Letter from L. Ron Hubbard to Peter Williams, 5 August 1964.
53. *The Anderson Report*, Chapter 6.
54. L. Ron Hubbard, HCO Bulletin, 11 May 1963.
55. ibid.
56. *Kangaroo Court*, op. cit., p. 13.
57. ibid., p. 16.
58. ibid., p. 17.

59. ibid.
60. *The Anderson Report*, Chapter 1.
61. ibid.
62. Russell Miller, *Bare-Faced Messiah*, Henry Holt and Company, New York, 1987, p. 250.
63. *Kangaroo Court*, op. cit., p. 19.
64. *The Anderson Report*, loc. cit.
65. *Kangaroo Court*, op. cit., p. 43.
66. *The Anderson Report*, loc. cit.
67. The original report was 173 foolscap pages plus appendices. The PDF available online is 234 pages in total.
68. *The Anderson Report*, Prefatory Note.
69. ibid., Chapter 6.
70. ibid.
71. ibid.
72. ibid., Prefatory Note.
73. ibid., Chapter 30.
74. ibid.
75. Kevin Anderson, *Fossil in the Sandstone: The Recollecting Judge*, Spectrum Publications, Richmond VIC, 1986, pp. 2–4.
76. *The Anderson Report*, Chapter 25.
77. ibid.
78. ibid., Chapter 2.
79. Russell Miller, op. cit., p. 253.
80. Jon Atack, *Let's Sell These People a Piece of Blue Sky* (2nd edn), Richard Woods, Worthing, 2013, pp. 177–178.
81. Jon Atack email to author.
82. Russell Miller, op. cit., p. 253.
83. *The Anderson Report*, Prefatory Note.
84. Peter Gillham Snr interview with author.
85. *The Anderson Report*, Recommendations, Chapter 31.

Chapter 9
1. Russell Miller, *Bare-Faced Messiah*, Henry Holt and Company, New York, 1987, p. 236.
2. L. Ron Hubbard Melbourne Congress, Welcome Address, 7 November 1959.
3. *Kangaroo Court*, Hubbard College of Scientology, Church of Scientology of California, 1967, pp3–4.
4. ibid., p. 3.
5. ibid.
6. ibid., pp. 3–4.
7. ibid., p. 3.
8. Simon Cooke, *A Meeting of Minds: The Australian Psychological Society and Australian Psychologists 1944–1994*, Australian Psychological Society, Carlton South, VIC, 2000, p. 108.
9. 'Bill empowers seizure of Scientology documents', *The Age*, 11 November 1965.
10. Jack Galbally speech to the Victorian Parliament, 7 November 1965.
11. Simon Cooke, op. cit., p. 109.
12. ibid.
13. Malcolm Macmillan interview with author.
14. ibid.
15. ibid. and Simon Cooke, loc. cit.
16. Malcolm Macmillan interview with author and Simon Cooke, ibid., p. 108.
17. 'Thousands of files in Scientology raid', *The Age*, 22 December 1965.
18. ibid.
19. 'Scientology ban now in force', *The Age*, 22 December 1965.
20. Howard Dickman's biography of Yvonne Gillham: http://scientolipedia.org/info/Yvonne_Gillham_Jentzsch
21. Letter from Annie Tampion to Henry Bolte, 12 July 1967.
22. Janis Grady (née Gillham) interview with author.
23. *Kangaroo Court*, op. cit., p. 3.
24. Jon Atack, *Let's Sell These People a Piece of Blue Sky* (2nd edn), Richard Woods, Worthing, 2013, p. 173.
25. See HCO Policy Letter, 5 April 1965, and HCO Policy Letter, 23 December 1965.
26. Peter Gillham Snr interview with author.
27. Terri Gamboa (née Gillham) interview with author.
28. Memo from the Chief Commissioner of Police in Victoria, 12 July 1966,
29. Letter from Treasure Southen to Premier Bolte, 17 January 1963.
30. Victoria Police CIB Report Form, Northcote District File no. 950/15/66.

31. ibid.
32. ibid.
33. Peter Gillham Snr interview with author.
34. HCO Ethics Order no. 60 Adelaide, 11 May 1966.
35. Terri Gamboa (née Gillham) interview with author.
36. Roy Wallis, *The Road to Total Freedom*, Columbia University Press, New York 1977, p. 193.
37. ibid., p. 194.
38. For full exchange between Lord Balniel and the Health Minister: www.cs.cmu.edu/~dst/Cowen/audit/balniel.html
39. Secretarial Executive Director 9 February 1966 Enquiry Rumour UK, as quoted in paragraph 181 in the Foster Report, December 1971.
40. ibid.
41. Russell Miller, op. cit., p. 254.
42. Project Pyschiatry – Secretarial Executive Director, 22 February 1966.
43. 'One man Britain can do without', *The People*, 20 March 1966.
44. HCO Policy Letter, 15 February 1966, Attacks On Scientology.
45. ibid.
46. Russell Miller, op. cit., pp. 255–256.
47. ibid., p. 165.
48. ibid., p. 273.
49. Jon Atack, *Let's Sell These People a Piece of Blue Sky* (2nd edn), Richard Woods, Worthing, 2013, p. 180.
50. Richard Behar, 'The thriving cult of greed and power', *TIME*, 6 May 1991.
51. HCO Executive Letter, 5 September 1966, How to do a Noisy Investigation.
52. Jon Atack's Scientology – The Church of Hate speech delivered at FECRIS, conference in Copenhagen May 2013. At the bottom of Jon's paper he references this quote with the following: Sefton Delmar's *Black Boomerang* and Christopher Felix's *The Spy and His Masters*. *Black Boomerang* describes the various false information tactics and dirty tricks used during World War II. Both these books, and a dozen more, were required reading on the *Confidential Information Full Hat*, the Guardian's Office 800-page intelligence course, of 9 September 1974. On page 8, 19 checklisted items are devoted to *The Spy and His Masters*. Over a dozen espionage terms are defined just for the first item. Demonstrations of 'a cut-out, building a cover' and various other spy operations are required. *Intelligence Specialist Training Routine Lying – TR-L, Confidential Information Full Hat* – GO Intelligence course 1974 Sept 9, Page 13, Drill 9. 'Purpose: to train a student to give a false statement with good TR-1. FBI 1977 seized raid document – Government Exhibit 236. For break ins, see *Hat Write-up Covering Functions Held by Info*, above and the Stipulation of Evidence in United States of America v Mary Sue Hubbard, et al., District Court, Washington, DC, criminal case no. 78–401. Hubbard's *Way to Happiness* urges followers not to tell 'harmful lies', which permits lying in defence of the cause.
53. HCO Policy Letter, 23 December 1965, Suppressive Acts, Suppression of Scientology and Scientologists, The Fair Game Law.
54. L. Ron Hubbard in the Scientology journal *The Auditor*, no. 31.
55. HCO Policy Letter, 18 October 1967.
56. HCO Policy Letter, 21 October 1968.
57. *The Cincinnati Enquirer*, 1 September 1979.
58. UN General Assembly Resolution on Southern Rhodesia.
59. Jon Atack, op. cit., p. 186.
60. Russell Miller, op. cit., p. 257.
61. ibid.
62. Jon Atack, op. cit., p. 186.
63. Jon Atack email to author.
64. Russell Miller, op. cit., p. 260.
65. Janis Grady (née Gillham) interview with author.
66. Russell Miller, loc. cit.
67. Jon Atack, loc. cit.
68. 'The case of the processed woman', *Daily Mail*, 22 August 1966.
69. Foster Report, Paragraph 11.
70. John McMaster quote as told to Russell Miller.

Chapter 10

1. Virginia Downsborough said he wouldn't get out of bed for three weeks in her interview with Russell Miller for *Bare-Faced Messiah*.
2. For a comprehensive history of Hubbard's drug taking read Jon Atack's paper 'Never Believe a Hypnotist' – an investigation of L. Ron Hubbard's statements about hypnosis and its relationship to Dianetics.

3.   Letter to Mary Sue Hubbard in 1967 as quoted in *Messiah or Madman?* (1987) by Bent
     Corydon and L. Ron Hubbard Jnr.
4.   Jerry Dorsman, *How to Quit Drugs for Good*, Random House, New York, 1998, p. 37,
     describes Pinks and Greys as Darvon. Gerry Armstrong, former archivist with the Church of
     Scientology, also told author he thought Pinks and Greys referred to Darvon capsules.
5.   Lawrence Wright, *Going Clear: Scientology, Hollywood & the Prison of Belief*, Alfred A.
     Knopf, New York, 2013, p. 93.
6.   Russell Miller's interview with Virginia Downsborough.
7.   www.scientology.org/faq/operating-thetan/what-is-ot.html
8.   Jon Atack, *Let's Sell These People a Piece of Blue Sky* (2nd edn), Richard Woods, Worthing,
     2013, p. 145.
9.   Flag Information Letter 67, 31 October 1977.
10. For L. Ron Hubbard's official version of the Xenu myth: http://jeta.home.xs4all.nl/scn/ot3/ot3.
     html
11. L. Ron Hubbard's Journal '67 – a taped lecture delivered in Las Palmas on 20 September 1967.
12. ibid.
13. ibid.
14. Lawrence Wright, op. cit., p. 96.
15. According to British Scientologist Neville Chamberlin as referenced in Janet Reitman's *Inside
     Scientology*, Houghton Mifflin Harcourt, New York, 2011, p. 90.
16. Janet Reitman, ibid.
17. Howard Dickman's biography of Yvonne Gillham: http://scientolipedia.org/info/Yvonne_
     Gillham_Jentzsch
18. Russell Miller, *Bare-Faced Messiah*, Henry Holt and Company, New York, 1987, p. 264.
19. Howard Dickman's biography, loc. cit.
20. *Sunday Mirror*, 24 December 1967 as quoted in Jon Atack, op. cit., p. 196.
21. Russell Miller, op. cit., p. 269.
22. Howard Dickman's biography, loc. cit.
23. Hana Eltringham interview with author.
24. Howard Dickman's biography, loc. cit.
25. ibid.
26. Janis Grady (née Gillham) interview with author.
27. Peter Gillham Jnr interview with author.
28. ibid.
29. Russell Miller, op. cit., p. 274.
30. Terri Gamboa (née Gillham) interview with author.
31. Janis Grady (née Gillham) interview with author.
32. ibid.
33. ibid.
34. Terri Gamboa (née Gillham) interview with author.
35. ibid.
36. Janis Grady (née Gillham) interview with author.
37. Terri Gamboa (née Gillham) interview with author.
38. ibid.
39. HCO Policy Letter, Penalties for Lower Conditions, 18 October 1967.
40. www.lronhubbard.org/ron-series/profile/humanitarian/solutions-to-administration.html
41. http://tonyortega.org/2013/11/07/statistically-speaking-jefferson-hawkins-takes-us-into-
     scientologys-numbers-fixation/comment-page-1/
42. Terri Gamboa (née Gillham) interview with author.
43. ibid.
44. Jon Atack, op. cit., p. 201, and FDA interview with McMaster in 1970.
45. Hana Eltringham, *Secret Lives – L. Ron Hubbard*, Channel 4 UK documentary.
46. Terri Gamboa (née Gillham) interview with author.
47. Peter Gillham Jnr interview with author.
48. Janis Grady (née Gillham) interview with author.
49. L. Ron Hubbard, 'Scientology and Your Children' ,*Communication*, September 1961.
50. Lawrence Wright, op. cit., p. 111. The story of Derek Greene was also confirmed to me by
     Janis Grady (née Gillham).
51. Hana Eltringham at a talk given in 2010 in Hamburg, Germany.
52. Hana Eltringham, op. cit.
53. Affidavit of Tonja Burden 25 January 1980.
54. Jon Atack, op. cit., p. 202, and FDA interview with John McMaster, 23 November 1970.
55. Terri Gamboa (née Gillham) interview with author.
56. Janis Grady (née Gillham) interview with author.
57. Lawrence Wright, *Going Clear: Scientology, Hollywood & the Prison of Belief*, Alfred A.
     Knopf, New York, 2013, p. 110, and Hana Eltringham correspondence with author.
58. John McMaster as quoted in Russell Miller's *Bare-Faced Messiah*, p. 273.

59. Lawrence Wright, op. cit., p. 111.
60. Hana Eltringham interview with author.
61. ibid.
62. As told to me by one former Sea Org member who requested anonymity.
63. Peter Gillham Jnr interview with author.
64. Alexander Mitchell, 'Over the side go the erring Scientologists', *Sunday Times*, 17 November 1968.
65. Alex Mitchell email correspondence with author.
66. Alex Mitchell, *Come the Revolution*, NewSouth Publishing, Kensington, 2011, p. 143.
67. Jon Atack, op. cit., p. 209.
68. Alex Mitchell, op. cit., p. 144.
69. UK *Daily Telegraph* Obituary for Major John Forte, 14 September 2012.
70. Alexander Mitchell, loc. cit.
71. Alex Mitchell, loc. cit.
72. Alexander Mitchell, 'The Odd Beginning of Ron Hubbard's Career', *Sunday Times*, 5 October 1969.
73. Alex Mitchell interview with author.
74. ibid.
75. Janis Grady (née Gillham) interview with author.
76. ibid.
77. Peter Gillham Jnr interview with author.
78. ibid.

Chapter 11
1. Statutory Declaration of Rex John Beaver, 17 October 1968, and interview with author.
2. *Daily Mirror*, Sydney, 9 September 1968.
3. Statutory Declaration of Rex John Beaver, loc. cit.
4. 'Bravery award for detective', *Daily Telegraph*, 22 December 1971.
5. 'More detectives come forward in Scientology', *Sydney Morning Herald* Probe, 22 October 1968.
6. 'New attack on cult likely', *Canberra Times*, 22 October 1968.
7. Statutory Declaration of Rex John Beaver, loc. cit.
8. ibid.
9. Rex Beaver interview with author.
10. Statutory declaration of Rex John Beaver, loc. cit.
11. ibid.
12. HCO Policy Letter, 15 February 1966, Attacks On Scientology.
13. George Munster, *Rupert Murdoch: A Paper Prince*, Penguin, Ringwood, 1987, p. 87.
14. Rex Beaver interview with author.
15. ibid.
16. Anne Deveson interview with author.
17. Statutory Declaration of Rex John Beaver, loc. cit.
18. *Hansard* NSW Parliament, 2 October 1968, p. 1489.
19. Statutory Declaration of Rex John Beaver, loc. cit.
20. ibid.
21. *Sunday Mirror*, 20 October 1968.
22. ibid.
23. *Hansard* NSW Parliament, 22 October 1968, p. 1863.
24. ibid., p. 1864.
25. *Hansard*, ibid., p. 1865.
26. *Sydney Morning Herald*, 23 October 1968.
27. *Sunday Mirror*, 27 October 1968.
28. ibid.
29. ibid.
30. Kenneth Robinson as quoted in paragraph 13 in the Foster Report, Enquiry into the Practice and Effects of Scientology, Report by Sir John Foster, KBE, QC, MP. Published by Her Majesty's Stationery Office, London, December 1971: www.xenu.net/archive/audit/fosthome.html
31. ibid.
32. Russell Miller, *Bare-Faced Messiah*, Henry Holt and Company, New York, 1987, p. 289.
33. 'Here to "fight back" says Scientologist', *The Sun* (Melbourne), 12 November 1968.
34. 'Bolte warns Scientologists they will be prosecuted', *Canberra Times*, 13 November 1968.
35. 'Cult chief invites prosecution', *The Age*, 13 November 1968.
36. 'Scientologists to investigate our leaders', *The Sun* (Melbourne), 13 November 1968.
37. Taken from the minutes of the National Conference of Health Ministers in June 1968 as published by the Church of Scientology in 1969.
38. 'WA to control cult', *Sydney Morning Herald*, 3 November 1968.

39.   'Scientology curb planned in SA', *The Advertiser* (Adelaide), 4 September 1968.
40.   Memo for the Secretary of the Department of Health, 14 January 1969.
41.   'Report on raid', *Canberra Times*, 15 October 1968, and memo from the Secretary of the Department of Health to the Minister for Health, 18 November 1968.
42.   Memo from the Secretary of the Department of Health to the Minister for Health, 18 November 1968.
43.   ibid.
44.   ibid.
45.   In Ian Tampion's letter to the Minister for Health on 18 December 1968 he refers to himself as Rev. In Peter Gillham's letter to the Minister on 13 November 1968 he refers to himself as an 'Ordained Minister'.
46.   Letter from Ian Tampion to Vance Dickie, 18 December 1968.
47.   Letter from Ian Tampion to the trustees of the Necropolis, 13 December 1968.
48.   'Check on cult meeting', *Canberra Times*, 8 October 1968.
49.   Peter Gillham Snr interview with author.
50.   ASIO memo on Hubbard Scientology Organisation, August 1968.
51.   *The Bridge*, Issue XVI, 1968.
52.   ibid.
53.   HCO Information Letter, 17 February 1969, Ron's Journal 1968, Australian–ANZO Supplement.
54.   ibid.
55.   ibid.
56.   ibid.
57.   John Forte, *The Commodore and the Colonels*, Chapter 5: www.cs.cmu.edu/~dst/Library/Shelf/forte/chapter5.htm
58.   Department of External Affairs Inward Cablegram from Athens Embassy, 4 February 1969.
59.   ibid.
60.   ibid.
61.   ibid., 22 February 1969.
62.   ibid.
63.   ibid., 19 March 1969.
64.   ibid., 21 March 1969.
65.   John Forte, loc. cit.
66.   ibid.
67.   ASIO Report from the London Office, 29 April 1969.
68.   Letter from Wayne Gibney to the UK High Commissioner of Australia, 27 April 1969.
69.   ASIO London Office Report, 27 May 1969.
70.   ibid., 6 October 1969.
71.   ibid.
72.   Minute from the Office of the High Commissioner for Australia, 10 July 1969.
73.   ASIO memo – Church of Scientology Demonstration Outside Australian Trade Commission Office, Los Angeles, California, 21 August 1969.
74.   Howard Dickman's biography of Yvonne Gillham: http://scientolipedia.org/info/Yvonne_Gillham_Jentzsch

Chapter 12
1.   'Project celebrity', *Ability Magazine*, 1955. For full list of targets go to www.xenu.net/archive/celebrities/
2.   Howard Dickman's biography of Yvonne Gillham: http://scientolipedia.org/info/Yvonne_Gillham_Jentzsch
3.   Peter Gillham Snr interview with author.
4.   Howard Dickman, loc. cit..
5.   Chris Many interview with Janet Reitman, *Inside Scientology*, Houghton Mifflin Harcourt, Boston, 2011.
6.   Skip Press, *Death by Devotion*: www.themortonreport.com/discoveries/stranger/death-by-devotion/
7.   Howard Dickman, loc. cit.
8.   ibid.
9.   Howard Dickman, loc. cit.
10.   Spanky Taylor interview with author.
11.   Lawrence Wright, *Going Clear: Scientology, Hollywood & the Prison of Belief*, Alfred A. Knopf, New York, 2013, p. 150.
12.   ibid, p. 151.
13.   'Perth police raid cult', *The Age*, 29 January 1969.
14.   *Canberra Times*, 28 March 1969.
15.   *Canberra Times*, 12 April 1969.
16.   *Canberra Times*, 4 December 1969.

17. As mentioned in The Church of the New Faith v Commissioner for Pay-roll Tax: http://uniset.ca/other/cs6/154CLR120.htm and letter from Tom Minchin to Lionel Murphy, 11 April 1972, Lionel Murphy Papers, National Archives of Australia.
18. GW Rogan memo to the Victorian Minister for Health, 5 January 1972.
19. Minchin's CV supplied to the Attorney-General's department in a letter on 18 August 1970, Lionel Murphy Papers, National Archives of Australia.
20. Chris Hurford, the then Federal Labor MP for Adelaide, confirmed to me that Dunstan only had two or three Labor branches in his electorate including St Peters. He says Dunstan would have attended St Peters' branch meetings.
21. 'Scientology link denied', *The Advertiser*, 10 April 1971.
22. Marjorie Fitzgerald interview with author.
23. Father James Minchin interview with author.
24. Eric Kleitsch interview with author.
25. Andrew Mack interview with author.
26. Reasons for Judgment – Mr C Zempilas SM, 2 December 1970, Lionel Murphy Papers, National Archives of Australia.
27. Bernard Doherty, *Spooks and Scientologists: The Monitoring of a Controversial Minority Religion in Cold War Australia 1956–1983*, Melbourne, 2015: www.cesnur.org/2015/doherty_scientology_tallinn_2015.pdf
28. Phillip Wearne death certificate.
29. Phillip Wearne affidavit, 6 January 1969.
30. Letter from Michael Graham to the Royal Commission on Intelligence and Security, 5 March 1975.
31. Letter from Tom Hughes to Tom Minchin, 24 December 1970; letter from Ivor Greenwood to Tom Minchin, 23 March 1972, Lionel Murphy Papers, National Archives of Australia.
32. Interview given by Senator Greenwood in September 1972, as transcribed in ASIO file on Scientology.
33. Tom Minchin letter to Lionel Murphy, 11 April 1972, Lionel Murphy Papers, National Archives of Australia.
34. 'Scientology makes a comeback', *The Australian*, 25 August 1972.
35. ibid.
36. ibid.
37. Lionel Murphy press release, 27 August 1972, Lionel Murphy Papers, National Archives of Australia.
38. 'Murphy gives church power to marry', *The Australian*, 13 February 1973.
39. The folder is now part of the Lionel Murphy Papers, National Archives of Australia.
40. *Freedom* magazine, ANZO edition, March–April 1973.
41. *Kangaroo Court*, Hubbard College of Scientology, Church of Scientology of California, 1967, p. 3.
42. *Freedom* magazine, ANZO edition, March–April 1973.
43. *Nation Review*, 28 April 1973.
44. TM Jensen letter to the Victorian Minister for Health, 15 June 1973.
45. ibid.
46. Jon Atack, *Let's Sell These People a Piece of Blue Sky* (2nd edn), Richard Woods, Worthing, 2013, p. 231.
47. 'Murphy gives church power to marry', *The Australian*, 13 February 1973.
48. Malcolm Macmillan interview with author.
49. Memorandum for the Secretary of the Department of Health, 29 April 1974.
50. 'Assembly passes scientology bill', *The West Australian*, 11 May 1973.
51. L. Ron Hubbard's Orders of the Day, 17 June 1971.
52. 'Scientology wedding', *Sydney Morning Herald*, 14 January 1974.
53. Executive Directive from L. Ron Hubbard – GO-ANZO-GO – 17 February 1974.
54. Enquiry into the Practice and Effects of Scientology, Report by Sir John Foster, KBE, QC, MP. Published by Her Majesty's Stationery Office, London, December 1971. Citation in notes, Chapter 9.
55. Peggy Daroesman, *Scientology in Australia and the USA 1974–82*, personal paper.
56. Peggy Daroesman. Her story has been confirmed for author by former Scientologist David Graham.
57. Jon Atack, op. cit., p. 232.
58. Russell Miller, *Bare-Faced Messiah*, Henry Holt and Company, New York, 1987, p. 314.
59. '5 Scientologists get jail terms for conspiring to rob, bug, spy on US', *Washington Post*, 7 December 1979.
60. Tony Ortega: http://blogs.villagevoice.com/runninscared/2011/11/paulette_cooper_scientologys_original_and_worst_nightmare_a_thanksgiving_tribute_by_the_village_voice.php
61. Lawrence Wright, op. cit., p. 119.
62. Tony Ortega: www.villagevoice.com/news/paulette-cooper-scientologys-original-and-worst-nightmare-a-thanksgiving-tribute-by-the-village-voice-6710895.

63.   ibid.
64.   *Lateline*: www.abc.net.au/lateline/content/2015/s4276151.html

Chapter 13
1.   Mike Rinder interview with author.
2.   ibid.
3.   ibid.
4.   ibid.
5.   ibid.
6.   ibid.
7.   ibid.
8.   Shannon Rae Butler, *Into the Storm: American Covert Involvement in the Angolan Civil War, 1974–1975*, The University of Arizona, Tucson, 2008, p. 191.
9.   Russell Miller, *Bare-Faced Messiah*, Henry Holt and Company, New York, 1987, p. 325.
10.   Mike Rinder interview with author.
11.   Russell Miller, op. cit., p. 326.
12.   Mike Goldstein, a drummer and member of the group, described them as awful in Russell Miller, op. cit., p. 325.
13.   Mike Rinder interview with author.
14.   Peter Gillham Jnr interview with author.
15.   ibid.
16.   Mike Rinder interview with author.
17.   Lawrence Wright, *Going Clear: Scientology, Hollywood & the Prison of Belief*, Alfred A. Knopf, New York, 2013, p. 130.
18.   Omar Garrison, *Playing Dirty*, Ralston-Pilot Publishers, Los Angeles, 1980, p. 84.
19.   Lawrence Wright, loc. cit.
20.   Janis Grady (née Gillham) interview with author.
21.   Russell Miller, op. cit., p. 328.
22.   ibid.
23.   Omar Garrison, loc. cit.
24.   Mike Rinder interview with author.
25.   Lawrence Wright, op. cit., p. 125.
26.   Stephen Kent, *Brainwashing in Scientology's Rehabilitation Project Force (RPF)*. Revised and Expanded Version of a Presentation at the Society for the Scientific Study of Religion, San Diego, California (November 7, 1997). Published by Hamburg Interior Ministry, 13 September, 2000.
27.   Jon Atack, *Let's Sell These People a Piece of Blue Sky* (2nd edn), Richard Woods, Worthing, 2013, pp. 325–326.
28.   ibid.
29.   According to Glenn Samuels, auditor on the *Apollo*, in Janet Reitman, *Inside Scientology*, Houghton Mifflin Harcourt, New York, 2011, p. 105.
30.   Jon Atack, op. cit., p. 236.
31.   Janis Grady (née Gillham) interview with author.
32.   Lawrence Wright, op. cit., p. 131.
33.   Russell Miller, op. cit., p. 334.
34.   ibid., p. 335.
35.   ibid.
36.   ibid., p. 337.
37.   Jon Atack, op. cit., p. 244.
38.   ibid.
39.   ibid., p. 257.
40.   Sentencing Memorandum: United States of America v Kember and Budlong, p. 26.
41.   Jon Atack, op. cit., pp. 259–260.
42.   Snow White Program order GO 732 WW: http://spyontology.files.wordpress.com/2014/04/guardian-order-732-20-apr-73-22snow-white-program22.pdf
43.   ibid.
44.   Lawrence Wright, op. cit., p. 123.
45.   United States of America v Mary Sue Hubbard et al. Stipulation of Evidence.
46.   ibid.
47.   ibid.
48.   ibid.
49.   Jon Atack, op. cit., p. 265.
50.   United States of America v Mary Sue Hubbard et al. Stipulation of Evidence.
51.   ibid.
52.   Lawrence Wright, op. cit., p. 122, and John Atack correspondence with author.
53.   GO 732 SWOTs www.xenu.net/archive/go/ops/go732/go732.htm
54.   ibid.

55. ibid.
56. ibid.
57. 'Man took secret file by fraud', *Sydney Morning Herald*, 11 April 1975.
58. ibid.
59. Peter Marsh (pseudonym) interview with author.
60. Submission from Michael Graham, Australian President of the Church of Scientology, to the Royal Commission on Intelligence and Security, 5 March 1975.
61. Letter from Michael Graham to Peter Barbour, 29 August 1974.
62. Letter from Peter Barbour to Michael Graham, September 1974.
63. Letter from Michael Graham to the Royal Commission on Intelligence and Security, 5 March 1975.
64. ibid.
65. ASIO Minute Paper Church of Scientology, 12 July 1978.
66. Letter from Michael Graham to the Royal Commission on Intelligence and Security, 5 March 1975.
67. ASIO memo 10 March 1970 in relation to blacklisting Wearne from any contact.
68. ibid.
69. ibid.
70. Jack Galbally speech to the Victorian parliament, 7 November 1965.
71. Letter from Michael Graham to the Royal Commission on Intelligence and Security, 5 March 1975.
72. Evan Whitton email correspondence with author.
73. ASIO letter to the Royal Commission on Intelligence and Security, 24 October 1975.
74. 'Scientologists issue writ against ASIO', *The Age*, 25 September 1979.
75. United States of America v Mary Sue Hubbard et al. Stipulation of Evidence.
76. ibid.
77. 'Scientologists plotted leak campaign', *Washington Post*, 24 November 1979.
78. Jon Atack, op. cit., p. 271.
79. United States of America v Mary Sue Hubbard et al. Stipulation of Evidence.
80. Russell Miller, op. cit., pp. 351–352, and Tony Ortega correspondence with author.
81. Janis Grady (née Gillham) interview with author.

Chapter 14
1. For Barry Hart's story, author relied on interviews he gave to Ray Martin on *60 Minutes* in 1980, Barry's unpublished manuscript, a speech he gave in Port Macquarie in 1996 and an interview with author.
2. The Honourable Mr Acting Justice JP Slattery, *Report of the Royal Commission into Deep Sleep Therapy*, 1990.
3. Royal Commission report, vol. 4., p. 25.
4. ibid., p. 37.
5. *Australian Dictionary of Biography*, Volume 17, Melbourne University Press, Carlton, 2007.
6. Susan Geason, *Dark Trance*, unpublished manuscript.
7. ibid.
8. Brian Bromberger and Janet Fife-Yeomans, *Deep Sleep: Harry Bailey and the Scandal of Chelmsford*, Simon & Schuster, East Roseville, 1991, p. 45.
9. Susan Geason, loc. cit.
10. Brian Bromberger and Janet Fife-Yeomans, op. cit., p. 60.
11. According to the conclusions made by Royal Commissioner Justice Slattery.
12. Royal Commission report, vol. 4 p. 26.
13. ibid.
14. ibid., p. 21.
15. ibid., vol. 1, p. 164.
16. Barry Hart, unpublished manuscript.
17. ibid.
18. ibid.
19. Susan Geason, loc. cit.
20. *Sydney Morning Herald*, 11 November 1975.
21. Barry Hart, loc. cit.
22. Royal Commission report, vol. 7, p. 18.
23. Marcia Fawdry interview with author.
24. Author interview with a relative of Rosa's who requested anonymity.
25. Brian Bromberger and Janet Fife-Yeomans, op. cit., p. 110.
26. Susan Geason, loc. cit.
27. Royal Commission transcript, pp. 5147–5148.
28. Rosa Nicholson, Royal Commission transcript, p. 5133.
29. Susan Geason, loc. cit.
30. Rosa Nicholson, Royal Commission transcript, pp. 5194–5195.

31. Rosa Nicholson, Royal Commission transcript, pp. 5192–5193.
32. Rosa Nicholson, Royal Commission transcript, pp. 5193–5194.
33. Janet Reitman, *Inside Scientology*, Houghton Mifflin Harcourt, New York, 2011, p. 86.
34. www.cchr.org.au/about-us
35. L. Ron Hubbard, Project Psychiatry, 22 February 1966.
36. ibid.
37. For the full memo and a summary of its implications: www.xenu.net/archive/go/projpsyc/projpsyc.htm
38. Lawrence Wright, *Going Clear: Scientology, Hollywood & the Prison of Belief*, Alfred A. Knopf, New York, 2013, p. 294.
39. L. Ron Hubbard, Hubbard Communications Office Policy Letter, 26 November 1970.
40. www.cchr.org/videos/psychiatry-an-industry-of-death/psychiatry-the-men-behind-the-holocaust.html
41. Peter Marsh (pseudonym) interview with author.
42. Rosa Nicholson, Royal Commission transcript, pp. 5125–5126.
43. Rosa Nicholson interview with Toni Eatts as quoted in Susan Geason *Dark Trance* manuscript.
44. Rosa Nicholson, op. cit., pp. 5206–5207.
45. ibid., pp 5147–5148.
46. ibid., pp 5175–5176.
47. ibid.
48. Susan Geason, loc. cit.
49. Marcia Fawdry interview with author.
50. ibid.
51. Rosa Nicholson, op. cit., p. 5044.
52. Susan Geason, loc. cit.
53. ibid.
54. ibid.
55. Rosa Nicholson, op. cit., pp 5149–5150.
56. Rosa Nicholson, Statement to the Royal Commission, 28 September 1988, p. 3.
57. Susan Geason, loc. cit.
58. ibid.
59. Jan Eastgate, Royal Commission transcript, pp. 13305–13306.
60. Susan Geason, loc. cit.
61. Jan Eastgate, Statement to the Royal Commission, 4 October 1989.
62. Peter Marsh (pseudonym) interview with author.
63. ibid.
64. Jan Eastgate, op. cit., pp. 13290–13291.
65. *The Chelmsford Report* – Citizen's Commission on Human Rights, 1986.
66. Jan Eastgate, Royal Commission transcript, pp. 13395–13396.
67. Peter Marsh (pseudonym) interview with author.
68. Royal Commission report, vol. 7, p. 26.
69. *The Chelmsford Report*, p. 16.
70. 'Zombie room outrage at hospital', *Sunday*, 22 October 1978.
71. Kevin Stewart, Royal Commission transcript, pp. 16512–16513.
72. Kevin Stewart, pp. 16470–16471.
73. ibid.
74. ibid.
75. ibid.
76. Royal Commission report, vol. 7, p. 108.
77. ibid., p. 101.
78. Susan Geason, loc. cit.
79. ibid.
80. Royal Commission report, vol. 7, p. 116.
81. ibid., p. 109.
82. Susan Geason, loc. cit.
83. Barry Hart unpublished manuscript.
84. Barry Hart interview with author.
85. Barry Hart, loc. cit.
86. '$60,000 awarded in test case', *Weekend Australian*, 19–20 July 1980.
87. Susan Geason, loc. cit.
88. ibid.
89. Anthony McClellan interview with author.
90. 'The Chelmsford File', *60 Minutes*, 28 September 1980.
91. Anthony McClellan interview with author.
92. Brian Bromberger and Janet Fife-Yeomans, op. cit., p. 151.
93. ibid., p. 153.
94. ibid.

95. ibid. and Royal Commission report, vol. 2, p. 130 – each has slightly different versions.
96. Margaret Como interview with author.
97. ibid.
98. Susan Geason, loc. cit.
99. Royal Commission report, vol. 1, p. 51.
100. ibid., p. 57.
101. ibid., pp. 62, 64.
102. ibid., vol. 7, p. 20.
103. GO 732 SWOTs www.xenu.net/archive/go/ops/go732/go732.htm
104. Peter Marsh (pseudonym) interview with author.
105. Royal Commission report, vol. 7, pp. 18–19.
106. Rosa Nicholson, op. cit., pp. 5194–5195.
107. ibid., pp. 5191–5192.
108. ibid.
109. ibid., pp. 5227–5228.
110. Marcia Fawdry interview with author.
111. Susan Geason, loc. cit.
112. *Sydney Morning Herald*, 10 March 1989.
113. Rosa Nicholson, op. cit., pp. 5232–5233.
114. ibid., pp 5224–5225.
115. Susan Geason, loc. cit.
116. Author interview with relative of Rosa Nicholson.
117. Susan Geason, loc. cit.
118. ibid.
119. Ron Segal interview with author.
120. ibid.
121. ibid.
122. ibid.
123. ibid.
124. ibid.
125. Ron Segal's assertion that B1 had no direct dealings with the Chelmsford operation has been confirmed with author by a former senior intelligence operative who worked there at the time.
126. Ron Segal interview with author.
127. Rosa Nicholson, op. cit., p. 5125.
128. Ron Segal interview with author.
129. ibid.
130. ibid.
131. Rosa Nicholson, op. cit., pp. 5203–5204.
132. ibid., p. 5189.
133. Author interview with relative of Rosa Nicholson.
134. Ron Segal letter to author.
135. Ron Segal interview with author.
136. Jan Eastgate email to author in 2010.
137. *Lateline*, 19 May 2010.
138. *Sydney Morning Herald*, 2 June 1989.
139. L. Ron Hubbard, HCO Bulletin, 5 November 1967.
140. For list of High Crimes see http://gerryarmstrong.org/50grand/cult/ise-high-crimes.html
141. Email from Kevin Rodgers of Brock Partners lawyers.
142. Pat Griffin interview with author.
143. Jan Eastgate evidence to Royal Commission.
144. *Impact*, edition 31, 1990.
145. ibid.
146. Email from Kevin Rodgers of Brock Partners lawyers.
147. *Freedom* magazine, vol. 31, No. 2.
148. ibid. and Church of Scientology press release, 19 August 1993 – 'Freedom Human Rights Leadership Awards'.
149. Toni Eatts award: www.freedommag.org/english/vol31i2/pdf/vol31i2.pdf
150. Rosa and Ron did receive awards in Australia in 1993, as did Pat Griffin and Toni Eatts.
151. Ron Segal email to author – Segal and Nicholson were given CCHR Human Rights Awards in Australia in 1993 as were Eatts and Griffin, but were not recognised with international awards as Eatts and Griffin were.
152. Email from Kevin Rodgers of Brock Partners lawyers.
153. Ron Segal interview with author.
154. ibid.
155. Author interview with relative of Rosa Nicholson.
156. Email from Kevin Rodgers of Brock Partners lawyers.
157. Author interview with relative of Rosa Nicholson.

158. ibid.
159. Email from Kevin Rodgers of Brock Partners lawyers.
160. ibid.

Chapter 15
1. Joe Reaiche interview with author.
2. ibid.
3. www.rugbyleagueproject.org/seasons/nswrfl-1978/round-6/eastern-suburbs-vs-parramatta/summary.html
4. Joe Reaiche interview with author.
5. John Quayle interview with author.
6. *Rugby League Week* – Phil Tresidder match review of match on 30 April 1978.
7. Joe Reaiche interview with author.
8. ibid.
9. John Quayle interview with author.
10. Bill Mullins's record of 104 tries was eventually broken by Anthony Minichiello.
11. Jon Atack, *Let's Sell These People a Piece of Blue Sky* (2nd edn), Richard Woods, Worthing, 2013, p. 372.
12. HCO Bulletin, 9 April 1960.
13. Joe Reaiche interview with author.
14. ibid.
15. For full list of questions go to: www.xenu.net/archive/oca/
16. Joe Reaiche interview with author.
17. This is the figure Joe Reaiche says it costs him and his wife to go up 'The Bridge'.
18. Margery Wakefield, *Understanding Scientology: the Demon Cult*, LuLu, Raleigh, p. 123: www.cs.cmu.edu/~dst/Library/Shelf/wakefield/us.html
19. As quoted from a 1998 edition of the book *A Scientologist Guide To Dissemination*, at https://exscientologists.co.uk/recruiting/
20. John Quayle interview with author.
21. Joe Reaiche interview with author.
22. ibid.
23. Chris Guider interview with author.
24. Author tried to contact Steve Stevens through the church and his former wife without success.
25. Joe Reaiche interview with author.
26. Comedian Harriet Littlesmith started doing Scientology services around the same time Joe Reaiche did.
27. Joe Reaiche interview with author.
28. ibid.
29. ibid.
30. ibid.
31. File note of the Foreign Investment Division of The Treasury, 31 October 1979.
32. http://tonyortega.org/2013/06/15/ot-powers-jon-atack-on-scientologys-promise-to-make-you-superhuman/
33. Joe Reaiche interview with author.
34. Graeme Wynn interview with author.
35. Michael O'Connor interview with author.
36. Joe Reaiche interview with author.
37. www.scientologyhandbook.org/assists/sh6_4.htm
38. Joe Reaiche interview with author.
39. ibid.
40. Graeme Wynn interview with author.
41. Joe Reaiche interview with author.
42. ibid.
43. ibid.
44. Chris Guider interview with author.
45. Roy Masters, 'Scientology's little big man keen to assist dragons', *Sydney Morning Herald*, 20 December 2008.
46. *Big League*, vol. 65, no. 21, 1984.
47. ibid.
48. Graeme Wynn interview with author.
49. Chris Guider interview with author.
50. ibid.
51. ibid.
52. ibid.
53. Brian Johnston interview with author.
54. Michael O'Connor interview with author.
55. ibid.

56. Graeme Wynn interview with author.
57. Chris Guider interview with author.
58. Brian Johnston interview with author.
59. Graeme Wynn interview with author.
60. Chris Guider interview with author.
61. Roy Masters statement to author.
62. For example, see Dr David Hogg's analysis: https://www.cs.cmu.edu/~dst/Narconon/sources/reports/hogg.htm
63. Chris Guider interview with author.
64. Graeme Wynn interview with author.
65. Brian Johnston interview with author.
66. ibid.
67. Chris Guider interview with author.
68. John Quayle interview with author.
69. Roy Masters statement to author.
70. Chris Guider interview with author.
71. ibid.
72. ibid.
73. www.rugbyleagueproject.org/matches/Custom/MTctMTIxLTQtLS0tLS00MjU2LS0tLS0tLS0tLS0t
74. Chris Guider interview with author.
75. Former St George official interview with author.
76. Steve Mortimer interview with author.
77. Warren Ryan interview with author.
78. Joe Reaiche interview with author.
79. Joe Reaiche email to author.
80. Pat Jarvis phone conversation with author.
81. Pat Jarvis email to author.

Chapter 16
1. In later years, Terri Gillham was known by her married name – Terri Gamboa.
2. Lawrence Wright, *Going Clear: Scientology, Hollywood & the Prison of Belief*, Alfred A. Knopf, New York, 2013, p. 169.
3. ibid., p. 170.
4. Terri Gamboa (née Gillham) interview with author.
5. ibid.
6. ibid.
7. ibid.
8. ibid.
9. Mark 'Marty' Rathbun, *Memoirs of a Scientology Warrior*, CreateSpace Independent Publishing Platform, 2013, Chapter 24.
10. *The Philadelphia Inquirer*, 3 January 2012.
11. *St. Petersburg Times*, 25 October 1998.
12. Terri Gamboa (née Gillham) interview with author.
13. ibid.
14. Mike Rinder interview with author.
15. Peter Gillham Jnr interview with author.
16. Terri Gamboa (née Gillham) interview with author.
17. ibid.
18. ibid.
19. ibid. Robert Vaughn Young in an affidavit put the loss at $50 million: www.xenu.net/archive/go/legal/rvy.htm
20. Homer Schomer testimony Church of Scientology of California v Gerry Armstrong: www.gerryarmstrong.org/50k/legal/a1/2524.php
21. ibid.
22. Terri Gamboa (née Gillham) interview with author – this story was confirmed to me by Homer Schomer.
23. Terri Gamboa (née Gillham) interview with author.
24. Lawrence Wright, op. cit., p. 171.
25. ibid., pp. 171–172.
26. Russell Miller, *Bare-Faced Messiah*, Henry Holt and Company, New York, 1987, p. 366.
27. Jon Atack, *Let's Sell These People a Piece of Blue Sky* (2nd edn), Richard Woods, Worthing, 2013, pp. 340–341.
28. Russell Miller, op. cit., p. 369.
29. ibid.
30. Flag Order 3879 'The Sea Org & the Future'.
31. *New York Times*, 29 January 1986.

32. Jon Atack, op.cit., p. 388 and Lawrence Wright, op. cit., p. 183.
33. Coroner's report: www.xenu.net/archive/hubbardcoroner/hubbard_toxicology_report.jpg
34. David Miscavige, Hollywood Palladium, 27 January 1986.
35. Lawrence Wright, op. cit., p. 191.
36. ibid.
37. ibid., pp. 192–193.
38. ibid., p. 191.
39. ibid., p. 193, and *Tampa Bay Times*, 29 September 2012.
40. Terri Gamboa (née Gillham) interview with author.
41. ibid.
42. Articles and Bylaws of CST lists trustees: www.savescientology.com/cstmemo.pdf
43. www.xenu-directory.net/documents/corporate/irs/1993-1023-cst.pdf
44. Terri Gamboa (née Gillham) interview with author.
45. Tony Ortega: http://tonyortega.org/2013/08/31/the-history-of-scientologys-weird-vaults-the-bizarre-battlefield-earth-connection/
46. Terri Gamboa (née Gillham) email to author.
47. Terri Gamboa (née Gillham) interview with author.
48. ibid.
49. ibid.
50. ibid.
51. ibid.
52. Terri Gamboa (née Gillham) email to author.
53. Terri Gamboa (née Gillham) interview with author.
54. ibid.
55. ibid.
56. ibid.
57. ibid.
58. ibid.
59. ibid.
60. ibid.
61. ibid.
62. ibid.
63. Terri Gamboa (née Gillham) email to author.
64. Terri Gamboa (née Gillham) interview with author.
65. Mark 'Marty' Rathbun, op. cit., Chapter 11.
66. Lawrence Wright, op. cit., p. 190.
67. Terri Gamboa (née Gillham) email to author.
68. Terri Gamboa (née Gillham) interview with author.
69. ibid.
70. ibid.
71. ibid.
72. Mark 'Marty' Rathbun interview with author.
73. Terri Gamboa (née Gillham) interview with author.
74. Howard Dickman's biography of Yvonne Gillham: http://scientolipedia.org/info/Yvonne_Gillham_Jentzsch
75. Spanky Taylor interview with author.
76. Nancy Many interview with author.
77. Janis Grady (née Gillham) interview with author.
78. Spanky Taylor interview with author.
79. ibid.
80. Terri Gamboa (née Gillham) email to author.
81. ibid.
82. Terri Gamboa (née Gillham) interview with author.
83. ibid.
84. ibid.
85. ibid.
86. Nancy Many interview with author.
87. ibid.
88. Terri Gamboa (née Gillham) email to author.
89. *St Petersburg Times*, 1 November 2009.
90. Marc Headley, *Blown for Good: Behind the Iron Curtain of Scientology*, BFG Books, Burbank, 2009, p. 111.
91. ibid., p. 118.
92. Janis Grady (née Gillham) interview with author.
93. Marc Headley, op. cit., p. 118.
94. ibid., p. 119.
95. Janis Grady (née Gillham) interview with author.

96.   ibid.
97.   ibid.
98.   ibid.
99.   Terri Gamboa (née Gillham) interview with author.
100.   *St Petersburg Times*, 1 November 2009.
101.   ibid.
102.   ibid.
103.   Terri Gamboa (née Gillham) interview with author.
104.   ibid.
105.   Janis Grady (née Gillham) interview with author.
106.   ibid.
107.   ibid.
108.   *St Petersburg Times*, 1 November 2009.
109.   Lawrence Wright, op. cit., pp. 225–226.
110.   Terri Gamboa (née Gillham) interview with author.
111.   Terri Gamboa (née Gillham) email to author.
112.   Lawrence Wright, op. cit., p. 231.
113.   ibid., p. 232.
114.   Terri Gamboa (née Gillham) interview with author.
115.   ibid.
116.   ibid.
117.   ibid.
118.   Terri Gamboa (née Gillham) email to author.
119.   ibid.
120.   ibid.
121.   ibid.
122.   Terri Gamboa (née Gillham) interview with author.

Chapter 17
1.   Sarah Palin Facebook post, 29 November 2010.
2.   Julian Assange interview with author.
3.   Julian Assange interview with Andy Greenberg, *Forbes*, December 2010.
4.   Letter from Helena Kobrin to David Gerard, 28 July 1995: http://suburbia.net/~fun/scn/pers/
      fun/950728-honote.txt
5.   Email from Helena Kobrin to Julian Assange, 5 May 1997: http://suburbia.net/~fun/scn/pers/
      fun/nots/970506-ausnet-ho.txt
6.   ibid.
7.   Suelette Dreyfus, *Underground*: www.gutenberg.org/files/4686/4686.txt
8.   Julian Assange interview with author.
9.   David Gerard post: http://ask.slashdot.org/story/10/04/07/1854219/how-did-wikileaks-do-it
10.   David Gerard interview with author.
11.   *Los Angeles Free Press*, 6 March 1970.
12.   ibid.
13.   *Rolling Stone*, 9 November 1972.
14.   Wendy M Grossman, *Wired* alt.scientology.war: http://archive.wired.com/wired/archive/3.12/
      alt.scientology.war_pr.html
15.   Wendy Grossman, *Net.Wars*, NYU Press, New York, 1997, Chapter 6.
16.   www.lermanet.com/cos/handlenet.htm
17.   Elaine Siegel letter: www.lermanet.com/cos/handlenet.htm
18.   ibid.
19.   Wendy M Grossman, *Wired*, op. cit.
20.   Alan Prendergast, 'Hunting rabbits, serving spam: the net under siege', *Westword*, 4 October
      1995.
21.   Wendy Grossman, *Net.Wars*, op. cit.
22.   ibid.
23.   *St Petersburg Times*, 10 November, 1991.
24.   Dennis Erlich affidavit, 16 November 1995: www.xenu-directory.net/documents/
      erlichd19951116.htm
25.   Denis Erlich email, 13 February 1995: www.xenutv.com/blog/category/legal-videos/
      individuals/dennis-erlich-raid
26.   *Washington Post*, 19 August 1995.
27.   Ann Brill and Ashley Packard, 'Silencing Scientology's critics on the Internet: a mission
      impossible?', *Communications and the Law*, pp. 9–10.
28.   *Washington Post*, 19 August 1995.
29.   ibid.
30.   Wendy Grossman, *Net.Wars*, op. cit.
31.   David Gerard interview with author.

32. Email from Helena Kobrin to David Gerard, 28 July 1995: http://suburbia.net/~fun/scn/pers/fun/950728-honote.txt
33. David Gerard interview with author.
34. http://suburbia.net/~fun/scn/pers/fun/vut/950814-dg-infotech.txt
35. Haddon Storey interview with author.
36. Author FOI request to Victorian Department of Education.
37. David Gerard email to author.
38. David Gerard interview with author.
39. David Gerard email to author.
40. Julian Assange interview with author.
41. Suelette Dreyfus interview with author.
42. Nieson Himmel as quoted in Russell Miller's *Bared-Faced Messiah*, Henry Holt and Company, New York, 1987, p. 117.
43. Suelette Dreyfus interview with author.
44. https://cryptome.org/0001/assange-cpunks.htm
45. Robert Manne, 'The cypherpunk revolutionary', *The Monthly*, March 2011.
46. Andy Greenburg, *This Machine Kills Secrets*, Penguin Books, New York, 2012, p. 113.
47. https://wikileaks.org/wiki/Talk:Church_of_Scientology_Office_of_Special_Affairs_and_Frank_Oliver
48. https://wikileaks.org/wiki/Church_of_Scientology_collected_Operating_Thetan_documents
49. WikiLeaks statement, 7 April 2008.
50. https://wikileaks.org/wiki/Scientology_threatens_WikiLeaks_over_secret_cult_bibles
51. Wendy Grossman, *Net.Wars*, op. cit.
52. Tony Ortega, 'Scientologists: How Many of Them Are There, Anyway?', *The Village Voice*, 4 July 2011.

Chapter 18

1. Andre Tabayoyon affidavit: www.xenu.net/archive/ronthenut/tabayoyo.htm
2. ibid. and another former Sea Org member has confirmed this story to author.
3. Lawrence Wright, *Going Clear: Scientology, Hollywood & the Prison of Belief*, Alfred A. Knopf, New York, 2013, p. 201.
4. John Barnes, *Sunday Times*, 28 October 1984.
5. 'The 1982 US Mission Holders' Conference, San Francisco', Appendix to the Latey judgement UK High Court, 23 July 1984.
6. Lawrence Wright, op. cit., p. 202.
7. *Washington Post*, 7 April 1989.
8. Tony Ortega's story in *The Underground Bunker*, 12 April 2015, quotes an assistant who saw them in bed together: http://tonyortega.org/2015/04/12/how-scientology-broke-up-tom-cruise-and-mimi-rogers-the-story-you-havent-heard/
9. Tony Ortega, ibid.
10. ibid.
11. ibid.
12. John Brousseau interview with author.
13. ibid.
14. ibid.
15. Andre Tabayoyon affidavit.
16. ibid.
17. Sinar Parman email to author.
18. John Brousseau interview with author.
19. Sinar Parman email to author.
20. Mark 'Marty' Rathbun interview with author.
21. Bruce Hines interview with author.
22. Andre Tabayoyon affidavit.
23. Joe Childs and Thomas C Tobin, *St. Petersburg Times*, 31 October 2009.
24. Patrick George, lawyer with Kennedys, email to author.
25. Richard Behar email to author.
26. *Forbes*, 27 October 1986.
27. Richard Behar, 'The Thriving Cult of Greed and Power', *TIME* magazine, 6 May 1991.
28. ibid.
29. Richard Behar acceptance speech at 1992 Leo J. Ryan Award presentation.
30. *New York Magazine*, 21 October 1991.
31. 'Scientology's Critical Ads', *New York Times*, 31 May 1991.
32. ibid.
33. Miscavige did a pre-recorded interview for Jonathan Stack's 1998 documentary *Inside Scientology*.
34. Mike Rinder interview with author.
35. ibid.

36. ibid.
37. David Miscavige, *Nightline*, ABC TV (US), 14 February 1992.
38. Mike Rinder interview with author.
39. ibid.
40. ibid.
41. Mark 'Marty' Rathbun, *Going Clear* documentary, 2015.
42. Mark 'Marty' Rathbun interview with author.
43. Thomas Keneally, 'Film: Nicole Kidman, From Down Under to 'Far Away', *New York Times*, 24 May 1992.
44. Mark 'Marty' Rathbun interview with author.
45. Mark 'Marty' Rathbun, *Going Clear* documentary, 2015.
46. Mark 'Marty' Rathbun interview with author.
47. ibid.
48. ibid.
49. Bruce Hines interview with author.
50. ibid.
51. ibid.
52. ibid.
53. ibid.
54. Former Kidman employee interview with author.
55. Lawrence Wright, op. cit., p. 282.
56. Former Cruise employee interview with author.
57. Former Kidman employee interview with author.
58. Former Cruise employee interview with author.
59. Tony Ortega, 'How Scientology Spied on Tom Cruise', *The Village Voice*, 13 January 2012.
60. Nora Crest interview with author.
61. Mark 'Marty' Rathbun interview with author.
62. Tony Ortega, 'Scientology, Winning! We Hear From the Church's #1 Student', *The Village Voice*, 12 January 2012.
63. Former Cruise employee interview with author.
64. Mark 'Marty' Rathbun interview with author.
65. Mark 'Marty' Rathbun: https://markrathbun.wordpress.com/2012/01/12/
66. Mike Rinder interview with author.
67. Former Cruise employee interview with author.
68. ibid.
69. Mark 'Marty Rathbun, op. cit.
70. Tony Ortega, *The Village Voice*, 12 January 2012, op. cit.
71. *Sydney Morning Herald*, 31 May 2008.
72. Andrew Morton, *Tom Cruise: An Unauthorized Biograhy*, St Martin's Press, New York, 2008, p. 184.
73. Lawrence Wright, op. cit., p. 246.
74. Amy Nicholson, '*Eyes Wide Shut* at 15: Inside the Epic, Secretive Film Shoot that Pushed Tom Cruise and Nicole Kidman to Their Limits', *Vanity Fair*, 17 July 2014.
75. Mike Rinder, *Going Clear* documentary.
76. Anne Summers, 'Portrait of an actress', *Sydney Morning Herald*, 1 February 1997.
77. Nicole Kidman, *Desert Island Discs*, BBC Radio 4, 20 November 1998.
78. Nicole Kidman interview with Liz Smith, *Australian Women's Weekly*, August 1999 (interview done in March 1999).
79. Mark 'Marty' Rathbun interview with author.
80. ibid.
81. ibid.
82. Mark 'Marty' Rathbun, *Going Clear* documentary.
83. Former Kidman staffer interview with author.
84. ibid.
85. Bryan Burrough and John Connolly, 'Talk of the Town', *Vanity Fair*, June 2006.
86. ibid.
87. Former Kidman staffer interview with author.
88. ibid.
89. Bryan Burrough and John Connolly, *Vanity Fair*, op. cit.
90. Mark 'Marty' Rathbun interview with author.
91. Bert Fields, lawyer for Tom Cruise, email to author.
92. ibid.
93. ibid.
94. Patrick George, lawyer with Kennedys, email to author.
95. www.ew.com/article/2001/02/06/tom-cruise-and-nicole-kidman-split
96. *New York Daily News*, 18 April 2001.
97. Former Kidman staffer interview with author.

98.   Mark 'Marty' Rathbun interview with author.
99.   ibid.
100.   ibid.
101.   *Hollywood Reporter*, 4 July 2012.
102.   ibid.
103.   John Brousseau interview with author.
104.   ibid.
105.   *Hollywood Reporter*, 3 November 2015, and *US Magazine*, 3 November 2015.
106.   Former Kidman staffer interview with author.
107.   Lawrence Wright, op. cit., p. 249.
108.   Tom DeVocht, *Going Clear* documentary.
109.   Mark 'Marty' Rathbun: https://markrathbun.wordpress.com/2012/10/09/the-scientology-inc-gates-of-hell/
110.   Lawrence Wright, op. cit., pp. 249–250.

Chapter 19
1.   Peter Barnes and Annette Sharp interviews with author.
2.   Eric Kleitsch interview with author.
3.   Mark 'Marty' Rathbun interview with author.
4.   Pamela Williams, *Killing Fairfax*, Harper Collins, Sydney, 2013, p. 132.
5.   James Packer interview with Mike Willesee, *Sunday Night*, Channel 7, 10 February 2013.
6.   *BRW Rich List* 2002.
7.   Paul Barry, *Who Wants to be a Billionaire? The James Packer Story*, Allen & Unwin, Sydney, 2009, pp. 126–127.
8.   ibid., p. 64.
9.   *Sydney Morning Herald*, 6 April 2002.
10.   Paul Barry, op. cit., p. 178.
11.   ibid., p. 183.
12.   Kerry Packer told this story on TV and is recounted in Paul Barry, ibid., p. 6.
13.   Paul Barry, op. cit., p. 193.
14.   Richard Guilliatt, *Sydney Morning Herald*, 5 May 2003.
15.   Pamela Williams, loc. cit.
16.   James Packer interview with Mike Willesee, loc. cit.
17.   Mark 'Marty' Rathbun interview with author.
18.   Mark 'Marty' Rathbun, *Memoirs of a Scientology Warrior*, CreateSpace Independent Publishing Platform, 2013.
19.   Mark 'Marty' Rathbun interview with author.
20.   Hubbard *Manual of Justice*, Hubbard Communication Office, 1959.
21.   AN Smith Lecture, 15 November 1972.
22.   Mark 'Marty' Rathbun interview with author.
23.   Bert Fields email to author.
24.   Patrick George email to author.
25.   Mark 'Marty' Rathbun interview with author.
26.   Targets, Defense, HCO Policy Letter, 16 February 1969.
27.   ibid.
28.   Mark 'Marty' Rathbun interview with author.
29.   Eric Kleitsch interview with author.
30.   ibid.
31.   ibid.
32.   ibid.
33.   Dean Detheridge email to author.
34.   ibid.
35.   Patrick George email to author.
36.   Eric Kleitsch interview with author.
37.   ibid.
38.   ibid.
39.   www.scientologynews.org/faq/what-is-the-rehabilitation-project-force.html
40.   Eric Kleitsch interview with author.
41.   'What is the Rehabilitation Project Force?': www.scientologynews.org
42.   Eric Kleitsch interview with author.
43.   Annette Sharp interview with author.
44.   ibid.
45.   ibid.
46.   ibid.
47.   Pamela Williams, op. cit., p. 133.
48.   *Daily Telegraph*, 21 December 2002.
49.   Richard Guilliatt, 'Shadow on the Son', *Sydney Morning Herald*, 5 May 2003.

50. James Packer interview with Mike Willesee, *Sunday Night*, 10 February 2013.
51. Pamela Williams, 'My Way', *Australian Financial Review*, 24 November 2006.
52. David Miscavige at the IAS Gala in October 2004.
53. Mark 'Marty' Rathbun interview with author.
54. Pamela Williams, *Killing Fairfax*, op. cit., p. 133.
55. Mark O'Brien and Anthony McClellan interviews with author.
56. Anthony McClellan interview with author.
57. Mark O'Brien interview with author.
58. ibid.
59. Alex Mitchell, *Crikey*, 20 February 2006.
60. Mark O'Brien interview with author.
61. Phillip Adams email to author.
62. Paul Barry, op. cit., p. 210.
63. Mark O'Brien interview with author.
64. Mark 'Marty' Rathbun interview with author.
65. Paul Barry, op. cit., p. 247.
66. Pamela Williams, op. cit., p. 130.
67. Pamela Williams, 'My Way', *Australian Financial Review*, 24 November 2006.
68. Lucy James interview with author.
69. ibid.
70. ibid.
71. Mark 'Marty' Rathbun: https://markrathbun.wordpress.com/2012/01/12/
72. Lucy James interview with author.
73. *Sydney Morning Herald*, 10 May 2008.
74. Mark 'Marty' Rathbun, *Memoirs of a Scientology Warrior*, op. cit., Chapter 25.
75. Mark 'Marty' Rathbun interview with author.
76. ibid.
77. Paula Froelich, 'Rupert Murdoch Attacks Scientology Because It Once Courted His Son Lachlan', *The Daily Beast*, 2 July 2012.
78. ibid.
79. Eric Kleitsch interview with author.
80. ibid.
81. ibid.
82. ibid.
83. Liz Kleitsch interview with author.
84. Eric Kleitsch interview with author.
85. ibid.
86. Text message from Eric Kleitsch.

Chapter 20
1. https://markrathbun.wordpress.com/2010/04/24/miscavige-meltdown/
2. Heather McAdoo phone conversation with author.
3. www.mikerindersblog.org/scientology-you-are-being-watched-247/
4. Mike Rinder interview with author.
5. http://tonyortega.org/2015/06/25/mike-rinder-and-reporter-man-convicted-of-hacking-was-working-for-scientology/
6. Matthew Goldstein, 'Hired Hacker Who Named Clients Now Fears Retaliation', *New York Times*, 8 July 2015.
7. Mike Rinder interview with author.
8. ibid.
9. ibid.
10. www.villagevoice.com/news/the-top-25-people-crippling-scientology-no-8-mike-rinder-6672762
11. Mike Rinder interview with author.
12. Joe Childs and Thomas C Tobin, 'Ex-Clearwater Scientology of officer Debbie Cook testifies she was put in "The Hole", abused for weeks', *Tampa Bay Times*, 9 February 2012.
13. ibid.
14. Tony Ortega, 'Scientology's Concentration Camp for Its Executives: The Prisoners, Past and Present', *The Village Voice*, 2 August 2012.
15. Lawrence Wright, *Going Clear: Scientology, Hollywood & the Prison of Belief*, Alfred A. Knopf, New York, 2013, p. 265.
16. Tony Ortega, *The Village Voice*, 15 February 2012; Tampa Bay Times, 9 February 2012; www.mikerindersblog.org/debbie-cook-revisited/
17. 'Scientology defectors describe violence, humiliation in "the Hole"', *Tampa Bay Times*, 12 January 2013.
18. http://tonyortega.org/2015/03/23/going-clear-mike-rinder-helps-us-understand-a-scientology-document-that-will-creep-you-out/

19.   Lawrence Wright, op. cit., p. 268.
20.   Mike Rinder interview with Tony Ortega: http://tonyortega.org/2013/01/29/mike-rinder-on-the-hole-and-how-he-escaped-scientology/
21.   Mike Rinder email to author.
22.   Lawrence Wright, op. cit., p. 336.
23.   Eventually broadcast on The Secrets of Scientology on BBC *Panorama* on 28 September 2010.
24.   Mike Rinder interview with author.
25.   ibid.
26.   ibid.
27.   ibid.
28.   ibid.
29.   John Sweeney, *The Church of Fear: Inside the Weird World of Scientology*, Silvertail Books, London, 2013, p. 294.
30.   Mark 'Marty' Rathbun: https://markrathbun.wordpress.com/2011/09/14/mike-rinder-the-antithesis-of-david-miscavige/
31.   Mike Rinder: www.mikerindersblog.org/disconnection-and-my-mother/
32.   Mike Rinder interview with author.
33.   Senator Nick Xenophon speech to the Australian Senate, 17 November 2009.
34.   Senator Nick Xenophon interview with author.
35.   Rohan Wenn interview with author.
36.   ibid.
37.   Senate *Hansard*, 17 November 2009.
38.   ibid.
39.   Rohan Wenn interview with author.
40.   ibid.
41.   Tony Ortega email to author.
42.   Statement from the Church of Scientology, 18 November 2009: www.news.com.au/national/church-of-scientology-response-to-nick-xenophon/story-e6frfkvr-1225799110442
43.   ibid.
44.   *Sydney Morning Herald*, 18 November 2009.
45.   www.crikey.com.au/2010/02/18/the-senate-lends-scientology-a-helping-hand/
46.   Rohan Wenn interview with author.
47.   www.news.com.au 17 March 2010.
48.   Senator Nick Xenophon interview with author.
49.   *Four Corners*, ABC TV, 8 March 2010.
50.   Mike Rinder interview with author.
51.   ibid.
52.   ibid.
53.   ibid.
54.   ibid.
55.   https://markrathbun.wordpress.com/2010/04/15/look-whos-disconnecting-now

ACKNOWLEDGEMENTS

This book would not have been published without the help and support of many, many people.

If Quentin McDermott and Caro Meldrum-Hanna from *Four Corners* had not generously shared their story leads and contacts I may never have ended up investigating Scientology. Those initial stories relied on the courage of Carmen Rainer and Scarlett Hanna to speak out in the face of one of the most intimidating organisations on the planet. It was their strength of character that put me on the path to writing this book.

John Bruce, my former boss at *Lateline,* and Alan Sunderland, the Editorial Director at the ABC, were rigorous and fearless when it came to helping me put together those initial stories. We were airing allegations that other international media organisations had been too afraid to run. John and Alan never shied away from running these stories despite the legal threats and complaints they had to deal with.

I'd also like to thank Tony Jones, Michael Doyle, Jo Puccini, Brett Evans, Suzie Smith, Alison McClymont, Chris Schembri and Margot O'Neill for their advice and encouragement at *Lateline*, and Michael Martin, Ross Duncan and Grant McAvaney from ABC Legal for helping to get these stories on air despite the threats of litigation. Rohan Wenn, who was an adviser to Nick Xenophon at the time, also proved a great help.

When I decided to write this book, three of the first people I wanted to talk to were Jon Atack, the author of *Let's Sell These People a Piece of Blue Sky;* Tony Ortega, the journalist and blogger who writes about Scientology daily at *The Underground Bunker*; and Mike Rinder, the former head of the feared Office of Special Affairs. All three, in their own ways, have made significant contributions to this book.

Jon Atack has an extraordinary knowledge of Scientology history and policy, and a penetrating critical mind. He helped me source documents, check facts, ask the right questions and put me in contact with key people. I regularly asked him annoying questions that he always answered with grace and good humour.

Similarly, I could always rely on Tony Ortega to generously share information, contacts and advice. Tony reports with great skill and courage about Scientology on a daily basis. As a battle-hardened reporter on one of the most adversarial beats a journalist could wish for, his experience and guidance were always appreciated.

Mike Rinder had a front row seat to some of the most extraordinary moments in Scientology's short but chaotic history – and he was always forthright in describing what he saw and experienced. Mike was at all times happy to be challenged on his version of events and his views about Scientology. The day he spent driving me around Clearwater (and across his spying neighbour's lawn!) proved invaluable, as did the dozens of subsequent conversations we had over the phone and email.

In the course of writing *Fair Game,* I came to rely heavily on the work of others, most significantly Russell Miller's biography of Hubbard, *Bare-Faced Messiah*, Lawrence Wright's *Going Clear* and Jon Atack's *Let's Sell These People a Piece of Blue Sky*. In a subject area where so many lies are told and myths are spun, these books were reliable sources to fall back on. Likewise, the quality journalism of Tony Ortega, as well as Thomas Tobin and Joe Childs at the *Tampa Bay Times*, and Chris Owen's historical analysis of Hubbard's war record provided another solid foundation on which to build.

Malcolm Macmillan and Roger Boswarva were a great help in understanding what went on during the Anderson Inquiry. Charlie Nairn was a joy to speak to about his illuminating off-camera conversation with Hubbard, as was Alex Mitchell, the intrepid reporter who tried to interview Scientology's founder at a urinal in a Corfu casino. Former private investigator Rex Beaver provided me with one of my favourite moments in researching this book. When I tracked down Rex, the man who had been hired by the Scientologists to spy on Rupert Murdoch in 1968, not only did he remember the assignment well, he had also kept his statutory declaration from the time, his notebooks and his payslips! He promptly scanned them and emailed them to me that afternoon.

The following people helped me track down contacts, get key bits of information or convince people to talk to me: Alison McClymont, John Cleary, Peggy Daroesman, John Stanley, Ian Heads, Margaret Como, Barry Hart, Carmel Underwood, Paul Schofield, Bonny Symonds Brown, Jennifer Robinson, Karen de la Carriere and Gráinne O'Donovan. Gráinne also played a critical role in helping me build the trust of key witnesses and source documentary evidence and contacts in the early stages of this project. I had only one conversation with Professor Stephen Kent at a cult conference in Copenhagen, but his wise words helped shape this book.

A big thanks to the former Scientologists who provided me with so many leads and so much information, among them Dean Detheridge, Paul Schofield, Carmel Underwood, Bruce Hines, John Brousseau, Marc Headley, Haydn James, Lucy James, Hana Eltringham, Nancy Many, Jesse Prince, Nora Crest, Spanky Taylor, Sinar Parman, Chris Guider, Valeska Paris, Joe Reaiche, Ramana Dienes-Browning, and Gerry Armstrong. Thanks also to Mark 'Marty' Rathbun for the two interviews he gave me that shed new light on James Packer's and Nicole Kidman's relationships to Scientology. There are also a number of people who I can't name who provided me with important information.

A special thanks to José Navarro, Terri Gamboa, Janis Grady, Ron Segal and Eric Kleitsch for trusting me to tell their stories in depth for the first time. Susan Geason very generously gave me access to her unpublished manuscript *Dark Trance*. Between us, I feel like we have unlocked the secrets of the true role the Scientologists played in uncovering the Chelmsford Hospital scandal. I hope to see her book published soon.

When you write a book like this you come to rely on librarians and archivists to help you uncover hidden gems. I still remember the sense of excitement I felt as I opened the ASIO files on Scientology. Michael Wenke at the National Archives of Australia made accessing these files a simple process. The Public Record Office of Victoria also provided me with many enjoyable moments as I discovered illuminating documents from the 1960s such as Hubbard's entertaining letter to Inspector Bent. I also appreciate the assistance I received from Cathy Beale and her colleagues at the ABC library in Ultimo.

The National Library of Australia's Trove website, which archives old newspapers and periodicals, was another invaluable resource. It is a crying shame that government budget cuts have threatened its ability to expand and add extra material.

A number of people read chapters and gave me important feedback over the long gestation period of this book, including Jon Atack, Tony Ortega, Mike Rinder, Julia Baird, Rodney Cavalier, Ian Heads, David Marr and Rhys Muldoon.

A big thanks to Brigitta Doyle, James Kellow and the team at ABC Books/HarperCollins*Publishers*. Thank you for having the courage to take on this book, for being patient as I did the research and for helping to make it better once I delivered it.

Finally, I'd like to thank my wife and family for putting up with the long periods of time I spent away from them as I tried to do justice to this important topic. Writing about Scientology is not for the feint-hearted, and I appreciate their love and support while I was working away at it.

Steve Cannane
London, 2016

INDEX

Printed in Great Britain
by Amazon